Victor Regnault and the Advance of Photography

The Art of Avoiding Errors

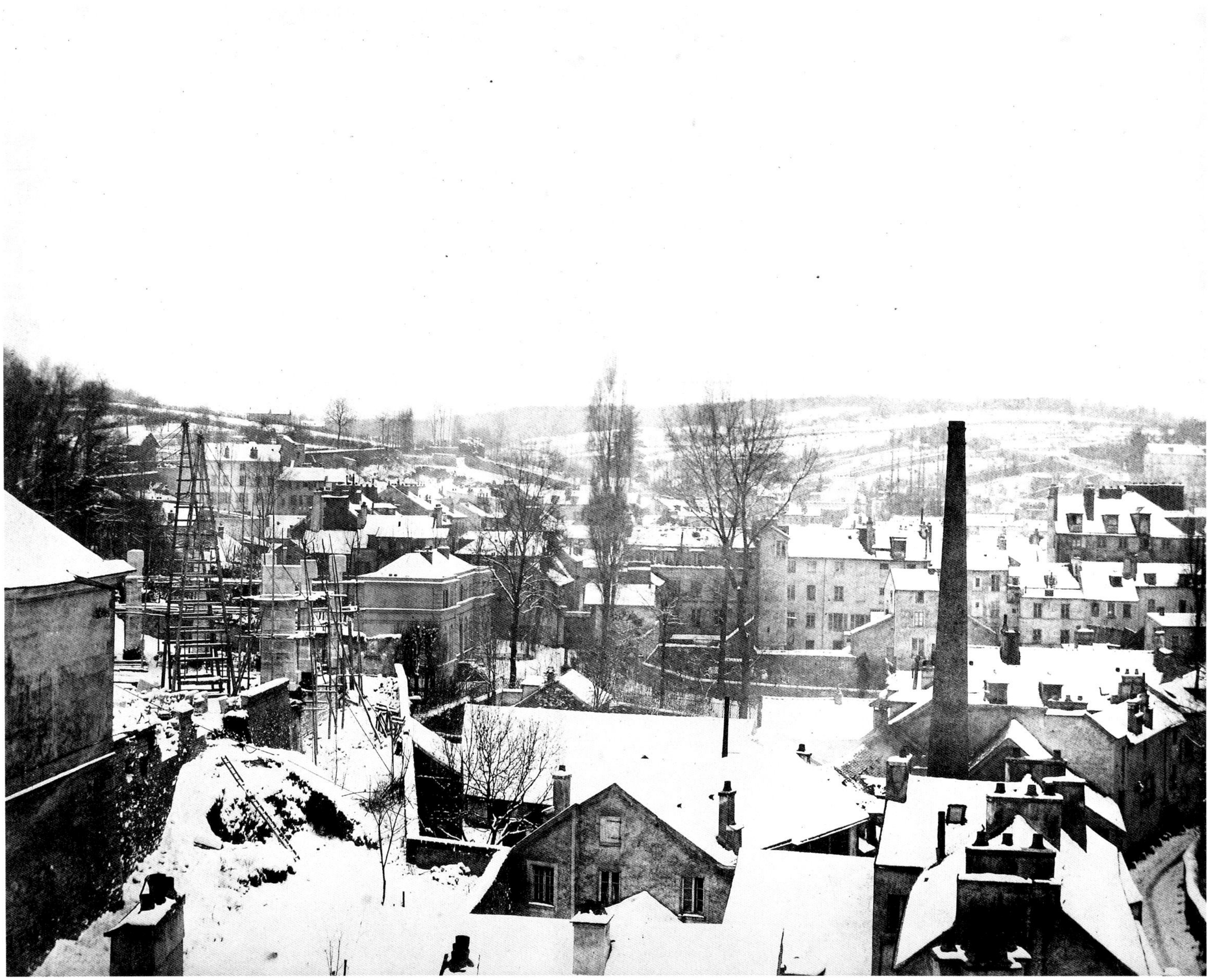

Victor Regnault and the Advance of Photography

The Art of Avoiding Errors

LAURIE DAHLBERG

Princeton University Press ❦ Princeton and Oxford

A note on the captions: the titles of Regnault's photographs have all been given posthumously. When possible, titles have been based on the extended descriptive captions that appear on the verso of some of the prints, which were probably added in the late nineteenth century. The term *calotype* (which describes a specific, patented process of paper negative photography) has been replaced by the more generic term *paper negative*.

Front cover: Victor Regnault, *The Marine Geographer Auguste Bravais,* c. 1851 (detail of fig. 40)
Back cover: Victor Regnault, *The Ladder,* 1853 (detail of fig. 87)
Frontispiece: Victor Regnault, *View of Sèvres from the West Wing of the Manufacture,* c. 1853. Salt print from paper negative, 13 x 17 3/8 in. (33 x 44 cm). Musée d'Orsay, Paris. 1983.159

Published by Princeton University Press, 41 William Street, Princeton, New Jersey 08540
In the United Kingdom: Princeton University Press, 3 Market Place, Woodstock, Oxfordshire OX20 1SY
pup.princeton.edu

Publication of this book has been made possible in part by a grant from the Publications Committee, Department of Art and Archaeology, Princeton University.

Printed and bound in Italy
10 9 8 7 6 5 4 3 2 1

Designed by Jean Wilcox
Composed by Tina Thompson
Printed by Trifolio, Verona, Italy

Library of Congress Cataloging-in-Publication Data
Dahlberg, Laurie Virginia, 1958–
Victor Regnault and the advance of photography : the art of avoiding errors / Laurie Dahlberg.
p. cm.
Includes bibliographical references and index.
ISBN 0-691-11879-5 (cl : alk. paper)
1. Photography—France—History—19th century. 2. Regnault, V. (Victor), 1810–1878. 3. Calotype—France. I. Title.

TR71.D34 2004
770'.944'09034—dc22 2004040046

Photography Credits: The photographers and the sources of visual material other than those indicated in the captions are as follows (numerals refer to plates).

Photo Bibliothèque Nationale de France, Paris (1, 13, 74, 87, 96, 97)
Courtesy of the J. Paul Getty Museum, Los Angeles (6, 26, 29, 67, 70, 71, 73, 84)
All rights reserved, The Metropolitan Museum of Art, New York (14, 16, 24)
Photograph © 2003 Museum of Fine Arts, Boston (32, 68, 69, 72)
Réunion des Musées Nationaux/Art Resource, New York. Photo: M. Beck-Coppola (88); B. Hatala (92); H. Lewandowski (frontis, 75–78, 93, 94); Jean L'hoir (25)
Photo: Lynn Rosenthal, 2003 (37, 44, 57, 60)
© The Royal Society, London (2, 12, 89)
Photo: Bruce M. White (28, 86)

CONTENTS

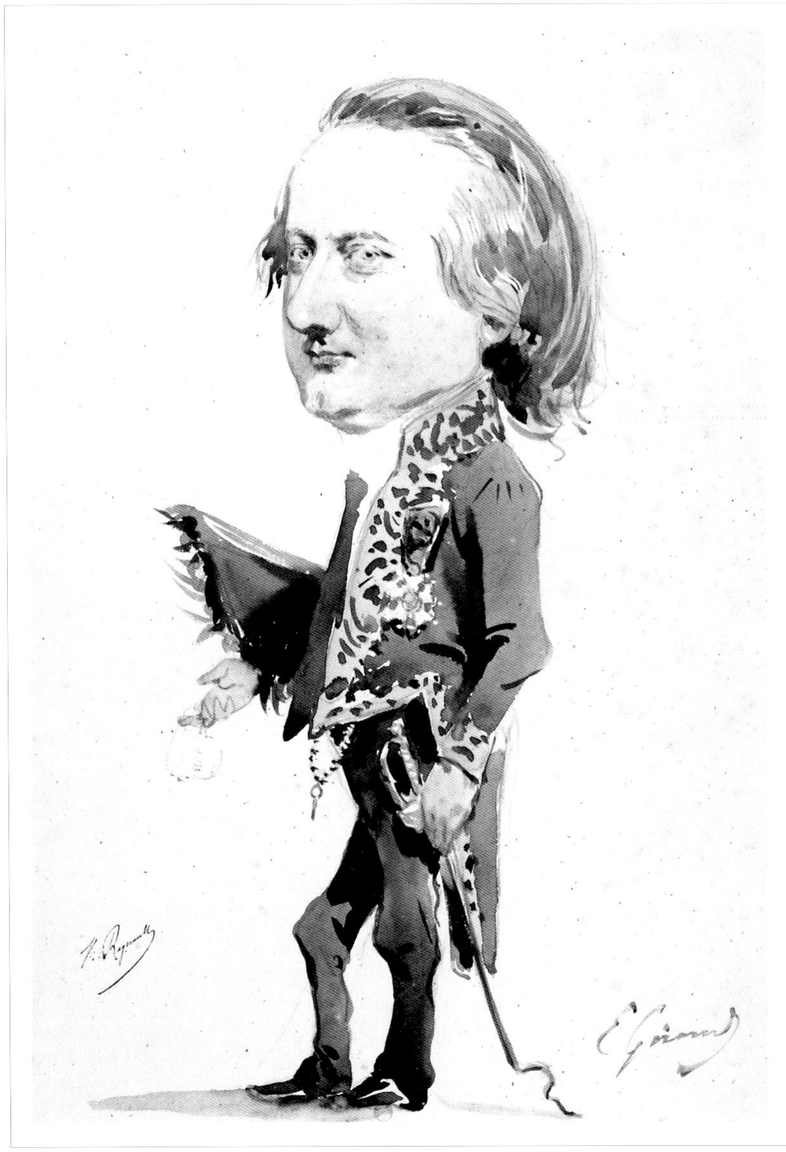

INTRODUCTION

Though known only among photographic specialists today, Victor Regnault (1810–1878) was once esteemed as the leader of the French photographic world, the soul of rationality in a chaotically emerging field. In 1857, when the celebrated portraitist Nadar filed suit for the exclusive use of his pseudonym, his eloquent statement to the court claimed Regnault as an artistic forefather.[1] While Nadar's homage was undoubtedly sincere, in placing Victor Regnault on his short list of mentors he also traded on the formidable weight Regnault's name then carried far beyond the small world of photography. To followers of science and academe in the 1850s, Regnault was recognized as the country's leading experimental physicist. In the world of beaux-arts, he was known as the director of the imperial porcelain factory at Sèvres. Observers of Second-Empire society knew him as an insider with access to the highest levels of Napoléon III's government. His inclusion in Nadar's professional genealogy recalls Regnault's prominence in still another career, this one devoted to the advancement of photography into all quarters of modern art and life. When the members of the Société Française de Photographie (S.F.P.) unanimously elected Regnault in 1855 as their first president, they recognized him as one of the most important, influential men in the field.

Regnault's fame in photography was short-lived, however, and even Nadar neglected to mention his former mentor in his 1900 memoir of his life in early photography.[2] It would even be safe

Fig. 1.
Eugène Pierre François Giraud (French, 1806–1881), *Portrait Chargé of Victor Regnault,* c. 1853. Watercolor on paper, 10 x 7 in. (25 x 18 cm). Bibliothèque Nationale de France, Paris. Cote Na 87

to say that Regnault's truly productive years in photography were well behind him when he resigned the presidency of the S.F.P. in 1868. Yet for a period of more than twenty years, beginning in the 1840s with the headlong rush to define the new field of photography, Regnault was never far from the heart of its developments.

Regnault had a unique part to play in the coming of age of photography. He was not a great inventor in the way of William Henry Fox Talbot or Hippolyte Bayard, or an influential teacher or writer like Gustave Le Gray, or a visionary entrepreneur, like A.-A.-E. Disdéri or Louis-Désiré Blanquart-Evrard. Unlike Nadar, he did not operate a studio or forge a distinctive visual style in photography; in fact, he never showed his photographs publicly in France. His greatest impact upon photography was as a facilitator—a powerful, diplomatic middle-man who influenced the new medium on all levels in his capacity as an academic scientist, a beaux-arts functionary, and an industrial engineer. By placing him at the head of their new organization in 1855, his S.F.P. colleagues recognized Regnault as a man propitiously placed to advance a medium that marked the intersection of modern science, art, and industry.

Part of this book's charge, therefore, is to sketch an institutional history of early French photography, through the prismatic lens of a key figure's activities. While ample primary material exists in relation to his life as a scientist in the Académie des Sciences (A.d.S.), and letters and other documents in the archives at Sèvres allow us to reconstruct a picture of Regnault the administrator, only a few pieces of correspondence are left that touch upon either his personal life or his activities in photography. The minutes of the monthly S.F.P. meetings published in the society's *Bulletin*—usually highly technical and procedural—are virtually the only traces left of Regnault the photographer, apart from the photographs themselves. To recognize the challenges Regnault faced as a photographic leader of the 1850s, it has been useful to revisit the unsettled culture of photography of the 1840s, as it existed prior to the establishment of the S.F.P. This was a period of contradictions, unfolding in a milieu characterized by both fraternity and bitter dissent. Sources for this period are necessarily limited, and the activities and concerns of most individuals who worked alone are lost to us. However, as terra incognita, photography encouraged its socially inclined practitioners to come together to share information, and the historical record thus represents this strata of early photographic practice: a largely elite, social photography that attracted gregarious, well-connected, wealthy amateurs and ambitious professionals of many kinds.[3] Taking shape in a casual context of roundtable dinners and private gatherings at the homes of enthusiasts, early Parisian photographic culture had few formal organizations to preserve its record, and we are left to piece together a view of the nascent world of photography from what remains of its pamphlets, manuals, and published articles.

Photography in France was in many ways plagued by contention, and its reception was famously conflicted. Exploring the implications of this ambivalence is vital to understanding why Regnault was chosen to shepherd photography into the legitimized, rationalized space of a quasi-professional society modeled on the Académie des Sciences. Introduced and advanced amid heated claims and counter-claims over priority of invention, photography spent its first decade stewing in rivalry, secrecy, rumor, and confusion. As one observer dolefully recalled, "On all sides, pitiful, fatal, and cruel circumstances surrounded the cradle of Photography."[4] The discord that greeted this new medium, however, was more than a squabble between competing inventors or factions that reductively cast photography as cultural scourge or savior. Photography was a lightning rod for wider, preexisting debates over the encroachment of technics and industry upon a culture still deeply attached to an agrarian, artisanal identity. Regnault's purpose as president of the S.F.P. was thus twofold: to guide and unify the field of photography by authoritatively presiding over discussions of technical, professional, and aesthetic concerns, and to promote the medium as a humanistic instrument, dutifully responsive to individual, creative intelligence.

Also of interest to the present study is Regnault's experience as director of the illustrious porcelain works, the Manufacture Impériale de Sèvres, not least because he joined a budding culture of amateur photography at the factory when he took up his post there in 1852. Practiced in an intimate, communal setting of men and women whose families had worked together for generations, photography fit comfortably into Sèvres's artists' practice of sketching for pleasure and amusement. Looking closely at this early flourishing of photography at Sèvres, however, divulges why it was late in being openly utilized for practical ends in the factory. Because ceramic fabrication and photography were both embattled by the arguments surrounding industrial production and reproduction, there is a strong correspondence between them, and during Regnault's tenure at Sèvres, the two fields were ultimately brought together in a subtly negotiated way that revealed the state's own equivocal relationship to technology. Regnault had been hired in part to bring modern production methods to a thoroughly resistant culture, a factory whose identity and traditions were unrepentantly based in an eighteenth-century veneration of deluxe handicraft. Modernization of any kind at Sèvres faced stiff critical resistance, parallel to that expressed by photography's vocal opponents. Critics of Sèvres echoed Charles Baudelaire's indictment of photography when they complained that under Regnault's direction, "the useful killed the pleasurable" and that the factory's products had devolved to "the bourgeois ideal of porcelain."[5] Latent anxieties over the industrial direction of the Manufacture spilled over in the higher administration when Regnault and Louis Robert, his *chef de peinture*, initiated a bitter, four-year struggle with the state's minister over the question of documenting and publicizing Sèvres's wares through photographs. Although the minister eventually relented, his staunch belief that the "vulgarization" of Sèvres wares by reproductive photography threatened the factory's reputation illustrates the contemporary ambivalence over industrial progress, even within a government committed to its advance.

Finally, with this book I have attempted to open Regnault's own photographs to study. Among his fellow photographers, Regnault's reputation as a consummate organizer, administrator, and technical expert overshadowed his activities as a passionate amateur photographer. Although he was quite productive, as his friend Paul Périer lamented in the pages of *La Lumière*, his work was known only to "a priviliged few." Still, nearly two hundred of his pictures, mostly portraits and landscapes, remain from three or four years of work in the early 1850s.

Beginning around 1847, following Blanquart-Evrard's improvements to the English paper-negative process, Regnault threw himself into the new art, initially working with portraiture. His personal portraits of family members and academic colleagues at the Académie des Sciences and the Collège de France constitute perhaps the most extensive group of intimate photographs of family and friends left to us from this era. These pictures present the opportunity to examine an important cultural phenomenon: the advent of domestic photography, a new and purely private means of constructing family identity through homemade images. If the commercial portrait was a conventionalized, publicly inscribed badge of bourgeois pride, the terms of the domestic photograph were quite different. Its production in the home, attended by the excitement of alchemical experimentation, made it a significant cooperative enterprise for the family, and underscored family roles as it called for their theatrical enactment before the camera.

Large-format landscapes (approximately 14 by 18 inches) were Regnault's most ambitious photographs. Considering these along with similar landscapes by his colleagues Périer and Count Olympe Aguado and other elite members of the S.F.P., I argue that the romantic landscape was especially meaningful to these men because of their material involvement—as scientists, bankers, and investors—in the industrial programs of the Second Empire. Regarding landscape as an aesthetically privileged subject, they followed the Barbizon painters of the previous generation in seeking a vision of unrefined nature in the rustic countryside outside Paris. And yet these photographs embody a crucial internal contradiction, given their production at a moment when the government was aggressively securing an industrial capitalist economy. With his state-commissioned research on steam engines, the fabrication of gas from coke, and other engineering projects, Regnault was particularly instrumental in this socioeconomic transformation.

Regnault continued to work in photography into the 1860s, as the earlier calotype and daguerreotype processes were supplanted by the wet collodion negative. But by this time, his professional life had become too demanding to allow him to pursue his hobby in the concentrated way of earlier years. Even at the height of his photographic ardor in 1853, he already worried that photography had cost him too much in time taken from his scientific research. The interface between Regnault's personal photography, his official work on behalf of photography's advancement, and his professional careers as a scientist and state functionary consequently brings a final issue to the fore: the evolution of photography as a leisure activity uniquely suited for the strenuously productive, capitalist modern age. Equal parts art, science, and industry, photography was distinct from older, more genteel activities of leisure like sketching and musical performance, in that it was literally as useful as it was pleasurable. To a nation increasingly driven by bourgeois priorities, individual prowess with implements of technology and science was valued as much as aesthetic judgment. In fact, it was only as a useful art that Regnault could justify his photography to himself, and he defensively insisted that he did not photograph "for amusement." With career goals in physics occupying the highest point on his horizon, it was inevitable that the obligations of his professional life would ultimately make him put aside personal photography. This circumstance makes Regnault's career a fitting opportunity to view photography from a perspective once suggested by Allan Sekula as a means to explore "the nature of work and creativity under capitalism."[6]

In the end, Regnault makes an irresistible figure through which to study the culture of early photography, for at the same time that he worked to mediate the problems surrounding the field of photography, he acutely reflected the contradictions and cross-purposes of the medium itself. He was, in effect, shaped, acclaimed, and disparaged by the same cultural forces that conjured photography. Individuals, though, are less flexible than the knowledge they produce and extend. Regnault's commitment to empirical method would ultimately be judged as his failing as times changed, while photography, with no commitments of its own, would continue to be adapted to new uses.

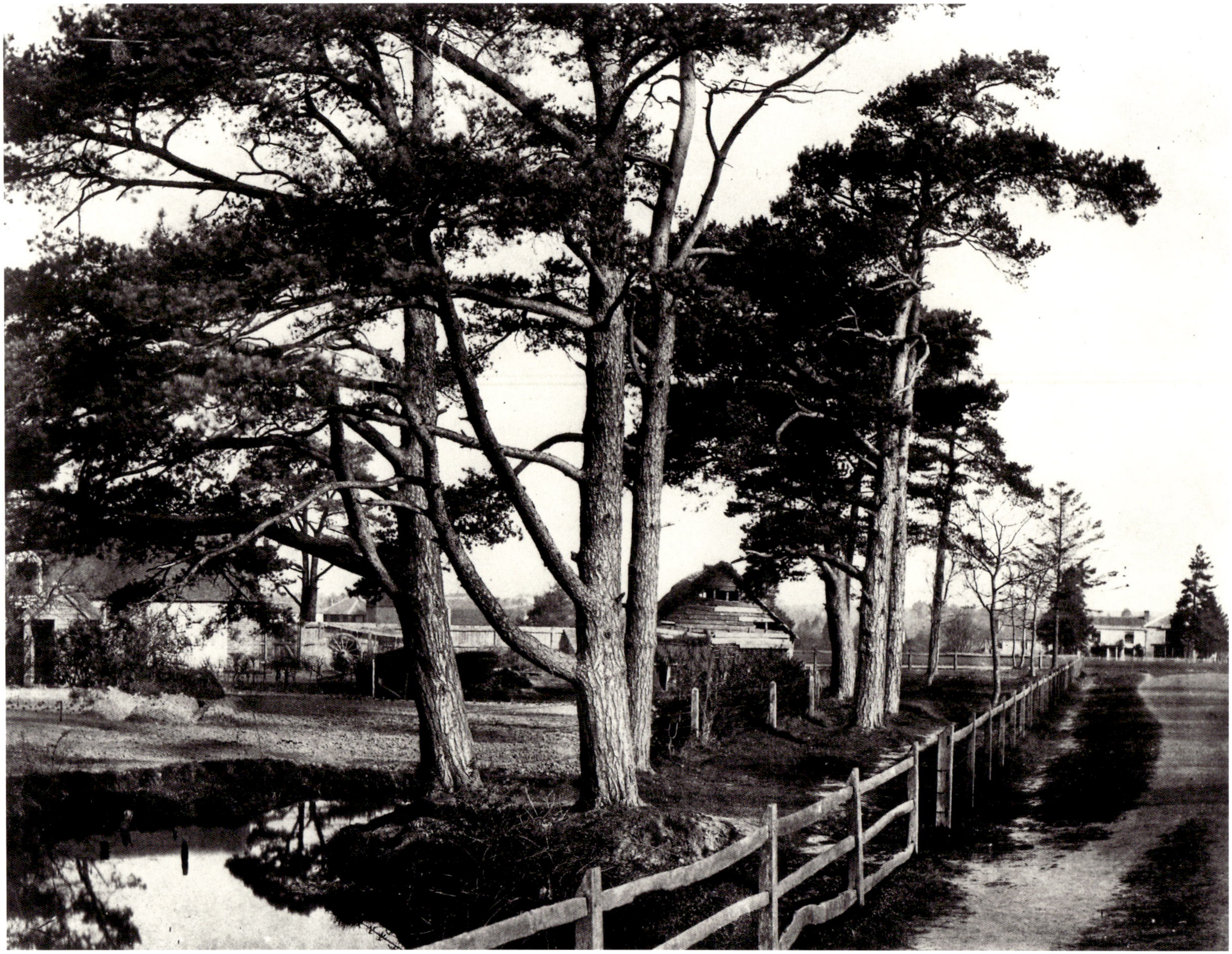

1 THE ART OF AVOIDING ERRORS

When Victor Regnault undertook his first experiments with photography, he was about to be elected to the Académie des Sciences. Two weeks before his thirtieth birthday in 1840, the academy unanimously elected him to one of the six seats in chemistry, although he would soon shift his primary interest to the emerging field of experimental physics.[1] An early self-portrait from about 1847 (fig. 3) shows the confident young scientist in the brilliant ascendancy of his career. The image resonates with conventions adapted from painting, recalling in simpler form the grand-manner portraiture of Anthony Van Dyck and Joshua Reynolds, as Regnault poses regally before a dramatically arranged curtain. With head tilted up slightly, a rather superior air accentuated by a high collar and wide cravat, the left hand stroking the chin in a gesture of private thought, he presents the image of a contemplative and sublimely self-possessed man whose mental focus is fixed upon some distant point.

In Alfred de Musset's characterization, France's economically thriving but morally vacant July Monarchy (1830–48) produced two kinds of men: vapid capitalists whose only joy was in making money and displaying wealth, and the "idle and tired" young men infected by the sickly lassitude that followed the collapse of the Revolution's illusions.[2] Regnault represents a third type: the man who stubbornly commits himself to proving that the sacrifices of his father's generation had not been in vain. Exemplifying the revolutionary ideal of advancement through personal merit, Regnault rose to a

Fig. 2.
Victor Regnault (French, 1810–1878) and John Stewart (British, 1814–1887), *The Moor, Hawkurst*, 1853. Salt print from paper negative, 15 1/8 x 11 3/8 in. (38.5 x 28.8 cm). Royal Society, London. MS 784.2

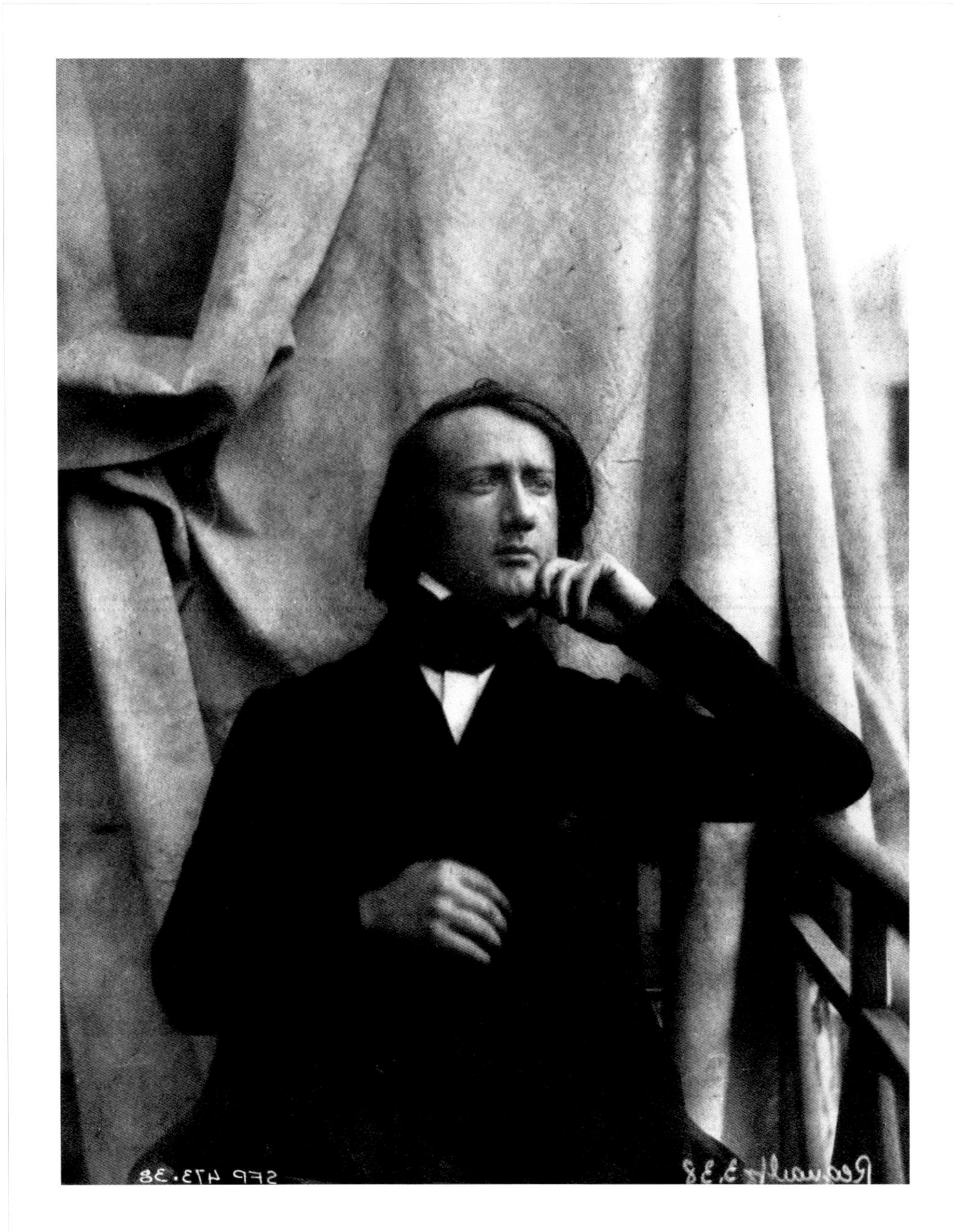

Fig. 3.

Victor Regnault, *Self-Portrait*, c. 1847. Modern print from paper negative, 6 5/8 x 5 3/8 in. (16.8 x 13.6 cm). Société Française de Photographie, Paris. 473.38

position of power and wealth through self-determination, astute ambition, extravagant diligence, and an almost religious faith in the value of empirical knowledge. In many ways, Regnault's professional accomplishments make him an exceptional figure, but he also represents a particular, radical drive and optimism shared by many scientists of his generation. Never before had science and engineering held such prestige and respect in France, just as they had never enjoyed so much independence from military concerns.[3] With the advent of the July Monarchy and continuing throughout the Second Empire (1852–70), careers in science brought power, influence, and the invigorating conviction that one's contributions would be instrumental in delivering a splendid future for France. For Regnault, this drive amounted to a kind of excess that was almost bound to come to grief, but not before it carried him briefly to the top of his field. At the time of his election, he was the youngest member of the A.d.S., succeeding upon his very first candidature, while other qualified hopefuls often waited decades to achieve that ultimate recognition.[4]

Biographers have found it irresistible to add dramatic emphasis to this poor orphan's rags-to-riches story, but it is true that his youth was spent in the bleak postrevolutionary "wreckage" described so bitterly by de Musset and other writers of the age. He was born Henry Victor Regnault on 21 July 1810, in Aix-la-Chapelle, in territory claimed by the French in 1794 and reclaimed by Prussia in 1815. Growing up in a bilingual region of mutable national boundaries and identities made an impression on the young Regnault, and he would forever cultivate an international outlook. Victor was the only son of André Privat Regnault, a military geographic engineer and captain in Napoléon's Imperial Corps, and Marie Thérèse Massardo, the daughter of a Belgian hotelier of Italian descent.[5] Captain Regnault died on the dismal retreat from Moscow in 1812, and his wife died seven years later, leaving behind the nine-year-old Victor and a younger sister. A fellow officer, Jean-Baptiste Clément, took an interest in the welfare of his comrade's son, and when Victor arrived in Paris at sixteen to make his way in the world, Captain Clément took the boy under his wing, placing him with a tutor to help him prepare for entrance to the École Polytechnique, Europe's most distinguished school of science and engineering. Regnault had an unshakeable faith that he was made for science, which made failure seem out of the question. He passed the *concours* (competitive examination) on his second attempt, and a few years later he would permanently join his future with his protector's family by marrying the Cléments' only child, Clémence.

Regnault arrived at the École Polytechnique at the opening of a new era of economic and professional opportunity, with the July Monarchy turning to the graduates of the *grandes écoles* (the top state schools) to implement an aggressive program of industrial development and public works. With a degree from the Polytechnique—the springboard for top careers in science, the military, engineering, civil service, and state administration—Regnault stood to overcome all the hardships of his childhood. While most of the graduates went on to careers in the military, the best students had their choice of careers in the Civil Corps.[6] Regnault surpassed the expectations of those around him by excelling not only at the Polytechnique, where he graduated third in his class of 126, but also at the state's top school for advanced engineering study, the École des Mines, where, had the authorities allowed it, he would have earned his basic engineering credentials in two years instead of the usual three or four.[7]

MATTER VERSUS SPIRIT

Years later, the eminent chemist Jean-Baptiste Dumas would describe his colleague Regnault as "the Personification of Science," as others would count him among "the lights of chemistry" and "the glories of physics."[8] Yet by the time of his death in 1878, accolades like these would be muffled in qualifiers, as the prevailing scientific outlook turned away from experimental to theoretical preoccupations.[9] Regnault's view of science was in fact a narrow one, based entirely in empirical practice, confined to the concrete and measurable; he distrusted theorization, and this prejudice would return to haunt him. At Regnault's eulogy, Dumas gave mixed praise when he noted that Regnault's work worshipped "the statue of Truth" but "banished the entire cult of the imagination."[10] Recounting the sentimental narrative of Regnault's youthful quest for admission to the École Polytechnique, Dumas denied that his colleague had been pursuing his dream, since Regnault "was never a dreamer." Regnault's contribution to science, Dumas concluded, was his precision, not his inventiveness, and he deserved recognition simply because he had mastered "the art of avoiding all errors."[11] At Regnault's centennial oration in 1910, Henri Le Chatelier went further in conflating Regnault the scientist with his method and cast him in contemporary terms of psychological disfunction. "Imprecision in Science disgusted him, as others would regard a stain on a beautiful garment," Le Chatelier observed, adding that Regnault's obsession with measurement went hand-in-hand with a "terror of vague imaginings."[12]

The image of Regnault as a hard-headed empiricist becomes a familiar refrain in reports of those who knew him. As scientific practice shifted and Regnault's star tumbled with the humiliating fall of the Second Empire, it became ever more popular to criticize his reliance on phenomenal observation as method without imagination, genius, or spirit. But the reaction against positivism had begun to form much earlier, taking on its edge as a minority opinion during the July Monarchy, when romantic literary rebels and other "defectors of the middle class" began sharp attacks on the articles of faith of the get-ahead era: progress, materialism, utility, rationality, technology, and science.[13] The philosopher Victor Cousin described the difference between "them" and "us" in these terms in 1845: "That which we call *les hommes positives* [men of fact], are men without imagination, who perceive only what they see . . . They can be seriously and profoundly honest [but] they shall never be poets or artists."[14]

This dichotomy that separates vision from imagination, granting privilege to one or the other, has famously been the plague of photography, and it has haunted the writing of Regnault's story as well. Ultimately, Regnault did not always behave as the empirical scientist, any more than he thought of himself as an artist in the primary sense of the word. Devoted though he was to empiricism, objectivity, and positive philosophy, these did not close his world view to subjective interpretation, art, or religion: he was an earnest believer in the felt, as well as the seen, albeit in those spheres of experience outside of hard science. Nevertheless, critics on many sides of the question of "progress"—understood by the government and its bourgeois constituency as the happy result of combining science, laissez-faire economics, technology, and liberal democracy—usually sketched the multifaceted tensions of the age as a conflict in black and white: matter vs. spirit, progress vs. tradition, technology vs. antitechnology, and vision vs. imagination.

Although the debate around early photography kept returning to the same polemical terms, Regnault—like so many others taking it up—showed remarkable flexibility in using photography, perhaps because it had virtually no history or tradition of its own. Around 1851, he assembled a photograph album consisting of some ninety-three pages of salt prints made from paper negatives. Regnault had already been practicing photography for a decade, beginning with the process of Louis-Jacques-Mandé Daguerre (1789–1851), which produced an image on a metal plate, before moving to William Henry Fox Talbot's process called "calotypy," which produced a paper negative that had been sensitized with silver salts, then exposed and chemically developed. Positive prints were normally created by contact printing the negative on another sheet of sensitized paper (salt prints). The so-called *Album Regnault* contains many of Regnault's own pictures—portraits, art reproductions, architectural views, cityscapes, documentation of scientific experiments—as well as prints by some of his colleagues in the new art, including Gustave Le Gray, A. Guillot-Saguez, Louis-Désiré Blanquart-Evrard, Alexis de Lagrange and his partner Lambrecht, and Talbot himself.[15]

Page eighty-one of the album features a curious arrangement of five photographs (fig. 4). A square full-length portrait of an unidentified man occupies the center of the page. Like many of Regnault's portraits, it was made outside his laboratory at the Collège de France. The young man, perhaps one of Regnault's students, is seated in profile. In an attitude of complete absorption, he reads from a sheaf of papers balanced on his knee. Behind him, on the table at his back, pushing into the picture, is a mechanical apparatus fitted out with a bell jar and glass cylinders: the vacuum pump Regnault pioneered

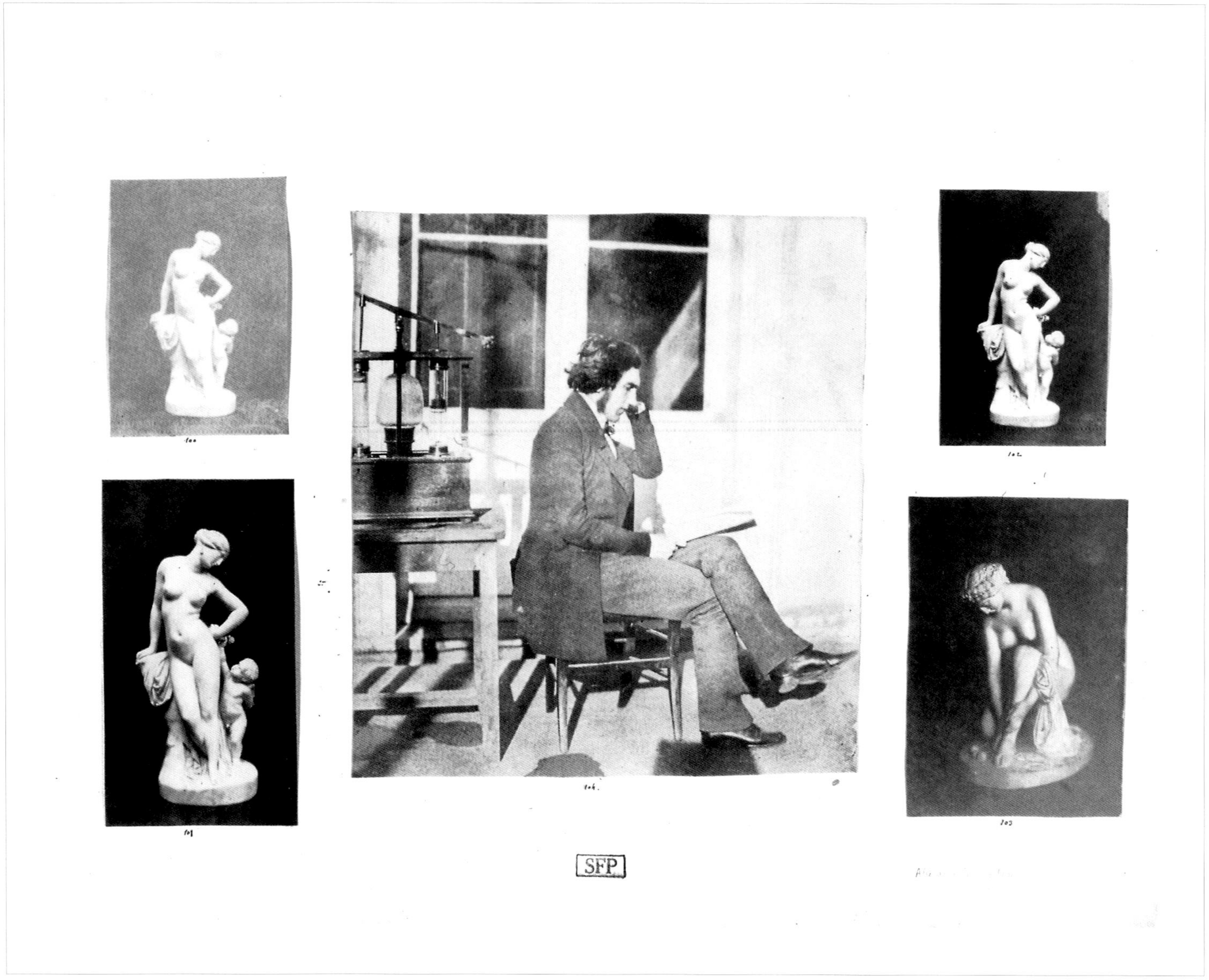

Fig. 4.

Victor Regnault, *Album Regnault*, p. 81, c. 1851. Albumenized salt prints from paper negatives, album dimensions unknown.
Société Française de Photographie, Paris

to impregnate his photographic paper with light-sensitive solution. In a playful gesture, Regnault surrounded this rather serious portrait of "l'homme positif" with four smaller images of erotic beauty: three prints of a Venus and Cupid statuette, plus a copy of James Pradier's comely *Atalante*. While these little prints, which demonstrate variations in developing or fixing solutions, record the actions of the scientist, they also speak of high art: the art of the sculptor and the promise of photography to educate the public through art reproductions. What's more, their placement, floating in the available space around the portrait, with three of the sculpted figures inclining their lusciously modeled, naked bodies toward the young savant, creates a composition that organically and ironically connects all five pictures, not unlike some humorous page layouts featured in the illustrated press of the day (fig. 5). We read these floating bodies as thought balloons, as if the serious young man finds his study of formulae and theorems crowded by irrepressible (and multiplying) thoughts of sex, and Regnault was no doubt in on his own jest. It's a montage that would have delighted the Dadaist Marcel Duchamp (1887–1968): the Bachelor (is he the flesh-and-blood man, the vacuum pump machine, or the shadowed presence of the man with the camera?) surrounded by his Brides-stripped-bare.

This album page could stand as an emblem for Regnault's relationship to photography, as well, for he thought of photography as the guiltiest of pleasures. Writing to his friend Sir John Herschel in 1851, he enviously described John Stewart's (Herschel's brother-in-law) more legitimate relationship to the medium: "Several times I have received news of Mr. Stewart, who definitively possesses this fatal passion for photography; he surrenders himself to it with the ardor of a new husband, and I don't doubt that he will obtain good results. As for me, I reproach myself everyday for the time I spent with it, and that I should have used to finish the works which have absorbed me for several years."[16] The work Regnault cited here was his scientific research, to which he had been wedded in the eyes of the academy for over fifteen years. Regnault was too self-abnegating not to feel guilt about taking time and attention from his proper profession and giving it to his pastime. As with many infidelities, Regnault's most intense year of photographic philandering (1851–52) coincided with a crisis in his marriage—to science. In the spring of 1851, with the French scientific world buffeted by the political struggles of the Second Republic (1848–51), Regnault wrote to his German mentor, Justus von Liebig about the impossibility of carrying out serious research in Paris, where "the existence of the savant is so agitated and wasted that it shall be difficult to undertake long-term projects."[17] Three months before Louis-Napoléon's coup d'état, he wrote to Liebig again with an air of futility: "Everyday I envy you your tranquility at Giessen; and to appreciate its true value, you would have to lead a year of the hellish life we are saddled with here . . . in Paris."[18] He concluded with a dire prediction: "My only ambition now is to make my position a little

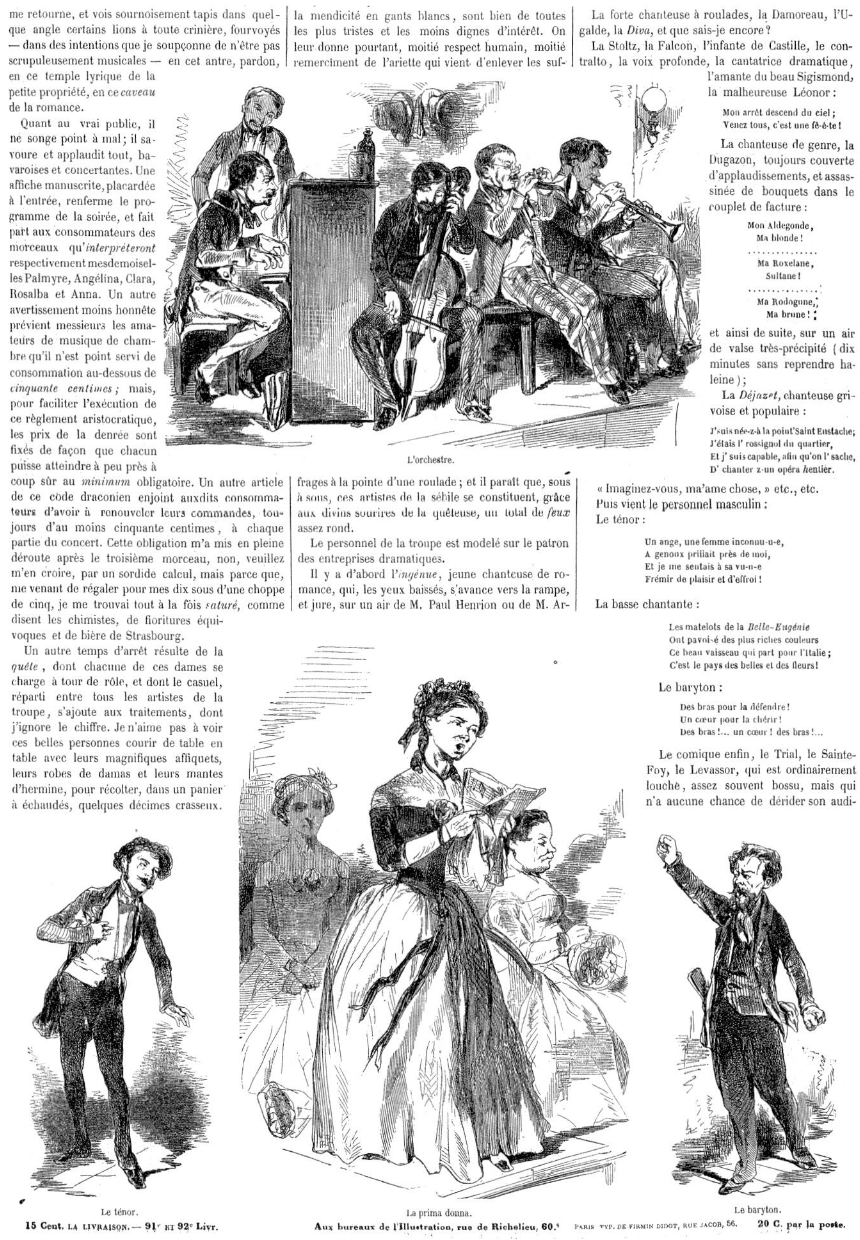

me retourne, et vois sournoisement tapis dans quelque angle certains lions à toute crinière, fourvoyés — dans des intentions que je soupçonne de n'être pas scrupuleusement musicales — en cet antre, pardon, en ce temple lyrique de la petite propriété, en ce *caveau* de la romance.

Quant au vrai public, il ne songe point à mal; il savoure et applaudit tout, bavaroises et concertantes. Une affiche manuscrite, placardée à l'entrée, renferme le programme de la soirée, et fait part aux consommateurs des morceaux qu'*interpréteront* respectivement mesdemoiselles Palmyre, Angélina, Clara, Rosalba et Anna. Un autre avertissement moins honnête prévient messieurs les amateurs de musique de chambre qu'il n'est point servi de consommation au-dessous de *cinquante centimes;* mais, pour faciliter l'exécution de ce règlement aristocratique, les prix de la denrée sont fixés de façon que chacun puisse atteindre à peu près à coup sûr au *minimum* obligatoire. Un autre article de ce côde draconien enjoint auxdits consommateurs d'avoir à ronouveler leurs commandes, toujours d'au moins cinquante centimes, à chaque partie du concert. Cette obligation m'a mis en pleine déroute après le troisième morceau, non, veuillez m'en croire, par un sordide calcul, mais parce que, me venant de régaler pour mes dix sous d'une choppe de cinq, je me trouvai tout à la fois *saturé,* comme disent les chimistes, de fioritures équivoques et de bière de Strasbourg.

Un autre temps d'arrêt résulte de la *quête*, dont chacune de ces dames se charge à tour de rôle, et dont le casuel, réparti entre tous les artistes de la troupe, s'ajoute aux traitements, dont j'ignore le chiffre. Je n'aime pas à voir ces belles personnes courir de table en table avec leurs magnifiques affiquets, leurs robes de damas et leurs mantes d'hermine, pour récolter, dans un panier à échaudés, quelques décimes crasseux.

la mendicité en gants blancs, sont bien de toutes les plus tristes et les moins dignes d'intérêt. On leur donne pourtant, moitié respect humain, moitié remercîment de l'ariette qui vient d'enlever les suffrages à la pointe d'une roulade; et il paraît que, sous à sous, ces artistes de la sébile se constituent, grâce aux divins sourires de la quêteuse, un total de *feux* assez rond.

Le personnel de la troupe est modelé sur le patron des entreprises dramatiques.

Il y a d'abord l'*ingénue*, jeune chanteuse de romance, qui, les yeux baissés, s'avance vers la rampe, et jure, sur un air de M. Paul Henrion ou de M. Ar-

L'orchestre.

La forte chanteuse à roulades, la Damoreau, l'Ugalde, la *Diva*, et que sais-je encore?

La Stoltz, la Falcon, l'infante de Castille, le contralto, la voix profonde, la cantatrice dramatique, l'amante du beau Sigismond, la malheureuse Léonor :

Mon arrêt descend du ciel;
Venez tous, c'est une fê-ê-te!

La chanteuse de genre, la Dugazon, toujours couverte d'applaudissements, et assassinée de bouquets dans le couplet de facture :

Mon Aldegonde,
Ma blonde!
. . . .
Ma Roxelane,
Sultane!
. . . .
Ma Rodogune,
Ma brune!

et ainsi de suite, sur un air de valse très-précipité (dix minutes sans reprendre haleine);

La *Déjazet*, chanteuse grivoise et populaire :

J'suis née-z-à la point'Saint Eustache;
J'étais l' rossignol du quartier,
Et j' suis capable, afin qu'on l' sache,
D' chanter z-un opéra *h*entier.

« Imaginez-vous, ma'ame chose, » etc., etc.

Puis vient le personnel masculin :

Le ténor :

Un ange, une femme inconnu-u-e,
A genoux priiiait près de moi,
Et je me sentais à sa vu-u-e
Frémir de plaisir et d'effroi!

La basse chantante :

Les matelots de la *Belle-Eugénie*
Ont pavoi-é des plus riches couleurs
Ce beau vaisseau qui part pour l'Italie;
C'est le pays des belles et des fleurs!

Le baryton :

Des bras pour la défendre!
Un cœur pour la chérir!
Des bras!... un cœur! des bras!...

Le comique enfin, le Trial, le Sainte-Foy, le Levassor, qui est ordinairement louche, assez souvent bossu, mais qui n'a aucune chance de dérider son audi-

Le ténor.

La prima donna.

Le baryton.

15 Cent. LA LIVRAISON. — 91e ET 92e Livr. Aux bureaux de l'Illustration, rue de Richelieu, 60. PARIS TYP. DE FIRMIN DIDOT, RUE JACOB, 56. 20 C. par la poste.

Fig. 5.

"Les Cafés," 1852. Steel engraving, *Tableau de Paris*, 1852. Vassar College Library, Poughkeepsie, N.Y.

more independent, that I might rid myself of some of the drudgery so largely and freely imposed on us by our government. Otherwise, a scientific career is ended, since the years flow past, [old] age approaches, and I have no more strength to lead the worrisome life to which I have been condemned for so long."[19]

Although he had consigned twenty years of his life to achieving a position within this world, he now expressed disenchantment and cynicism about the ostentatious, even factitious, aspect of the French Institute and considered the position of the state-supported French academic scientist to have been badly compromised. Thus it happened that, just as Regnault had a lapse of faith in his profession, a surge in the energy of the French photographic world transformed his sporadic, ten-year side interest in photography into a concentrated passion. This was 1851, a year that photographic leader Jules Ziegler predicted would be "a glorious year" for photography.[20] Ziegler was right; historians now mark this moment as a turning point, when the photographic world began to coalesce socially and institutionally.[21] Regnault probably began to assemble the *Album Regnault* in this year, too, and it reflects his place inside that emerging social realm: trading pictures with other photographers, collecting the technical information to caption their prints, comparing their process results with his own, even including portraits he made of them in the album.[22] Although he was reluctant to confess the pleasure he took in photography—he insisted to Liebig, for example, that he had taken up photography not as a diversion, but for its usefulness in his scientific work—Regnault was becoming more involved in this world and had even begun to make some photographs for their beauty, not their utility. By 1855, he would find himself the leader of the "official" French photographic world, when he was elected to preside over the Société Française de Photographie (S.F.P.), soon to be the most influential photographic institution in Europe.

Leading up to this point was a decade of turmoil brought on by what photography was (an imperfect instrument for which everyone imagined some immediate use) and by the way it exploded upon the scene (an imperfect instrument with virtually no industry or institutions to support the demands quickly thrust upon it). As even the earliest reports of 1839 tell us, the public announcement of a photographic process launched a marketing bonanza of colossal proportions. In *Daguerréotypomanie* (fig. 6), the comic lithograph by Théodore Maurisset (active 1835–59), thousands of people crowd around a series of daguerrean spectacles, products, and commercial opportunities. Out of the surging multitude, men emerge bearing pallets and wheelbarrows weighted down with giant box cameras. Others happily shoulder the cumbersome outfits, still marked with large price tags—"250F," "300F COMPLETE,"—on their backs, or set themselves up for business on the spot. One dapper gentleman hobbles away with a massive camera wedged under his arm, ironically marked "PORTABLE APPARATUS FOR TRAVELING." A high-wire act performs off to one side, but the real entertainment lies in the number and

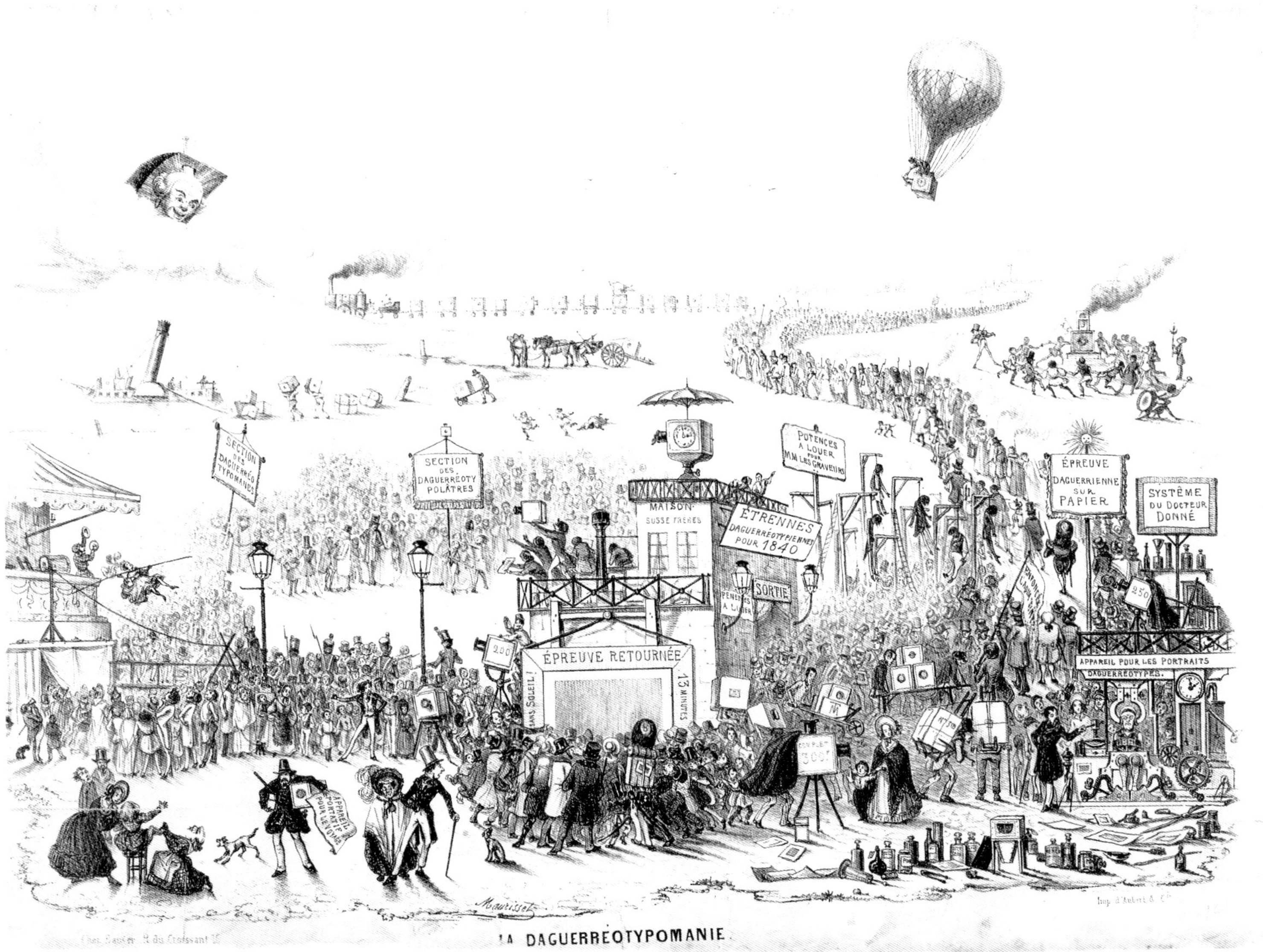

Fig. 6.

Théodore Maurisset (French, active 1835–59), *Daguerréotypomanie*, 1839. Lithograph, 10 1/4 x 14 1/8 in. (26 x 35.7 cm).
The J. Paul Getty Museum, Los Angeles. Gift of Samuel J. Wagstaff, Jr., 84.XP.983.28

variety of budding daguerreotypists scrambling to attempt the ridiculously impossible feat of capturing the motions of the aerialist. A daguerreotype studio, conveniently situated near the action, bears a notice, "WINDOWS FOR RENT," advertising that the best camera views to the scenery and sunny studio rooms can be had for a price. Hundreds of figures, herded beneath a pair of banners designating "DAGUERREOTYPE MANIACS" and "DAGUERREOTYPE LOVERS" await their turns to enter the Maison Susse Frères studio, passing before a giant mirror inscribed "PROOFS TURNED OUT IN 13 MINUTES, WITHOUT SUN!" and a huge sign advertising "DAGUERREOTYPE NEW YEAR'S GIFTS FOR 1840." The crowd exits from this establishment in a queue that extends two-abreast over the plains to a distant town, miles off. Gamely mocking his own professional predicament, the artist depicts the satisfied "daguerreotypomaniacs" as they file blithely past the casualties of the new fad: a crowd of disconsolate printmakers who press toward a row of scaffolds. There a placard announces "GALLOWS TO RENT FOR ENGRAVERS"—an opportunity that has already enticed several unfortunate souls. Displayed outside another shop marked "APPARATUS FOR PORTRAITS—DAGUERREOTYPES" is an elaborate pillory for immobilizing portrait sitters and a collection of no fewer than twenty vials, flasks, and apothecary jars—just the basics necessary to get started.

A comic exaggeration, to be sure, but Maurisset's print was inspired by an actual incident, which underscores the very real market for all things daguerrean, that took shape within days of the public announcement of the details of the process on 19 August 1839. Contemporary reports recount that when Susse Frères first placed a daguerreotype portrait in their shop window (reputedly the first so displayed), a near-riot ensued in front of the shop; authorities had to be summoned to control the crowd.[23] Most amazing is that "daguerreotypomania," more than a mere fad, would become a durable obsession of the modern age that would stir the emotions of opposing camps for more than a century. If in 1839 a mob of Parisians struggled to catch a glimpse of a single, uncanny daguerreotype portrait gleaming in a shop window, some nineteen years later the critic Victor Fournel would be tormented by a simulacrum of the mob, its painfully ordinary faces immortalized in fatuous individual portraits, loaded cheek-by-jowl into gaudy studio vitrines, assaulting the innocent glance of each passerby.[24]

But in 1839 such commercial saturation was more than a decade away. While the Maurisset print makes sport of the self-satisfied neophytes trotting off with their expensive toys, what it does not show are the frustrations and the hapless failure that attended so much early photography. The 1840s were spent in frenetic, disorganized, and atomized photographic activity, with few established experts or channels of contact for new photographers. Failure did not necessarily dampen the hopes of novices, however, for as the veterans of that early period were so fond of recounting, the truly marvelous quality of the successful plate was an end that justified any disappointment and expense along the way.

PHOTOGRAPHY AND THE ACADÉMIE DES SCIENCES

The first body in France to provide institutional support to the fledgling medium was the Académie des Sciences, and it remained one of the most important channels of technical information through the 1860s. Regnault, elected to the A.d.S. in July 1840, missed the academy's first presentations on the daguerreotype in the previous year. Like most devotees of the new medium, he depended on the A.d.S. for the latest photographic information, and he would eventually become one of the resident photographic experts. Between 1839 and 1850, the A.d.S. heard 230 papers, letters, and reports related to photography, which were duly published in its weekly *Comptes rendus*. Moreover, any research presented to the A.d.S. was usually treated to a thorough technical examination by a committee, which reported its findings and gave advice on improvements. To have the country's best scientific minds focusing their knowledge and experience on every item that came before them was invaluable to the technical advancement of photography. Still, the A.d.S. could serve photography only incompletely: its meetings were closed to the public; nonmembers needed a sponsor to present their papers; its communications naturally had a scientific focus, as opposed to an artistic or commercial one; and, being responsible for all branches of science, its time for any given subject was limited.

The big announcement in August 1839, which divulged the chemical recipe and technique used by Daguerre, was actually the A.d.S.'s second official communication on Daguerre's process. Rumors had been circulating about the supposed means of fixing the image in the camera obscura for at least four years, as Daguerre quietly investigated avenues to profit from the process he had devised with the late Joseph-Nicéphore Niépce. When Daguerre privately brought his daguerreotypes before three members of the A.d.S.—François Arago, J.-B. Biot, and Alexander von Humboldt—the men were astounded by the clarity and perfection of the images, which included architectural and landscape views, and even an image of the moon. These were objects that could withstand the lengthy exposures, which Daguerre optimistically estimated at eight to ten minutes under good conditions.[25] The three scientists envisioned a host of useful and fascinating applications, and Biot remarked that Daguerre had done nothing less than place an "artificial retina" at the disposal of physicists.[26]

Arago, an elected statesman as well as the Académie's perpetual secretary, immediately began brokering a government pension for Daguerre and his partner's heirs. On 7 January 1839, Arago made the first presentation of Daguerre's work before the A.d.S., which he described in both artistic and scientific terms, but the details of the process were withheld while the state's negotiations with Daguerre were pending. Nevertheless, the daguerreotype specimens themselves were a sensation, and the interval between the initial January "preview" and the 19 August disclosure of the process itself created a fever of public curiosity. Intended or not, that official silence functioned as a masterful stroke of public manipulation, but it had another unexpected effect: the report of a process that generated a positive image on a silvered plate brought other inventors of photographic processes and equipment out of the woodwork, creating a cacophony of voices calling attention to their different techniques and processes. Notably, Hippolyte Bayard managed to accomplish his own unique photographic process in this brief interim, but the government's grandstanding support of Daguerre precluded appropriate recognition for the unlucky Bayard.[27] Several weeks after Arago's preliminary announcement in January, journalist Jules Pelletan counted three such "pretenders" who had already appeared, and he predicted that the public would now "see inventors rushing forth from every corner."[28] For would-be inventors, it was a question of pride as well as profit, particularly as Daguerre (it was believed) audaciously presumed to name the new process after himself. Outraged allusions were made to Christopher Columbus, robbed of the glory of being namesake to his own New World, and a contingent quickly emerged that characterized Daguerre as a huckstering usurper who had exploited the untimely death of his partner, Niépce, the true genius behind the process.[29]

The most determined counter-inventor was the Englishman William Henry Fox Talbot (1800–1877), who had been privately working for several years, with measured success, on a paper photographic process. Like Daguerre, Talbot realized that he needed an advocate inside the A.d.S. to make headway with his claim, and he approached Biot, an old friend of his own technical advisor, Sir John Herschel (1792–1817). Arago and Biot were known as professional rivals with a certain history, but there was never any serious conflict between them over the Daguerre/Talbot contest. Arago was not about to yield an inch in his support for Daguerre, having gone to great trouble to bring Daguerre's process forward as the nation's gift to the world. Biot, on the other hand, had no real personal stake in Talbot, although the men were acquainted through British scientific circles. Thus, while giving Talbot an ear in the A.d.S., Biot was still careful to maintain his neutrality. From 1839 to 1841, he corresponded with Talbot frankly and in good faith, giving advice and reporting on the A.d.S.'s continuing discussion of Talbot's claims. He also examined Talbot's techniques and personally presented each of Talbot's letters and his own findings to the academy, but he would not enter the debate as a partisan. However, Biot did express frustration over the rivalry between Daguerre and Talbot—and other photographic inventors, for that matter—and he plainly felt that Talbot's reluctance to reveal his methods was harmful to scientific progress, as well as to Talbot's own best interest.[30] More than once, he urged Talbot to simply have done with it and publish explicit descriptions of his methods.[31] By the end of almost three years of Talbot's protracted struggles with the academy, Biot was evidently tired of acting as an intermediary. When Talbot sent Biot some photographic papers and instructions for their use in 1841, Biot politely declined to examine them himself but instead passed them on to Regnault, a recent convert to the new art, who happened to be in competition with Talbot and Biot for the Royal Society's Rumford Medal that year.[32] Assuring Talbot that his samples would be "very well used," Biot described the recipient as "one of my youngest colleagues . . . a clever physicist as well as an experienced chemist, who had already made, for his own interest, some very successful Daguerreotype proofs."[33]

With his immersion in the activities of the French scientific establishment and his command of chemistry and optics, it is not surprising that Regnault joined the many scientists who were experimenting with photography.[34] Beyond their interest in the new medium as a synthetic application of the laws of physics and chemistry, Regnault and his colleagues recognized photography's consonance with the philosophy of empirical method.[35] To a man whose entire work consisted of establishing scienfic proofs through precise observation and measurement, photography would have appeared a godsend, a new, infallible tool of visual, incremental notation. Yet even though the crystalline detail of Daguerre's process was superior in terms of legibility, Regnault was more interested in Talbot's process, which offered the endless reproducibility of the paper negative and the album-friendly format of a paper positive. But Talbot, determined to elicit some form of recognition for his work, had placed a broadly written patent on his process. It would take several years of effort by French inventors to circumvent Talbot's claim, culminating in 1847 with a "new" paper process that Regnault would help to legitimize.

After experimenting with Talbot's own papers, Regnault evidently continued to work privately (outside of the patent restrictions) with the calotype.[36] In September of 1846, the A.d.S. received an intriguing letter: the report of a new paper process from Louis-Désiré Blanquart-Evrard (1802–1872), a businessman from Lille, who may have already known Regnault through Frédéric Kuhlmann, the Lille chemist who taught Blanquart-Evrard chemistry.[37] For several months, Blanquart-Evrard engaged the academy with a series of impartial, tantalizing communications pertaining to a new process for paper photography. His first short note was accompanied by two small paper photographs that demonstrated printing variations "depending entirely upon the will of the operator."[38] The image featured Blanquart himself jauntily posed amid a haphazard arrangement of the familiar and disparate props of the artist's studio—a globe, guitar, palette, tapestries, plaster masks, anatomical cast, wine glass, and carafe. The explanatory note, which advertised a photographic process responsive to the photographer's taste and intention, and the picture itself, clearly referencing the medium's use by artists, showed the newcomer's artistic orientation. Blanquart-Evrard finally addressed details of the process to the A.d.S. on 25 January 1847, and in April, Regnault was asked to lead the examining committee, jointly formed of members from the academies of science and beaux-arts, for the process.[39] There is a portrait of Regnault and three members of this committee, made by Blanquart-Evrard during a three-day workshop before the committee at the Collège de France (fig. 7). Regnault, dressed to assist the messy technical operations, cuts a casual figure with his shirtsleeves rolled to the elbow, wearing a sporty cap, sitting next to his colleagues with their waistcoats and top hats. After learning the process under Blanquart-Evrard's direction, Regnault tested it with his students at the Collège, who quickly mastered it.[40]

With the positive results reported by Regnault and confirmed by the committee, and with the inventor's willingness to freely publish details of the process, the joint academies were eager to endorse Blanquart-Evrard's process and to grant that it was sufficiently different from Talbot's to elude the English patent restrictions.[41] The news that Blanquart-Evrard had at last "awoken Mr. Talbot's 'sleeping beauty'" was greeted most enthusiastically in France. The photography writer Louis Figuier, however, wrote a scathing commentary on this turn of events in his 1851 photographic manual, asking how the A.d.S. could validate a method, practically identical to Talbot's own, when Blanquart-Evrard did not even have the courtesy to mention the rightful inventor's name in his mémoire. How was it, Figuier demanded, that this man, "no more than a drapery merchant from Lille," now deserved "the honors of a celebrity"?[42] The A.d.S.'s decision not to question Blanquart-Evrard's process as infringing on Talbot's patent was unquestionably self-serving and possibly actionable, but Talbot had given up on getting his due in France. He laconically responded, said Figuier, "like a nobleman," by simply sending "two or three of his photographs to a few friends in Paris that [make] the prints of Blanquart-Evrard singularly pale by comparison."[43] Figuier's comments are an early invocation of the metaphor of class that divided photography in two camps: a photography of the enlightened individual and a photography of the vulgar masses. Reconciling these two stubbornly held concepts would occupy photography's promoters for more than a century.

While rivalries and competition had always been an essential part of the scientific world that helped parent photography, photography differed from most lines of research pursued by the academy in that it was always clear that it stood to be a money-maker of the first order. One did not need to be a scientist to practice it; on the contrary, it attracted practitioners from all classes and backgrounds, and so it rapidly moved from being a medium shared by science and art to one dominated by commerce. With the variety of people ready to use it—from artists to pornographers to zoologists and all points in between—it was evident that photography could never be delimited or regularized by the Académie des Sciences.

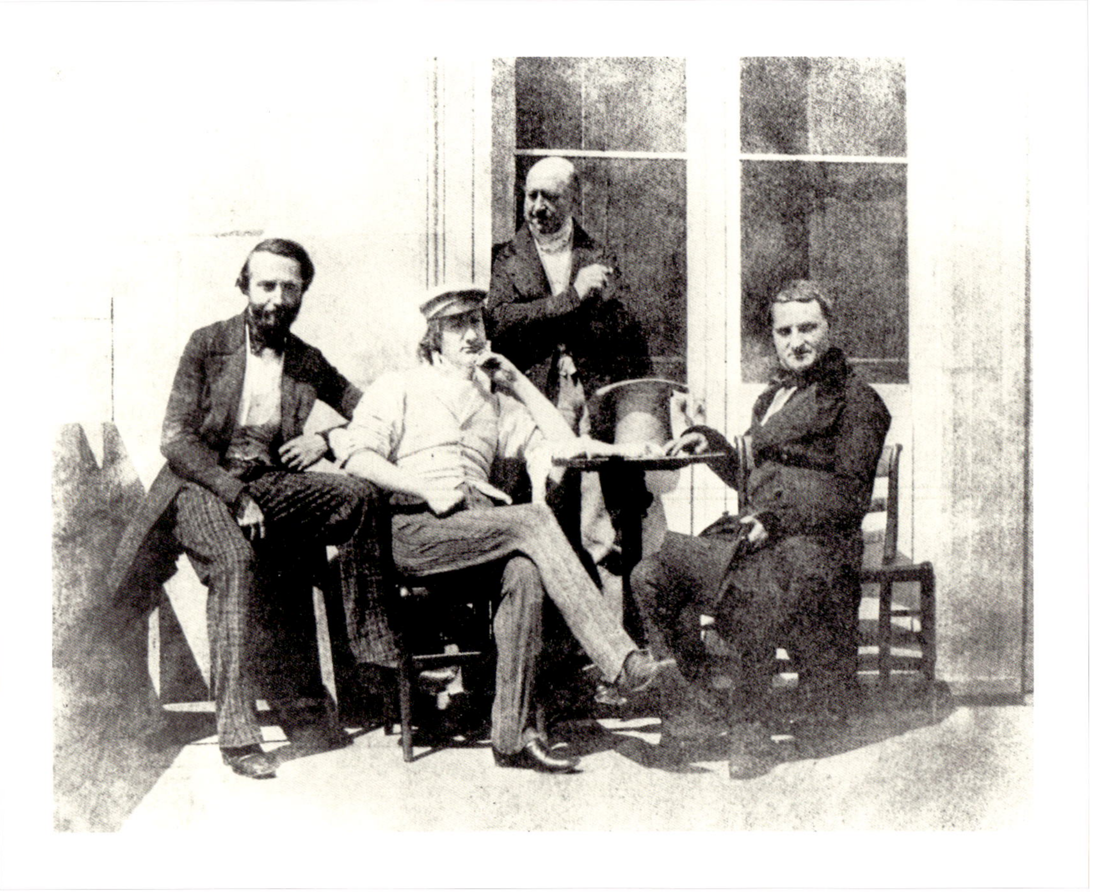

Fig. 7.

Louis-Désiré Blanquart-Evrard (French, 1802–1872), *Blanquart-Evrard Process Demonstration, Collège de France*, April 1847. Salt print from paper negative, $7^{1}/_{8}$ x $5^{7}/_{8}$ in. (18.2 x 15 cm). Société Française de Photographie, Paris

IMMERSION IN PHOTOGRAPHY AND THE SOCIÉTÉ HÉLIOGRAPHIQUE

Although he had been experimenting with the medium since 1840, the appearance of a dependable paper process was apparently the stimulus for Regnault's real immersion in photography. By 1850, in addition to his frenetic activities in research, teaching, and publishing, he was regularly practicing photography using Blanquart-Evrard's techniques, adding his own modification of sensitizing the paper by using the vacuum pump. By 1851 he had also devised another substantial improvement: substituting pyrogallic acid (pyro) for the gallic acid normally called for as a developer. He passed his results with pyro along to Gustave Le Gray (1820–1882), who advised the change in the 1852 edition of his popular manual of photographic method.[44]

A third innovation by Regnault dating from the same time—a method of making line illustrations from photographs—may have occurred to him through a photographic exercise connected with a new course in acoustics he was offering at the Collège de France in the 1850–51 academic year.[45] A group of ten pictures illustrates stagings of acoustic experiments that must have concerned sound more than sight, and what exactly he sought to show in the photographs is not immediately apparent. Taken outdoors in the open area adjacent to his apartments and laboratory at the Collège, they document Regnault's assistants and colleagues performing a series of manipulations on seemingly improvised objects—strange hybrids of musical and scientific instruments. One man draws a violin bow across a tall rod held upright in a bowl of water (fig. 8); another, dressed in a frock coat and top hat, strikes a hammer against the rim of a metal bowl while pivoting a large open cylinder at the bowl's edge (fig. 9). Another uses the violin bow, perhaps to demonstrate the action of vibration on grains of sand scattered across the surface of a metal sheet, where sound waves are amplified by a tube held perpendicular to the surface (fig. 10). Without macro lenses, strobe lighting, or instantaneous exposure, early photography was incapable of depicting the physical principles of acoustics demonstrated in these experiments. These photographs therefore served as illustrations of experimental procedure, not as visual proof of the physics at work.

Regnault may have been thinking about photography and its pedagogical uses for some time. His first textbook, *Cours élementaire de chimie* (1847), had been a fantastic success—in part because of its inspired use of engraved illustrations interspersed throughout the text (fig. 11).[46] In 1851 he described a similar project for a physics book to Liebig.[47] This time, however, he wanted to illustrate the book with engravings based on photographs, for which he devised an ingeniously simple method.[48] The photograph was traced with indelible ink, then washed in a cyanide bath, leaving behind only the marked outlines, which became the basis for engraving. But like many other subsidiary projects, Regnault's plan for an illustrated physics text was ultimately shelved; other work commissioned by the government was more pressing.

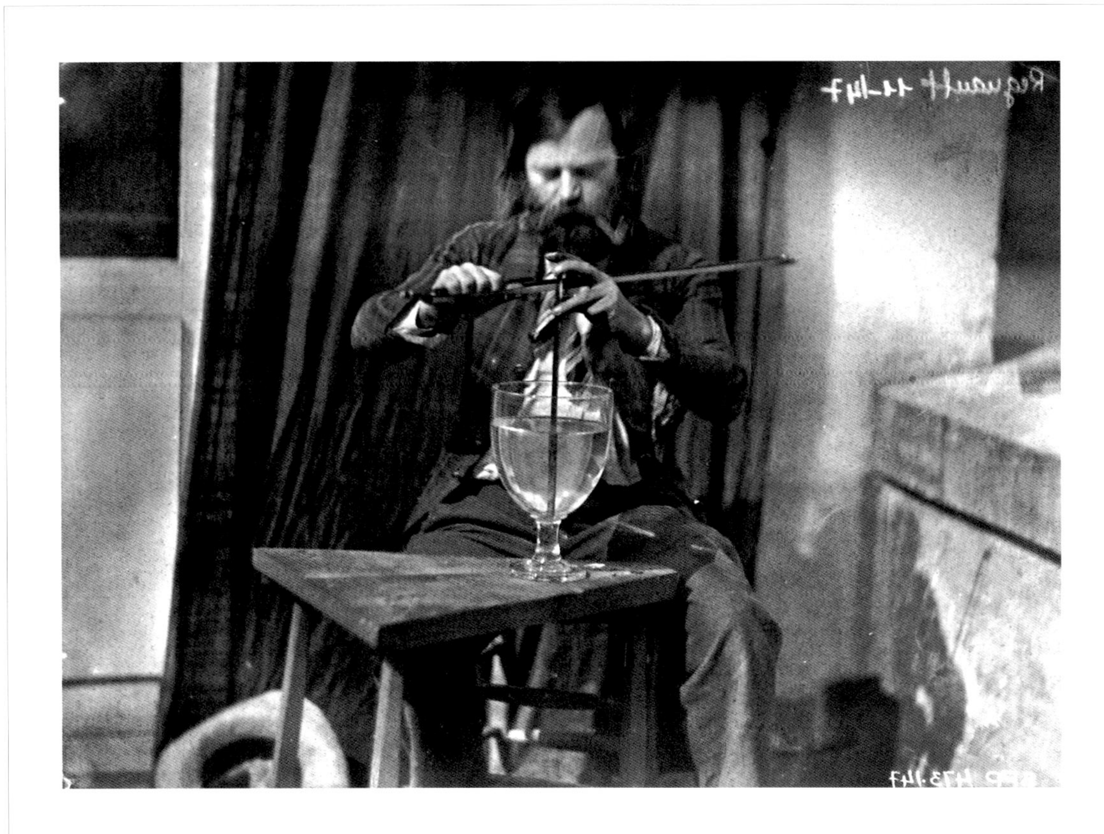

Fig. 8.

Victor Regnault, *Acoustic Experiment*, c. 1850. Modern print from paper negative, 5 5/8 x 4 in. (14.4 x 10.2 cm).
Société Française de Photographie, Paris. 473.147

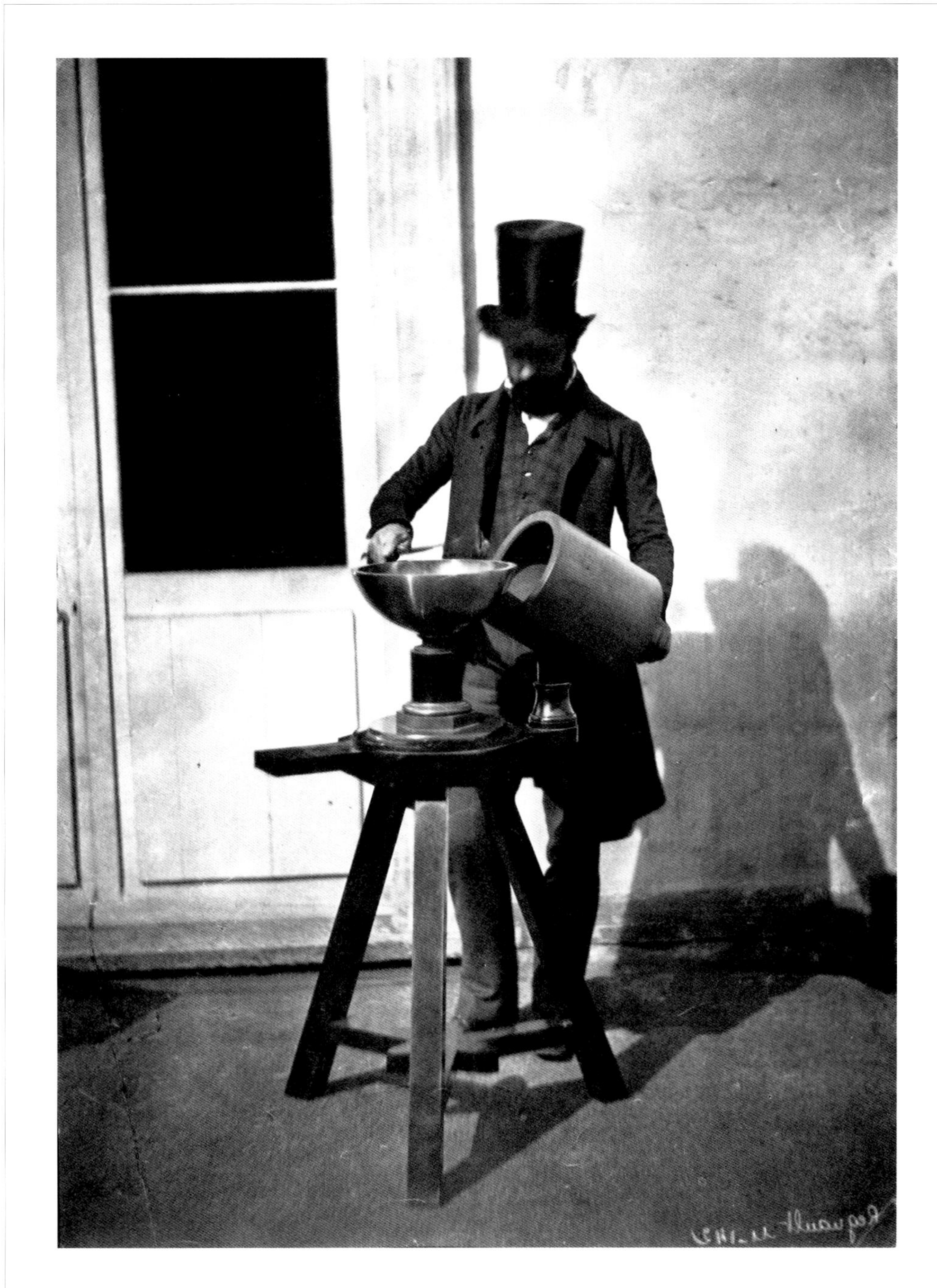

Fig. 9.

Victor Regnault, *Acoustic Experiment*, c. 1850. Modern print from paper negative, $7^1/_2$ x $5^3/_8$ in. (19 x 13.7 cm).
Société Française de Photographie, Paris. 473.142

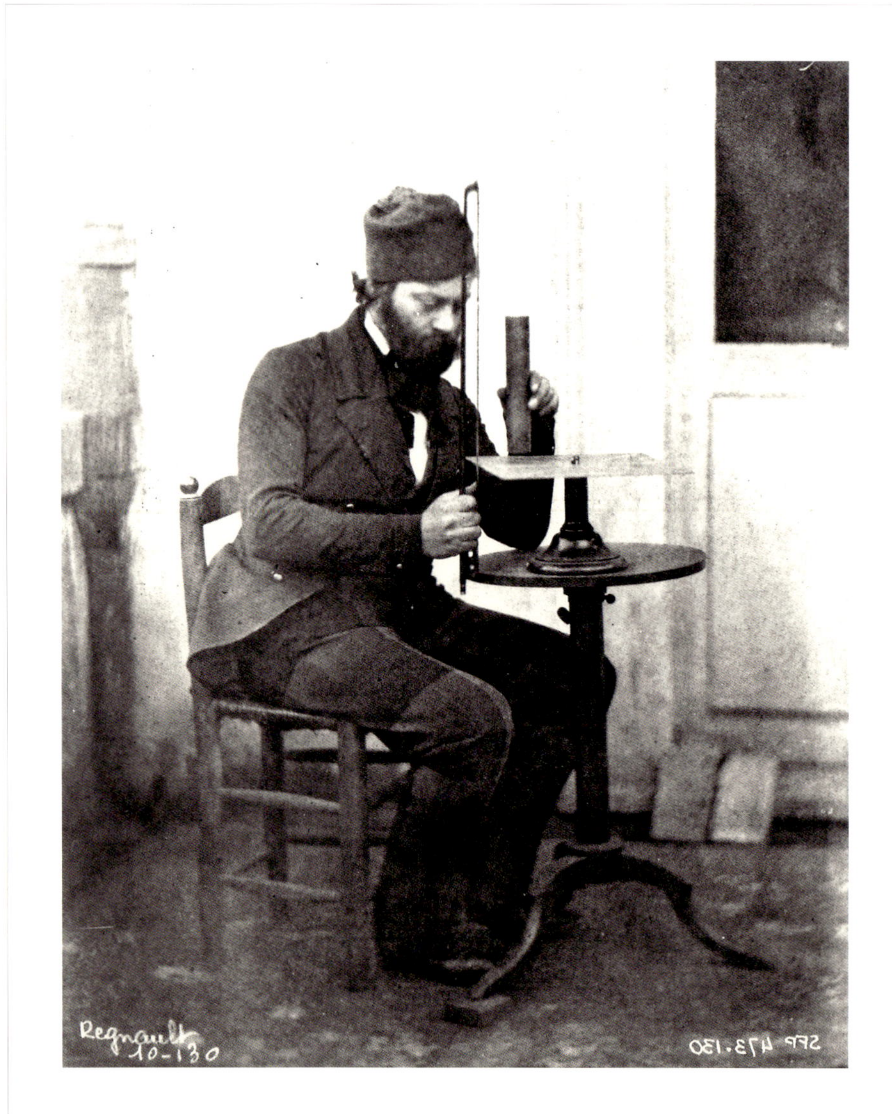

Fig. 10.

Victor Regnault, *Acoustic Experiment*, c. 1850. Modern print from paper negative, 6 x 4 3/4 in. (15.1 x 12.2 cm).
Société Française de Photographie, Paris. 473.130

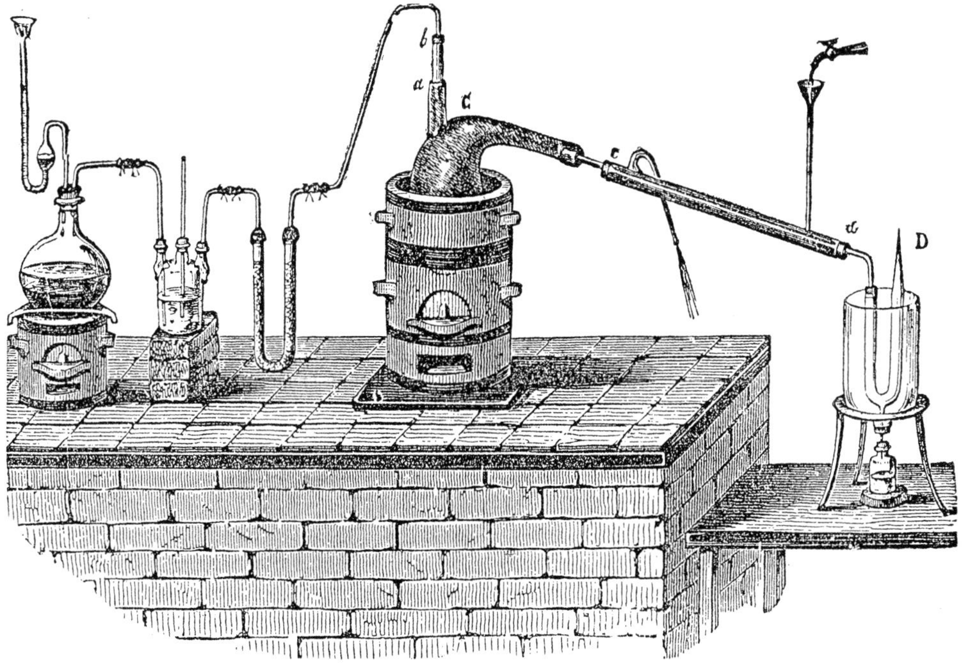

Fig. 11.

Illustration. Victor Regnault, *Cours élementaire de chimie*, 2d ed., 1853

Regnault did not bring any of these innovations before the Académie des Sciences. Instead, he shared them with a new body of colleagues, the Société Héliographique (1851–53?), the first official photographic society in France. Surprisingly little is known of the society, despite the fact that the weekly newspaper *La Lumière* was launched as its official publication.[49] The founding of the Société Héliographique in January 1851 marked the end of photography's troubled childhood and the attainment of its majority, its independence from the parental shelter of the Académie des Sciences. While the A.d.S. continued to receive papers dealing with photography, these were increasingly directed toward the interests of science proper: astrophotography, microphotography, lens refraction, and the like. With its diverse membership drawn equally from the arts, sciences, and letters, the Société Héliographique functioned differently; it was like a salon of variously talented, well-heeled, and professionally successful men, who met to discuss informally matters relevant to photography. The membership list of this society presents a cross-section of the Paris cultural elite: the diplomat art lover Baron Louis Gros (first president); art world figures like the painter Jules Ziegler, Léon de Laborde (curator at the Louvre), the painter Eugène Delacroix (1798–1863), and the architect César Daly; critics and writers such as Jules Champfleury, Francis Wey, and Maxime du Camp, and scientific savants like Regnault and Edmond Becquerel. André Gunthert has recently shown that despite the Société Héliographique's clubby organization (the group was more fraternal than professional), there were pronounced internal tensions over the society's direction and focus. In addition, the group faced some hostility from the wider photographic community over its perceived snobbery and artistic emphasis, noted in its promotion of calotypy and the consequent disregard for daguerreotypy and the new collodion process.[50]

Still, the Société Héliographique was intended to be more than a social club or booster organization. Following the first article of its statutes ("to hasten the perfection of photography"), the members were to form committees to examine, report on, and find solutions to all manner of problems still bedeviling photography, particularly paper photography, which was the method used by most members.[51] It appears, however, that these good intentions remained more or less inert, although Regnault eagerly shared his own findings with the group.[52] Reported in *La Lumière*, the society's minutes show him frequently coming forward as a technical expert on matters of chemistry and optics, and as an intermediary of Blanquart-Evrard, with whom he had maintained contact since their association in 1846–47. Regnault is also gradually revealed as the unnamed expert on photographic papers, one of the society's resident authorities that editor F. A. Rénard boasted about in the lead article of the inaugural issue of *La Lumière*. Authors' dedications in books from Regnault's photographic library witness his growing stature in French photographic circles in the early 1850s.[53] At this point, he was clearly pursuing photography for its practical and scientific applications, while also venturing into the terrain of artistic expression. By the summer of 1852 he had obtained a second, larger camera and had begun making ambitious, Barbizon-inspired landscapes.

Early on, Regnault's photographic contacts had extended beyond France; his scientific career had introduced him to the British scientists and photographic aficionados Sir John Herschel and Sir David Brewster (1781–1868) in the early 1840s. Through Herschel, Regnault met John Stewart (1814–1887), and probably other British photographers. Regnault and Stewart would develop a warm friendship based upon their mutual fascination with photography. In 1852 Stewart wrote to Herschel with new directions for paper photography he had learned from Regnault, and in December of that year, Stewart loaned nine of Regnault's landscapes for the world's first grand-scale photographic exhibition at the London Society of Arts.[54] Following upon this entrée to British photographic circles, looking forward to a big photographic season, Regnault wrote to the newly formed London Photographic Society in March, offering to trade some of his prints for "fifty sheets of the best English negative paper," an offer that was accepted but apparently never carried through.[55] That summer (1853) Stewart and Regnault would meet at Herschel's country house in Kent for a week of photographic excursions, which yielded a group of at least seven collaborative pictures, all landscapes and architectural studies (figs. 2 and 12).

Ultimately very little mention was ever made in the press of Regnault's own photographs, even though in 1851 and 1852 he was making them by the dozen.[56] "The whole photographic world talks of the masterpieces by Mr. Regnault, of the Institut," wrote the photographic publisher N.-P. Lerebours in 1852, to which he added, "I have not been lucky enough to see them."[57] Regnault evidently did not contribute to the Société Héliographique's albums and his name never appears in *La Lumière*'s (or any other journal's) exhibition reviews, which indicates that he did not publicly exhibit his own work in France. The reports of the Société Héliographique's "photographic soirées"—private evenings hosted in members' homes, evidently consecrated to the discussion of pictures—produced virtually the only words written by Regnault's contemporaries about his photographs, and these are few indeed. Regnault chose to keep his photography private, sharing it almost exclusively with these photographic colleagues and his family, and not with the salon-going public, although thirteen of his unsigned images were published in Blanquart-Evrard's portfolio editions.[58]

Why the Société Héliographique dissolved after fewer than two years is not entirely clear. Janet Buerger points to a split occurring within the group as early as 1852, but most members chose to support the original group for another year or two.[59] Still, the feuds and competitive tussles that Buerger and André Gunthert describe within and without the Société Héliographique, which hampered the

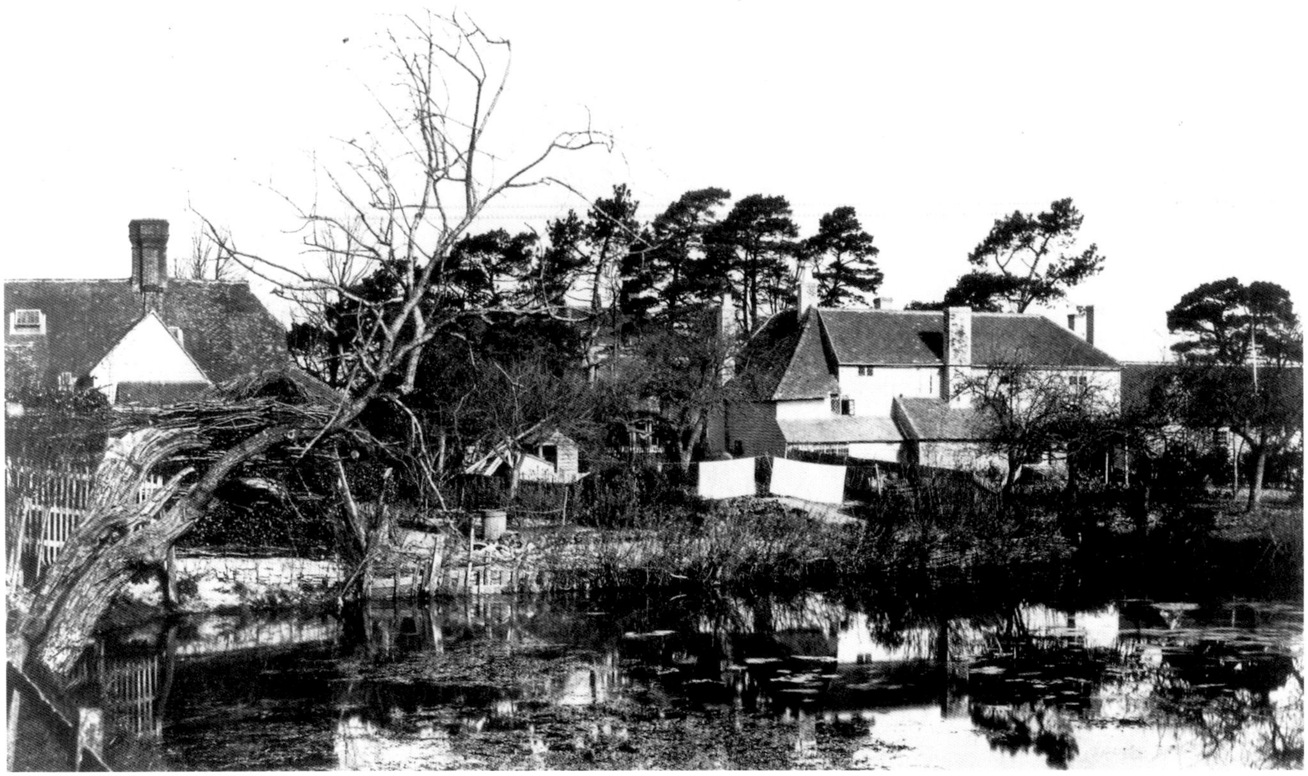

Fig. 12.

Victor Regnault and John Stewart, *The Lime Pond, Hawkurst*, 1853.

Salt print from paper negative, 15 x 10 in. (38 x 25.5 cm). Royal Society, London. MS 784.3

society's ability to carry out its objectives in furthering the art, portray an environment that was as chaotic as it was vibrant. With the continuing stream of new equipment, alternative processes, burgeoning scientific and commercial uses of photography, and recalcitrant technical problems, there remained a need for a financially secure, dependable organization with a stable membership capable of definitively examining and organizing this flood of information.

THE SOCIÉTÉ FRANÇAISE DE PHOTOGRAPHIE

On 15 November 1854, a group of interested persons, including some former members of the Société Héliographique, founded the Société Française de Photographie. Its first order of business was to make itself an official institution by drafting no fewer than sixty statutes, compared with the Société Héliographique's eighteen. In fact, the new society was to depart from the Société Héliographique in some crucial ways. Eschewing the open membership of the earlier club and modeling itself instead upon the Académie des Sciences, the S.F.P. was to be an elite, quasi-professional society. Annual dues of eighty francs helped maintain the exclusivity (the Société Héliographique had been free), as did its hierarchical membership, which was composed of three ranks: *membres titulaires* (incumbents), *correspondants* (corresponding members), and *associés amateurs* (amateur associates). Members in all three categories had to be put forward by two incumbents, then ratified by a two-thirds majority of members assembled. It was, as Buerger remarks, a "rule-loving" group, determined to succeed where the unregulated Société Héliographique failed.[60]

Although Regnault is listed as a founding member in the S.F.P.'s prospectus, he was not on the steering committee, nor was he among the first to actually sign on. His official membership was announced at the second meeting, and he was elected president two months later, on 16 March 1855. In proposing the nomination, acting president Eugène Durieu reminded voters of how important Regnault was to the society, as "one who occupies so high a position in science, and whose personal taste for photography is so well known."[61] The vote was unanimous. It was an inspired choice, one that illustrates the forethought and practical concerns of the collective members. Rather than bestow the position on a wealthy benefactor as the Société Héliographique had done (Col. de Montfort and the Baron Gros), the new society showed its pragmatism in electing the man who would be the most useful to the society's concrete aims. Regnault was not someone who would have time to involve himself with the society's ordinary business—that was Durieu, a retired state official, who remained the president of the administrative committee. But having been appointed director of the Sèvres porcelain factory in 1852, Regnault now had the highest connections in the official worlds of science and beaux-arts, which also enriched his substantial political contacts. Moreover, his experience with all kinds of technology and industrial engineering made him extremely knowledgeable about practical questions facing photography as an emerging industry; his word was as important to the paper manufacturer Canson as it was to the members of the S.F.P. With his frequent travels to Great Britain, he would also help mend old fences and forge links with the British photographic world (the London Photographic Society elected him an honorary member in June 1855).[62] Most of all, he was a peerless technical expert on photography, with an encyclopedic knowledge of photography that his fellow society members called upon at virtually every meeting of the S.F.P. Totaling the sum of Regnault's knowledge and contacts, which extended throughout so many circles of art, science, industry, and government, he was probably the most powerful man in French photography.

As the activities of the S.F.P. unfolded, it became evident that it operated primarily from a scientific point of view, but the founding document's stated goals for the society and its journal (the *Bulletin de la Société française de photographie*) articulate a dual purpose: to consider all that interests photography from the perspective of both science and art. Regnault, however, steeped in the aims and protocols of the A.d.S., ran the society as an institute committed to furthering the technics of photography. The society's minutes show that no meeting went by without an extensive discussion of a technical question or the appointment of a commission to examine a process, a piece of equipment, or a problem of photography, while comments on aesthetics or pictorial values were very rare.[63] In 1855 Regnault was chiefly occupied with a campaign to convince French paper manufacturers to improve and standardize their papers for use by photographers (undertaken, as it happened, on the eve of the decline of paper negative photography).[64] A more universal concern taken up by the S.F.P. was the permanence of photographic positives. In spite of his meticulous methods and insight into chemistry, like most calotype photographers, Regnault struggled with the problem of fading in his photographs. This led him to design a pair of competitions in 1856, funded by the Duc Albert de Luynes, a wealthy philanthropist/archaeologist interested in the industrial arts. The first, carrying a hefty prize of eight thousand francs, was a competition to perfect a photomechanical process, envisioned by Regnault as a carbon-based photogravure or photolithographic process.[65] The second, worth two thousand francs, was simply a competition for the greatest improvement brought to the permanence of positive prints. Both prizes were eventually awarded to Alphonse Poitevin (1819–1882).[66]

Like his predecessors in the Société Héliographique, Regnault realized the importance of his society to the history of photography, and seized the opportunity to build a collection of photographs and photographic literature. He considered part of the society's charge to be museological and intended that the society's physical expansion one day accommodate a gallery and ample room for collections.[67] Yet Regnault's most memorable act as the society's president was perhaps his campaign to have photography admitted to the beaux-arts section of state exhibitions. This cannot really be called Regnault's personal crusade, though, unlike his attempts to improve commercial paper manufacture. The official acceptance of photography as one of the fine arts was a key issue for the S.F.P., which mandated Regnault to pursue this objective. The society's early discussions on the subject show him taking a cautious position, urging members to consider both the advantages and disadvantages of being included in the annual Salon.[68] Nevertheless, he may have begun using the weight of his government position to effect photography's inclusion when he was appointed to the Imperial Commission organizing the 1855 Exposition Universelle—in fact, photography was included along with the other fine arts in the initial regulations outlining the arts exhibition.[69] Soon, however, the decision was reversed without explanation, and photography was demoted to its usual place in the industrial products section of the exposition. In 1857, Regnault took the S.F.P.'s renewed demand to Count Alfred de Nieuwerkerke, the state's Director General of beaux-arts. Nieuwerkerke flatly refused, informing Regnault that the Minister of State, Achille Fould, had explicitly authorized the refusal.[70] Undaunted, Regnault asked his constituents to return the measure to committee and draft a formal statement asserting photography's "certain and incontestable right" to take its place alongside printmaking in the next salon.[71] It seems likely that at this point Regnault may have taken the matter up directly with Fould, with whom he had frequent—and not always pleasant—dealings about Sèvres, but the record is silent on their discussion of photography. But on the occasion of the next salon, in 1859, photography was finally admitted under the same roof as the other fine arts, if under the terms of compromise: photography was installed in an area next to the other galleries, but was served by a separate entrance. The significance of this compromise, grudging though it was, was not lost on either photography's promoters or its detractors, and it is no coincidence that the 1859 salon occasioned Charles Baudelaire's excoriating digression on photography. The official acceptance of photography as a fine art had begun.

One of the peculiarities of Regnault's photographic career is that his own photography was beginning to subside by the time he was elected president of the S.F.P. On this account, the *Bulletin* reported a telling disclaimer in Regnault's brief acceptance speech of the presidency: "M. Regnault thanks the Société for the honor it has conferred in electing him its president. He regrets that his occupations do not permit him to show an assiduousness equal to his zeal for photography, and would be happy to take a more active part in the work of the Society that he follows with the most lively interest."[72] As before, Regnault felt his photography—his guilty pleasure—must yield to his proper obligations. In

1854, that meant preparations for Sèvres's participation in the Exposition Universelle of 1855. As usual, he did not show his work in this exhibition, although it was mentioned in a review of the Exposition by S.F.P. Vice President Paul Périer. There Périer described Regnault as one of photography's best-kept secrets, introducing his name in a list of some prominent photographers who preferred the more "artistic" calotype process: "Such is the opinion of our excellent and illustrious President, M. Regnault, who in his rare hours of leisure makes prints of the first quality, known to too few privileged persons, but who above all . . . speaks to us of art, as if he never had any other religion, and as if he were not already one of Europe's glories in rigorous science."[73]

It was not just Regnault's passion for art that Périer found remarkable; it was the coexistence of artistic sensitivity with an equally strong feeling for that which seemed its opposite: his other religion, rigorous science. If Regnault had once been conflicted by his two passions, he resolved the matter through deliberate choice. This usually meant setting aside photography in favor of scientific work, although he kept photography well in his thoughts. Taking a vacation in 1857 along the coast of Ireland, he did not bring his camera, but he did make notes of the sites that offered picturesque subjects for photography.[74]

There were several reasons why Regnault's photographic activity dropped off after 1855. His obsessive work led not only to physical exhaustion but also to increasingly serious injuries from fires and accidents in the lab, including a catastrophic explosion in 1856 that left him unconscious for a week.[75] Although he resumed his official duties after several months, this head injury required a long convalescence, which also may have interrupted his photography. He still continued to direct the S.F.P., though, and throughout the 1860s he contributed to the technical discussions reported in photography periodicals like the *Bulletin*, *Cosmos*, and *La Lumière*. Although none of his images from the wet-plate era are known to survive, Regnault did not lose interest in photography with the waning of calotypy; his participation in discussions on collodion photography confirms that he was fully experienced with the process that superceded the calotype.[76] When Regnault's son Henri, now a Prix de Rome winner and successful painter, toured Spain and North Africa in 1869, he asked his father for advice on making photographs. Regnault wrote back with detailed instructions for several variants of the collodion process, and his annotated recipes leave no doubt that he had worked with them himself: "This collodion spreads very well, doesn't tear during washing, and when dry, gives a very smooth surface, though a little opaque. Seven plates were thus treated; they were all successful. They give very fine prints, taking on a beautiful black, in development with gallic and pyrogallic acids."[77]

By 1868, in declining health, widowed, and with mental illness and/or other degenerative diseases indicated in three of his four children, Regnault stepped down from the presidency of the S.F.P., although the society voted to keep him as honorary president. He maintained his interest in the S.F.P. and photography into the 1870s. In 1873 he wrote with some advice on preparing dry plates; he also took the opportunity to urge the society back to the methods he had used when he was president, habits he had formed long ago when learning the art of avoiding all errors. The minutes noted that "M. Regnault, on a more general order of business, calls the attention of the society to the interest there would be in adopting a general and uniform system [for reporting] the formulae and research of photography."[78] The society politely thanked him for the suggestion and promised to bring it before the appropriate committee.

Surveying the vagaries of his photographic career, one sees that it was engendered by his scientific activities, just as it was curtailed by them. Back in 1851, when he saw his future as a scientist threatened by the political uncertainties and tedious obligations imposed upon him by the government, photography had served as an engrossing diversion while he looked for a way to increase his professional independence. He thought he had found it when the new government of Louis-Napoléon offered him the directorship of the Manufacture Nationale de Sèvres in 1852. To his surprise, while this position would ultimately burden him with more official duties than before, it also introduced him to a photographic coterie in the factory setting, where, surrounded by artists, it became possible and even practical for him to explore both the useful and pleasurable ends of the medium.

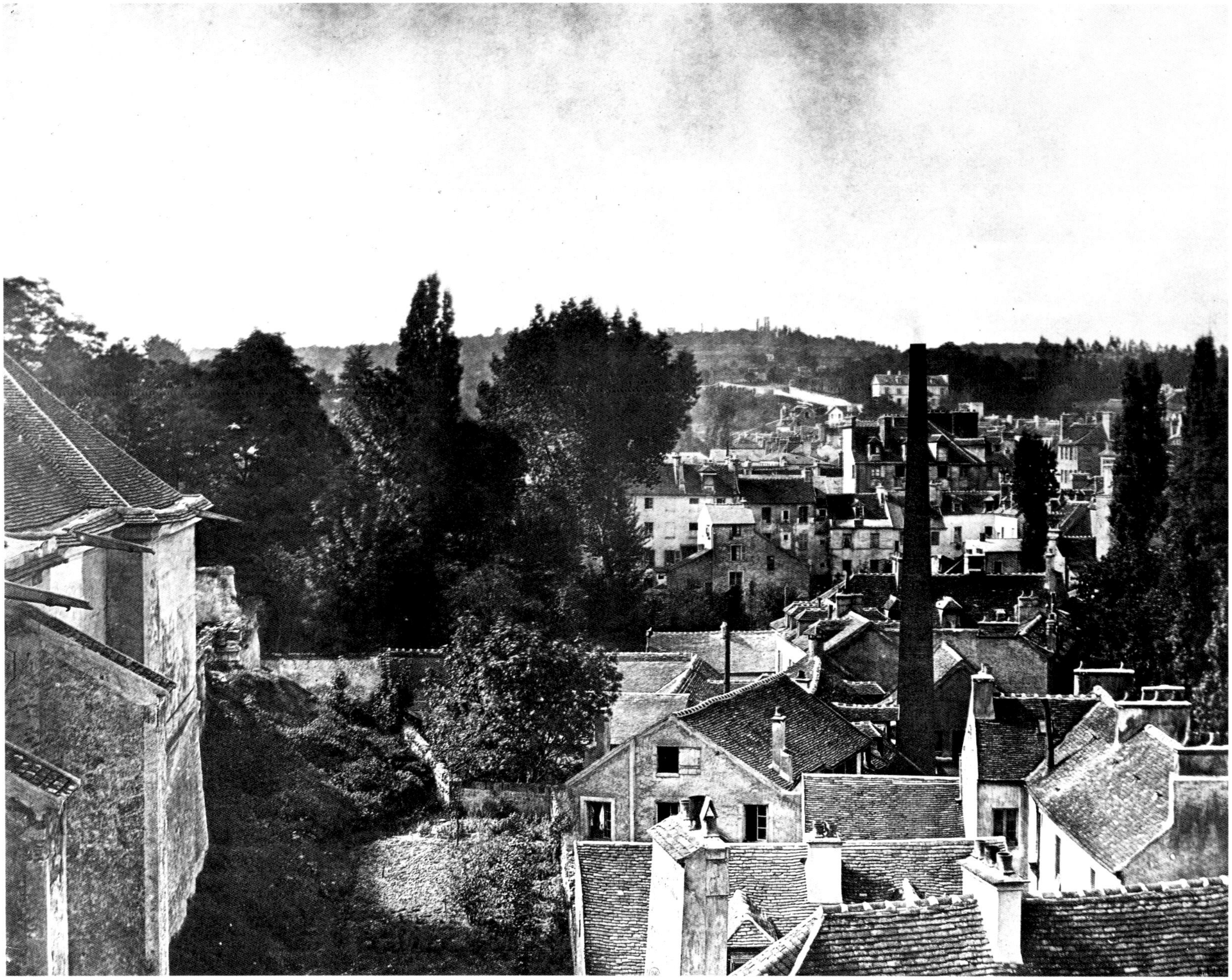

2 THE BULL IN THE CHINA SHOP:

PHOTOGRAPHY AT THE MANUFACTURE DE SÈVRES

By 1852, when Regnault was appointed to direct the national porcelain works at Sèvres, the factory already had an acute dilemma. This was a problem of reconciling two competing demands: to retain the traditional artistic distinction of Sèvres craftsmanship and to modernize by developing new industrial techniques. The competition at the Manufacture de Sèvres between the precious human touch and the soulless efficiency suggested by new technology was another version of the conflict between art and industry that was then being conspicuously waged around photography. As in photography, the question of modernization at Sèvres was vociferously debated in print by connoisseurs, critics, and the educated elite. In addition, as a state institution the prominent Manufacture was a convenient symbolic target for critics of Napoléon III.

Although Second Empire critics frequently accused the Manufacture de Sèvres of being diverted from its true—that is, traditional—path by the Faustian promises of industrial progress, it is now evident that Sèvres actually remained one of the most technologically conservative ceramic producers in Europe.[1] It was true that since the reign of Napoléon I (1804–14), each administration had encouraged scientific research and technological development at the factory, in keeping with an earlier pattern of government interest in promoting the collaboration of science and industry.[2] However, genuine innovation and unfettered application of new tools, materials, and production methods were greatly

Fig. 13.
Victor Regnault, *View from the West Wing of the Manufacture de Sèvres,* c. 1853. Salt print from paper negative, $13^{1}/_{2}$ x $15^{7}/_{8}$ in. (34.3 x 40.4 cm). Bibliothèque Nationale de France, Paris. Eo 219 Fol: A.11648

tempered by old habits and the factory's recalcitrant identity as a royal workshop—problems both material and abstract.

Regnault thus faced several sources of resistance to his initiatives: the culture of the factory itself, the nostalgia of connoisseurs and critics for the ideal of eighteenth-century Sèvres, and the uncertainty of government officials who oversaw a factory they scarcely understood. Moreover, in addition to the very practical fear of altering or abandoning the techniques and products that had carried Sèvres to the forefront of the decorative-arts world, there was a more ambiguous concern for protecting the image of the Manufacture, which was as crucial as the actual quality of the products to Sèvres's continued success. In 1863, attempts to install a studio for reproductive photography in the factory would redouble the debate over the control and protection of the Manufacture's public image.

PHOTOGRAPHY AND SOCIALITY AT SÈVRES

When photography first appeared in the factory around 1850, it was strictly as a social and leisure activity—not as a medium being investigated for its industrial applications, as one might expect. Stranger still, when Regnault and the head of the painting studio, Louis Robert (1810–1882), attempted to apply it to practical use in the factory, they were rebuffed by their superior, the maréchal J.-B.-P. Vaillant, Minister of the Emperor's Household and Fine Arts. This conflicted reception parallels the tenuous position of all new technology at Sèvres, which in turn reflects the state's equivocation over its own mandate for technological advancement.

As one of three state manufactures, the Sèvres factory was directly tied to the country's political upheavals. Its transformation from Manufacture "Royale" to "Nationale" to "Impériale" took place in just six years. As each new regime assumed power, the factory was given a thorough housecleaning; personnel might change, new decorative programs for the state's porcelain were ordered, and old stock bearing the iconography of the previous regime was destroyed. In April of 1852, four months after his coup d'état, Louis-Napoléon named Victor Regnault to be director of the Manufacture Nationale de Sèvres, filling a post left open by the recent death of the previous director, Joseph Ebelmen. But other changes were in the offing, for within the year the head of state would transform himself into Napoléon III, resurrecting his uncle's empire, and the factory would face a new round of changes.

When Regnault arrived at Sèvres that spring, he found that photography had preceded him. Louis Robert, recently promoted to head the painting studio, was already using the fine linen letterhead left over from the factory's previous royal incarnation as the paper base for photographic negatives and prints (fig. 14). Robert, a chemist and a specialist in stained glass technology, and Jules Dieterle

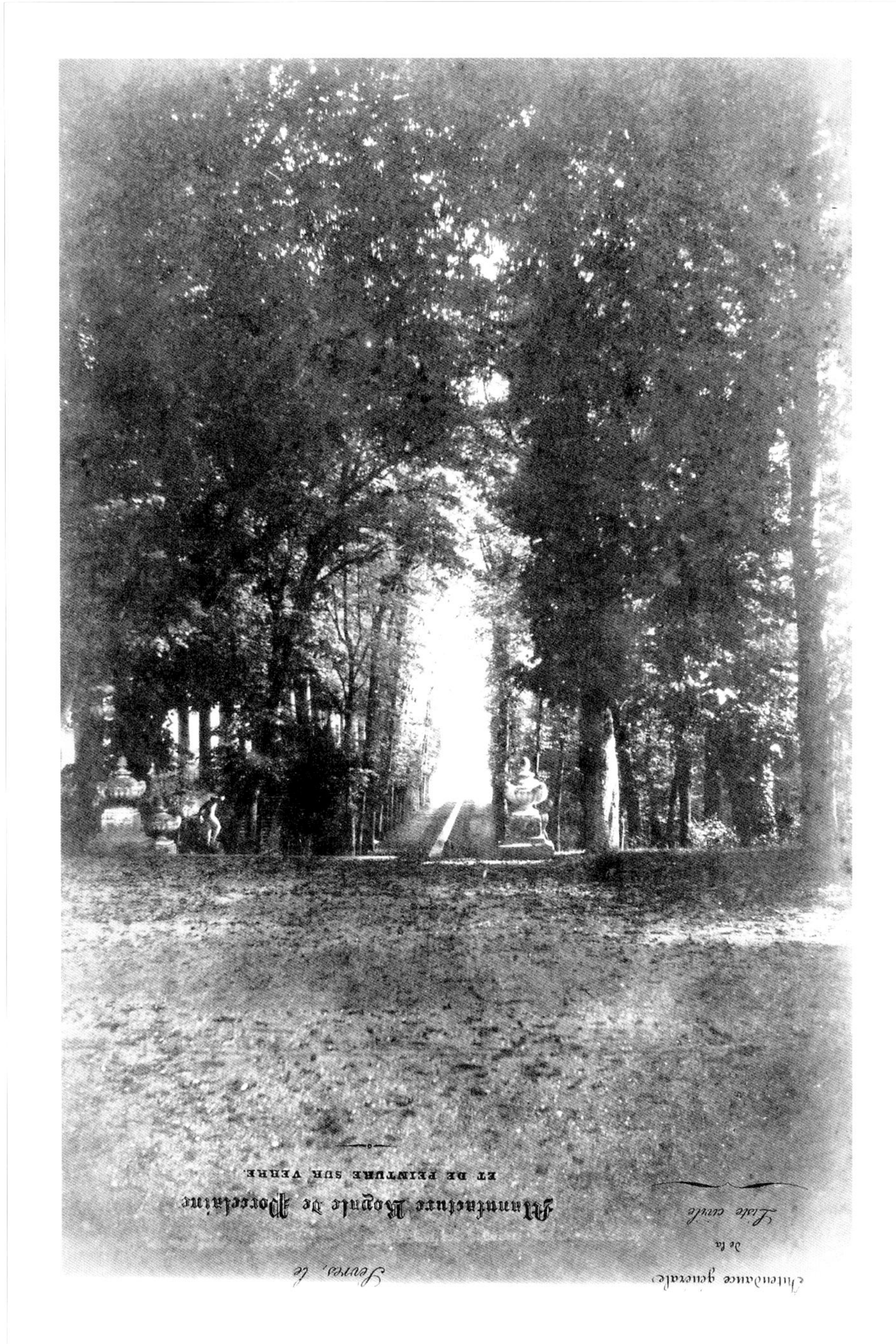

Fig. 14.

Louis-Rémy Robert (French, 1810–1882), *Garden of the Château de Saint-Cloud*, c. 1851. Salt print from paper negative, $12^{1}/_{4}$ x $7^{7}/_{8}$ in. (31.2 x 20 cm). The Metropolitan Museum of Art, New York. Purchase, the Horace W. Goldsmith Foundation Gift, 1995, 1995.104

(1811–1889), the factory's artistic director, probably began experimenting with photography when Sèvres's production slowed during the Second Republic (1848–52).[3] Although Regnault may have been surprised to find even one accomplished photographer on his staff in 1852, conditions at the factory made it a likely place for the efflorescence of this new medium, especially after Blanquart-Evrard's paper process of 1847 skirted Talbot's patent restrictions on calotypy and created an alternative to the cumbersome methods of daguerreotypy. The Manufacture provided a large laboratory with running water, ready access to chemical components, and a large stock of free paper, and a camera obscura was on hand as standard equipment for the artists. Robert was fully ready for photography; if he needed further assistance, he could consult his former professor, the chemist and early photographic authority J.-B. Dumas, who, having married the factory director's daughter, happened also to live in Sèvres.

Photography quickly found a place as social expression at the factory, where it dovetailed with the preexisting forms of self-representation that acted as part of the social glue preserving the institution's stability. This social aspect was a feature of the factory's special character as a family: a highly organized, stratified, insular community of laborers, artisans, office workers, artists, and scientists. Historians note that the family was the model for the earliest type of industrial management in France, but in the case of Sèvres, kinship was as real as it was metaphorical.[4] The factory's social completeness was enhanced by the fact that it hired nearly as many women as men; depending on the factory's economic health, two hundred or more people might be employed full-time. Many workers spent their entire lives there, married within the factory's population, and lived on the factory grounds or in the surrounding village. Jobs were handed down in families; a child would learn a skill at the parent's knee and be duly prepared to assume a regular place in the atelier. Some workers could boast a Sèvres lineage going back five generations, and it was not unusual for an atelier to be composed largely of kinfolk.

Some may have found the atmosphere at Sèvres painfully insular, but there was compensation in the comfort of the factory's paternalism and the pride to be taken in collectively representing what was arguably Europe's premier porcelain establishment. As a kind of family, the factory needed emotional connection as much as bloodlines, and there was indeed a great deal of intimate, self-reflexive interaction and expression among the employees. Communal theatricals, seasonal fêtes, music, and especially drawing and painting were common collective amusements. A humorous atelier sketchbook in the Manufacture archives illustrates this convivial closeness; composed jointly by the artists of the painting studio, it is filled with self-referencing cartoons and comic narratives, including a demonic caricature of Louis Robert menacing the dream life of his painters (fig. 15). It is not difficult to imagine how photography, especially portraiture, found a place in this communal setting as a means of serving the

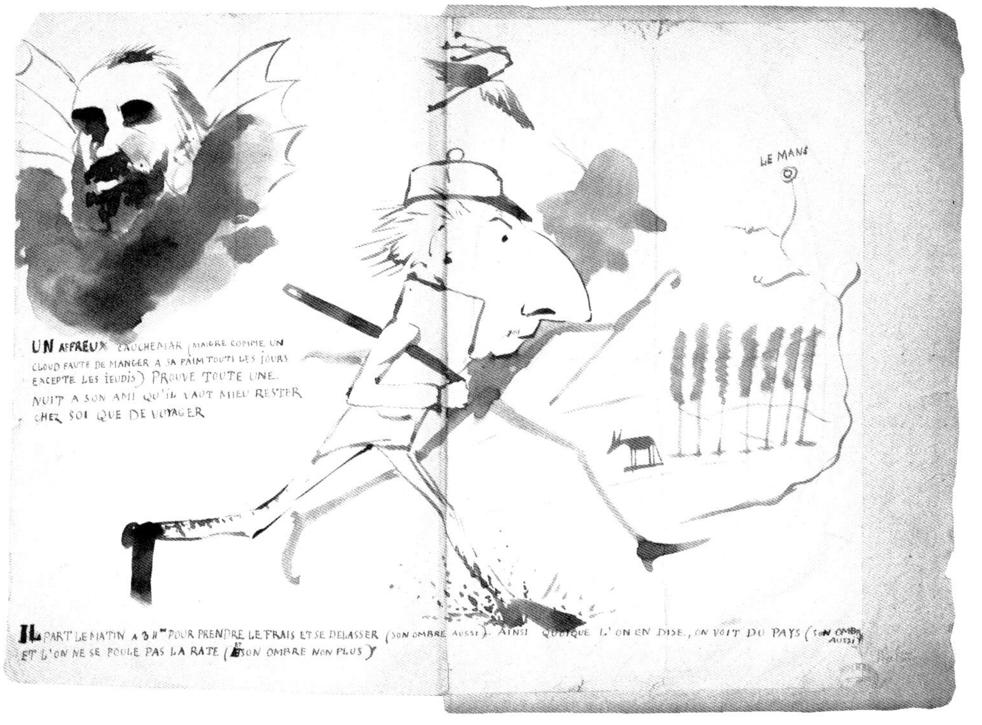

Fig. 15.

Sèvres atelier sketchbook, c. 1860. Watercolor and ink on paper, dimensions unknown.

Manufacture Nationale de Sèvres Archives

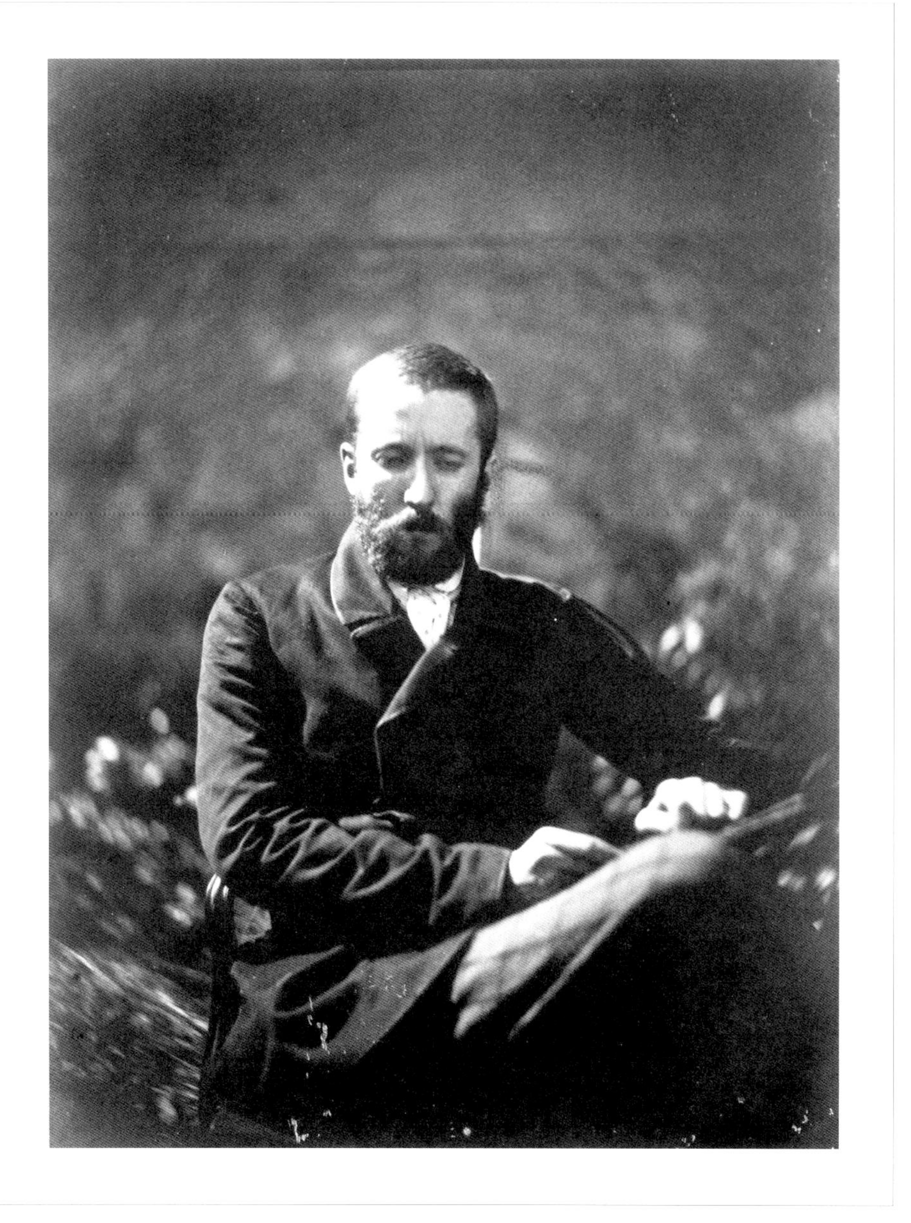

Fig. 16.
Louis-Rémy Robert, *Alfred Thompson Gobert*, c. 1851. Salt print from paper negative, 8 7/8 x 6 1/2 in. (22.6 x 16.8 cm).
The Metropolitan Museum of Art, New York. Purchase, Joyce and Robert Menschel, Mrs. Harrison D. Horblit and Paul F. Walter Gifts, and Rogers Fund, 1991, 1991.1044

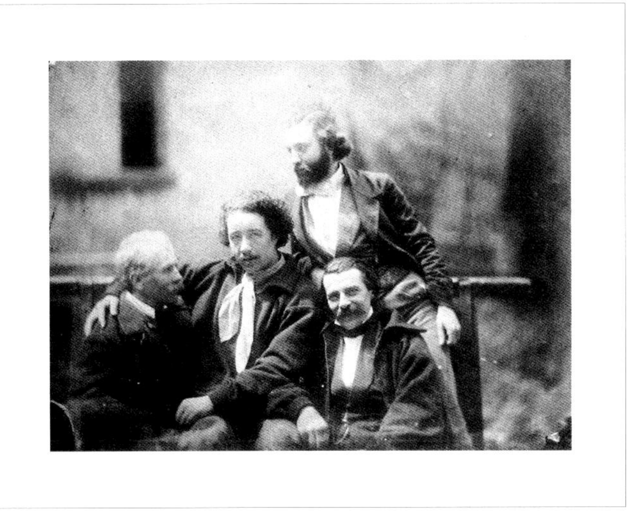

Fig. 17.
Attributed, Achille-Louis Bonnuit (French, 1833–after 1894) and Jean-Charles-Gérard Derischweiler (French, 1822–after 1884), *Members of the Sèvres Painting Studio*, c. 1859. Albumenized paper print from glass negative, 5 x 6 3/4 in. (12.6 x 17.3 cm). Manufacture Nationale de Sèvres Archives

intimate connections between the workers and their institution. Above all, portrait photography was collaborative and concretely productive: it documented personalities, expressed relationships, signified fondness and recognition, created sentimental mementos, and generally witnessed the significance of certain people, places, and things. For this group of early experimenters, it was also thrillingly modern, unpredictable, and a source of shared enjoyment.

Louis Robert's photographs depict his immediate family—his wife, daughter, and son-in-law (all Sèvres painters)—and his extended family of fellow employees (fig. 16).[5] He had ample experience as a portraitist, having sketched and painted since childhood under the instruction of the artists in the factory, including his grandfather, father, mother, and uncle. Robert had even exhibited pastel portraits of his Sèvrian friends and relatives in the salons of 1848, 1849, and 1850, although these were years when the Salon was unjuried. Expanding his practice to include photography probably enabled him to obtain photographic models for working in pastel, while making photographs for their own sake. Several colleagues, including Jules Dieterle and the painters Alfred Thompson Gobert (active 1849–91) and Jules André (active 1840–69), evidently assisted Robert's experiments with photography. It is likely that they, too, tried their hands at photography, and within ten years at least a few more artists and workers at the factory were making photographs of themselves and each other (fig. 17).[6] Most of Robert's factory portraits look like early trials with the calotype, showing long exposures, the distortions of a crude lens, opaque shadows, and overexposed highlights. Even in these experimental pictures, Robert chose framing, pose, and background carefully, using garden settings, other rustically picturesque settings like ancient stone courtyards, and even an elaborately painted architectural backdrop.

Robert and Regnault both made large numbers of photographs on the grounds of the factory, depicting some of the same structures. They made many views from the factory's upper windows: Regnault facing west, photographing from one of the laboratories (fig. 13), and Robert facing east, photographing from his apartment windows (fig. 18); these may have been their default views for testing new papers and process variants. Other features on the grounds made visually interesting subjects that were also filled with the detail of daily life in the factory: the royal courtyard, the main drive, the factory's complex roof lines, the area of the kiln sheds, the wooded slope being harvested for fuel rising behind the factory (fig. 19), and the main building pictured from numerous angles and viewpoints (figs. 20 and 21). They photographed in all seasons.

Regnault was partial to genre subjects, and several times he photographed picturesque scenes of the workers at rest: laborers relaxing in the brickyard, the carpenter and his wife sitting in the shade of the carpentry shop, a man in a workman's blouse looking over the cold frames of his garden, and two men sitting in the doorway of a workers' entrance, cleaning vegetables (fig. 22). These images present a surprisingly cozy view of life at the factory, given the difficulties Regnault was having in managing his workers in the shadow of his predecessor, the beloved Alexandre Brongniart, who had presided over the Manufacture from 1800 to 1847. When Regnault moved to Sèvres, his responsibilities did not end with fulfilling the expectations of the state. His new employees also expected him to assume the complex role of "father" to the factory's population, and they felt betrayed by his first preemptory acts on behalf of the state: the reduction in pay for voluntary overtime work to two-thirds the regular rate, and the attempted surveillance of attendance in the painting studio, which surely placed him at odds with Robert.[7] While waiting for the state's minister to settle this matter, Regnault took a trip to London in July of 1853, where he intended to photograph with John Stewart. Jules Dieterle wrote to him every few days, keeping him informed of the latest factory news, and gently reminded him of another side of his responsibilities: "Take good care of yourself and remember that you have a very large family, of which all the children are neither lovable nor pretty, but in the end, you accepted it thus. It is called the Manufacture Impériale de Sèvres."[8]

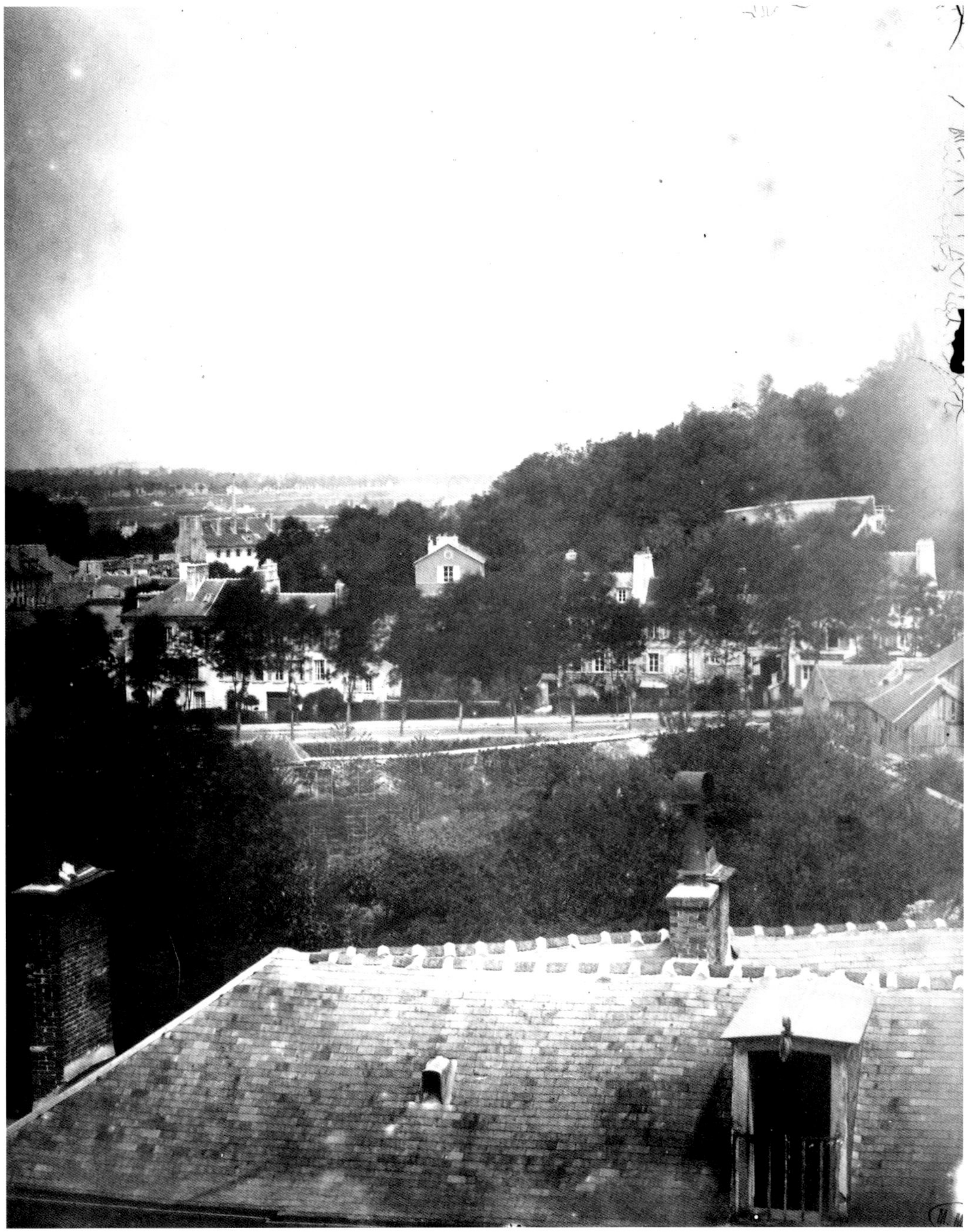

Fig. 18.

Louis-Rémy Robert, *View from the East Wing of the Manufacture de Sèvres*, c. 1855. Albumen print from glass negative, $12\frac{5}{8}$ x $10\frac{1}{4}$ in. (32 x 26 cm). Ville de Sèvres Archives. 5 fi 2259

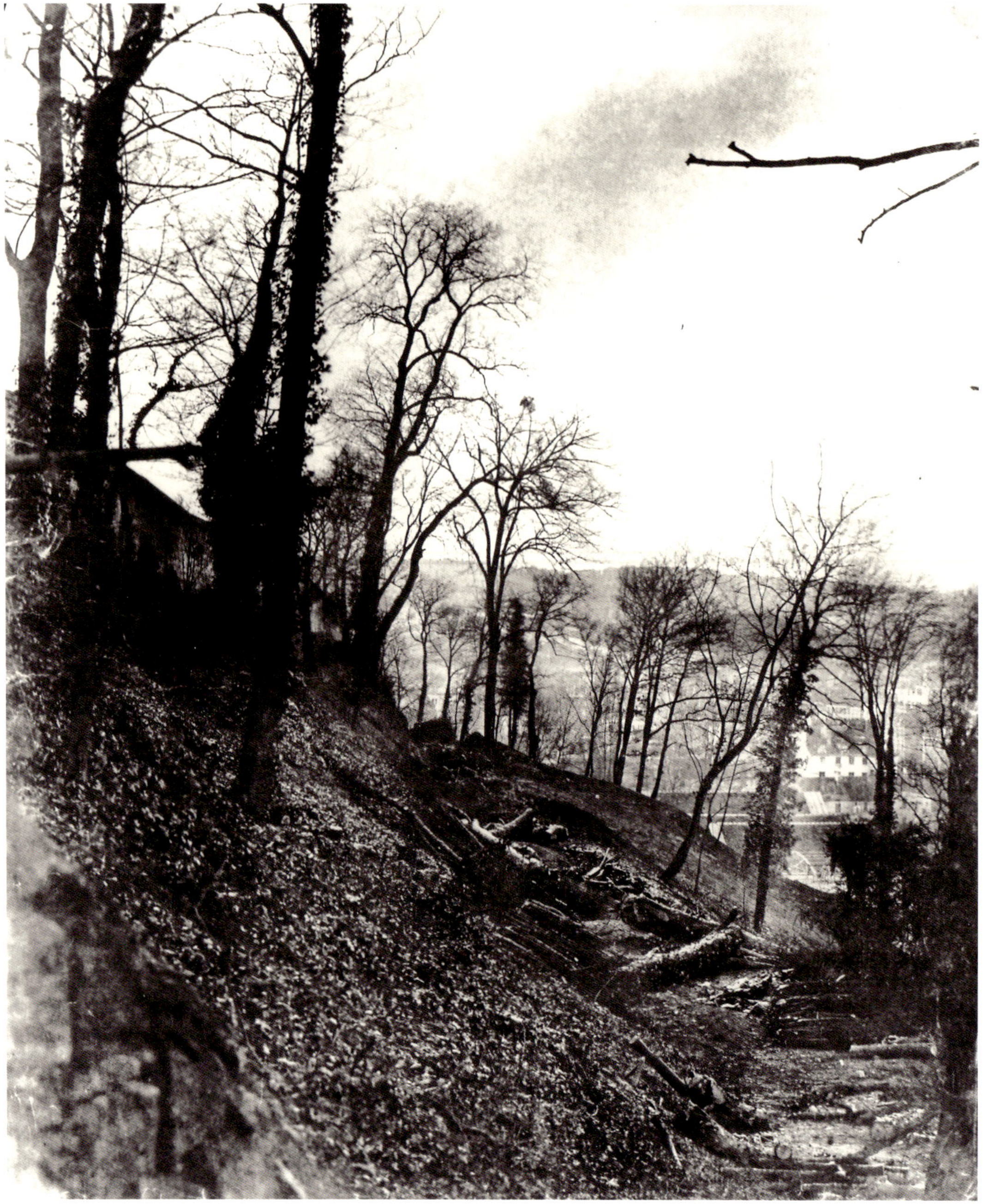

Fig. 19.

Victor Regnault, *Woodcutting behind the Manufacture de Sèvres*, c. 1852. Modern print from paper negative, 17 x 14 3/8 in. (43.2 x 36.4 cm). Société Française de Photographie, Paris. 473.174

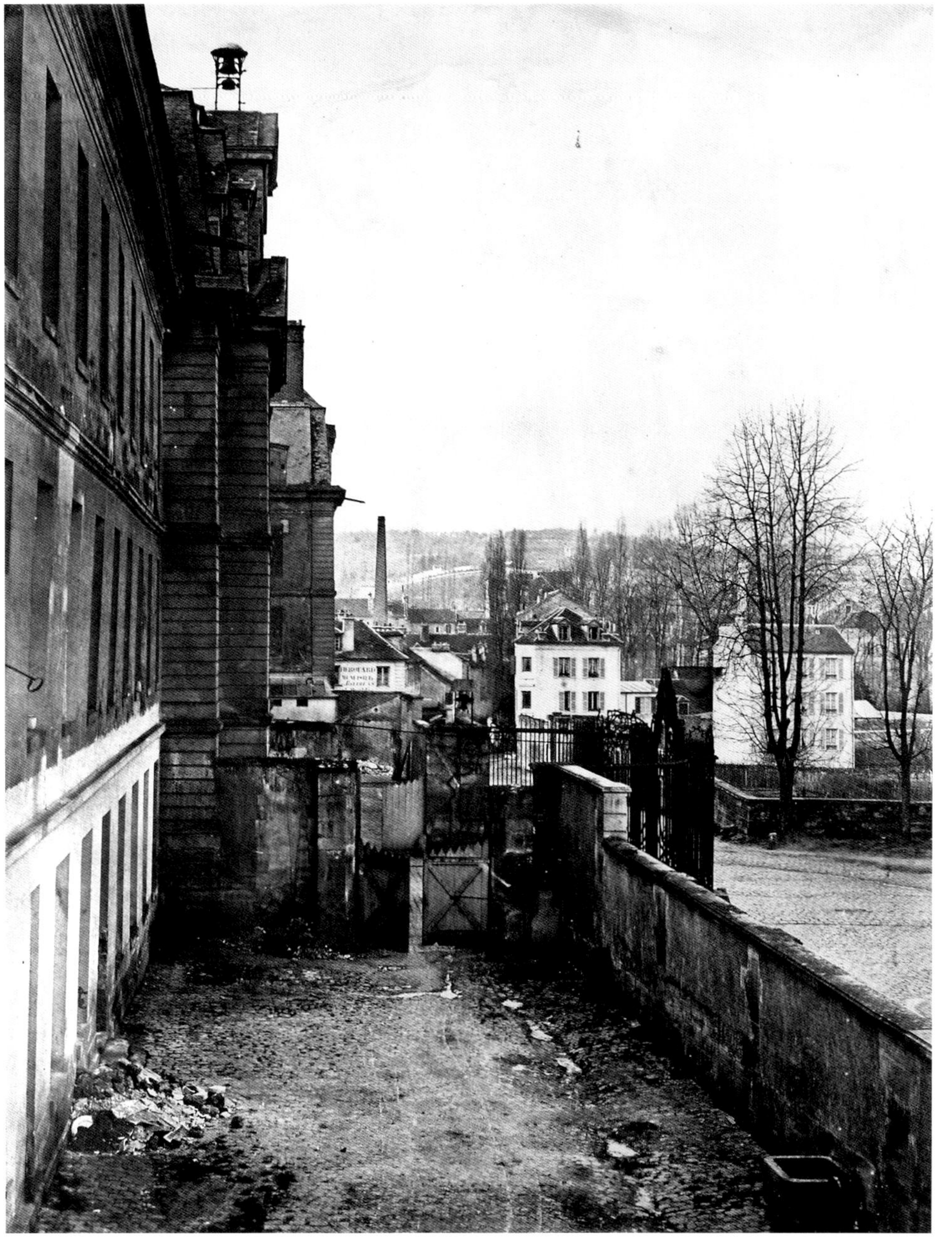

Fig. 20.

Victor Regnault, *View of Sèvres from the Facade of the Manufacture de Sèvres, Facing West*, c. 1852. Salt print from paper negative, $17^{3}/_{8}$ x $13^{1}/_{2}$ in. (44 x 34.5 cm). Collection of Richard and Ronay Menschel, New York

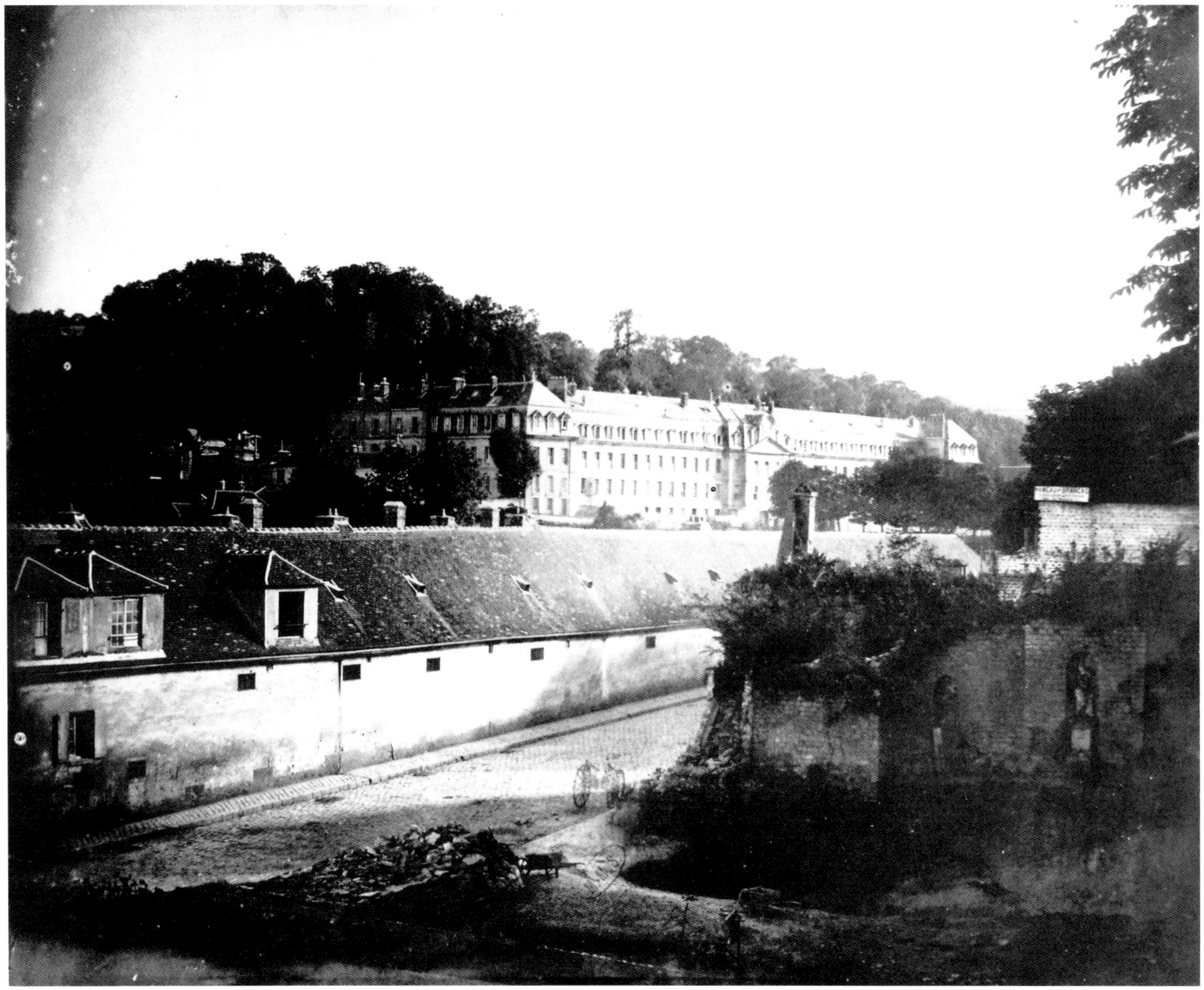

Fig. 21.

Victor Regnault, *The Manufacture de Sèvres from the Entrance of the Parc de Saint-Cloud*, c. 1852. Salt print from paper negative, dimensions unknown. Ville de Sèvres Archives. 5 fi 1-2366

Dieterle spoke several times of their shared interest in photography, closing one letter, for example, with "a multitude of photographic wishes."[9] The extent of Dieterle's own photographic activity is unknown, but he did appear before the camera several times, even posing for Regnault in pseudo-Turkish costume, wearing a fez and holding an ornate, long-stemmed pipe (fig. 23).[10] His letters to Regnault show how much photography had become part of their daily lives and the stuff of personal reciprocity, as when he playfully remarked: "I hope, monsieur, that, as here, the sun is shining brightly in London . . . that you have recovered from the bad crossing, that your health be good, that your negatives do not tire you too much, and that I shall be able to enrich myself with their positives."[11]

It would ultimately take years for Regnault to grow into the paternal role that his staff expected him to assume, but photography proved to be particularly helpful in facilitating his entry into the factory's tightly knit social ranks. It provided a common ground that brought together his staff's diverse expertise in art, technology, science, and design. At the same time, it gave Regnault a less formal point of contact with his *chefs* (studio managers) and artists, a proscribed collegial arena, ostensibly apart from the politics and power relations of the factory, in which he and the others could nurture the reassuring conceit of a fraternity of knowledge and experience based on their mutual fascination with the new art. The exchange of photographs nourished friendship, since pictures underscored the bonds of the community; held sentimental, pictorial, and practical meaning; and yet could be given and received casually. Moreover, two subjects Regnault was photographing in 1853—views from the banks of the Seine at Sèvres and Meudon, and views in the Parc de Saint-Cloud—reappeared as themes for several coffee services of 1854, which suggests that Regnault and his artists were sharing pictorial ideas as much as photographs. Photography was the means by which he began to negotiate a relationship with his senior employees based on mutual respect, while he slowly acquired the tact, wisdom, and experience to be accepted as their leader.

THE CULTIVATION OF PROGRESS

Given the vigorous amateur practice of photography within the factory walls in 1852, why did it still take a decade for practical photographic applications to appear at Sèvres? In short, photography's progress in the factory was actually impeded as much as it was impelled—for all the forces that would nourish its practical investigation at Sèvres, there were opposing conditions and policies that hampered its practice, beginning with the factory's place within a vast bureaucracy.

The factory had been acquired by Louis XV in 1753; with its budget underwritten by the monarch and pampered by legislation that protected it from competition with private industry, Sèvres

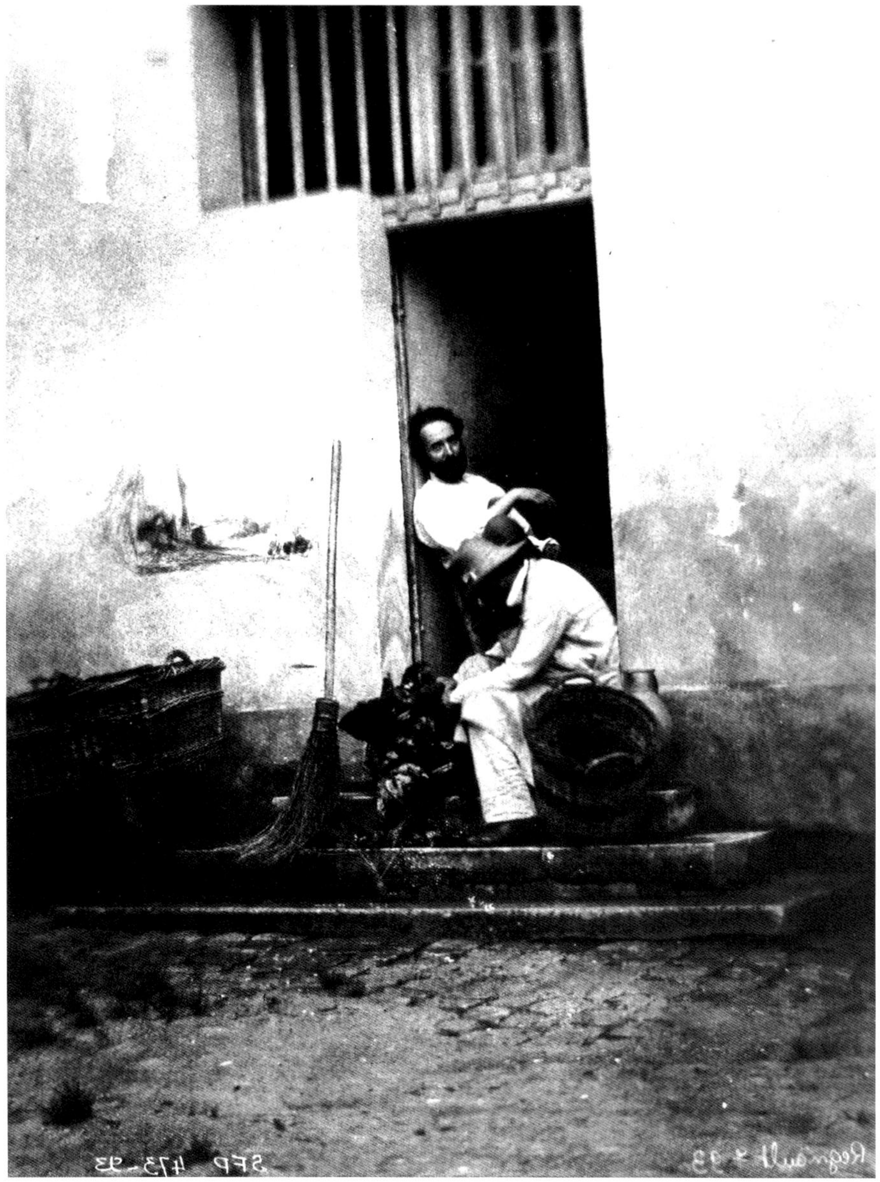

Fig. 22.

Victor Regnault, *Cleaning Vegetables, Sèvres*, c. 1853. Modern print from paper negative, $7\frac{7}{8}$ x 6 in. (20 x 15.2 cm).

Société Française de Photographie, Paris. 473-93

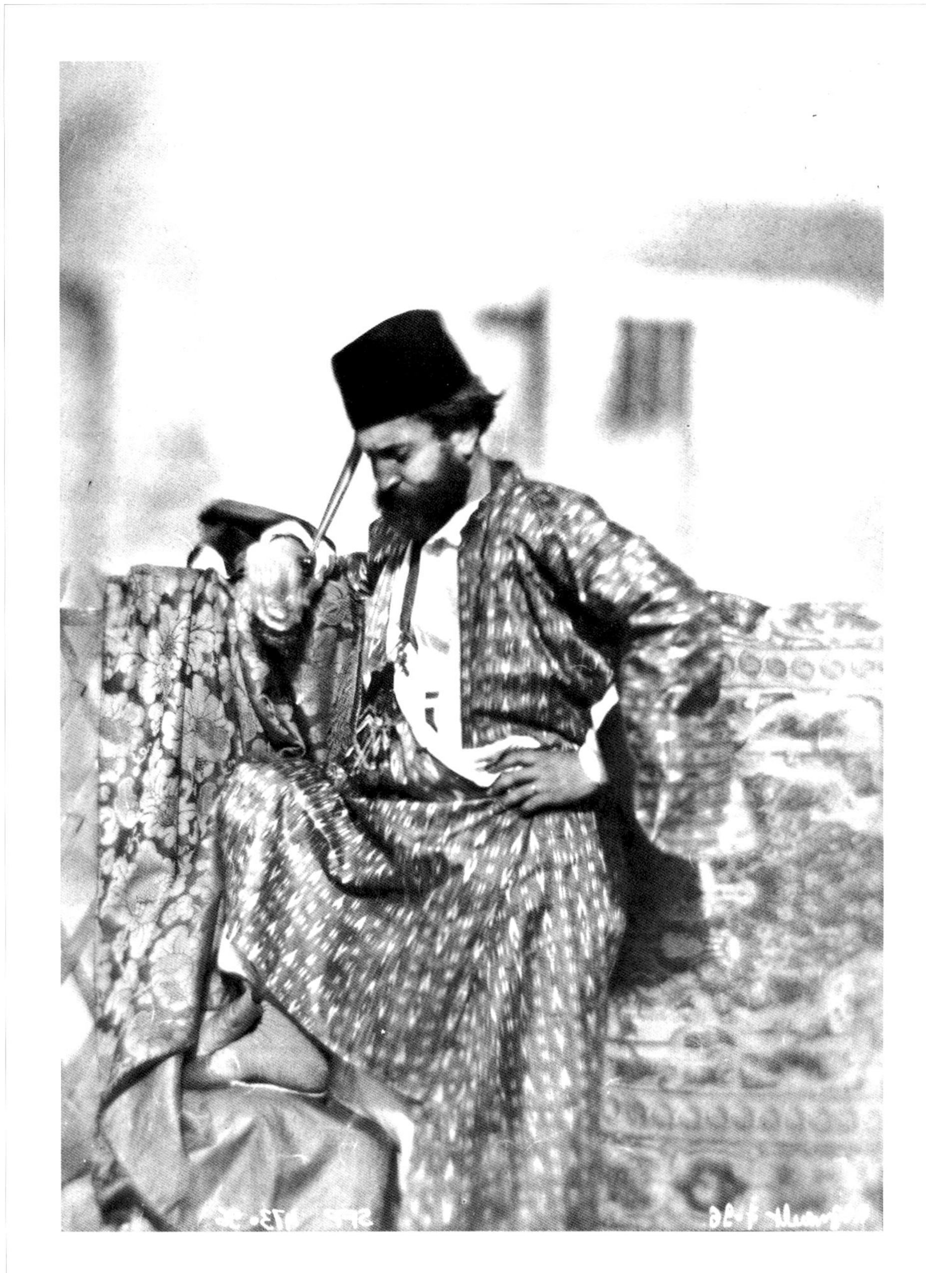

Fig. 23.

Victor Regnault, *Jules Dieterle in Turkish Costume*, c. 1852. Modern print from paper negative, $7^{7}/_{8}$ x $5^{3}/_{4}$ in. (19.9 x 14.6 cm). Société Française de Photographie, Paris. 473.96

could flourish in a way that its competitors could not, and it built an incandescent reputation on the artistic and technical quality of its products. Like the royal tapestry factories of Gobelins and Beauvais, the Manufacture de Sèvres was supposedly a commercial venture, with public salesrooms at Sèvres and in Paris, but in practice, the factory's first responsibility was to supply furnishings for the royal residences and provide the royal gifts by which the crown conveyed recognition and respect.[12] Although the factory's sales were sustained by its famous tableware, by the nineteenth century, Sèvres's workshops included ateliers of sculpture, stained glass, enameling, and metalsmithing, which produced furnishings and grand objects like armoires, floor clocks, and cathedral windows.

The first golden age of Sèvres ended with the Revolution, when the state support of the Manufacture was seriously debated by politicians hostile to the factory's royal history and the very idea of elite luxury in a democratic society. Yet while the new government(s) did revoke certain of the factory's privileges, there was sufficient support to maintain the Manufacture's operating budget.[13] In its half-century of existence, the factory had secured an international reputation rivaling even that of Bavaria's Meissen, thereby setting a standard of excellence for all of French porcelain. In 1800, Napoléon Bonaparte proposed a new director for the factory: Alexandre Brongniart (1770–1847), a geologist and academician from an illustrious family of scientists and architects. This signaled a departure; while chemists had been on the Sèvres payroll for years, there had never been a scientist at the head of the factory. French industry had been notoriously slow to alter the existing cottage and guild-based systems of production, and it would be Brongniart's charge to make the Manufacture de Sèvres a testing ground for all information related to ceramic technology, with the goal of modernizing the entire industry.[14] The changes at Sèvres—reflections of the cultural ascendance of science and rationalism—were even carried into new decorative styles, which traded sensuous, lighthearted Rococo imagery for crisply painted historical and allegorical narratives related to the actual exploits of the Empire (figs. 24 and 25).[15] Yet the factory could not abandon its original emphasis on opulence and exquisite craftsmanship without forfeiting its traditional clientele. Rather than sacrificing traditional deluxe handcraft to the efficiency of modern production methods, Brongniart ultimately retained most of the old methods of fabrication, to which he added further expenditure on behalf of industry: the investment of resources in scientific research, which created new choices for glazes, pastes, and fabrication and firing techniques. But the audience for Sèvres's virtuoso performance had supposedly changed. If the fruits of these labors were formerly enjoyed only by the wealthy few, the new Sèvres was to make its discoveries and progress accessible to French private industry. For the moment, Brongniart was prepared to satisfy two distinct demands: to maintain an elite product line at exclusive prices, and to serve the commercial market by sharing technical research with private manufacturers.

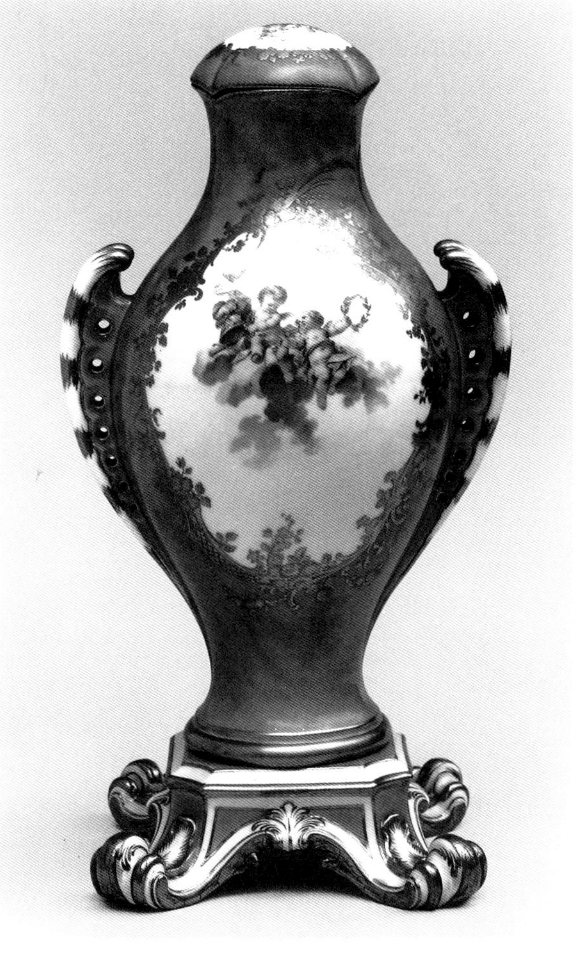

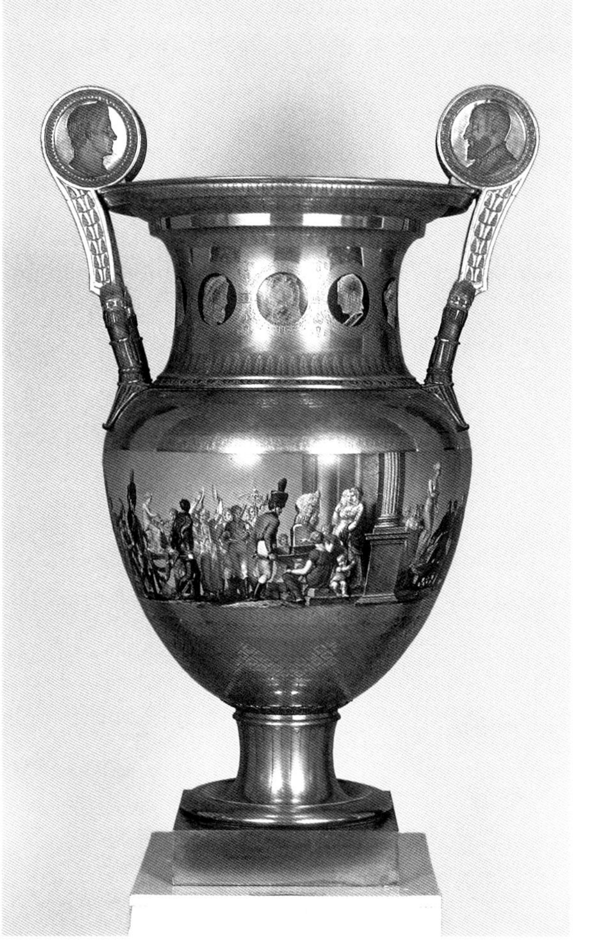

Left: Fig. 24.

Vase, *Urne Antique*, Manufacture de Sèvres, c. 1755–60. Soft-paste porcelain, height 11$^{3}/_{4}$ in. (30 cm).
The Metropolitan Museum of Art, New York. Gift of the Samuel H. Kress Foundation, 1958, 58.75.112 a, b

Right: Fig. 25.

Vase, *Étrusque à Rouleaux*, Manufacture de Sèvres, 1813. Hard-paste porcelain, height 47$^{1}/_{4}$ in. (120 cm).
Musée National de Céramique, Sèvres. Inv. 1823

The direction of the Manufacture de Sèvres would rest in Brongniart's hands virtually until his death in 1847, in part because he had realized that, beyond accommodating the state, the Manufacture's future depended on maintaining the public's faith in its significance as a French institution. In 1830, navigating the choppy waters of the July Revolution, he wrote a treatise on the Manufacture that anticipated and defended the institution against a renewed assault on its state subsidy. There he described the factory's new direction and purpose as cultivating a proper, efficacious balance between scientific and artistic concerns, giving a hearty reaffirmation of the sovereign place of art and the individual artist in the factory's philosophy.[16] Downplaying the factory's role as the royal gift shop, judiciously placing potential technological development beneath the "talents of the hand" and the artist's "individual merit," Brongniart made the traditions of Sèvres seem secure at the same time that he touted the factory as a progressive institution that would deliver the entire ceramic industry into the modern era.

Late in 1838, Brongniart must have heard the talk passing around the Académie des Sciences about a means to fix the image in the camera obscura, particularly since his son-in-law J.-B.Dumas was involved in behind-the-scenes testing of Daguerre's process.[17] As rumors became public information in a succession of presentations before the A.d.S. in 1839, Brongniart could not have overlooked the new medium's noisy promise to become the century's definitive union of science, art, and industry.

PHOTOGRAPHIC APPLICATIONS

It is likely that the academician Brongniart—who had pledged himself to the advancement of industrial art—was present for the most widely anticipated scientific presentation of the century, when François Arago finally disclosed the particulars of Daguerre's process to a standing room–only crowd of members of the academies of science and art on 19 August 1839. On that day, Arago read the report he had given a few weeks earlier to the chamber of deputies, which signaled some of the potential applications of photography. First among them was its usefulness to archaeology and historical preservation as a faithful copyist.[18] On other matters related to the fine arts, Arago quoted from a testimonial letter that had been solicited from the respected academic painter Paul Delaroche (1797–1856). Recognizing the practical value to artists of collecting photographs as low-cost, unimpeachably accurate models, Delaroche effectively anticipated the modern photographic reference library.

From these simple suggestions one could imagine two clear applications for photography in the factory at Sèvres. Photographic documentation was perfectly suited for the factory archives, which had been limited to collecting working drawings of the Sèvres products that continually left the ateliers. The photographic inventory had been such a natural subject that Daguerre, Talbot, and Hippolyte Bayard all demonstrated it in some of their earliest photographs. It would nevertheless take twenty-five years to introduce photographic cataloguing at Sèvres. Photographs would also have made excellent pictorial resources for the Sèvres artists, particularly since Brongniart's art direction followed the contemporary taste for realism and optical accuracy in subject and style of decors, such as the elaborate topographic landscapes currently popular in the factory stock.[19] In fact, it had long been common for factory artists to use the camera obscura, which was ideal for rendering precise drawings of architecture, monuments, landscape, and still life, in the reduced size required by the porcelain object—without the investment of hours of labor. Photographs could also have produced such small-scale, highly detailed models, and they might also have reduced the frequent cost of sending artists out in the field to obtain authentic drawings on site. Robert's father-in-law, Denis Riocreux, the factory's curator and librarian, already maintained extensive pictorial files for the artists' consultation, composed of landscape prints like the *Voyages pittoresques* editions, archeological sites and foreign views, among others. But he was curiously slow to add photographs, despite the fact that by 1852, Robert was busy creating a photographic stock of important architectural monuments like Versailles, the Château de Saint-Cloud, and long-neglected medieval sites in Normandy and Brittany—all of which were typical motifs for Sèvres's wares. These pictures are strangely absent from the factory archives, and photographs only regularly began to enter the factory's picture files in the late 1860s.[20]

Photographic printing on ceramic was probably one of the earliest intentions behind attempts to fix the camera-obscura image, an idea that may have inspired Thomas Wedgwood's frustrated photographic experiments around 1800.[21] The development of vitrifiable photography (photoceramic) would also seem to have been close to Sèvres's interests, where it might have been used as a method of underpainting, if not a substitute for the finished porcelain painting. In many cases, Sèvres painters, particularly the decorators who applied borders and repeating motifs, were already acting as mere "mechanical" copyists. However, no mention of photoceramic research has been found in the Manufacture archives and laboratory notes. This is in keeping with the well-documented resistance to all kinds of mechanical "transfer printing" at Sèvres, and the disfavor that greeted mechanical printing is a prologue for photography's equivocal reception at Sèvres in the 1850s and 1860s.

By the time photography arrived on the scene, Brongniart had already experimented with transfer printing, a new area of technology based on lithography and engraving being vigorously pursued by the English.[22] In France, however, transfer printing was tartly observed to be "a process, unfortunately, more democratic than artistic."[23] It was therefore not used at Sèvres, except in the rare case of large numbers of identical monograms and simple borders; an 1860 survey of the factory reported that

Sèvres still utiltized handpainting almost exclusively.[24] A viable photoceramic process had been developed in 1854 by Alphonse Lafon de Camarsac (1821–1905), who fancifully advertised his process as "inalterable, like the paintings of Sèvres."[25] But photoceramic printing would also be excluded from Sèvres's methods, since the factory's identity was so closely associated with "the talents of the hand." The factory did not even open a lithography studio until after the Second World War, and even then its operation was "practically clandestine," as it was deemed unworthy of the Manufacture's traditions.[26]

As new director Regnault experimented with vitrifiable photography, but his interest was evidently more on the side of photography than ceramics, since it was one solution to a question that plagued photographers: how to make photographic images that were permanent and fadeless. He probably experimented first with the original process that Lafon de Camarsac presented to the A.d.S. in 1855.[27] In 1865, Regnault presented his own method of vitrifiable photography to the A.d.S., which differed in its simplified operations from the methods of both Lafon de Camarsac and Alphonse Poitevin.[28] Yet no amount of technical improvement—short of reproducing the full color spectrum—would push photoceramic beyond the status of a novelty, even in the wider world of the commercial ceramic industry. Its most significant niche remained the creation of permanent, weatherproof images for memorials and headstones.[29]

TECHNOLOGY AND THE "DECLINE" OF SÈVRES

The sudden death of Joseph Ebelmen, Brongniart's hand-picked successor, had effected Regnault's call to Sèvres. With this swift appointment of one of the nation's most prominent scientists to the post of Director of the Manufacture de Sèvres, the new president Louis-Napoléon showed his commitment to maintain the national manufactures and his intention to continue Sèvres on its course as a research institution. Regnault had been chosen chiefly because he was a meticulous experimental scientist, but he was also an experienced promoter of technological progress, since his research always anticipated potential industrial development. Moreover, he was a faithful worker for the state; from his days as a student engineer, he had patiently devoted himself to each new government's initiatives to study foreign technologies and deliver them to French industry.

Within a few months of his appointment, Regnault had creatively interpreted this scientific mission according to his own objectives and had put the Sèvres craftsmen to work "in moments of leisure" making precision scientific instruments for international export, a practice that was soon quashed by Achille Fould, the watchful minister of state, who felt the factory had no business extending its resources into this obscure, utilitarian area of production.[30] Regnault's endorsed research included experiments with new kiln fuels, and his greatest successes, the creation of *pâte colorée* (colored paste) and the rediscovery of a formula for *pâte tendre* (soft paste), which had been lost since its discontinuation in 1804. In this program of experimentation, Regnault followed the direction charted for the Manufacture over five decades earlier by Napoléon I and Alexandre Brongniart. Fifty years was ample time for the critics hostile to industrial development at Sèvres to rise to a state of exasperation with the scientific interests of the factory's administration. In 1862, the critic Adalbert de Beaumont lambasted Sèvres for its preoccupations with science, but placed the blame on the temper of the century. His view, which became a familiar refrain in criticism of Sèvres, was that any scientific considerations must be strictly held in the service of the art of the piece, meaning its form and color. "But," he asked, "is it thus at Sèvres? Certainly not . . . since the beginning of the century, the question of science has dominated the question of art in the most regrettable way."[31]

In 1866, the critic Philippe Burty gave another withering summary of the factory's "decadence" in the course of the century, which began when Napoléon promoted technology ahead of art, "chiefly for the purpose of beating the English." But, he added, "The useful killed the pleasurable, at the same time that the pedantic stifled that conventional, but exquisite, antique style . . . The architect ejected the decorator and the sculptor, the savant oppressed the artist, and the studio was overcome by the laboratory."[32] Burty's comments condemned the whole sweep of Sèvres's output since 1800, and his belief that science had bullied art into submission at the Manufacture de Sèvres was shared by many writers of the period.

Given Burty's harsh view of Sèvres's industrial direction, it is interesting to note that he was a great collector of photography and one of its most intelligent critics. But Burty accepted the technical and industrial as part of photography's nature, just as he considered photography a necessarily lower branch of the arts. Unlike photography, however, whose "tradition" was unclear and even denied, Sèvres's future demanded some rapprochement with its concrete past. Burty felt particularly protective of the Manufacture, since he judged it to be one of the most important French sources of influence and recognition in Europe.[33] The French were inclined to think of the Manufacture de Sèvres—supported in large part by public taxes—as truly theirs, a national treasure, which made the factory's performance any citizen's proper business. Critics who reviewed the Manufacture's displays at any of the national or international exhibitions were more personally invested in Sèvres than in private industry. By the same token, the three national manufactures necessarily represented the polity and bore the consequences of the government's current standing with the people. Finally, the course of the Manufacture in the nineteenth century had attracted public attention as a marker for something further: the ideal of modern progress.

Brongniart had featured this ideal, cast in a blindingly optimistic light, at the center of his 1830 history and prospectus for the factory. By 1860, the repercussions of change in the name of progress were too well known to allow such unclouded faith. Whereas complaints against the new order of modernity in France had once been dismissed as rebellious nay saying from the Romantic intellectual fringe, wider cultural reaction and resistance could now be perceived, manifesting in ways that ranged from retrenchment into dreams of the nation's grand dynastic past to the resurgence of Catholicism, a hostility toward industry, or a distrust of science.[34] With Regnault's administration, the factory received the full force of the gathering backlash against the ideal of industrial progress, which at worst was seen as annihilating a tradition of art made more precious by a veil of nostalgia.

The state-run Manufacture de Sèvres had become, like photography, a focus for anxieties over the encroachment of the technological and industrial upon the domain of art. This tension was evident in more than the resistance to new technologies and methods of production. Critics associated the factory's *juste milieu* (a conservative, fashionably "realistic" art style) artistic direction with a materialist perspective, from which they extrapolated a whole trajectory of decline. Comparing the transient conquests of history and science to the "living facts" of art, Burty opened his discussion of Sèvres's decorative subjects with this declaration: "Material facts are relative—intellectual [ones are] absolute."[35] What worried critics like Burty and Adalbert de Beaumont was the thought that at Sèvres, "art"—that supreme product of imagination—had devolved to the handmaiden of technology: the form and decoration of pieces had become merely the excuse to show off a variety of technical achievements. "Art" and "technology" were necessarily complex categories, laden with associations both symbolic and concrete, that attracted each other in a natural dialectic. To those treading anxiously on the threshold of the industrial age, "art" might romantically represent the ancient individualistic desire to recreate what was beautiful or unique in nature; "technology," on the other hand, might stand for inexorable change that was capable of leveling individuality.

This was an intractable problem for the Manufacture. For despite Brongniart's intentions to find an optimal synthesis of tradition and innovation that would satisfy both old and new demands, these ill-defined tendencies were now embraced by their proponents as fully fledged, antithetical doctrines. If anything, the force of tradition at Sèvres was growing stronger in relation to the technological inroads occurring there and elsewhere; on this account, one need only recall that Regnault's most urgent (and acclaimed) research was on the recreation of the eighteenth-century formula for soft-paste porcelain. Even Regnault's efforts to utilize the steam engine in the factory were stymied by the Manufacture's old principles of deluxe handcrafting; in 1860, the writer J. Turgan reported that the use of an externally powered potter's wheel was "hardly possible" at Sèvres, since the workers, also being artists, needed to personally control all aspect of production.[36] In his glowing tribute to the Manufacture—perhaps written in defense of Regnault—Turgan insisted that Sèvres was "more prosperous than ever," but never mentioned the question of a balance between art and industry.[37] Philippe Burty, on the other hand, concluded his 1866 critique of Sèvres with some open advice to the Manufacture on how to reverse its declining prestige. "Let an artist be placed at the head of the works . . . [and] expend on behalf of the beautiful what is now spent for what you call the useful. . . . Lastly, repudiate the term industrial art, which was invented of late years to apply to your art productions."[38]

To retain the precious respect of critics, the Manufacture needed to protect its fine art traditions, especially where it concerned what was most visible: the decoration of its pieces. What mechanical printing and vitrifiable photography had to offer—namely, uniformity and cheap reproducibility—was, to use Burty's disparaging sense of the word, "useful."

THE *ATELIER DE PHOTOGRAPHIE*

Using photography as a means of decorating wares was one thing, but to use the medium in its humble function as scribe was another, and it is perplexing that photography took such a hesitant path into the documentary service of the Manufacture, particularly since Louis Robert had featured some of the wares in several early photographs. Novices in photography usually began with stationary objects, and a few of Robert's early calotypes depict still lifes of objects borrowed from the factory's collections and ateliers. One tightly framed picture of orientalist objects has the appearance of an artist's étude, in which Robert was testing his grasp of composing with shape, texture, value, and space in photography (fig. 26). By 1855, he had begun a more focused project: the documentation of wares that the Manufacture would show in the 1855 Exposition Universelle. The Exposition Universelle would be the French response to the 1851 Great Exhibition of the Works of Industry of All Nations, where the English had flaunted their industrial superiority.[39] As France lagged behind England in heavy manufacturing, its hopes for economic power and international recognition rested in its ability to succeed as a producer of art and luxury goods that possessed the cachet of French taste.[40] Sèvres's role as flagship of the national manufactures made it imperative to maintain its international leadership as a tastemaker, even though only a small part of its wares was produced for the commercial market. Understanding these conditions, the Exposition's Imperial Commission—which seated Regnault and twenty-nine other notables of art and science—lavished attention on the fine arts section of the exhibition. A crucial component would be the display for the Manufacture de Sèvres (fig. 27). For this public spectacle of such political significance Regnault and his staff prepared an exhibit of 195 of the most extravagant objects ever made in porcelain.

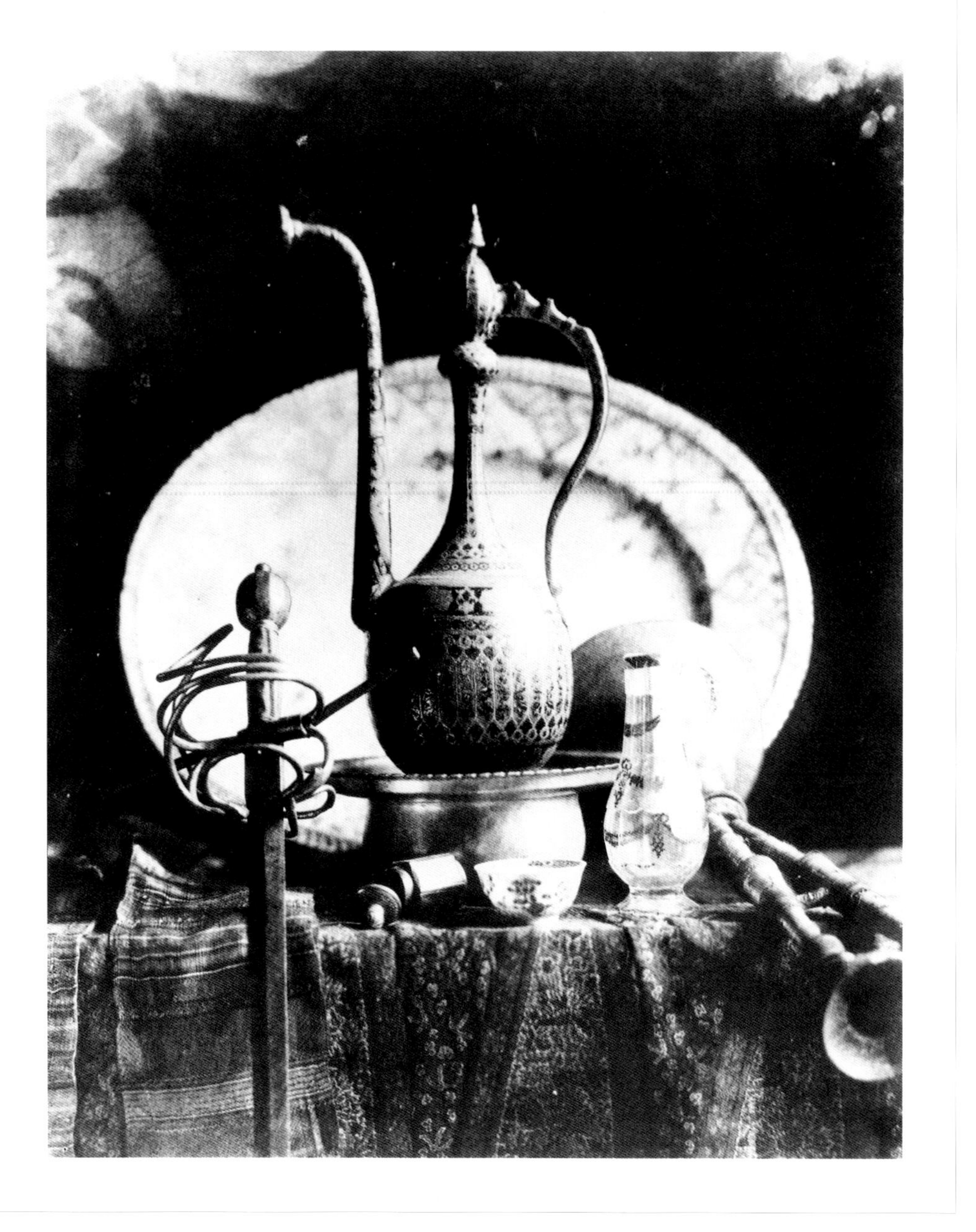

Fig. 26.

Louis-Rémy Robert, *Still Life with Orientalist Objects*, c. 1850–55. Salt print from paper negative, 13 x 10 3/8 in. (32.9 x 26.3 cm). The J. Paul Getty Museum, Los Angeles. 84.xp.370.21

As the exhibition approached, Robert thought to produce a permanent photographic record of some of the most important of these unique pieces. He had already sought out Hippolyte Bayard to teach him the albumen-on-glass-negative process, perhaps for this purpose, since glass could yield a finer degree of detail than paper negatives.[41] The result was a group of at least seventeen salt prints that was offered for sale in the Sèvres section of the exhibition. The decision to market the prints as "art reproductions" may have inspired Robert to create more than simple descriptive documents, to make the photographs themselves reflect the luxury and perfection of the porcelain. To that end, he labored over the photographs as objects in themselves: lush, dramatic, balanced, flawlessly exposed, toned with gold chloride or other chemical agents, and perfectly suitable for framing (figs. 28 and 29). As with the earlier picture of oriental objects and textiles, Robert took pains composing the images, arranging vases and biscuit figurines singly or in complex groups before a dark drapery. They were lit from the left side, allowing a dramatic play of light and shadow over the fine modeling of the wares. A small measuring stick in the lower-left corner provided scale.

Robert's inspiration for the general project probably came from two illustrated catalogues that had been published for the Great Exhibition of 1851 (though he surely also knew Jules Ziegler's photographs in the latter's *Études céramiques* of 1854).[42] *The Official Descriptive and Illustrated Catalogue of the Great Exhibition of the Works of Industry of All Nations*, a presentation set of eleven volumes, was illustrated with 154 photographs by Hugh Owen (1804–1886) of Bristol (calotypes) and by Claude-Marie Ferrier (1811–1889) of Paris (salt prints from albumenized glass plates). Owen's and Ferrier's pictures were less artistically ambitious than Robert's, however. In Ferrier's photograph of Sèvres porcelain, for example, no attempt was made to suggest an environment for the pieces; they were photographed on the floor, against a blank wall, as specimens that received no additional comment from the photographer (fig. 30). Nothing interfered with the photograph's purpose as an objective, indexical record.

This was not the case with the illustrations in Matthew Digby Wyatt's *The Industrial Arts of the Nineteenth Century* (5 vols., 1851–53), a commercially printed catalogue of the exhibition that was far more sumptuously contrived. Folio-sized, the book's showy chromolithograph plates featured close views of groups of objects filling the entire frame (fig. 31). A dramatically upswept velvet curtain fills the shallow space behind the pieces and spills over the tabletop, while the eye-level view monumentalizes the objects, which appear to be only inches away from the picture plane. These illustrations were more likely the model followed by Robert. Choosing between one and ten objects for his arrangements, he varied the kind of objects displayed together, from statuettes to large vases to small enameled boxes. The biscuit figures—graceful nude bathers and winged nymphs—add animation to the formal arrange-

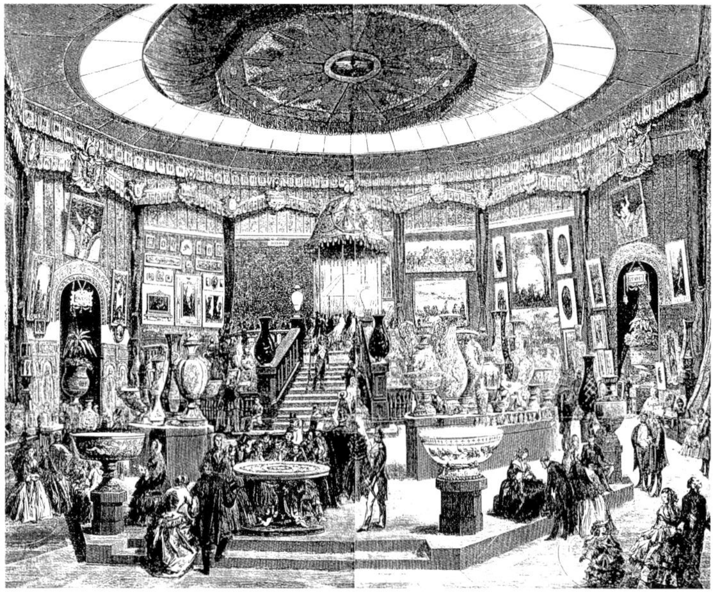

Fig. 27.
E. D. Renard (French, active 1850s), *Exposition des Manufactures Impériales de Sèvres*, 1855. Steel engraving, reproduced, *L'Illustration, Journal Universel*. Firestone Library, Princeton University

ments, as they move cautiously through the landscape of fragile porcelain vases, jewel boxes, and tableware (fig. 32). The photographer compensated for the lack of color by chemically toning the pictures to shades of eggplant or warm reddish-brown, which sets them distinctively apart from the strident multicoloring of the English chromos. In tempting the viewer with seductive, illusionistic displays of desirable, if prohibitively expensive goods, these opulent spreads pique acquisitive appetites like the Dutch "laden table" still lifes they imitate. But what could not be attained in reality could be virtually attained for the price of the photograph. Robert proudly printed each image with his name, the series title, and date in the lower corners of the negative.

Nothing of the cost or sales of Robert's photographs is known. Artists at the magazine *L'Illustration* used them as the models for the engravings accompanying a review of the Exposition, which informed readers that photographs could be purchased at the Manufacture's display.[43] Whether or not they were commercially successful, Robert showed them in photography exhibitions several times in the next three years, where they earned critical praise. Reviewing photography at the Brussels Exhibition of

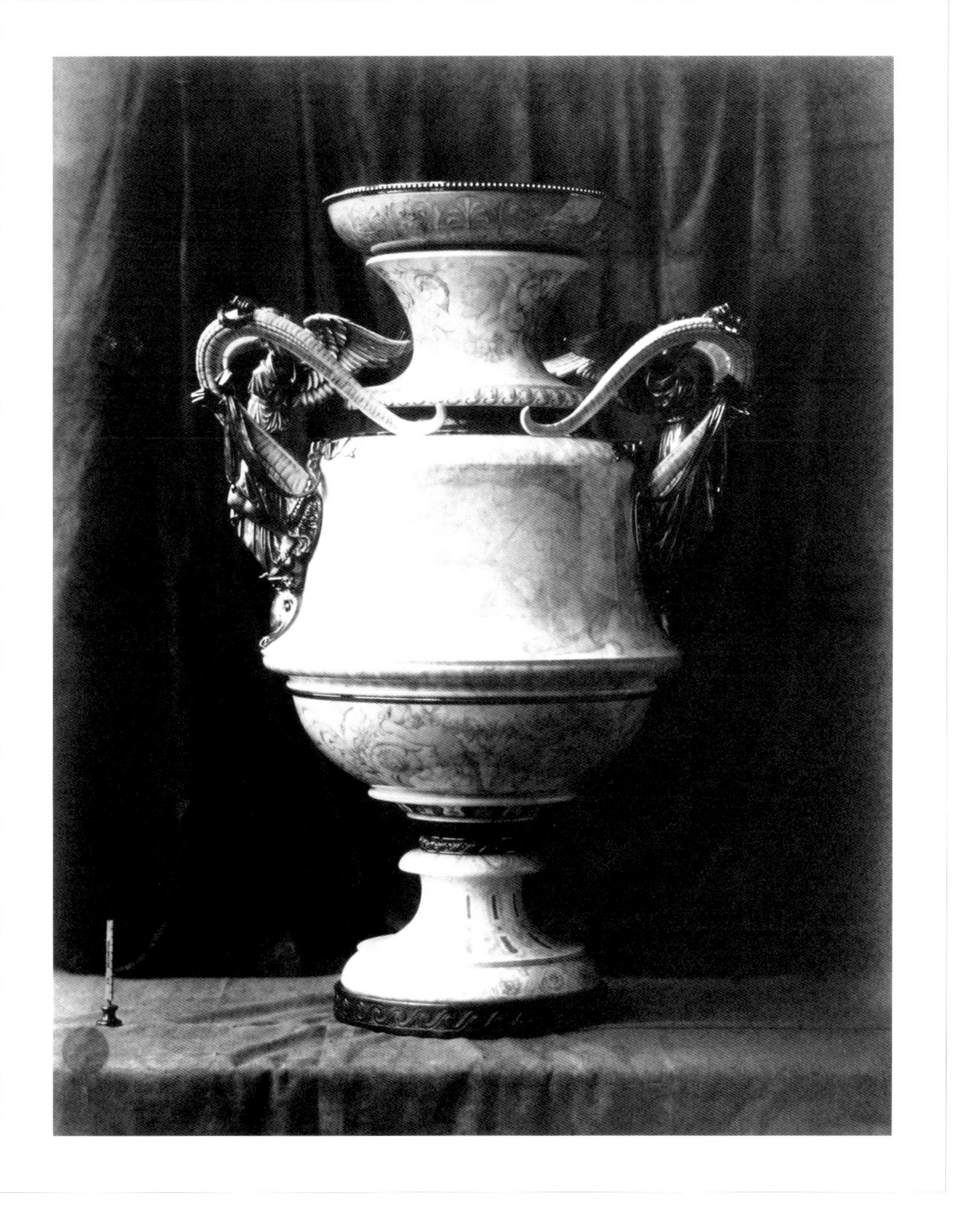

Fig. 28.

Louis-Rémy Robert, *Vase Mansard*, 1855. Albumenized paper print from glass negative, 12 5/8 x 10 1/4 in. (32 x 25.9 cm).
The Art Museum, Princeton University. Museum purchase, gift of the Florence Gould Foundation, x1993-147

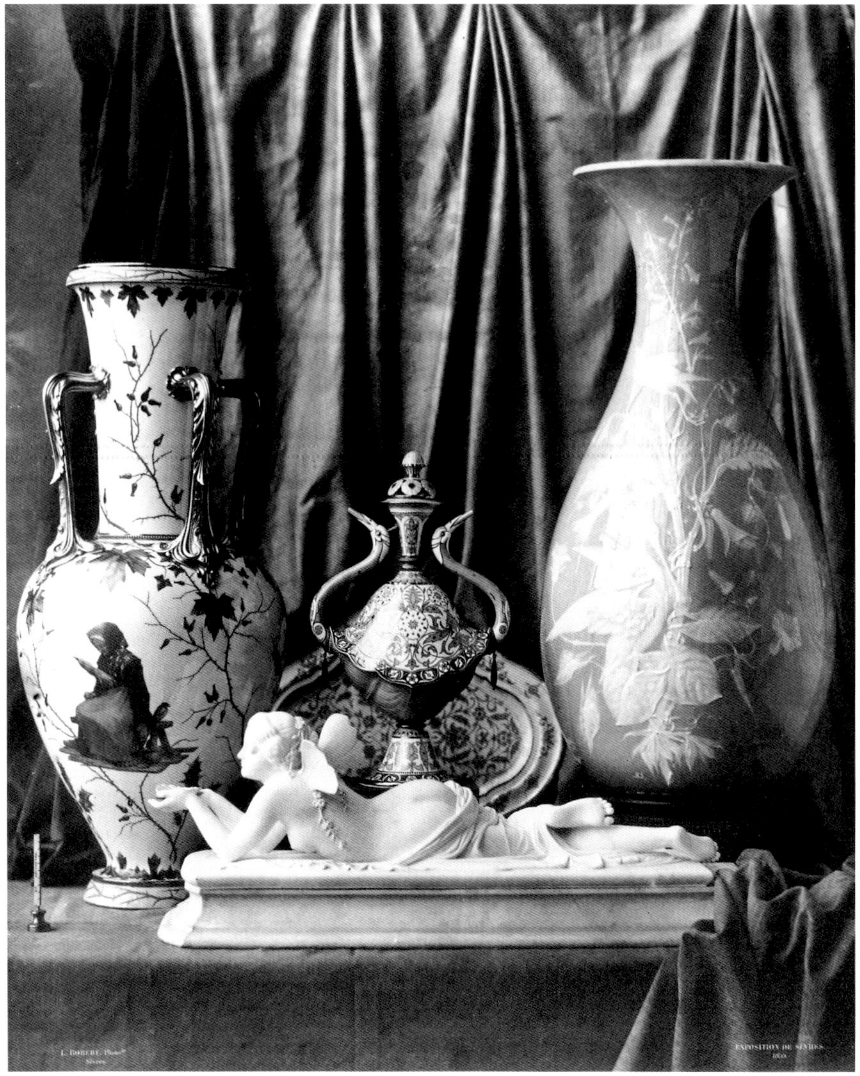

Fig. 29.

Louis-Rémy Robert, *Still Life: Decorative Arts, Sèvres*, 1855. Albumen print from glass negative, 12 3/8 x 10 in. (31.3 x 25.5 cm).

The J. Paul Getty Museum, Los Angeles. 84.xp.960.40

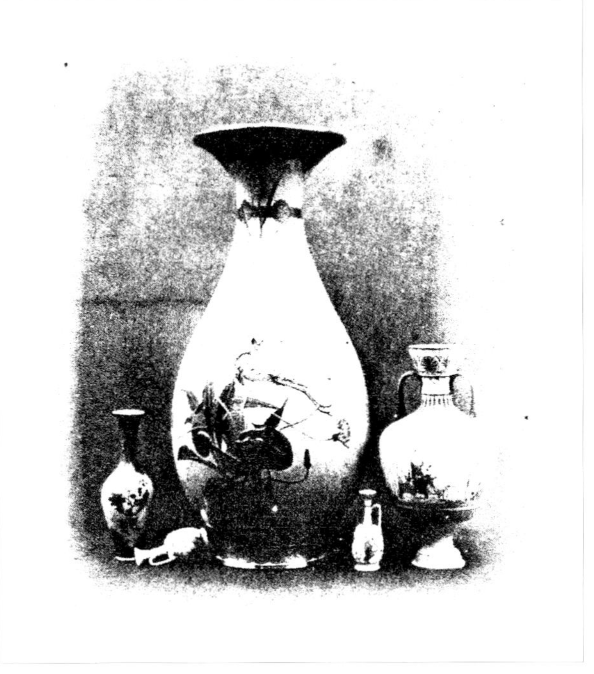

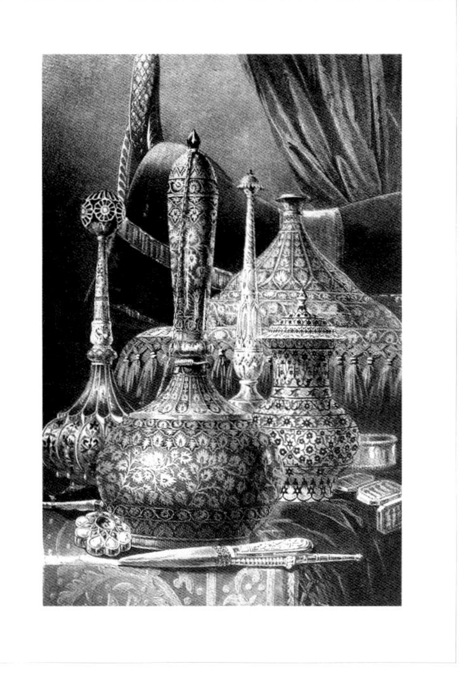

Left: Fig. 30.

Claude-Marie Ferrier (French, 1811–1889), *Porcelain of Sèvres, Great Exposition*, 1851. Salt print from paper negative, dimensions and location unknown

Right: Fig. 31.

Francis Bedford (British, 1816–1894), *Group of Indian Objects Principally Enamelled*. Chromolithographic illustration plate 152, Matthew Digby Wyatt, *The Industrial Arts of the Nineteenth Century* (London: Day and Son, 1851–1853). National Gallery of Canada Library and Archives, Ottawa

Industrial Arts in 1856, Humbert de Molard offered Robert's medal-winning photographs as a critical standard for judging other works of their kind.[44] In 1857, a reviewer for the second S.F.P. salon described Robert's pictures as "little masterpieces" that demonstrated the importance of the artist's unique subjectivity, even in art reproduction: "M. Robert knows how to prove—by the composition of the tableau, the disposition of each object, and above all, by the clearly understood distribution of light—just how great a part is played by the intelligence and feeling of the artist, even in reproductions of still lifes."[45]

Robert seems to have put aside further work on a photographic catalogue of Sèvres wares until 1863, when he petitioned J.-B.-P. Vaillant, the new minister of the Emperor's Household and Fine Arts, for permission and funds to operate a photography studio within the factory. This request—copying state collections by photography—was not unprecedented. Robert himself had supposedly received permission to photograph the factory's products in 1855, and the Louvre had sporadically allowed photographers partial access to its collections in the 1850s.[46] Although bureaucrats had been slow to investigate the possibilities of photography, there was nothing radically new in Robert's request.

This makes the minister's vehement resistance to the idea all the more intriguing. In his letter to Vaillant, Robert had stressed three ways in which the photographs could be of service. First, he cited them as valuable teaching tools—references for the factory's artists and designers that would complement the engravings and drawings already collected by the factory's library. They would also furnish accurate documentation of the history of the factory's production. Finally, Robert reminded the minister that the photographs would witness the generosity of the state in supporting the factory—they could be used as persuasive tools in disputes over the state's funding of the factory. It was too expensive to make gifts of actual porcelain to legislators, but one could court them with collectible photographic testaments to the factory's achievements. Robert alluded to his own costs as the obstacle to continuing the series.[47] He included several of the meticulously crafted 1855 prints with his letter.

Robert's request provoked a strong rebuke from the minister, who did not bother to reply to Robert but wrote a terse letter directly to Regnault. In this letter he pointed out the disadvantages he saw in Robert's proposal: the cost, which Robert had mentioned, yet neglected to address; the relatively small benefit to the factory; and the consequent "vulgarization" of the factory's unique models. Regnault's response dismissed the minister's first two objections outright. He took Vaillant's last point, the question of vulgarization, to be the real heart of the problem. Writing a few years earlier on the subject of photographic reproduction and painting, the critic Henri de Lacretelle had discussed the issue of mass reproduction as a double-sided coin: "There are two senses to the word 'vulgarize'; if sometimes it

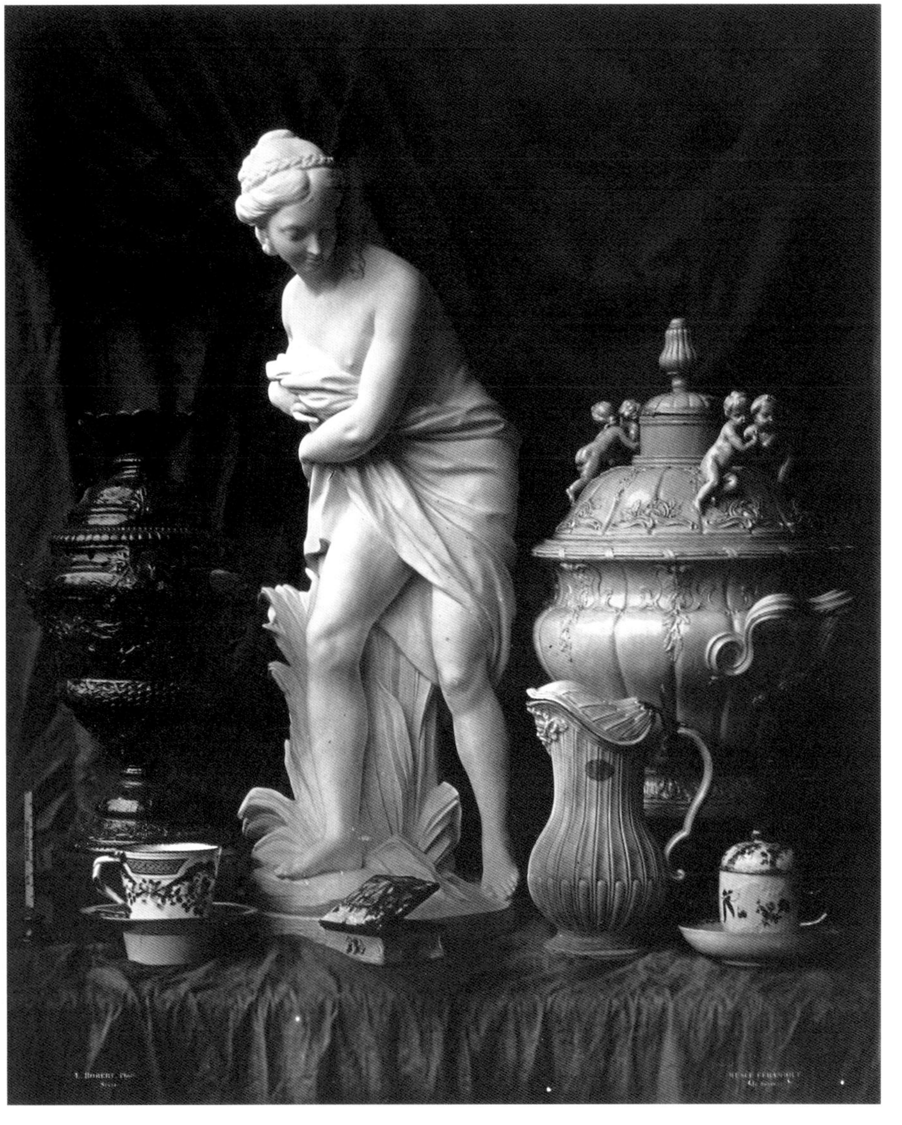

Fig. 32.

Louis-Rémy Robert, *Still Life of Sèvres Porcelain*, 1855. Albumenized carbon print (1865), 12 x $9^{3}/_{4}$ in. (30.4 x 24.7 cm).
Museum of Fine Arts, Boston. Abbott Lawrence Fund, 1981.91

means that in multiplying, it diminishes, and in spreading something out, it lowers it, it also signifies that it brings familiarity, and thus appreciation; that it brings understanding, and thus calls forth more intelligence."[48] An energetic champion of photography, Lacretelle felt that the "understanding" fostered by widespread dissemination of reproductions was so socially beneficial that the fear of debasing the original became a negligible concern. Photography, Lacretelle enthused, would soon be to the visual arts what the printing press had been to the written word.

Two problems were embedded in Regnault and Vaillant's debate about vulgarization and photography, although only one was addressed directly. This was the question of whether the models and designs of Sèvres, once so closely guarded, could be copied by private industry if photographs were publicly available. Regnault dismissed this concern, first by falsely denying the photograph's utility for copying sculptural forms. He then changed tack and argued that artists—including British designers—already had ample opportunity to copy Sèvres's wares by sketching them in public exhibitions and in collections like those of the South Kensington Museum.[49] Taking up Robert's point, Regnault emphasized the propagandistic value of the photographs, as publicity that would serve the Manufacture's advocates in the perennial struggles over the factory's budget: "This . . . is *important evidence* in the permanent trial that [the Manufacture] has with its detractors. The public can judge if it is advancing or in decadence. It is a *powerful stimulant* for its artists who will be able to hope that their personal works shall not remain completely unknown, etc. [emphasis original]."[50]

Like Brongniart before him, Regnault believed that the taxpaying public had to be actively drawn to support the Manufacture. Confident that the factory's enemies were confined to a handful of critics and politicians, Regnault was willing to place the case before the public, especially a public that had been primed and educated by the generous circulation of photographic reproductions. Visits to the factory were restricted to those with the Minister's written consent, and to own Sèvres porcelain was a luxury reserved for the wealthy, but through photographs anyone could possess a bit of the Manufacture's image and cultivate an amateur appreciation. This publicity was more than simple product advertising; it was a way to combat the recalcitrant image of the factory as an outdated, elitist institution.

The subtext beneath the debate over vulgarization and photography was really the question of image. The Manufacture's image was not simply its own; it belonged also to its patron, the state, which expected a return on its investment, particularly in the form of international public prestige. On this account, Robert's suggestion for a photographic studio was particularly ill-timed, coming on the heels of the Manufacture's embarrassing performance at the 1862 Universal Exhibition in London. There Sèvres's reputation had been dealt a serious blow when France was widely acknowledged to have stumbled as the leader in decorative arts. In an unfortunate coincidence, Robert's own photographs of Sèvres's porcelain, exhibited in the Exhibition's photography section, won a medal for photographic excellence while the wares themselves were panned, even by French critics. The most vigorous stream of criticism came from Adalbert de Beaumont, who wrote a thirty-five page criticism of Sèvres in the *Revue des deux mondes* in which he castigated the Manufacture for its pretentious decoration and absorption in technical feats.[51] The Goncourt brothers, disgusted with what they called the "bourgeois ideal of porcelain," privately accused Sèvres of the irreparable ruin of French taste.[52]

Thus by 1863, the Manufacture was in an impossible position, despised by aesthetes like the Goncourts for pandering to middle-class taste, but also criticized and mistrusted by politicians and reformers who saw it as a budget-draining dinosaur whose "theoretical experiments" were too rarefied to benefit private industry. Making matters worse, adversaries of Napoléon III were only too happy to seize on the perceived weakness of the Manufacture de Sèvres as evidence of the decadence of the reign. In such a climate, Vaillant was forced to scrutinize every decision regarding the Manufacture. This was particularly true of the decision to conjoin the Manufacture's vulnerable image with a medium that was itself under attack. As others have noted, Napoléon III and his government were also implicated in French attacks on photography, in that photography served as a trope for any technological change that was being underwritten or supported by the emperor.[53] By using photography—frequently cast as the embodiment of cheap, tawdry commercialism—to publicize its wares, would the Manufacture, and by extension, the government, be risking further damage to its reputation? Was it wise to link it with a medium that was itself the center of a debate not just on vulgarization, but vulgarity? Vaillant's objection to opening a photography studio at Sèvres thus concerned both the fear that competitors could use photographs to copy Sèvres's models, and that the Manufacture's elite image could be damaged by entrusting it to the standard-bearer of modern, counterfeit experience: photography.

Until the advent of photography, the average person could encounter the works of the country's finest porcelain producer on limited occasions at exhibition, in grand public settings, or as engravings in books—all high culture contexts that elicited a reverential response. Ordinary reproduction photographs, like the 1851 prints by Owen and Ferrier, offered no such cues; in fact, their reductive two-dimensional, monochromatic representations fundamentally altered the appearance and effect of the works they reproduced. That anyone might claim familiarity with an object, based on such diminished representations, and the casual way in which photographs could appear, disappear, circulate, and proliferate, effortlessly snatched the object's image from the control of cultural authorities like museums, academies, and connoisseurs. Seventy-five years later, this challenge would become the subject of

Walter Benjamin's Marxist critique, "The Work of Art in the Age of Mechanical Reproduction," (1936) but it was already being rehearsed in critical debates of the 1850s and 1860s.[54]

The photographic reproduction of Sèvres wares was one more small step on a path—welcomed by some, but alarming to a vocal contingent of writers—that appeared to be leading to the disintegration of distinctions between the upper and middle classes. Capitalism, industry, photography—these served the financial interests of the wealthy and the aristocracy at the same time that they served the more varied interests of the middle class. But the middle class stood to gain more from these resources, to be able to cover more social ground in its lengthening strides. Scientific discovery served industrial growth, which was a boon for the nation; increased production and foreign and domestic trade yielded tax revenues that enriched government coffers, but it also feathered the beds of mostly middle-class industrialists, some of whom used their wealth to purchase the honorifics that had once belonged exclusively to the clergy and aristocracy, just as they began laying their tables with Sèvres's wares as soon as income permitted.[55] Year by year, industrial development brought more of the experiences and objects that had been the marks of aristocratic distinction into the hands of the middle class, and this was one reason why eighteenth-century Sèvres became so prized, and the current output of Sèvres so disdained, during the Second Empire. Despite the respect still commanded by the factory name, setting one's table with Sèvres was no longer a guarantee of impeccable taste; that honor was now reserved for the original, increasingly rare soft-paste.[56] Thus it happened that Regnault's revival of soft-paste appealed to a clientele that, on its way up, did not know, or could not afford, better—not one that had already arrived. Like that ersatz soft-paste, photography was not the same as the original, but it was inspiring fuel for social aspiration.[57] For a reasonable price, anyone could enjoy a visit to ancient Rome through stereographs, study the drawings of Raphael in albumen prints, or masquerade as one's betters in a sumptuously appointed portrait studio.

Under these circumstances, trying to enlist photography in the service of the beleaguered factory was like rushing to the scene of a burning house armed with gasoline, for even as Robert was making his first reproduction photographs in 1855, criticism of photography's cheapening effect on French taste was mounting, especially as the less-expensive glass negative processes superseded the more precious calotype and daguerreotype. Robert had consequently been very cautious and solicitous in wording his initial proposal to Vaillant. It was important to convince the minister that his photographs were more than shoddy mechanical reproductions, but he still did not dare proselytize about the art or artistry of photography.

For the moment, Vaillant denied Robert's 1863 request, on the grounds that the consequences had not yet been sufficiently studied.[58] Two years later, however, Regnault finally convinced the minister to approve partial funding. Vaillant grudgingly allotted a skeletal budget for equipment, and a scarcely adequate sum for making two prints from each negative, expressly reserved for the factory's own use.[59] Regnault forwarded Robert's specimens for Vaillant's inspection in 1867, and must have felt vindicated when the minister wrote back to say that, having judged the quality of the photographs for himself, he could now see the collection's value. He asked for two additional collections of all the photographs: one for his personal library, and one for the Louvre's.[60]

What had changed? The immediate embarrassment over Sèvres's performance at the 1862 Exhibition had passed, and Sèvres had been somewhat redeemed at the 1867 Exposition Universelle.[61] Vaillant was also genuinely impressed with the quality of Robert's photographs, although this should not have been a surprise, since he had seen the 1855 series. Yet Vaillant would still not allow the photographs to be published; he merely wanted his own private collection. He made this request, with increasing irritation, four times in the next two years; Regnault stubbornly refused to respond. The minister's patience ended in 1870 when he received a request for a complete collection of the Sèvres photographs from an art school in Origny that had somehow acquired two of Robert's photographs—which surely confirmed his fears of photography's uncontrollability. Believing that the Manufacture was casually circulating prints while refusing his request for a set of his own, Vaillant demanded a full report on the photographic atelier. Regnault's bridling response reminded the minister of his own refusal to increase the budget beyond the regulated two prints per negative, despite repeated requests for either more funds or an arrangement to publish the photographs. "Thus," Regnault stated flatly, "it is impossible for us to make a gift of collections of our photography, neither to the Minister, nor to schools of art. . . . After this explanation, I think that Your Excellence will admit that the Manufacture de Sèvres cannot give a free collection of our prints to the school at Origny. The Maison of the Emperor will have to pay the cost of this gift, and soon every school of design in France will be making the same demand."[62]

In the eighteen years since Regnault's arrival at the factory, photography at the Manufacture had graduated from purely personal aims, both private and social, to a use that existed on a fault line between the public and private, which ultimately broached the question of access to both government property and high culture. Photography's place within a state-run beaux-arts institution had as much to do with the simmering dynamics of class and institutional power as with outward questions of policy. Photography itself reflected the conflicted regard for the democratic ideals that were so deeply enmeshed in the rhetoric of post-revolutionary France. By 1860, photography had already seen three developments in its reception: the initial delight attending its introduction, the subsequent backlash against its imputed deleterious effects, and an acceptance—happy or grudging—of photography as a given condition of the modern world. In this third phase, photography officially gained its limited place within the conservative institution of the Manufacture de Sèvres.

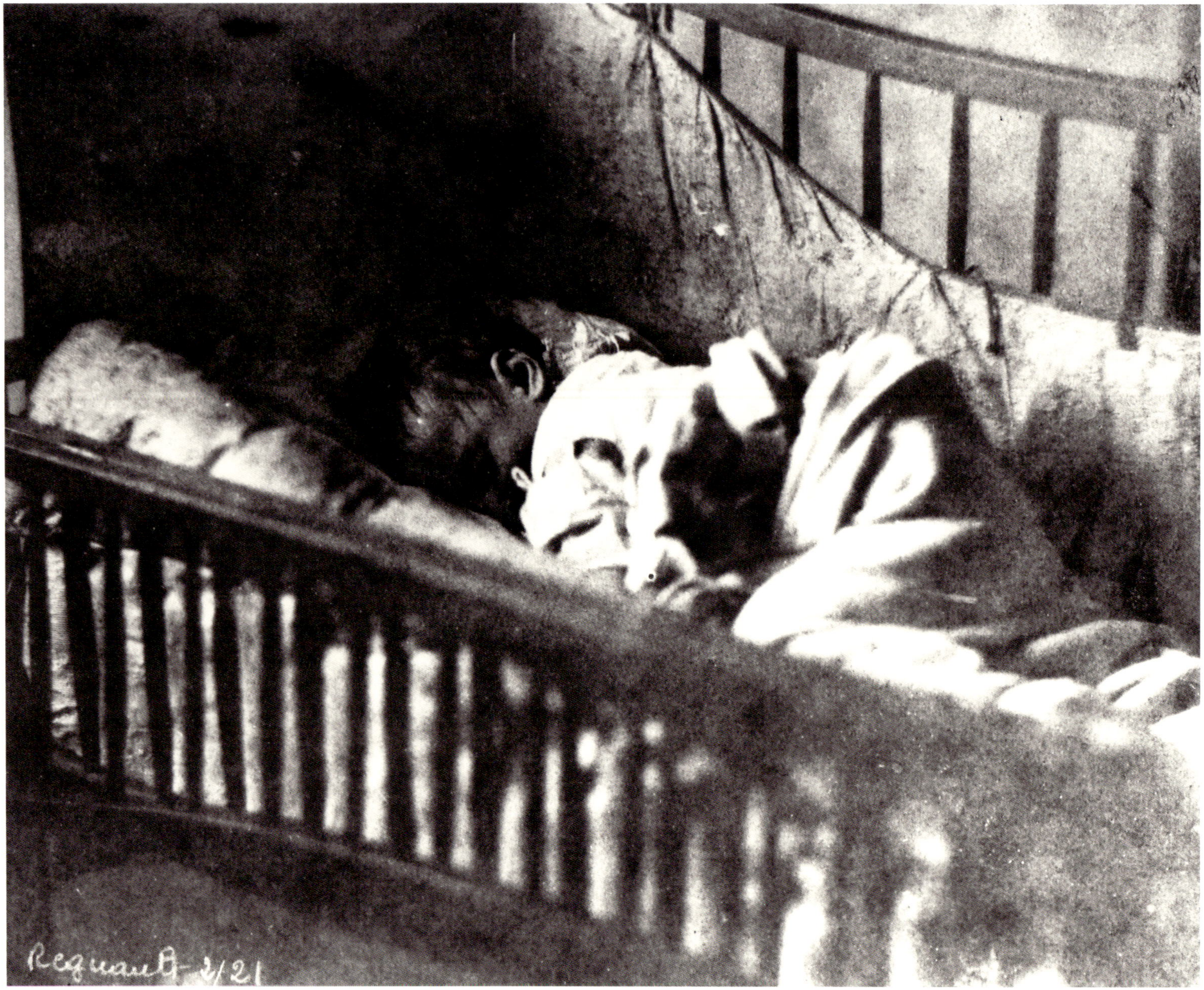

3 FRATERNITY AND FAMILY

Regnault was ready to apply photography to any subject—scientific documentation, architecture, landscape, still life, art reproduction—but he made far more portraits than any other kind of image. A group of noncommercial portraits so extensive at this early date is uncommon, and it initially led me to ask whether Regnault was working as an "amateur professional," that is, receiving an informal clientele without asking for payment. But the identities of his portrait subjects suggest that this was a personal project. The sitters were drawn from two distinct spheres of Regnault's life: his public, professional life as an academic scientist, and his private life as a man with a growing family.

Regnault's portraits are unusual in several ways. First, he used the calotype process, which was unpopular with most portraitists for reasons that will become clear. Further, the portraits show a remarkable range of intentions, from artful "high concept" images to offhand pictures of anyone who happened to be present when the camera was ready. More importantly, Regnault's portraits—particularly the domestic portraits—exhibit a degree of intimacy, emotion, and animation rarely seen in portraits by his peers, and they may form the most extensive collective family portrait of the era. In fact, his substantial work as a maker of "domestic portraits" is so unique that is difficult to find a parallel among his contemporaries. Portraiture from the 1840s and 1850s was almost always the product of commercial photographers, and the photographers named in their time and ours as masters of the genre were

Fig. 33.
Victor Regnault, *Eugène Regnault in His Crib*, c. 1852. Modern print from paper negative, $4^{7}/_{8}$ x $6^{1}/_{8}$ in. (12.4 x 15.5 cm). Société Française de Photographie, Paris. 473.21

professionals: David Octavius Hill and Robert Adamson in Edinburgh, Albert Sands Southworth and Josiah Hawes in Boston, Nadar in Paris, and Antoine Claudet in London, among others. In pose, setting, and expression, their portraits are infused with the public character of the sitting in the professional studio.

Despite the fact that photographic portraiture was a veritable wonder in the 1840s, disdain for it as simply "common"—meaning both the product and the social act itself—was already being expressed in print by the early 1850s. Though he never exhibited them, Regnault did share his portraits at a private gathering of members of the Société Héliographique in 1853. Reporting on this meeting at *La Lumière* editor Ernest Lacan's home, a writer for the journal commented that Regnault's portraits "merit the most sincere praise," but showed more enthusiasm for his "delicious copy" of an Ary Scheffer (1795–1858) drawing.[1] Like his fellow amateurs, Regnault, too, reserved his greater artistic ambitions for landscapes, and he pursued his portraiture as a personal attachment that usually had little to do with morally elevated fine art as it was understood within his circle. When we consider the state of professional portraiture at this time, and the ambivalent status of portraiture in the photographic salon culture, Regnault's portraiture stands out as a highly personal, even idiosyncratic body of photographs.

PROFESSIONAL PORTRAITURE

Having solved the initial problem of unbearably long exposures, by 1844 photographers had established numerous portrait studios in Paris, and photographic portraiture would grow into an industry of unimagined profits and proportions by 1850.[2] There was one small way, however, in which the portrait industry was a victim of its own success. Commercial portraiture may have been practiced in the bustling milieu of thousands of eager customers and a robust legion of professionals, but the public's love affair with it was countered by disdain from the small world of artistic photography—the world of photographic clubs, salons, and newspapers. This disapproval may seem paradoxical coming from photography's most vocal defenders (most of them writers in *La Lumière*), but their criticism of the portrait industry was actually the opposite of the antitechnology view expressed by writers like Baudelaire. Both sides agreed that the bulk of commercial portraiture was utterly artless, but whereas the adversaries of photography loathed the medium for its mindless, technological mesmerism, photographic proselytizers like Lacan, Francis Wey, and Henri de Lacretelle (1815–1899) feared that commercial portraiture—the medium's greatest presence in the public realm—was damaging the image of photography. Believing that the public's indiscriminate appetite for portraits encouraged the proliferation of third-rate operators and threatened the development of truly artistic photography, Wey and others attempted to establish higher goals for portraiture.

Scorning the daguerreotype portrait as "the bloodiest critique of that which one could call 'material' or rather, 'materialist' truth," Wey complained that most portrait photographs were artistic failures because they were unselectively detailed, too explicit, and therefore, *vulgaire* (banal).[3] In his 1851 theorization of portraiture in *La Lumière*, Wey condemned purely mechanical reproduction as antithetical to the concept of resemblance. Instead, Wey recalled David Hume's philosophy of identity in supposing that "resemblance differs from material fact. It is an abstract idea: the result of an interpretation, it is not essentially subordinated to an absolute precision; rather, it is liable to assume a stronger similitude from some deliberate inaccuracies."[4] He described such an interpetation as analagous to memory, and in a reversal of conventional wisdom, he argued that a mental concept of resemblance could indeed be transmitted by photography, provided the photographer combined his own sensitive response to the model with a firm understanding of the principles of art. He concluded, "In order to compete with art, photography must appeal to feeling [and] to the artist's knowledge," which would naturally extend the "moral reach" of the new medium.[5]

The photographer's psychological and aesthetic insight was therefore key to the notion of an artistic photography. Apologists for photography-as-art would always be hindered by the presumption that photography precluded the intervention of the artist's hand, but they could convincingly argue that the photographer could approach his creative act from an elevated moral plane, just like any other artist. In America, photography was widely understood through the precepts of transcendentalism as being a divine creation, but in France, critics often dismissed it as mere material—all flesh and no spirit.[6] Photography's defenders working against this belief therefore described it with the vocabulary of the spiritual, ethereal, and super-real. In proposing a metaphysics of photographic portraiture, these advocates were struggling to lift photography beyond the gravitational pull of the material world from which it came. Paraphrasing Wey's ideas in more mystical language, Henri de Lacretelle insisted, "It is not the flesh . . . but the transparency of the soul upon that flesh . . . to which one must first devote oneself," and he called for the photographer to prepare himself for the moment when "the whole soul shows itself in the face."[7] A decade after Wey first spoke of the portrait as a "spiritual interpretation," studio photographers Ernest and Fréderic Mayer and Louis Pierson reiterated the concept, exhorting the photographer to enter the portrait session in a state of heightened awareness and to manipulate external conditions until the image on the ground glass resonated with "the impression he feels in his soul facing the model."[8] The portrait produced in this moment of sensitivity and recognition would stimulate a response of intuitive understanding—a pseudo-memory—in the viewer.[9]

Writers on photography also gave practical advice on how the sensitive portrait was best obtained: through the knowing use of artistic principles and physiognomic theory, the suppression of detail, a personalized approach to pose, and "taste" in lighting and accessories. The legendary portraitists were always invoked, particularly Anthony Van Dyck, Peter Paul Rubens, and Titian. Rhetorically addressing the masters of the past, photography critic Henri de La Blanchère wondered of portraiture, "What was it then, what is it still, in the hands of great masters?—if not an ensemble of general lines, and never a microscopic study . . . O, magnificent portraits of Raphael, Van Dyck, Caravaggio, when shall we know enough to sacrifice in order to arrive at your effect!"[10]

THE PORTRAIT AND CALOTYPY

By the mid-1850s, photographers could choose from three major processes: daguerreotype, calotype, and wet plate (glass negative). Of the average daguerreotype portrait, Wey had famously quipped that it left its subjects looking like "fried whiting stuck to a silver plate."[11] The calotype, with its broad rendering of light and dark, uneven tonalities, and matte surface, seemed to represent an antidote to the problems so often diagnosed in daguerreotype portraiture. Back in 1840, William Henry Fox Talbot had even imagined that, with his exposures under three minutes, he could at least beat Daguerre in claiming portraiture for the calotype, but improvements were already on the way that would make daguerreotype portraiture the bread and butter of the emerging photographic market.[12] While Talbot's lightweight paper process would be adopted by travelers and embraced by artistic photographers who appreciated the paper negative's softer rendering of landscape, it would never be widely used by portraitists. Apart from the regional success of Hill and Adamson in Edinburgh, calotype portraiture languished.

This is rather remarkable, considering what the calotype would have offered to consumers of portraits, namely lightweight flexibility, which made it suitable for mailing and pasting in albums, and reproducibility. These conveniences, however, were overshadowed by two impediments to paper portraiture in France. First was the Talbot patent, which practically pushed the English process from public view, and even after Blanquart-Evrard's patent-busting improvements of 1847, the calotype never achieved the widespread use of Daguerre's process.[13] Second, having been nurtured on the vibrant detail of daguerrean portraiture, consumers expected a sharpness and tonal range the calotype could not easily deliver. As photographic entrepreneur N.-P. Lerebours observed, while "portraits on paper, obtained by bright light" were "strongly suited to the taste of artists," they simply did not appeal to the average person.[14] In his 1852 article discussing the merits of "Paper, Plate, or Glass?" Lerebours gave little credence to critical hopes attached to paper portraits: "Since the presentation of several beautiful portraits on paper, you hear it said on all sides by those in the know: 'The reign of the plate is over, before long all proofs will be on paper or glass!' We believe this moment, if indeed it will ever come, is not even close."[15] He then went further in practically dismissing paper portraits altogether: "We have . . . admired the beautiful portraits on collodion . . . by M. Le Gray, from 1850, and since then by two or three persons . . . But after that, is there really, besides some truly rare exceptions, anything to cite in the way of photographic portraits?"[16]

Lerebours took note of the greater technical difficulties of calotype portraiture, but he located the real source of the general preference for daguerreotypes in the daguerreotype's quasi-divine direct action. Voicing the popular conceit that daguerreotypy acted as a kind of natural magic, he observed, "It's the image of a father, of a mother, of a son, that paints itself, that dispatches its luminous reflections to the sensitized plate, without the intermediary of any material agent."[17] In Lerebours's view, the positive paper print was one step removed from the immediacy of the negativeless daguerreotype image. Because the physical or metaphysical emanations of the portrait sitter were trapped in the calotype negative, they were absent from the positive print. Wey, on the other hand, unequivocally recommended the paper process for artistic reasons, but apart from a few exceptions like Victor Laisné (born 1807), the calotype was mostly ignored by commercial portraitists in France.[18] When the sharp, economical wet-plate process arrived on the scene in the mid-1850s, it replaced daguerreotypy in most studios virtually in one fell stroke.

It was thus left largely to amateurs to investigate calotype portraiture, though in France it appears that Regnault was one of the few to do so. This may be because many amateurs practicing calotypy—people like Paul Périer, Paul Delondre, Henri de La Blanchère, André Giroux, E. Mailand—held landscape photography to be the higher artistic calling.[19] The preference for landscape was reinforced by the salon culture that nourished amateurs, which gave less incentive to work in portraiture. With rare exception, critics reserved their lengthiest and most substantive commentary for landscapes, and it was not uncommon for them to admit a casual disinterest in—or contempt for—the whole genre of portraiture. In 1858, for example, a reviewer of the annual S.F.P. fundraising sale and exhibition expressed his great relief at the small number of portraits on view and noted besides, "there are so few of them that depart from mediocrity that the public seem[s] scarcely to regret their absence."[20] This writer was of course describing the sophisticated, self-selecting "public" of photography aficionados, not the ordinary consumers that so avidly patronized the portrait industry. One further problem may have dampened the reception of portraits within salon culture, particular in regard to exhibition. To expose images of friends and loved ones—particularly women—to the indiscriminate gaze of strangers was considered by some an indelicacy, although portraits of public figures were certainly acceptable.[21]

Thus, the first generation of photographers with high-art aims, including Regnault, may have had difficulty seeing the portrait apart from either a utilitarian or a purely private frame of reference. As the source of income for hundreds of shoddy commercial operators who had no concern with art, portraiture was tainted by its ubiquity in the marketplace. Lacan summed up the problem in 1856: "Until today the portrait has been considered one of the most lucrative applications of photography . . . but outside of the benefits . . . the photographer can derive from it, and the satisfaction . . . that one experiences in recognizing one's own image reproduced on a silver plate or a piece of paper, one scarcely sees anything else in a photographic portrait."[22]

Portraiture was consequently conscripted to two debased and codependent needs: the support of commercial photographers and the gratification of private vanities. Apart from celebrity portraiture, portrait photographs were never entirely comfortable in the public arena, although they had an undeniable and beloved place within the private realm.

PHOTOGRAPHS AND FRIENDSHIP

In 1851 Regnault wrote to Sir John Herschel to thank him for the hospitality he had received in London, probably on a visit to see the Universal Exhibition. He enclosed a gift of photographs (landscapes) and took the liberty of sending along a set of portraits of J.-B. Biot "for the other savants in London," whose names he stipulated on each portrait.[23] This gift of Biot's portrait was a kind of double homage, first to Biot, who at age seventy-seven was the grand old man of French science, and second, to the chosen men who would be able to appreciate the respect implicit in Regnault's presentation to them. Biot, of course, had played an important role in the birth of photography, particularly as the channel for Talbot's challenge to Daguerre, and we can only speculate that one of those portraits was intended for Biot's unfortunate correspondent.[24] The remarkably fierce portrait of Biot—the only portrait Regnault ever signed and dated—is a three-quarter length seated view (fig. 34). Biot holds a large volume casually on his lap and looks out beyond the frame with a penetrating gaze.

Although he claimed to have taken up photography for use in his scientific work, the large number of portraits Regnault had begun producing around 1850 belies that pragmatic motivation. The Biot portrait was part of an extensive series of pictures of colleagues in the Académie des Sciences, the Collège de France, and probably the Société Héliographique, which allowed Regnault to combine the pleasure of photography with his social and professional activities. The pictures became personal

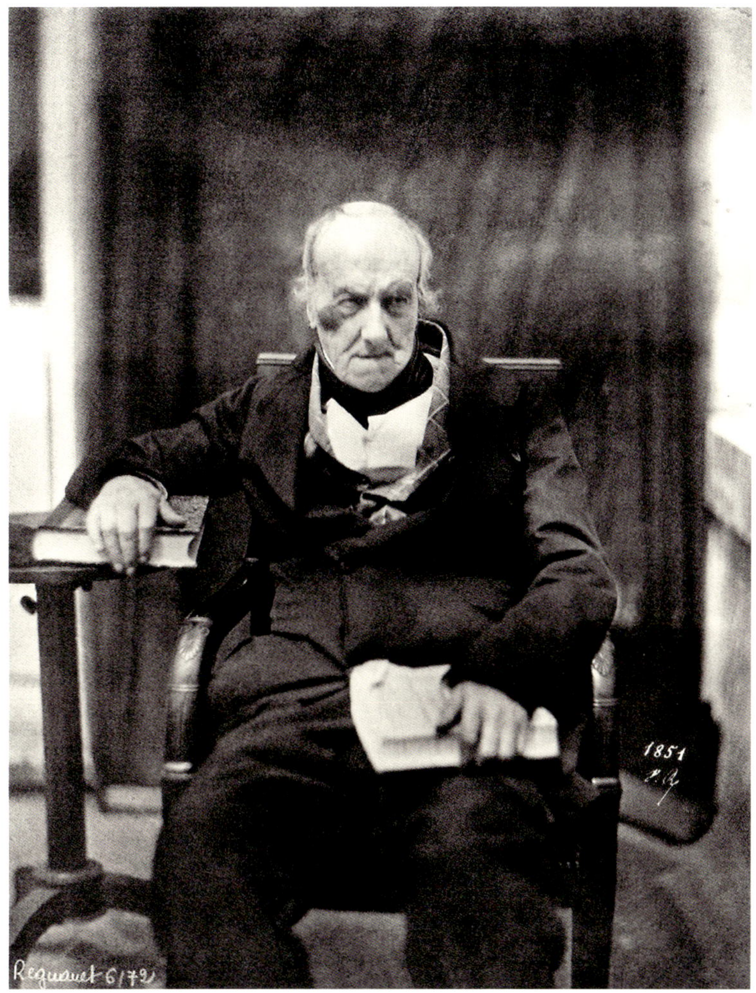

Fig. 34.

Victor Regnault, *Jean-Baptiste Biot*, 1851. Modern print from paper negative, $7^{5}/_{8}$ x $6^{1}/_{4}$ in. (19.4 x 15.9 cm).

Société Française de Photographie, Paris. 473.72

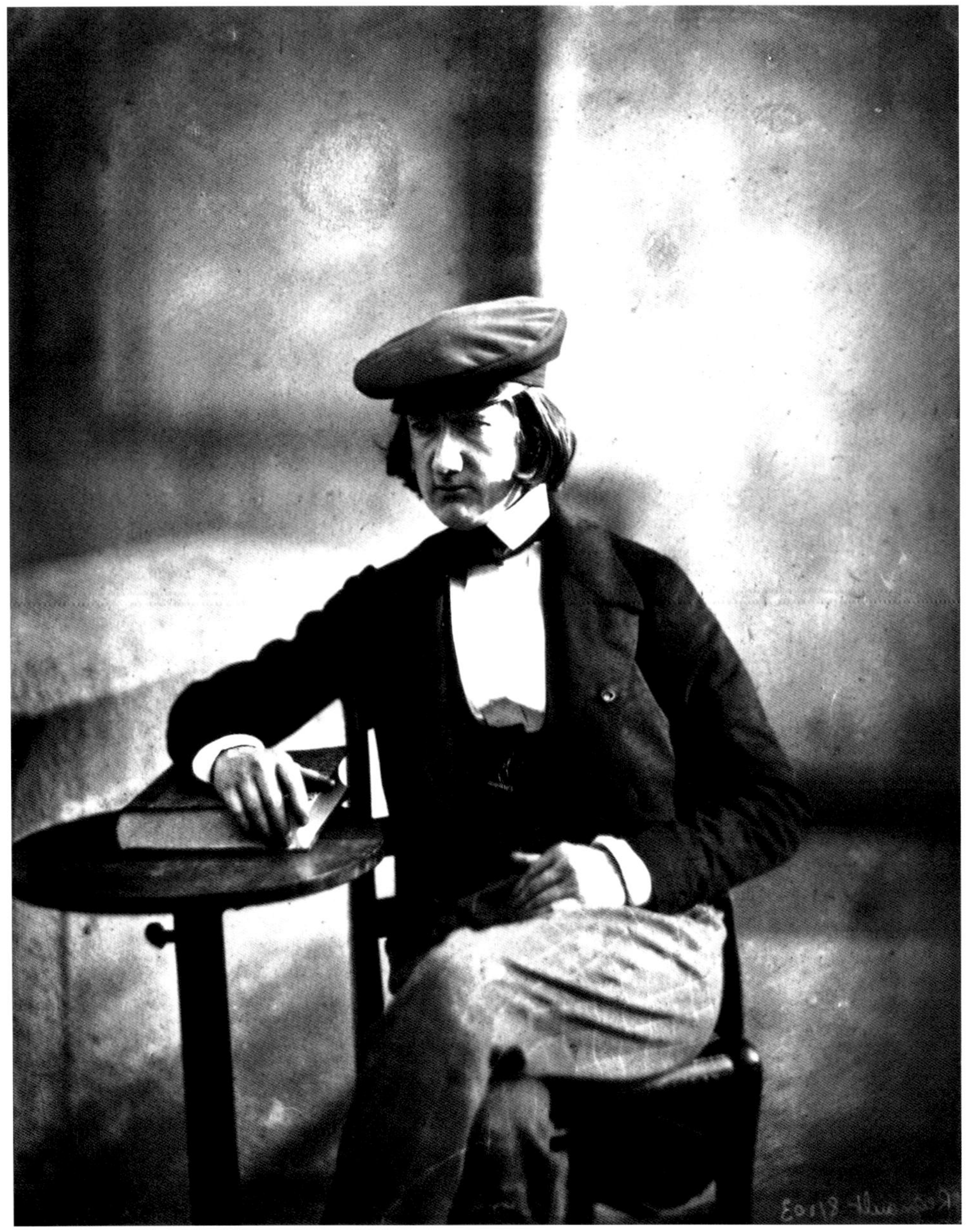

Fig. 35.

Victor Regnault, *Self-Portrait*, c. 1851. Modern print from paper negative, $8\frac{1}{4}$ x $6\frac{1}{2}$ in. (21 x 16.5 cm).

Société Française de Photographie, Paris. 473.103

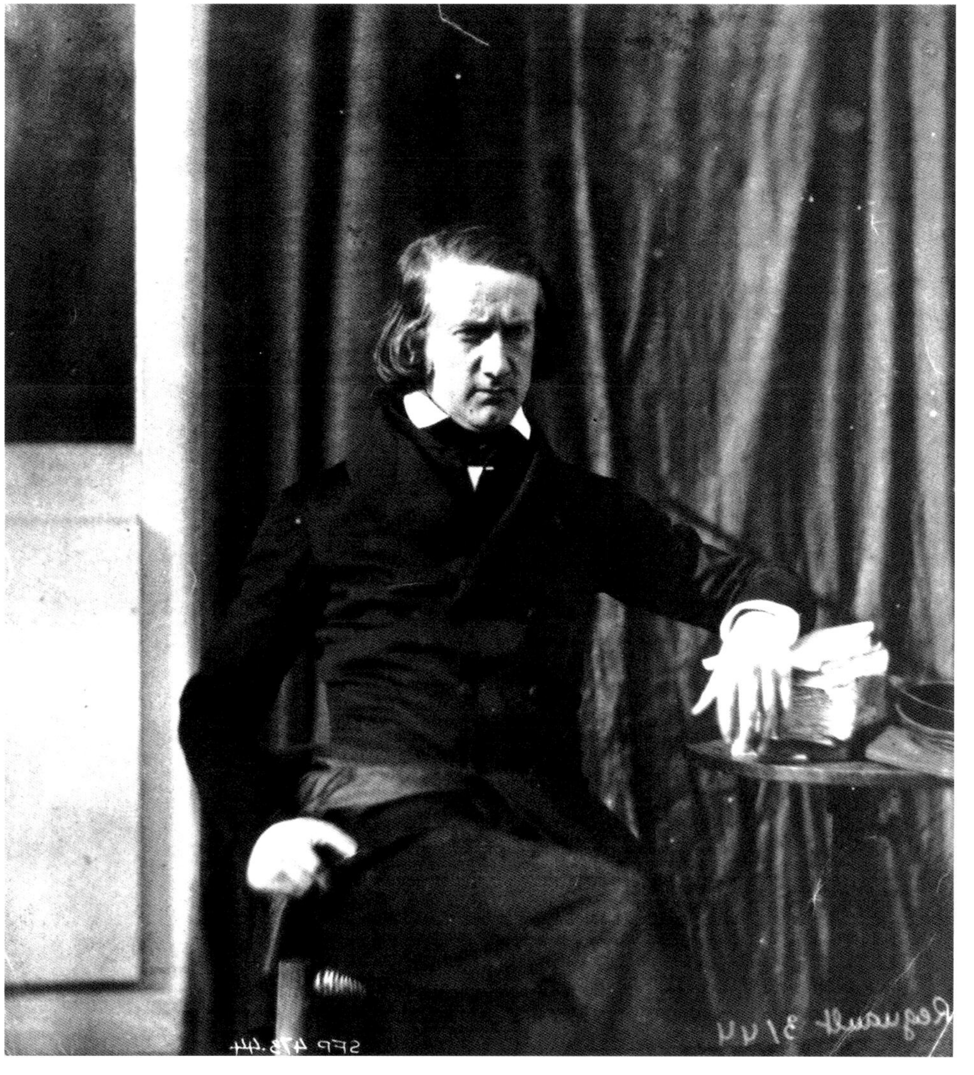

Fig. 36.

Victor Regnault, *Self-Portrait*, c. 1851. Modern print from paper negative, $6^{1}/_{4}$ x $5^{7}/_{8}$ in. (16 x 14.8 cm).

Société Française de Photographie, Paris. 473.44

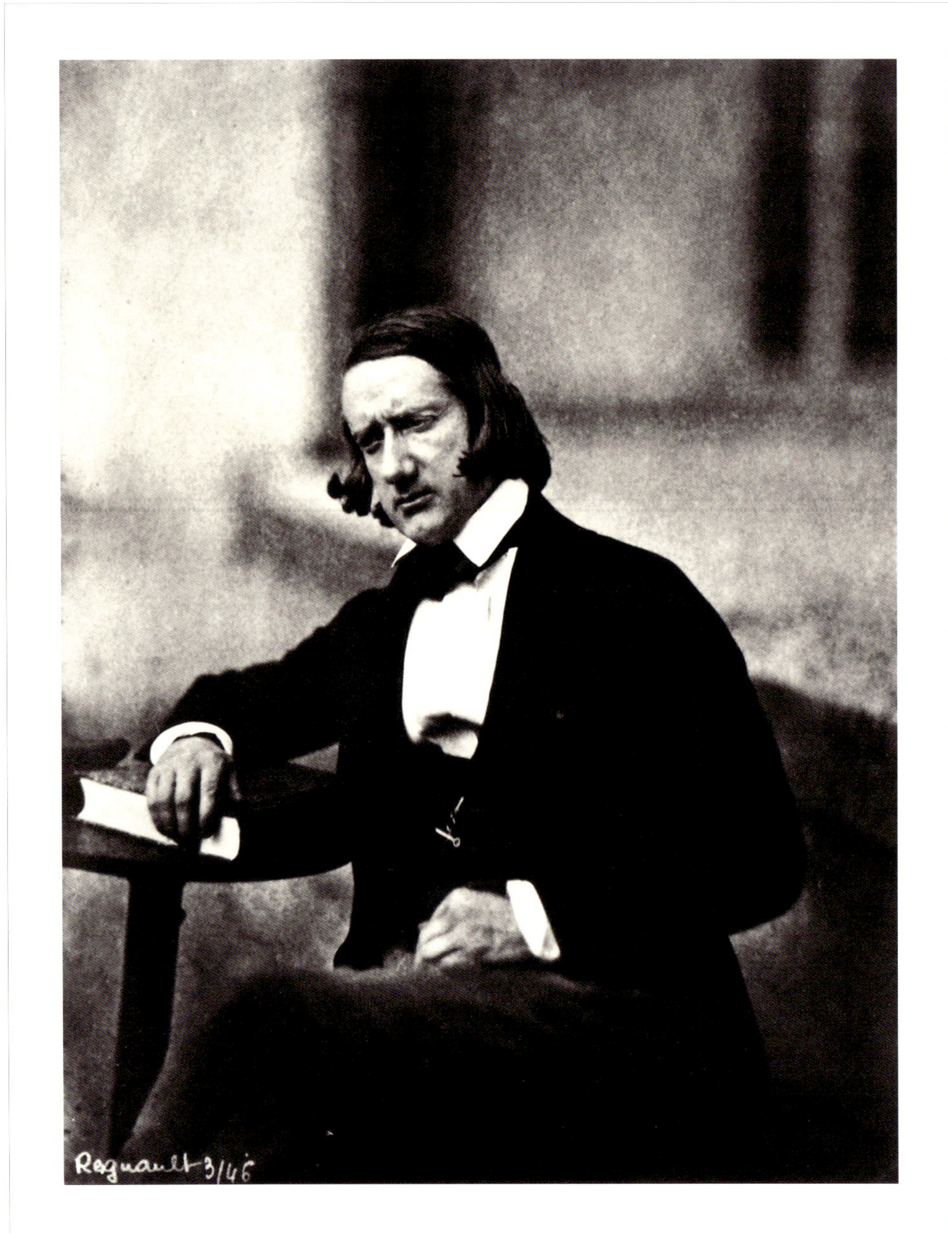

Fig. 37.

Victor Regnault, *Self-Portrait*, c. 1851. Modern print from paper negative, 7 3/4 x 6 in. (19.9 x 15.2 cm). The Philadelphia Museum of Art. Purchased with funds contributed by the American Museum of Photography, 1971, 71-4-46

mementos, some of which he placed side-by-side with family photographs in his only surviving photograph album. Still reluctant to admit his guilty pleasure in photography, he told Justus von Liebig: "I am devoting myself to this art, not for amusement, but because I am shooting a great part for the drawings in my work on Physics," which he spontaneously contradicted by adding, "When the weather improves a little, I will make my own portrait and send you an example."[25] A group of eight self-portraits from this period—experimenting with different poses, backgrounds, costume variations (with and without hat), props, and lighting possibilities (figs. 35, 36, and 37)—shows Regnault occupied with the subjective and unscientific questions of self-presentation before the camera. And while only a handful of photographs remotely linked to his physics experiments exist, more than 150 portraits survive.

Why this profusion of portraits? One answer is implied by Biot's photograph: Regnault made portraits as expressions of esteem and respect. Like all academics living in the capital, he had a professional life freighted with entangling alliances and the political intrigues of the academy, though he liked to think of himself as fiercely independent. It was true that he almost always worked alone and declined to accept students into his own laboratory. As a young academic in 1841, he had naively insisted to Liebig that "I, myself, march under the banner of no one."[26] But as the scientific establishment began to recognize him with positions and honors in the mid-1840s, his pride and gratitude bound him to the exclusive, masculine world that now received him so warmly. At the same time he took up photography for scientific illustration (photographing acoustic experiments), he also began to use it to recognize his friendships within the French Institute and with other men of intellectual mark.[27]

Only about a quarter of these seventy-plus portrait subjects have been identified. Liebig was apparently one of the early sitters; writing to him in March 1851, Regnault described this now-lost portrait as "not a great success as a photograph, but . . . a very strong likeness," which might be taken to mean a mediocre exposure, but otherwise a solid portrayal of Liebig's physiognomy.[28] The series includes many fellow scientists and other academics at the Collège de France.[29] Regnault made most of the portraits outside his apartments at the Collège, which made it possible to catch professors for sittings between lectures.

The project recalls the popular thematic print collections known as *galeries contemporaines* that featured prominent figures of the day. And although the breadth of this project could be taken to indicate more sweeping plans to, say, create a collective portrait of the Académie des Sciences, or supply photographic models for a commercial publishing venture, this was not the case. This was a highly selective series, not an inclusive one, and many of the Académie's most illustrious figures are missing, such as François Arago, the perpetual secretary, whose role in mediating the purchase of Daguerre's invention was so well known.[30]

There was an obvious model available to Regnault when he undertook this series: Hill and Adamson's elegant portraits of the Edinburgh intelligentsia. Hill and Adamson's portraiture of the mid-1840s was well-known in Great Britain, where Regnault had photographic contacts, including Sir David Brewster, an avid admirer of the Scottish calotypists.[31] Hill and Adamson's portraits had also been presented by Arago at a meeting of the Académie des Sciences in 1844, so Regnault had undoubtedly seen examples by these recognized masters of calotype portraiture.[32] Yet Regnault's portraits are nothing like Hill and Adamson's, except in motivation, since both series began as gestures of personal respect and recognition. Visually they could hardly be more different. Unlike Hill and Adamson's consistently elegant and painstakingly arranged portraits (fig. 38), Regnault's portraits of his colleagues are unceremonious, offhand, and unaffected. Hill and Adamson constructed virtually every aspect of their portraits with studious precision—pose, elaborate accessories, camera distance, and angle. Regnault's method was as simple as theirs was complex.

In most of his pictures, a single figure was photographed in an open-air setting, standing or seated before a dark cloth backdrop, a wall, or a set of double doors. Whereas Hill and Adamson strove to re-create the look of an intimate, often opulent interior in their outdoor studio by structuring a shallow space with pieces of fine furniture and heavy draperies, Regnault almost never concealed the spare outdoor setting of most of the portraits, which consequently appear casually improvised. Bricks can be seen anchoring the plain cloth that was occasionally hung behind the sitter; furnishings, when present at all, consist of a functional, adjustable table and simple wooden chairs that look hastily borrowed from a nearby classroom or laboratory. Table legs are shimmed with blocks of wood upon the uneven ground, and often the sitter's coat, hat, or umbrella lies nearby, as if the sitting took place spontaneously during a casual visit (fig. 39). Few of these images have the studied elegance of Regnault's earliest self-portrait, which he may have made as an aide-mémoire for his wife's cousin, Eugène Amaury-Duval (1808–1885), who was painting his portrait in 1847.[33]

Accessories and props—even books, meaningful as they were in Regnault's circle—appear infrequently. In several instances the sitters were photographed with signifying objects: a sextant for the marine geographer Auguste Bravais (fig. 40), jars of specimens for the pisciculturist Victor Coste, and a common chemist's flask for Graham (fig. 41). Never adept at fitting these objects comfortably into the image, Regnault seldom used them. One of Regnault's most unusual portraits depicts Jules Ziegler (1804–1856), a painter, decorator, designer, ceramicist, and all-around art-world figure, who Regnault may have known through a long mutual association with Amaury-Duval (fig. 42). The signification of pose, costume, and accessories is particularly dense in this portrait, perhaps in keeping with Ziegler's

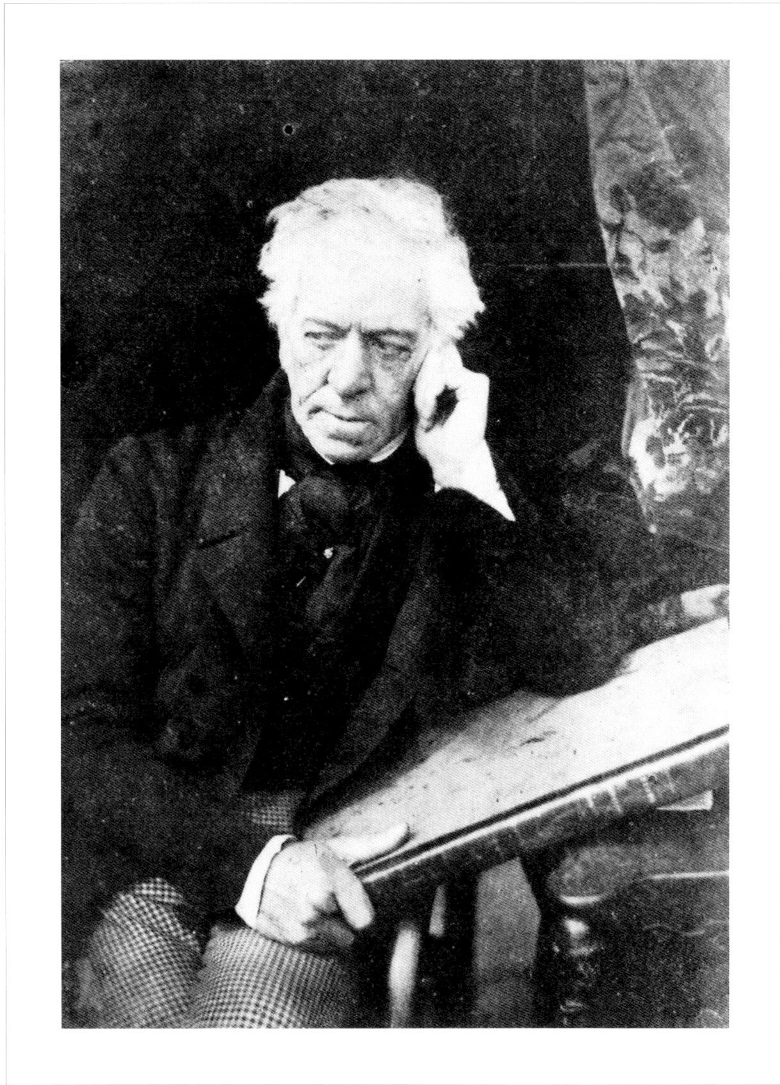

Fig. 38.

David Octavius Hill (Scottish, 1802–1870) and Robert Adamson (1821–1848), *Sir William Allen (1782–1850), President of the Academy of Fine Arts*, 1843. Salt print from paper negative, 7 1/2 x 5 1/2 in. (19.1 x 14.1 cm). National Gallery of Canada, Ottawa. Gift of Dorothy Meigs Eidlitz, St. Andrews, New Brunswick, 1968, P68:046:73 DME

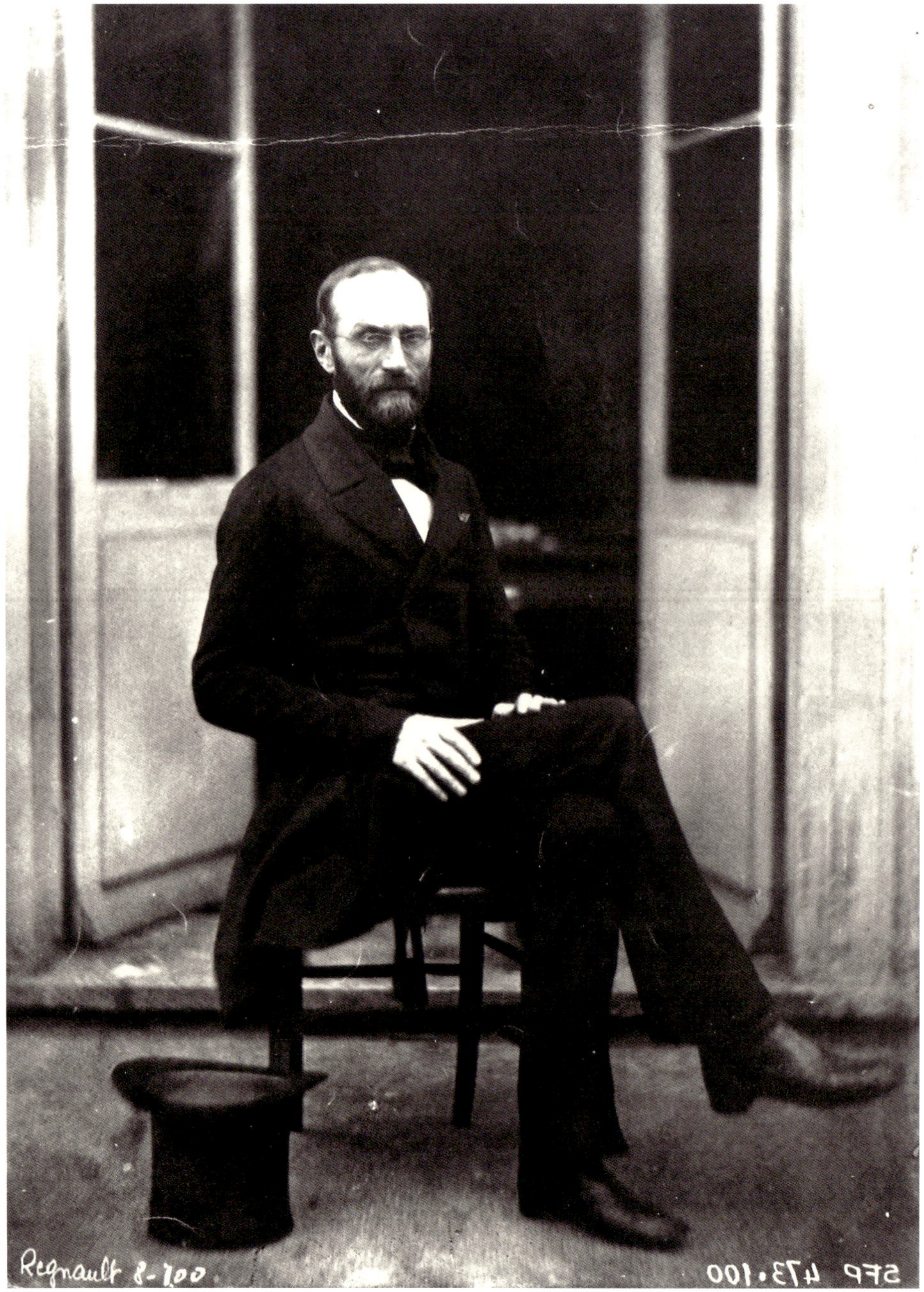

Fig. 39.

Victor Regnault, *Unidentified Man*, c. 1851. Modern print from paper negative, 7½ x 5½ in. (19.3 x 14.2 cm).

Société Française de Photographie, Paris. 473.100

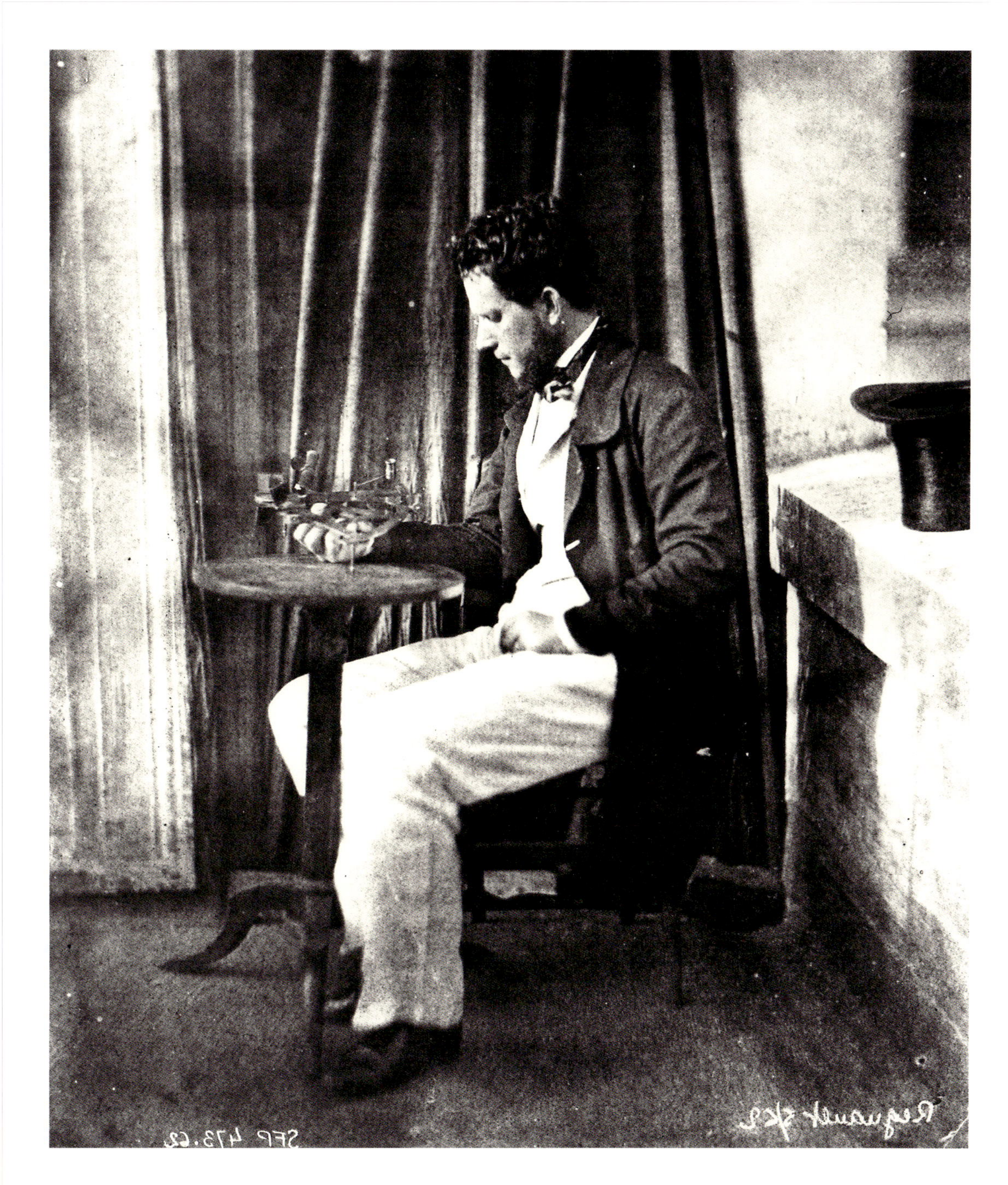

Fig. 40.

Victor Regnault, *The Marine Geographer Auguste Bravais*, c. 1851. Modern print from paper negative, $7^{3}/_{8}$ x $6^{1}/_{4}$ in. (18.8 x 15.9 cm). Société Française de Photographie, Paris. 473.62

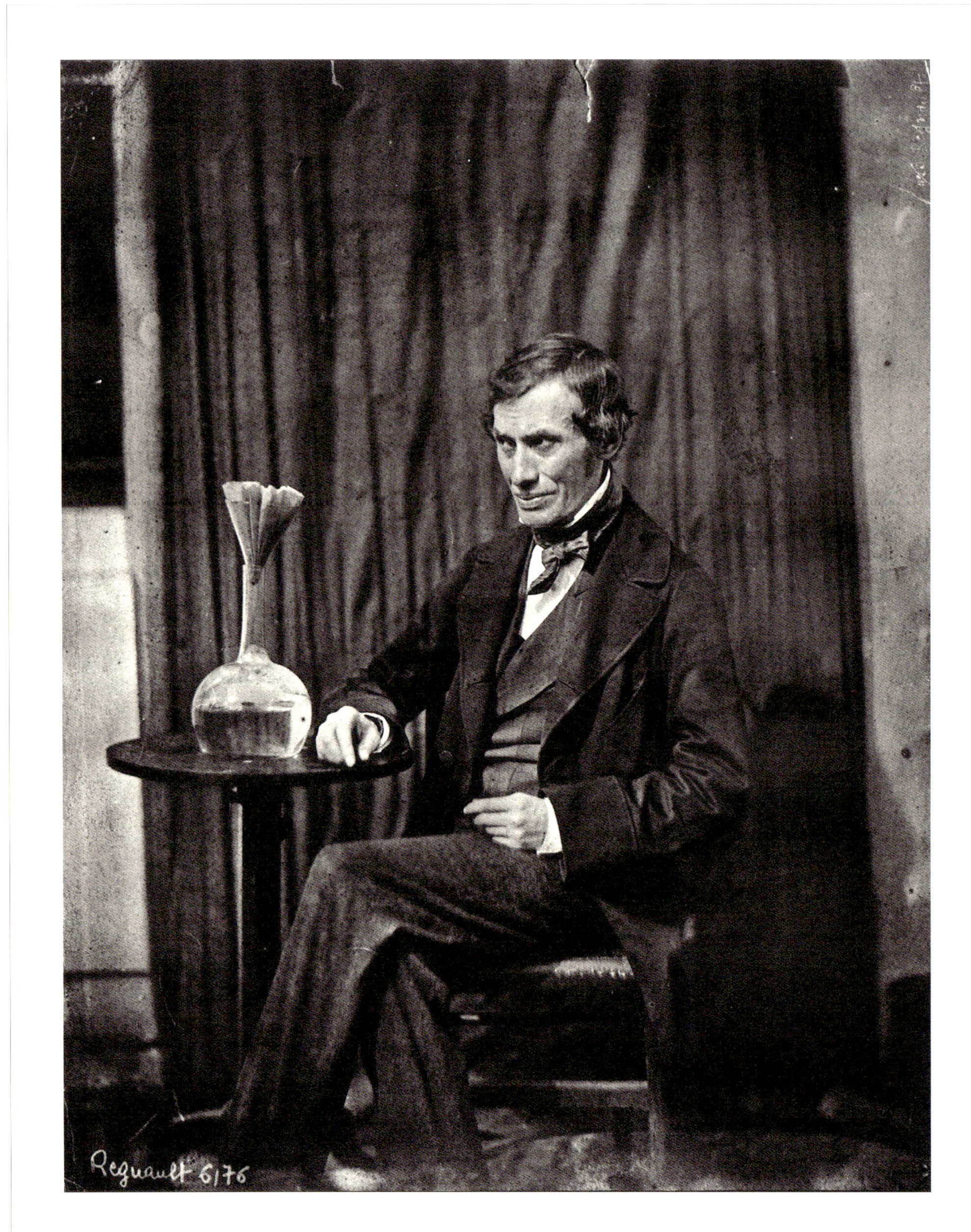

Fig. 41.

Victor Regnault, *The Chemist Thomas Graham*, c. 1851. Modern print from paper negative, $7^{7}/_{8}$ x $6^{1}/_{2}$ in. (20.1 x 16.4 cm). Société Française de Photographie, Paris. 473.76

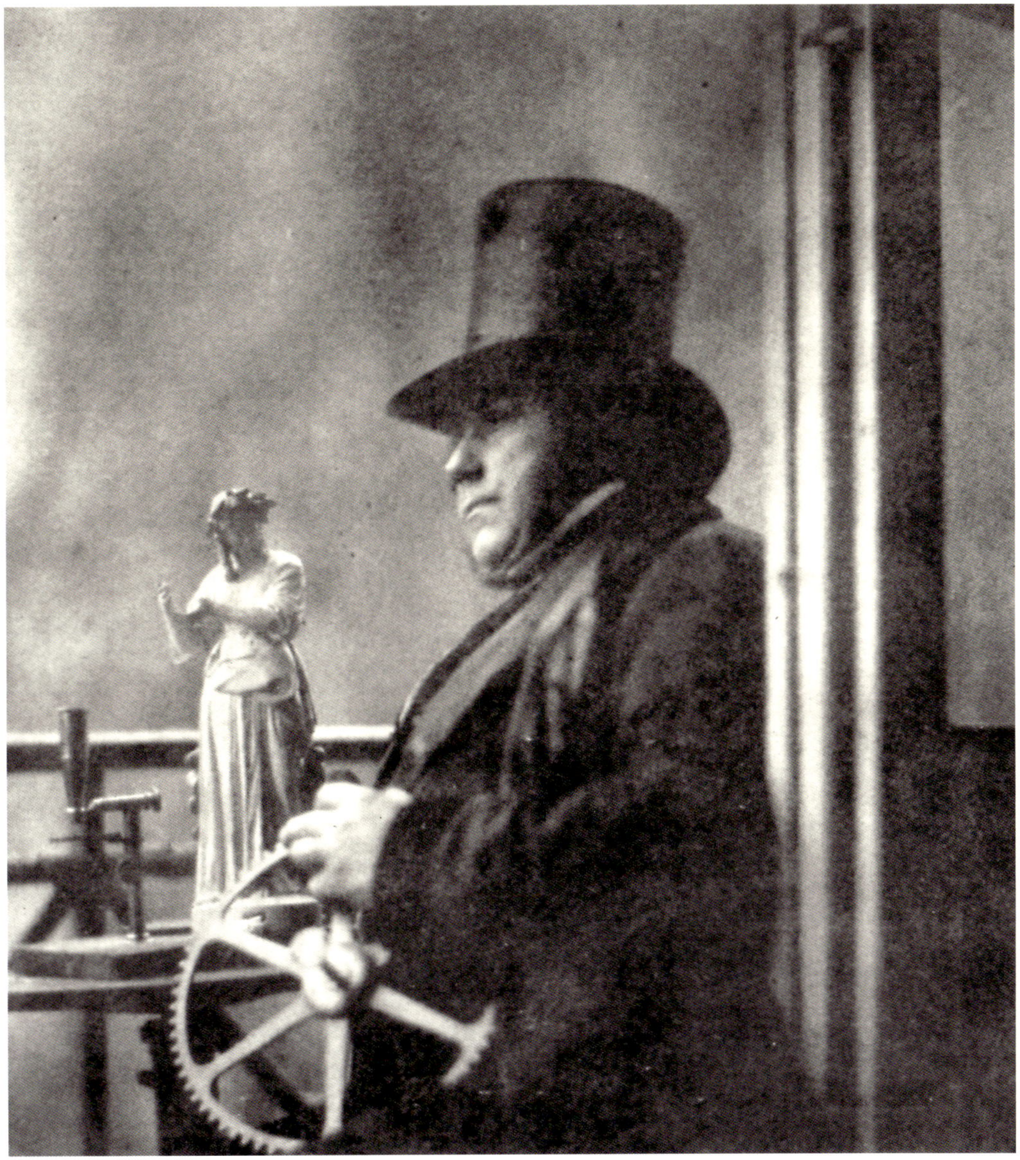

Fig. 42.

Victor Regnault, *Jules Ziegler*, p. 13, *Album Regnault*, c. 1851. Modern print from paper negative, 5 1/4 x 4 3/4 in. (13.4 x 12.1 cm).

Société Française de Photographie, Paris

multifaceted identity. Around the time of this sitting, Ziegler was also a leader of the artistic phalanx of the emerging photographic world—a founding member of the Société Héliographique—but his profession in ceramics seems to be the key reference in Regnault's portrait. Photographing indoors in ambient light, looking onto a shallow balcony, Regnault portrays Ziegler in profile, clad in overcoat and high top hat, leaning heavily against the doorframe. On a table to his right are a porcelain statuette and small mechanical brace; he holds a large cogwheel against his body—perhaps in reference to Ziegler's contributions to industrial ceramic fabrication.[34] Although Regnault has tried to contrive a scene in which we glimpse a man absorbed in solitary thought, replete with the signs of his professional identity, the quirky staging of the photographic moment insistently intrudes, and we cannot forget the photographer's presence.

This meta-awareness, a sense of being present not in the scene but at the enactment of the scene, is characteristic of much early photography, and it turns upon questions of acting and directing. Many early photographers whose work was strongly directorial, like Hill and Adamson and Julia Margaret Cameron (1815–1879), strove to conceal the directing presence behind the work, with varying degrees of success. Since Regnault's works were implicitly about the photographer's relationships with his colleagues, he usually took the opposite tack, openly acknowledging the contact between himself and his sitters.

The physical attitudes in the portraits also differ from the scrupulously posed works by Hill and Adamson. The Scottish partners worked with a consistent, if broad vocabulary of pose, reiterated throughout their hundreds of portraits, drawn mostly from the fine art tradition. In Regnault's portraits, the inconsistency of poses suggests he may have given his friends minimal direction, or even let them position themselves for the camera. Sometimes fully relaxed and natural, at other times stiffly formal and awkwardly self-conscious, these poses index his sitters' sense of ease with the new ritual of posing for the camera. With a prim placidity, the Saint-Simonist economist Michel Chevalier waits patiently for the exposure to be over (fig. 43). One colleague slouches thoughtfully in a chair next to the vacuum pump Regnault used for preparing photographic paper (fig. 44), while another faces the camera with pleasant frankness, hands resting comfortably on his thighs (fig. 45). A page from the *Album Regnault* shows this pair of portraits: Henri-Hureau de Sénarmont, sternly at attention and adopting the officious hand-in-vest pose so famously used by Napoléon, and the careworn Henri Milne-Edwards, with his head casually framed by the door behind him, who looks passively distracted (fig. 46). The painter Amaury-Duval—himself a successful portraitist—presents a flinty self-possession, with furrowed brow and angular limbs betraying the tension of holding perfectly still for the exposure (fig. 47). Regnault's former drawing master, Carl von Steuben (1788–1856), appears to be taking a pinch of snuff in his

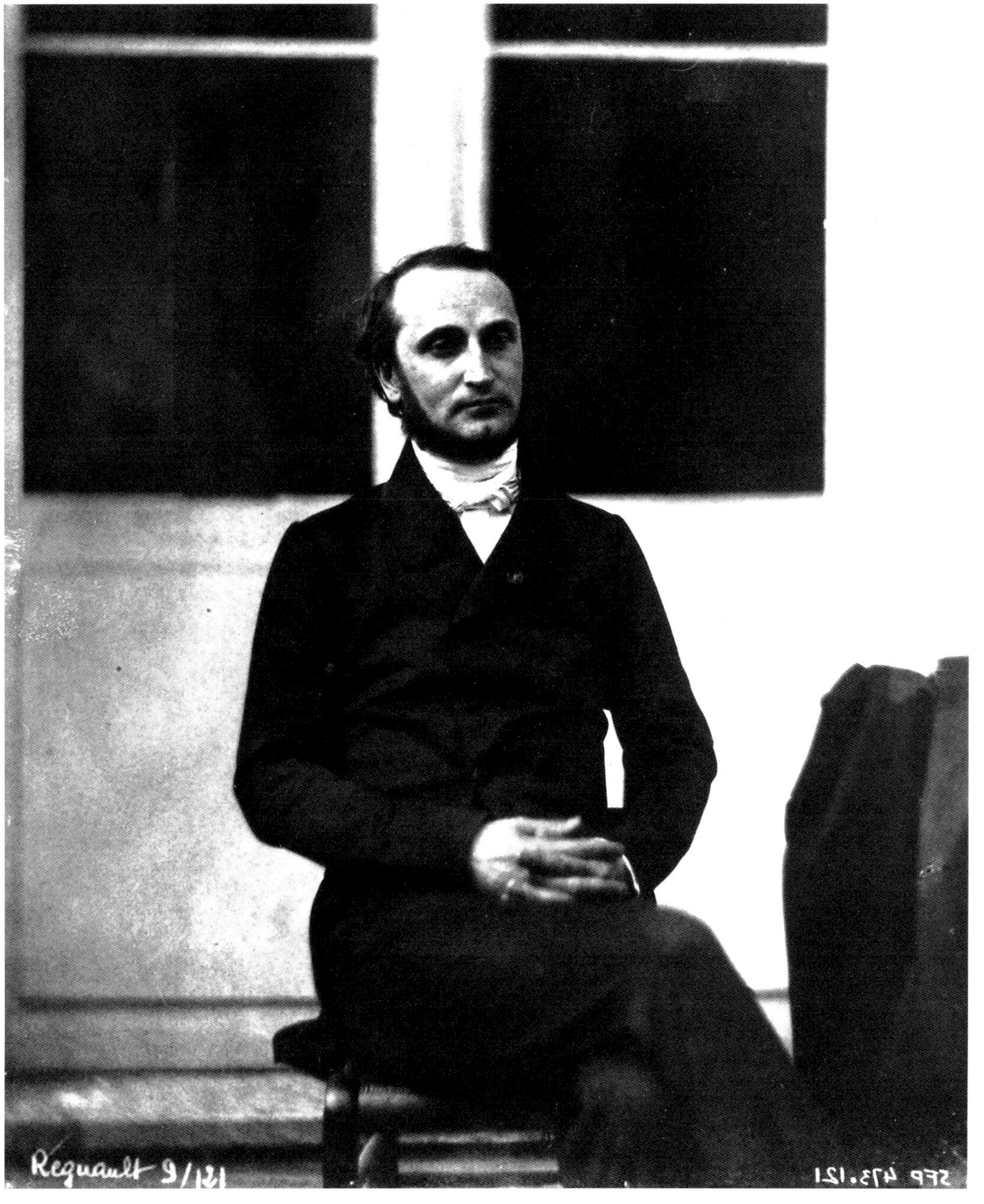

Fig. 43.
Victor Regnault, *The Economist Michel Chevalier*, c. 1851. Modern print from paper negative, $7^{1}/_{4}$ x $5^{3}/_{4}$ in. (18.3 x 14.7 cm).
Société Française de Photographie, Paris. 473.121

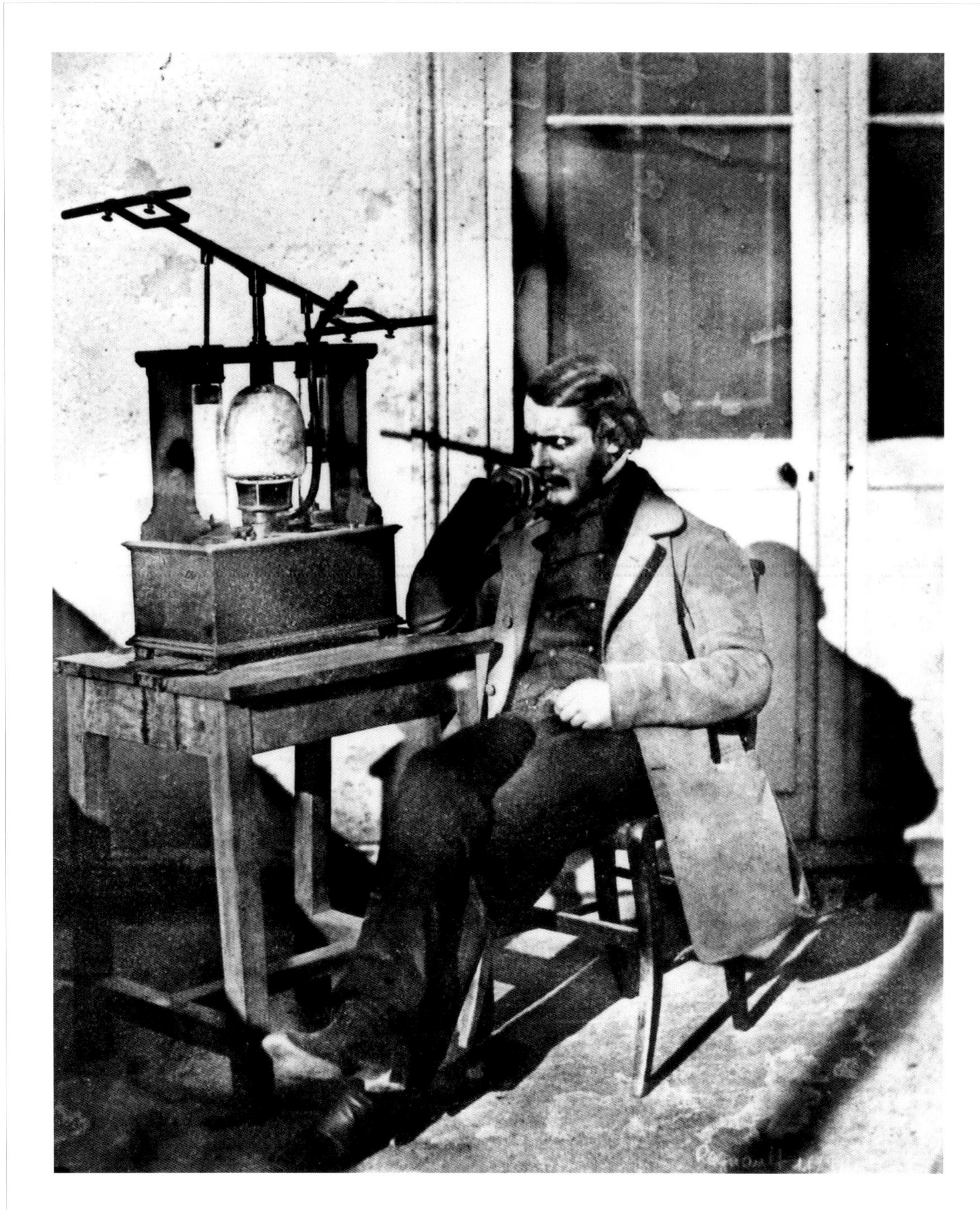

Fig. 44.

Victor Regnault, *Man with Vacuum Pump*, c. 1851. Modern print from paper negative, 7 1/8 x 6 in. (18.2 x 15.4 cm). Philadelphia Museum of Art. Purchased with funds contributed by the American Museum of Photography, 1971, 71-4-55

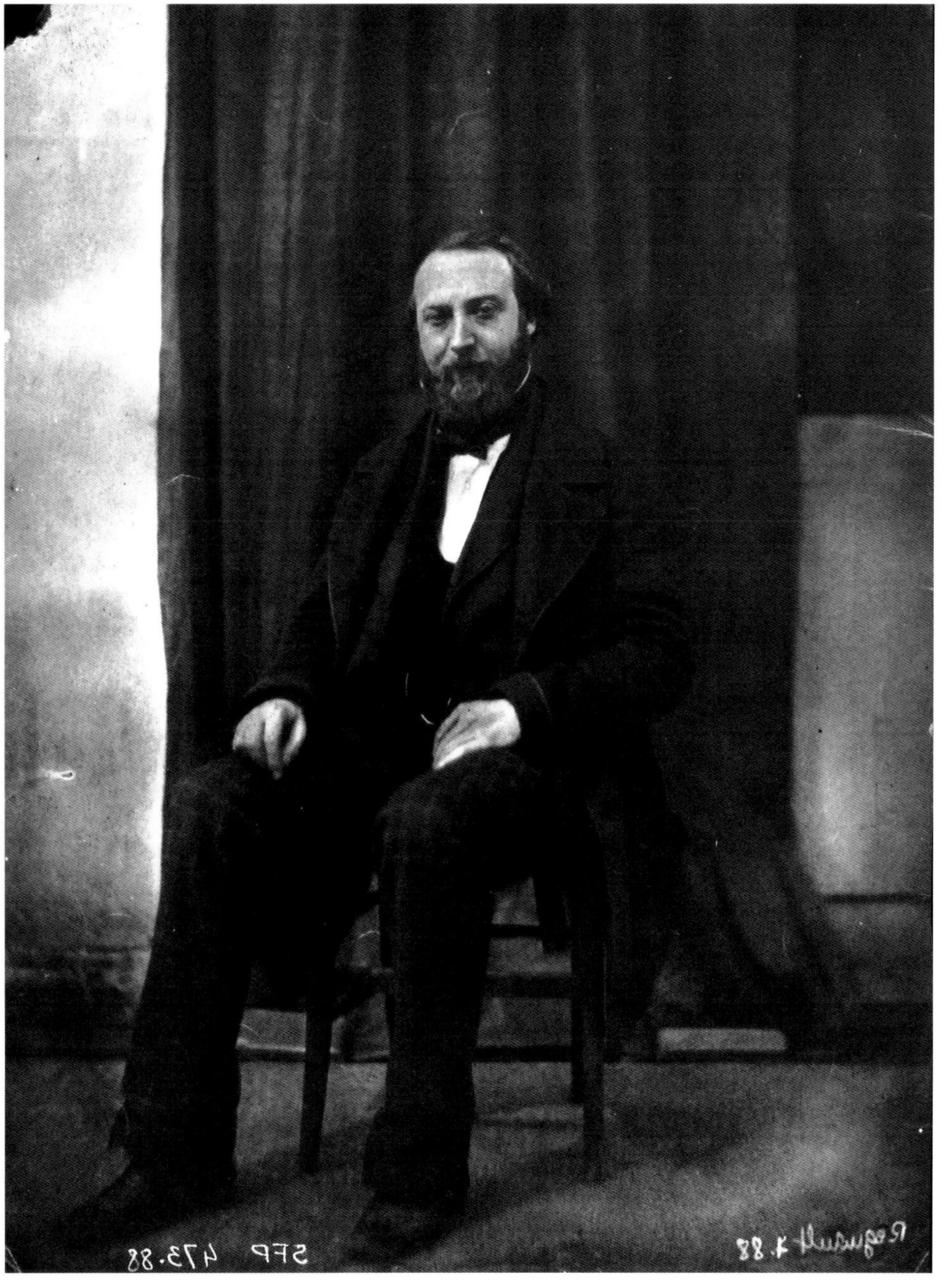

Fig. 45.

Victor Regnault, *Unidentified Man* [*Fréderic de Reiset?*], c. 1851. Modern print from paper negative, 7 1/8 x 5 3/8 in. (18.2 x 13.5 cm). Société Française de Photographie, Paris. 473.88

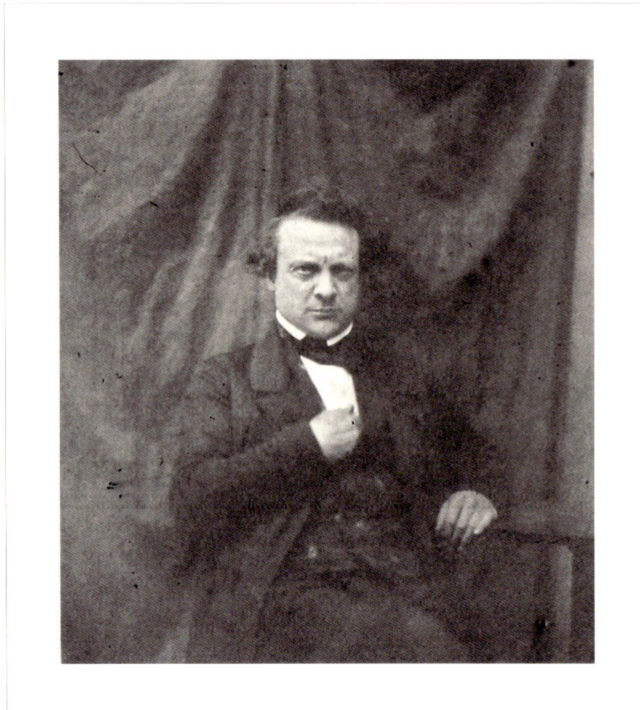

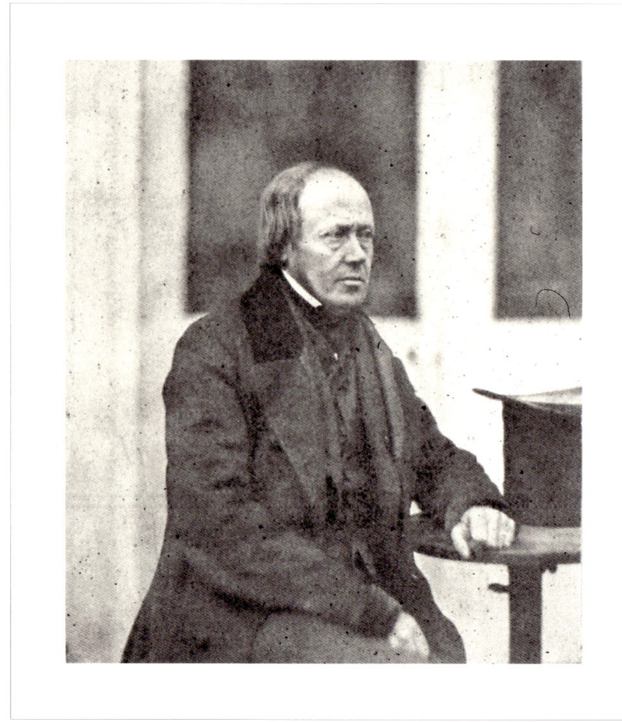

Fig. 46.
Victor Regnault, *Henri-Hureau de Sénarmont* and *Henri Milne-Edwards*, p. 80, *Album Regnault*, c. 1851. Salt prints from paper negatives; left: 6 x 5 3/8 in. (15.1 x 13.5 cm); right: 6 1/8 x 5 1/8 in. (15.6 x 13 cm). Société Française de Photographie, Paris

fingers (fig. 48). In a second portrait of Steuben, Regnault comes close to the casual, affective feeling of the modern snapshot (fig. 49). Seated before a rosebush in full bloom, with a young woman standing behind him, Steuben gazes at a flower he holds by the stem. The girl looks on over his shoulder, steadying her body against his in a casual, familial embrace.

On rare occasions, Regnault attempted a grander effect, using strong chiaroscuro as the means of infusing the portrait with vigor and drama. A bust-length view of an unidentified academician, posed in Regnault's apartment at the Collège, is one of the photographer's most polished efforts (fig. 50). Standing before the camera in a commanding, full-frontal pose, the man rests his right arm on a mantlepiece; the right hand drapes gracefully over the edge of the mantle, illuminated by a strong

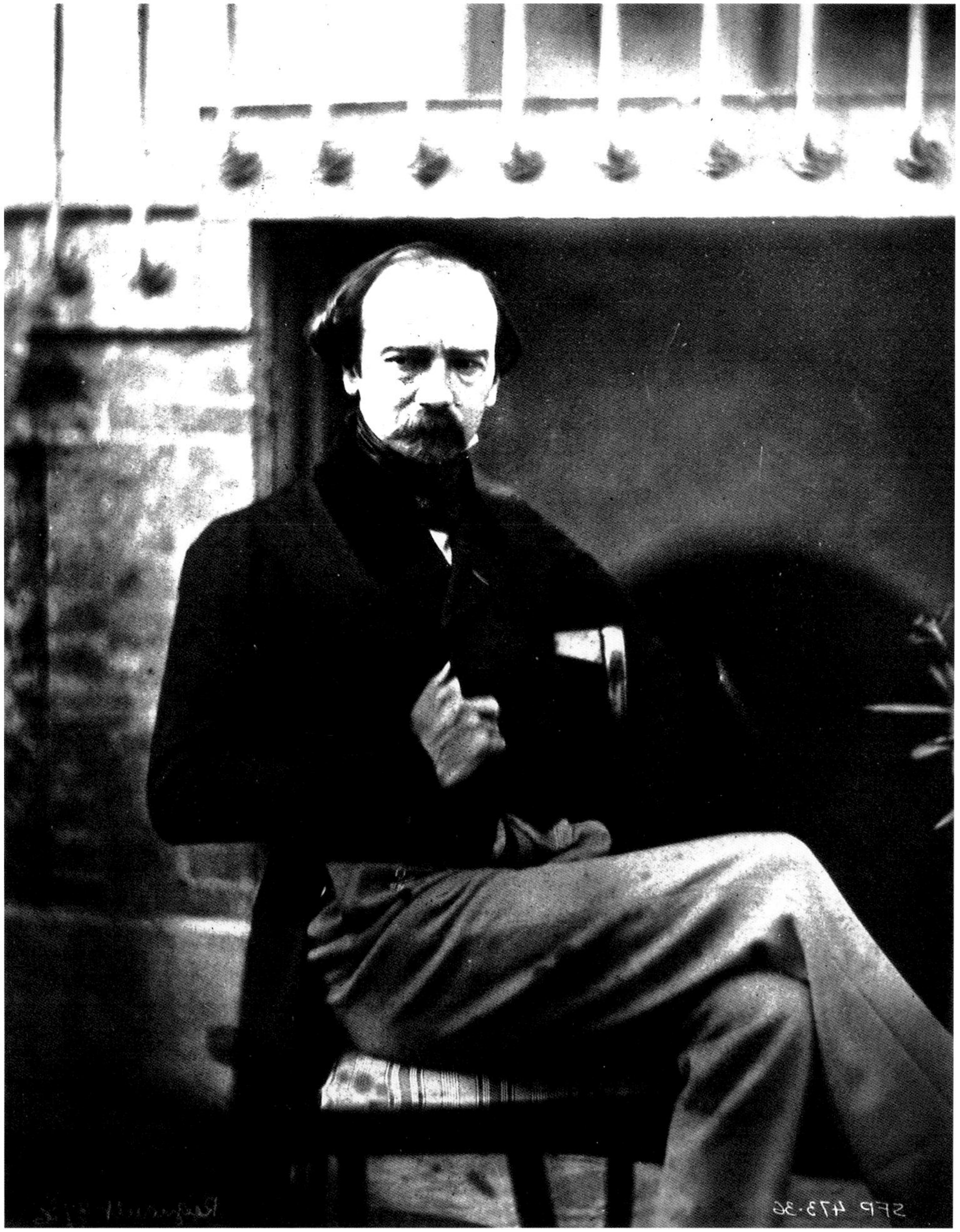

Fig. 47.
Victor Regnault, *The Painter Eugène Amaury-Duval*, c. 1852. Modern print from paper negative, $7^{3}/_{8}$ x 6 in. (18.6 x 15.2 cm).
Société Française de Photographie, Paris. 473.36

raking light. The left half of his face is saturated in sunlight; the right half is plunged into deep shade. Highlights touch upon the rich satin of his cravat, a stickpin, and the elegant sweep of a watch chain. The figure is further set off by the irregular shapes of light and shadow cast on the rear wall by the curtains and window casement, which create a glowing frame for the crown of the head, accentuated, as the experts dictated, as the seat of the intellect.

Although there is an overriding modesty in Regnault's portraiture, the striking individuality expressed in his sitters' poses and expressions—unusual for its time—reminds us that Regnault was once hailed as an inspiration and a master portraitist by Nadar.[35] By preferring to put aside the conventions of grand style portraiture in his series of savants and notables and photographing his sitters "as is," Regnault seems to have cared more about representing their plain substance and less about glossing the images with signifiers of profession and status. We might consider this series in light of Regnault's current troubles within the academy, for in the midst of this project he was facing a real crisis of faith in his future in French science. As a mature scientist in 1851, Regnault looked frequently back on his youthful experience of studying with Justus von Liebig in the laboratory at Giessen, which he considered the greatest stimulus to his career as a scientist.[36] There he had been impressed by the internationality of Liebig's laboratory, which operated in a system more open, more financially vulnerable, and more independent than that of French science.[37] Regnault had maintained a warm correspondence with Liebig since 1835, and his letters illuminate the evolution of his attitude toward the culture of French science. Letters of the 1830s and early 1840s show Regnault confident and full of ambition, even while he complained of narrow-minded colleagues and powerful, capricious professors. Annoyance was gradually replaced by bitterness in the 1850s, as Regnault, now an established physicist disabused of any naïveté, came to understand the government's support of the Académie des Sciences as a devil's bargain, and his complaints became self-searching ruminations on this troubling state of affairs.

He had hoped to loosen the government's ties on his research by accepting the position of director at Sèvres in 1852, where he would put several critical miles of distance between himself and the insular environment of the A.d.S., but he discovered too late that he was now subject to even more government interference and tedious administrative obligations. Having served barely more than a year at Sèvres, Regnault tendered his resignation over a dispute with the minister of state; it was refused, and, as he told Sir John Herschel's wife, he found himself more trapped in his position than ever.[38] His letter to Lady Herschel of 1853 also included a surprising confession of his dissatisfaction with life in the academy. Explaining his refusal to accept the nomination for the post of perpetual secretary, vacant since Arago's recent death on October 2, Regnault described his distaste for the artifice and pomp of academic

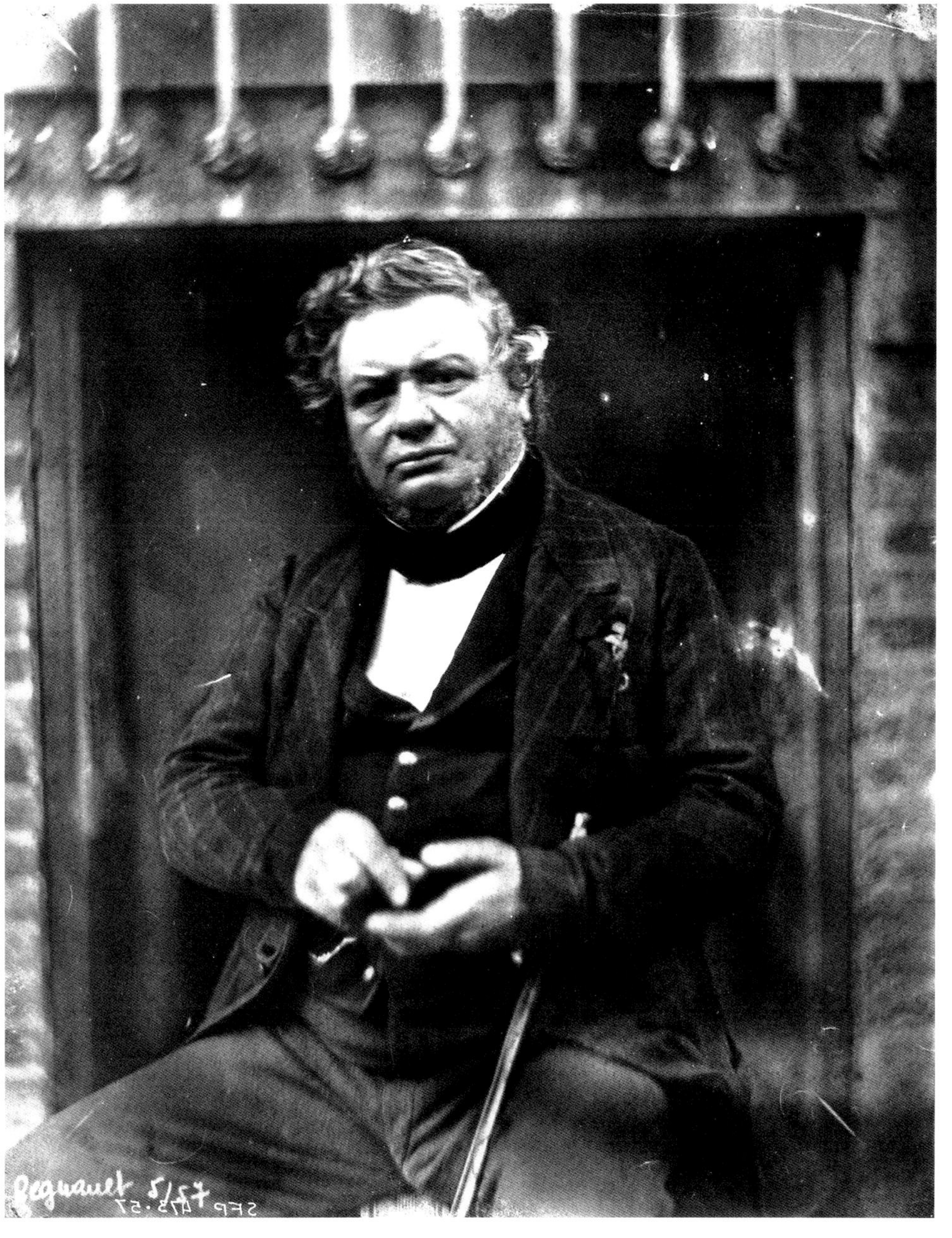

Fig. 48.

Victor Regnault, *The Painter Carl von Steuben*, c. 1852. Modern print from paper negative, 8 1/4 x 6 3/8 in. (20.9 x 16.3 cm). Société Française de Photographie, Paris. 473.57

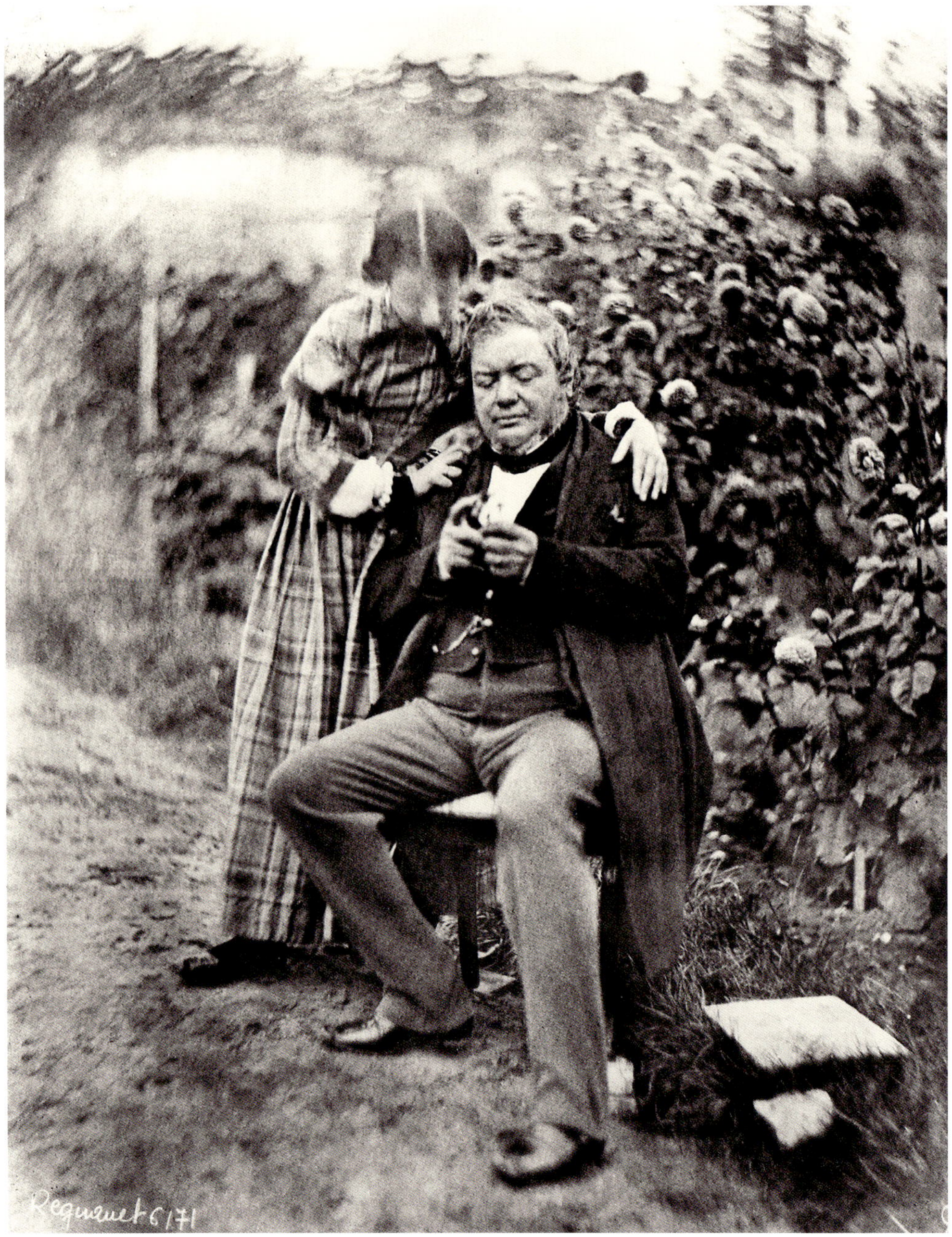

Fig. 49.

Victor Regnault, *The Painter Carl von Steuben and an Unidentified Girl*, c. 1852. Modern print from paper negative, $7^3/_4$ x $6^1/_4$ in. (19.8 x 16 cm). Société Française de Photographie, Paris. 473.71

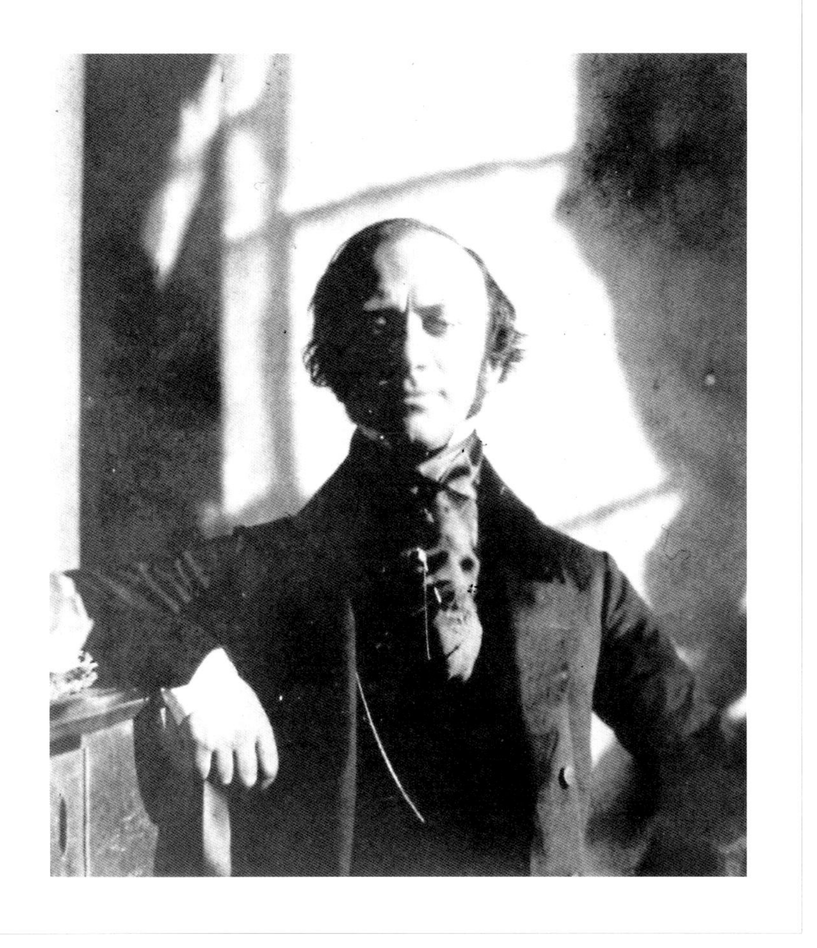

Fig. 50.

Victor Regnault, *Unidentified Academician*, p. 9, *Album Regnault,* c. 1851. Salt print from paper negative, 6 1/8 x 4 3/4 in. (15.5 x 12.2 cm). Société Française de Photographie, Paris

celebrity: "I have an instinctive horror of all positions that put one constantly on display, and which do not at all suit my vagabond, even a little bohemian, spirit. Besides, in our academic organization, the position is rather more literary than scientific. I have a horror of phrases and phrase-makers, and it gives me gooseflesh when I imagine that I would have to pass entire months stringing together words, to summon feelings up cold, and to 'decorate all the virtues' of a man, more or less one whose scientific work hasn't the least interest to the listener, who comes to witness an exercise of literary acrobatics."[39] He added in jest, "If I knew English, I would leave this minute for Australia."[40]

Laboring under the multiplying pressures and constrictions brought on by official patronage and by his obligations as a high-ranking scientist, professor, and government functionary, Regnault still cherished the essence of the intellect as something pure and noble. The portraits of his colleagues—his fellows, in the confraternal sense of the word—reference the ideal of the individual, unvarnished and uncompromised by stylish conventions. The series might have been a kind of personal antidote to the artificiality of the A.d.S. In the French Institute's world of shifting alliances, Regnault's invitation to a portrait sitting could be a gesture of respect, approval, or homage, and the collecting of the portraits a meaningful act of synthesis and consolidation. Created at a time when he and other French scientists were beginning to question the A.d.S.'s insularity, Regnault's portraits crossed national and disciplinary boundaries to describe an ideal international family of men of intellect. The collection fixed a Polish literatus, a French economist, a Scottish chemist, an English naturalist, and a German orientalist as complementary figures in an academy of Regnault's own design.

DOMESTIC PORTRAITURE

Today home photographers take their cues from a well-worn set of motifs and themes that have become inscribed as domestic photography's "natural" subjects—holidays, family vacations, birthday parties, children, pets. With so few practitioners in the genre in 1850, Regnault was working in an arena that was still mostly unmarked by photography. The antecedent for his practice was therefore not photographic, except to the extent that he borrowed the vocabulary of studio portraiture; it has more in common with the modest sketchbook, in which the artist or amateur privately hones his skills at the same time that he sketches the family conveniently at hand. The indexical power of photography, however, adds something else, infusing the portrait with an ineluctable sense of the sitter's presence, which obscures the act of crafting the object.[41]

Although their original meaning—their private significance—is mostly lost to us, Regnault's domestic portraits inspire questions about the meanings and social utility of this emergent family ritual. They also illustrate a pictorial genre under construction, where we can study the borrowings and improvisations of the photographer as he and his family perform their family narrative for an elite audience: themselves. To possess the means of private self-representation was a luxury; the rarity and independence of taking photographs at home allowed its makers to escape the ordinary limitations of conventional commercial portraiture. Regnault's domestic portraits were intended for and retained in this private arena. He approached the subject like a collector gathering a pictorial inventory of friends and family, beginning around 1850, at the same time that he was photographing his academic colleagues. The family photographs do not represent an extended record over time, but form a large group of pictures made within two or three years at most.[42]

Considering how far early photography was from the casual ease and habit of modern snapshot photography, Regnault's effort, by which he produced some sixty family pictures, stands out as significant and represents a substantial investment of time spent with the family. Since the early nineteenth century, novelists, playwrights, and other writers had been describing a cultural trend that accompanied the rise of the bourgeoisie—the decay of family intimacy created by the loveless *mariage de raison* (marriage of convenience) that treated marriage and the family as the raw materials of social ascension.[43] Jules Michelet, one of Regnault's colleagues at the Collège de France, was particularly concerned with the contemporary professional man, distanced from his family by his pursuit of wealth and career.[44] With his oppressive work schedule, Regnault might easily have been one of the casualties whose home life Michelet envisioned in such dismal terms: "Even at the hour of relaxation, he speaks little, he is lost in thought. Success in business, invention in science, are achieved at a high price.... Alone among his family, he who makes their glory or their fortune risks becoming a stranger to them."[45] This was not to be the case for Regnault, however, and photography became a means that both witnessed and extended his involvement in domestic life.

Against the odds and despite the demands upon his time, Regnault was a devoted family man who enjoyed spending time with his wife and children, assumed the moral education of his sons, and cherished the drawings, cards, and letters his offspring gave him. This close relationship with the family was made possible by the fact that his family lived where he worked—first at the Collège de France, then at the Manufacture de Sèvres; he could and did see his wife and children throughout the day. One might imagine, too, that Regnault's past as an orphan heightened his attachment to family. His marriage seems to have been based on an intimate rapport, since he and his wife had known each other since childhood, when Regnault arrived in Paris under the protection of her father. Clémence Clément and Regnault wed in 1837, and he became son-in-law of the family that had treated him as a surrogate son.[46] After the death of Captain Clément, the three elder Duval women—Madame Alexandre Duval and her daughters Adèle Duval Clément and Malvina Duval Mazois—became members of Regnault's own household. When the extended Regnault family moved to the director's apartment at Sèvres in 1852, they made a strong impression on Jules Dieterle's daughter Louise, who described them in her memoirs some seventy years later: "How brilliant and lively was the Regnault family in those days! First, I see Mr. Regnault: slim, blond, with long locks, of a rather neglected appearance, with an air of a German student about him. He had, it seemed, a greatly logical sensibility; his conversation was animated and passionate."[47]

Louise Dieterle was also struck by the mutual devotion between Regnault and the Duval women, and remembered how "Mr. Regnault often teased his 'wives' as he called them, that is to say his wife; her mother, Madame Clément; her aunt, Madame Masoin [*sic*]; and Madame Alexandre Duval, her grandmother."[48] This was a family in which the ties never loosened; in fact, the Duval women eagerly assisted Clémence and Regnault in all the duties of parenting their four children. Two or three years after the family moved to Sèvres, they were also joined by Regnault's sister, Thérèse; her husband, the architect Alexandre Laudin; and their young daughter. Once practically without kin, Regnault now found himself the patriarch of a thriving clan living under his roof, and with the equipment and laboratory there on the premises, making photographs of his family surely happened naturally.

The earliest family portraits, made at the Collège de France around 1851, include photographs of Madame Regnault, the four surviving children (Léon, Henri, Alice, and Eugène), and their nurse. Photographing loved ones, particularly children, took on a sense of urgency in an era of high mortality. (No images exist of the Regnault's youngest child, who died in infancy in 1852, at about the time Regnault was immersed in family photography.) Like commercially made portraits, Regnault's pictures witnessed the importance of his family members and provided a psychological insurance that the present would not be completely effaced by the future, but their effect is distinct from the simple studio likeness. These privately produced images address the warm, familial relationships of their subjects with seemingly little pretense or circumspection.

The vocabulary of gesture, expression, and body language in Regnault's images is subtly different from that of commercial portraiture. In professionally made portraiture of the period, the image was construed as if for a public audience. Figures in groups look either at the camera or beyond the frame; they rarely look at each other. This assured that the commercial image would be subdued, dignified, and appropriate for public company, even if the portrait was meant for private use. The commercial portrait was, after all, delivered through the intervention of a virtual stranger, often of a different social class. The very act of dressing for the occasion, traveling to the studio, waiting in the salon while other customers were served, and finally being studied and posed by the photographer constituted a public event of some complexity, which some likened to a visit to the doctor's office.[49] Portrait sitters either looked directly at the camera, frankly and politely submitting themselves to the gaze of a future audience, or looked away, having their gazes directed to different points outside the frame, which placed them at a dignified remove from the sometimes awkward here-and-now of the portrait setting. A glance shared between sitters—an internal gaze—was rarely shown in the commercial portrait because it made the photographer/viewer party to a private relationship, an intimate moment of emotional contact between real persons. Instead, familiarity, warmth, and empathy were typically signified in studio portraits through a limited vocabulary of gestures: a hand placed upon a shoulder or an inclination of the body (fig. 51).

Greater intimacy is on view in Regnault's domestic photographs. Family members were used to the ritual of picture-making; photographing at home allowed Regnault to combine his love of photography and family, while simultaneously creating a family document that could be appreciated by everyone. Unlike the typical professional photographer who strove to achieve the most conventional portrait with as few trials as possible, Regnault's project was casual, personal, and ongoing, which left its participants with room to experiment—to play, although "playing" at this time was limited by exposures between five and twenty seconds and by a more circumspect code of conduct than we follow today.[50]

Still, even Regnault's most casual domestic photographs were in some way contrived, constructed by the photographer to embody personal and cultural beliefs he held about his family. The posing of individuals and groups raise several recurring themes: the tenderness of motherhood, the precious bonds between siblings, respect of the elders, and a husband's fascination for his wife as model/muse. Most of the images were made as single figure portraits, which are more formally and conventionally composed; those featuring multiple figures are less so. A group portrait of Madame Regnault, the nurse, and the three youngest children has the pedestrian look of modern family snapshots, with the same typical problems. Henri's head casts a shadow across his mother's face, all eyes squint in the sun's glare, the nurse stiffly braces herself against the back of Alice's chair and vainly attempts to hold the thumb-sucking Eugène still for the camera (fig. 52). Clémence Regnault often appears completely at home in the photographic moment, as she gazes at her children with a smiling expression of unselfconscious happiness (fig. 53). In one portrait, she holds her three-year-old daughter on her lap, embraces her with both arms, and presses her face close to Alice's bonnet; they clasp hands across Alice's lap (fig. 54). Body language in other portraits is similarly demonstrative and casual in the portrait of seven-year-old Henri leaning against his mother, as she drapes an arm around his shoulder, holding him close to her side (fig. 55). A

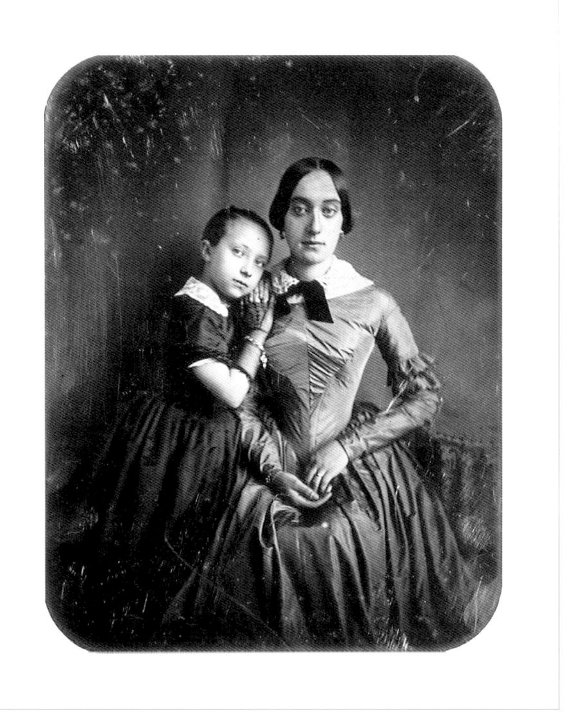

Fig. 51.
Jean-Baptiste Sabatier-Blot (French, 1801–1881), *Portrait of a Woman and Sabatier's Daughter*, c. 1852. Daguerreotype, full plate. International Museum of Photography and Film at George Eastman House, Rochester, N.Y. 76:168:16 (62.17)

more mature and restrained code of manners operates in the portrait of Madame Regnault and thirteen-year-old Léon (fig. 56). For this image, Regnault made an effort to appropriate the conventions of the studio portrait, hanging a dark drapery background and including a few basic furnishings: two plain wooden chairs, a bare table, and a porcelain statuette. Mother and son sit close to each other at the table, their heads subtly inclined as if in conversation, but with eyes cast down to avoid the sun's glare. Léon's military-style school uniform gives him the air of a young soldier and suggests his imminent adulthood. Unlike Madame Regnault with the younger children, they do not touch, but the end of her shawl has chanced to drape over her son's knee. The strangest note is the inclusion of the large statuette on the table between the two sitters. Such objects were common in studio photographs, where they were meant to signify good taste while imitating the decor of the drawing room. Although it may have been added to lend some of this professional ambiance to the sitting, the statuette, so out of place as an objet d'art on this bare wooden table in the outdoor setting, ultimately calls attention to the fact that this is not a professional studio. Frozen in a rhetorical gesture, its head at eye level with Clémence and Léon, and

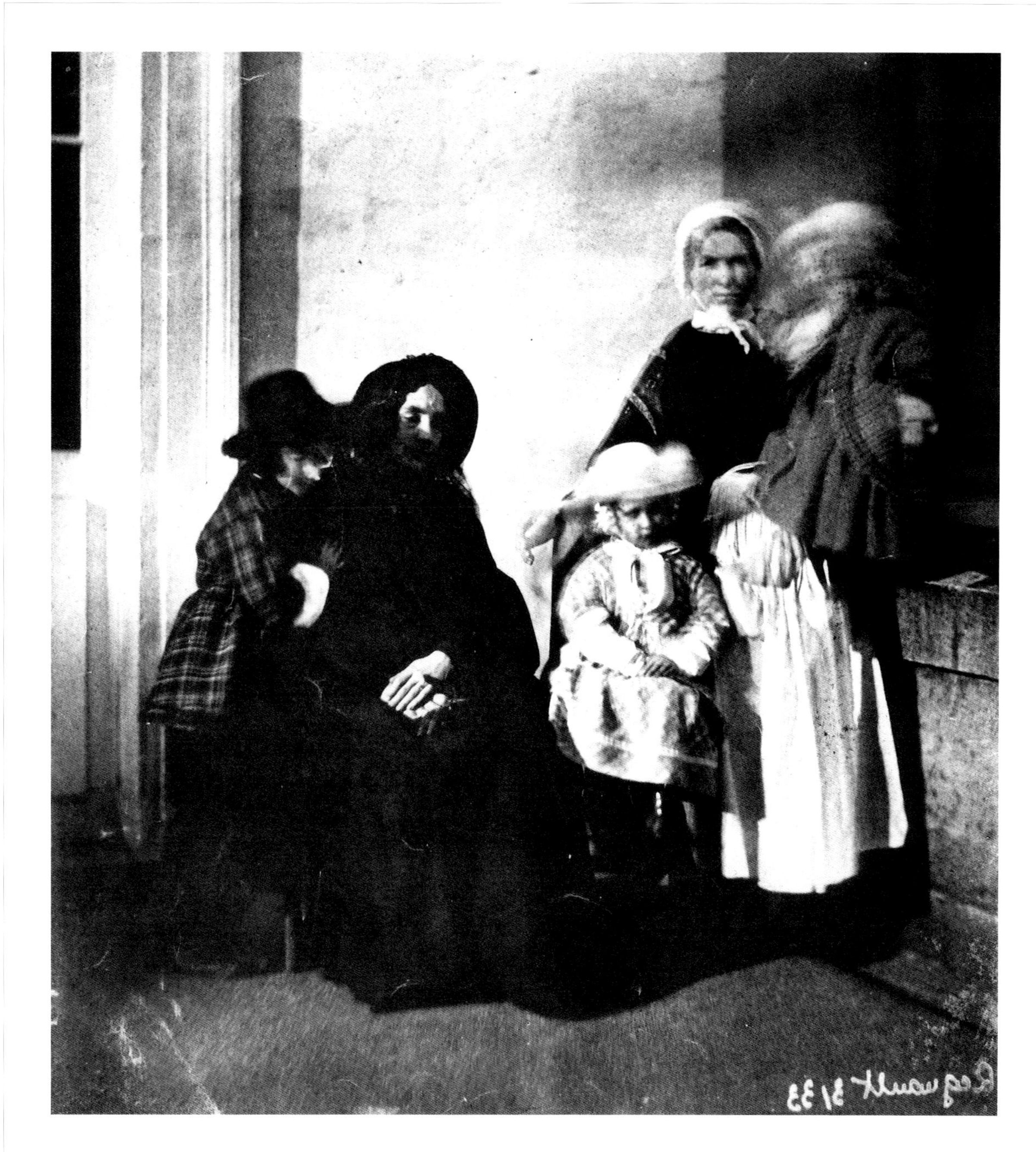

Fig. 52.

Victor Regnault, *Madame Regnault and Her Family*, c. 1852. Modern print from paper negative, 6¼ x 5⅝ in. (16 x 14.4 cm). Société Française de Photographie, Paris. 473.33

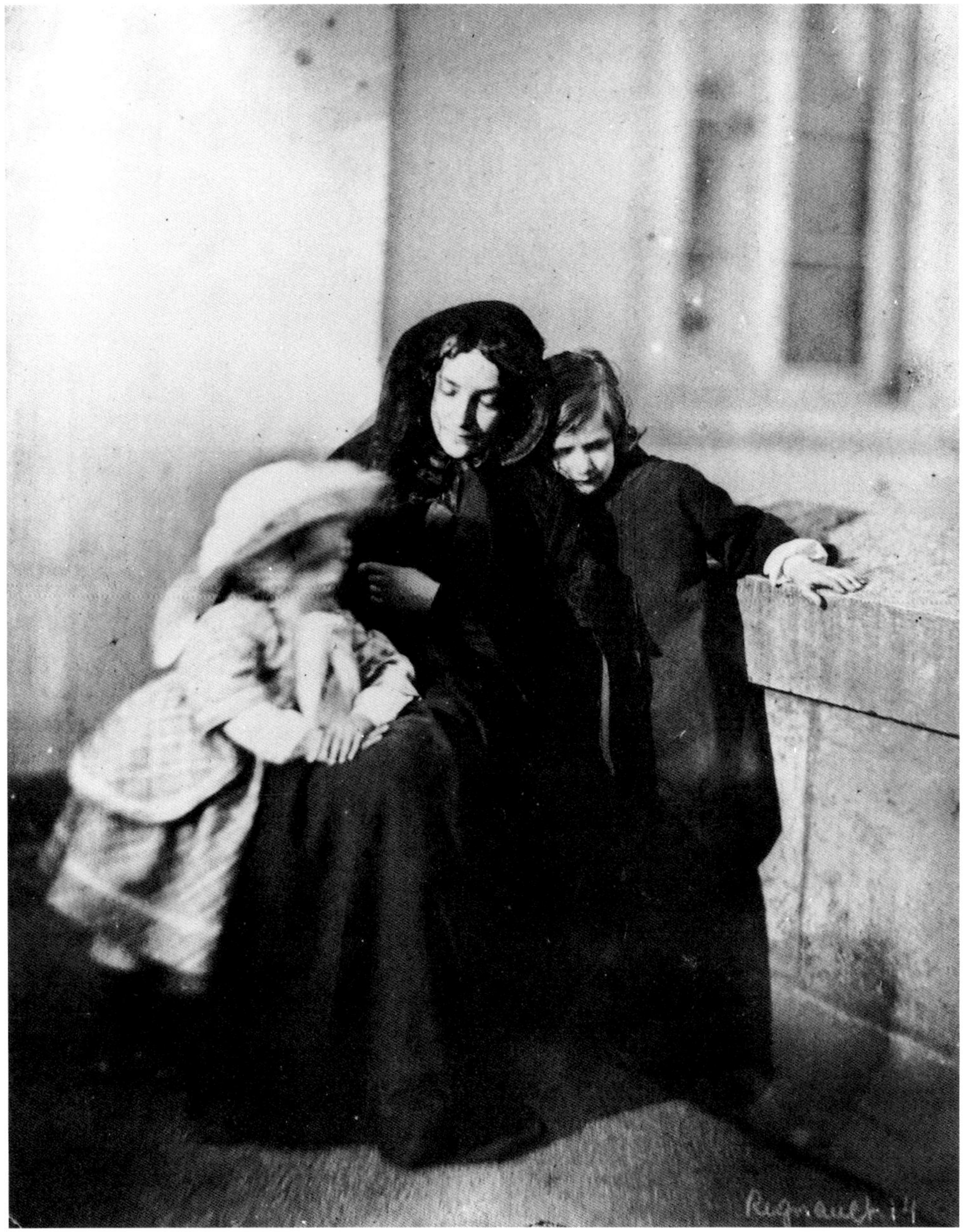

Fig. 53.

Victor Regnault, *Madame Regnault and Her Children, Henri and Alice*, c. 1852. Modern print from paper negative, $6^{1}/_{2}$ x $5^{1}/_{4}$ in. (16.5 x 13.2 cm). Société Française de Photographie, Paris. 473.14

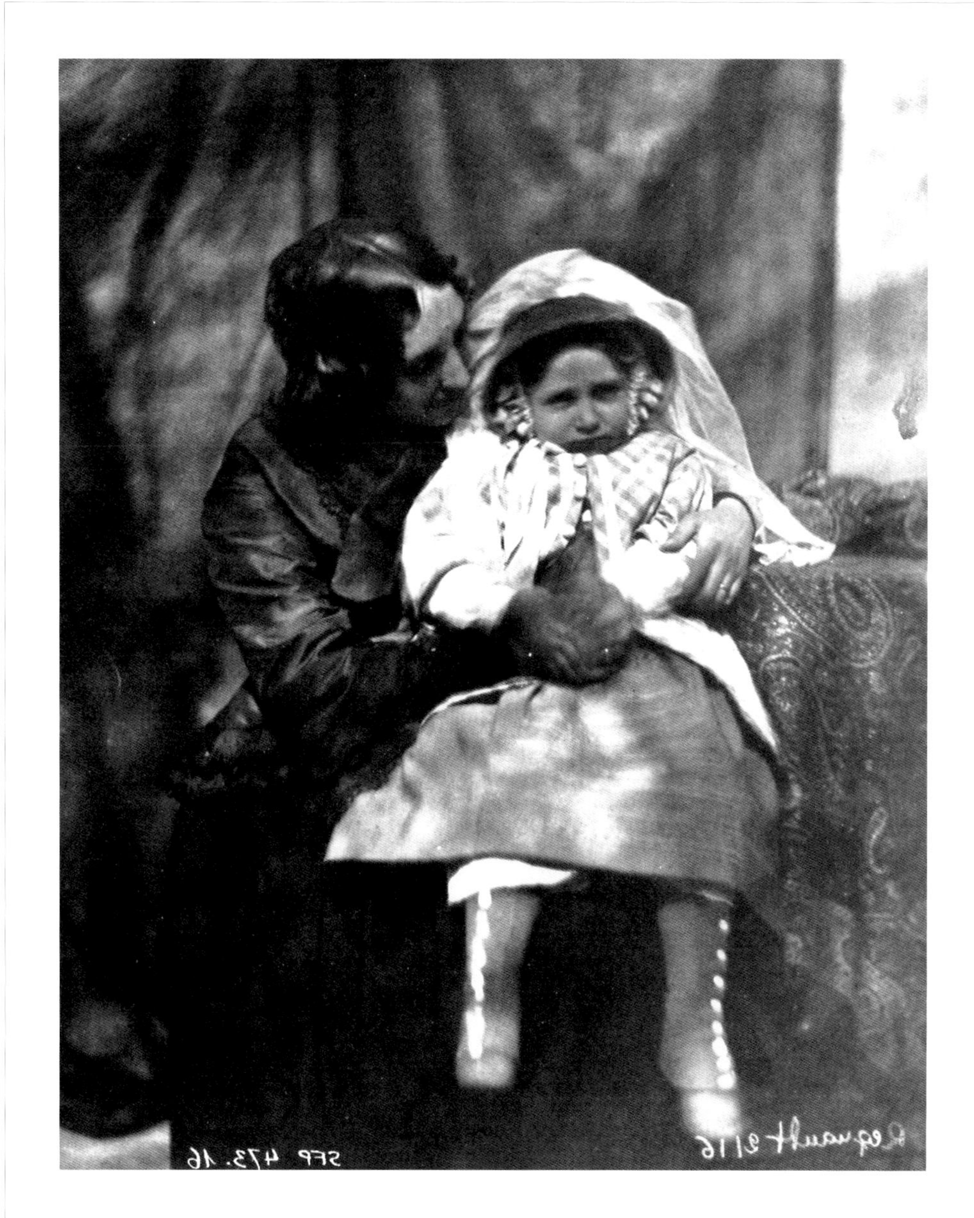

Fig. 54.

Victor Regnault, *Madame Regnault and Her Daughter Alice*, c. 1852. Modern print from paper negative, 6 x 4 3/4 in. (15.3 x 12.2 cm). Société Française de Photographie, Paris. 473.16

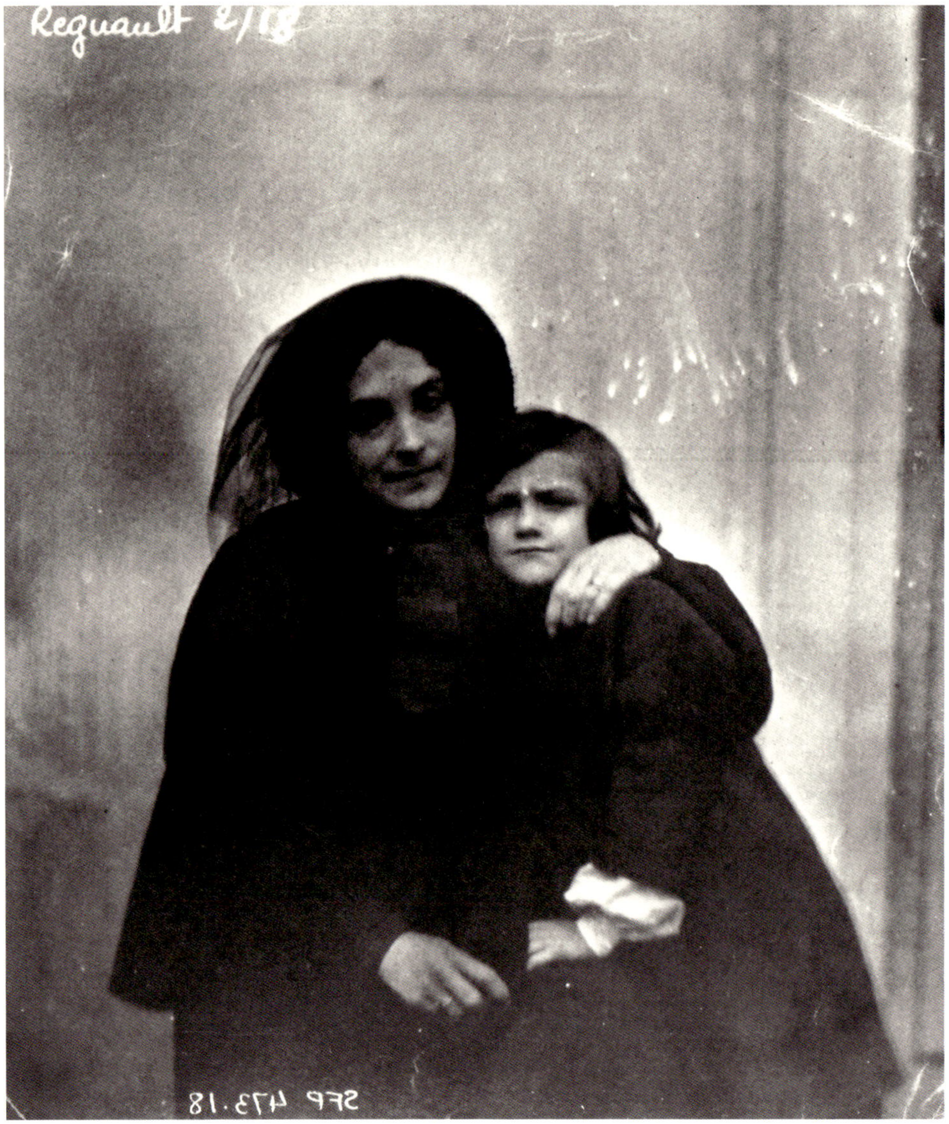

Fig. 55.

Victor Regnault, *Madame Regnault and Her Son Henri*, c. 1852. Modern print from paper negative, $4^{7}/_{8}$ x $4^{1}/_{4}$ in. (12.3 x 10.9 cm). Société Française de Photographie, Paris. 473.18

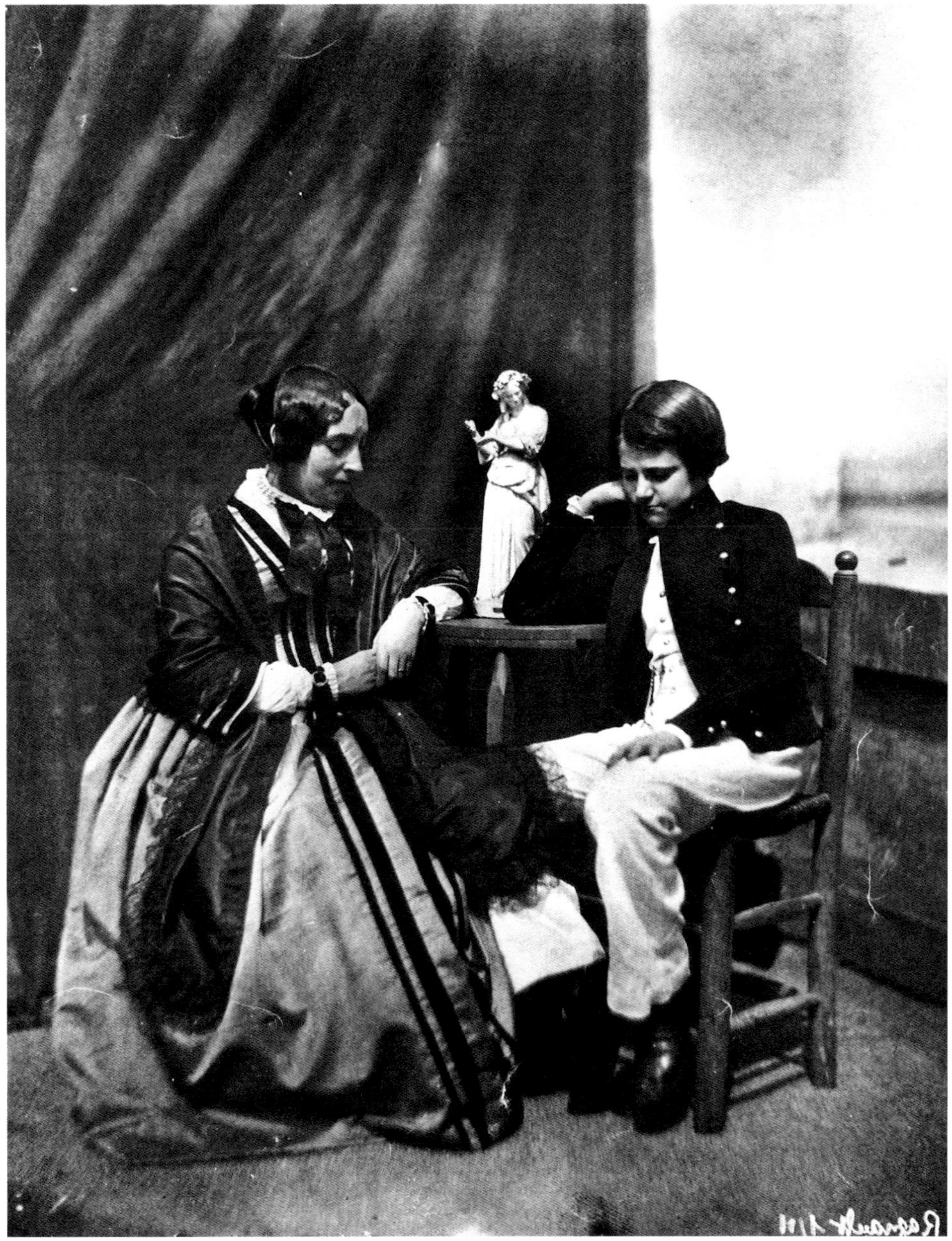

Fig. 56.

Victor Regnault, *Madame Regnault and Her Son Léon*, c. 1852. Modern print from paper negative, $7^{1}/_{2}$ x $6^{1}/_{4}$ in. (18.9 x 15.8 cm). Société Française de Photographie, Paris. 473.11

sharing their downcast gazes, the statuette becomes a third party—an animated chaperone—to this demure tête-à-tête between a mother and her maturing son.

Most of Regnault's portraits of individual children are somewhat stiff; it would not have been easy for a child to hold a pose of even five seconds, which may explain why there are so few pictures of the two youngest, Alice and Eugène. Regnault once solved this problem by photographing the two-year-old Eugène asleep in his crib (fig. 33); there the exposure could be as long as necessary to succeed in the dim available light of the nursery. He had more success posing the other children in pairs, which animated the pictures by providing a meaningful family context and a more complex physical relationship between two figures. On several occasions, two children were posed together in a single chair, which allowed a tighter shot and suggested a homey narrative through this mise-en-scène. Fraternal ties, for example, were simultaneously acted out and memorialized in the closely framed portrait of Léon and Henri seated together (fig. 57). Holding Henri on his lap, Léon embodies the role of the loving, selfless, and protective elder brother. The book he holds on his knee is a rhetorical note that implies his duty to instruct and guide his younger sibling. With Regnault's own past as an orphan who put his first wages toward a dowry for his sister, he had already impressed his eldest son with a solemn sense of fraternal obligation when he chose Léon to be Henri's godfather. Though it was conceived by the father, not the son, this picture resonates as a pictorial vow accepting that charge.

Despite the evident freedom Regnault enjoyed in setting up his pictures, the portraits were staged according to certain rules that had as much to do with cultural proprieties involving age, class, and gender as with the status and personal dignity of individual family members. Any desire to satisfy compositional niceties had to first accommodate these powerful social givens, which may explain the lack of experimentation and variation within the pictures of the family elders. Whereas Clémence appears in many attitudes and formats, with and without the children, the elders of the family were always photographed individually. Regnault photographed his wife's grandmother, Madame de l'Écotay Duval, in the half-light of the sitting room, swathed in ribbons and fancy stuffs, half-hidden under a voluminous paisley shawl; her aged face is barely visible in the shadow cast by her deep bonnet (fig. 58). Fantastic shadows, enhanced in pencil on the negative, play across the wall behind her. The image calls to mind Louise Dieterle's description of her as an overly proud woman who sat in her room year round, fully dressed as if ready for a brisk promenade outdoors.[51]

Of the elder women, Madame Clément was Regnault's preferred subject. In one portrait, he seated his mother-in-law indoors next to an open window, using a subdued raking light to give a delicate modeling to the face (fig. 59). The interior setting locates Madame Clément reassuringly at the

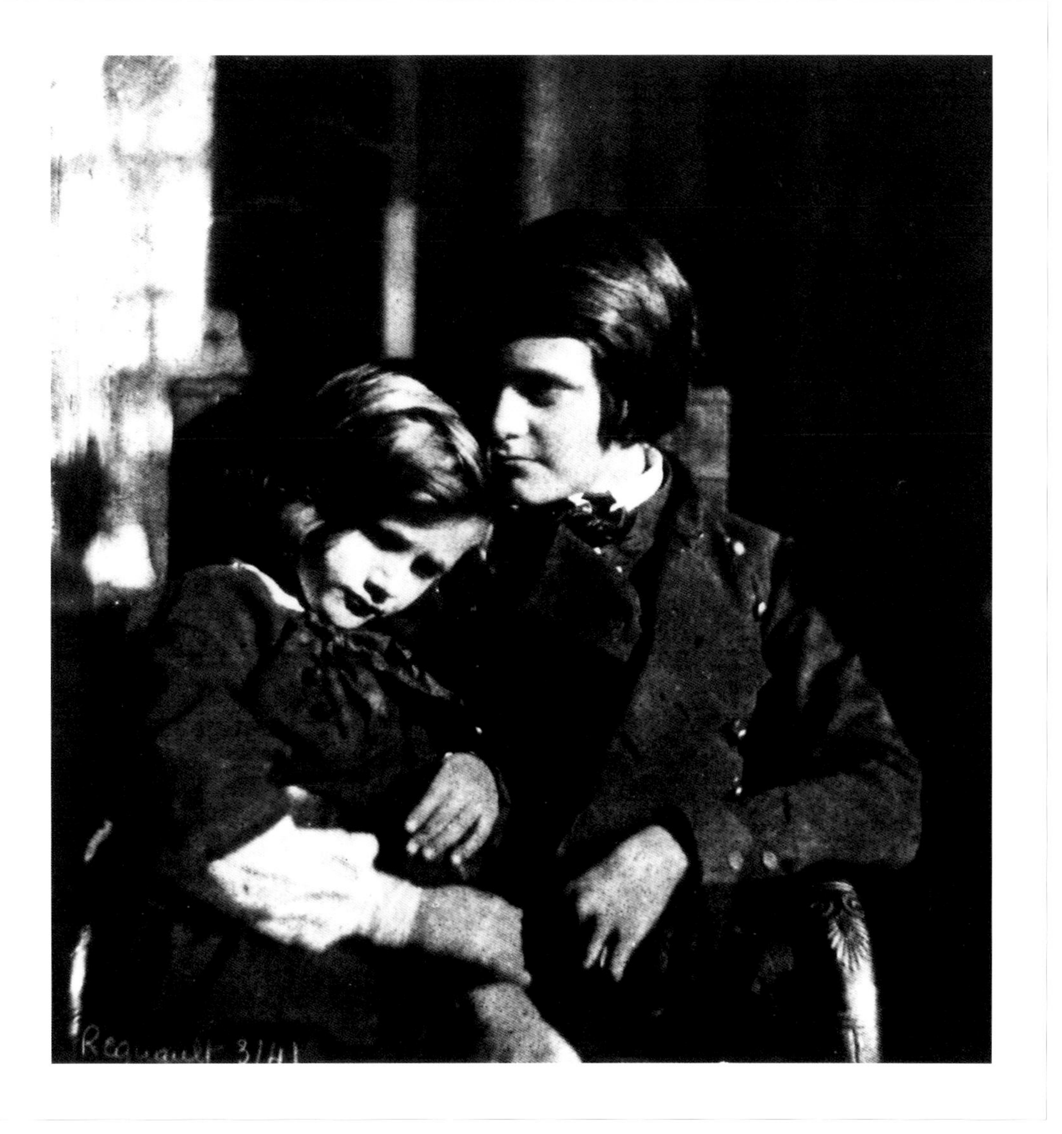

Fig. 57.

Victor Regnault, *Léon and Henri Regnault*, c. 1852. Modern print from paper negative, $5\frac{1}{4}$ x $5\frac{1}{8}$ in. (13.4 x 13 cm).
The Philadelphia Museum of Art. Purchased with funds contributed by the American Museum of Photography, 1971, 71-4-49

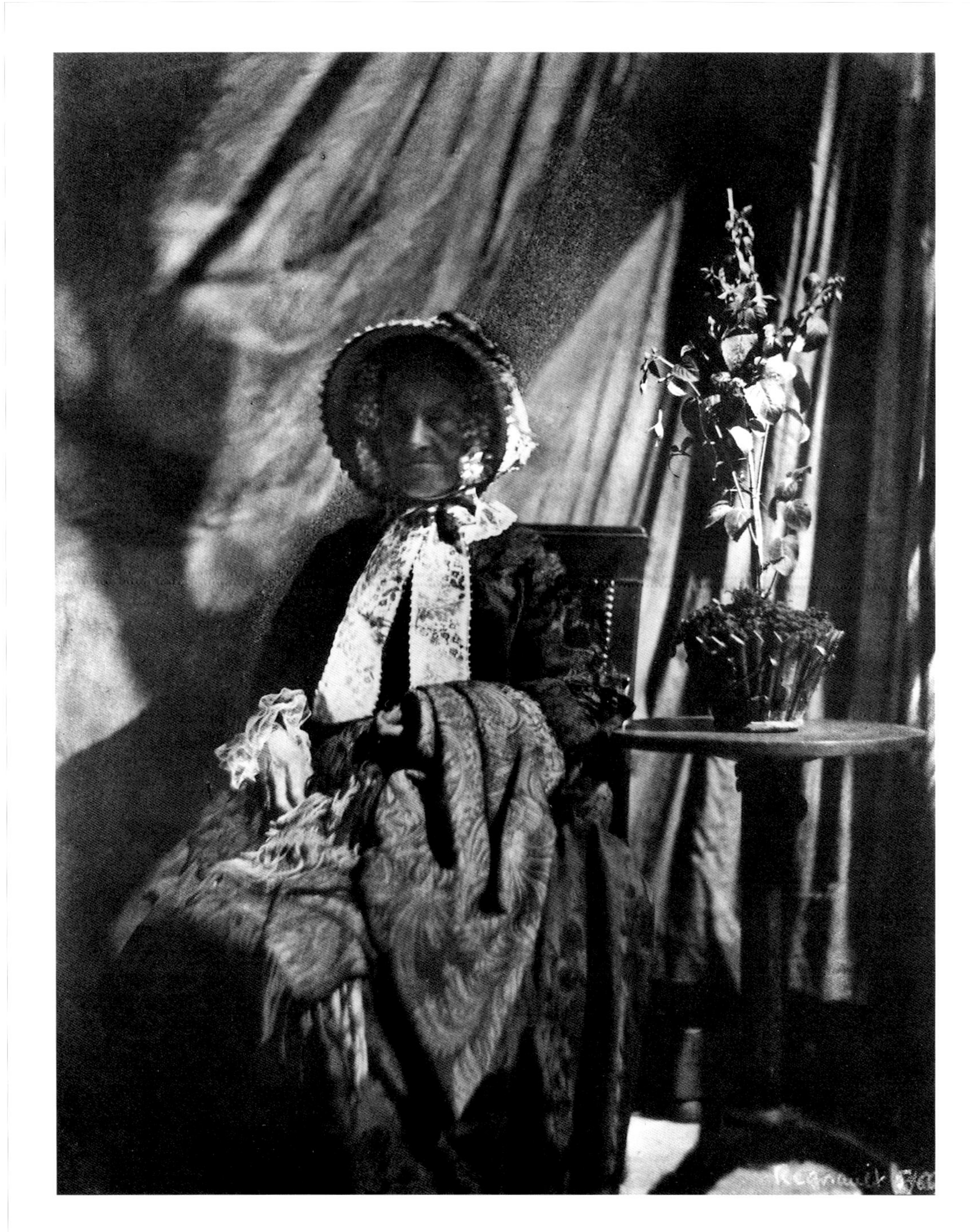

Fig. 58.

Victor Regnault, *Madame Regnault's Grandmother, Madame de l'Écotay Duval*, c. 1852. Modern print from paper negative, $7^{1}/_{2}$ x 6 in. (19.1 x 15.1 cm). Société Française de Photographie, Paris. 473.66

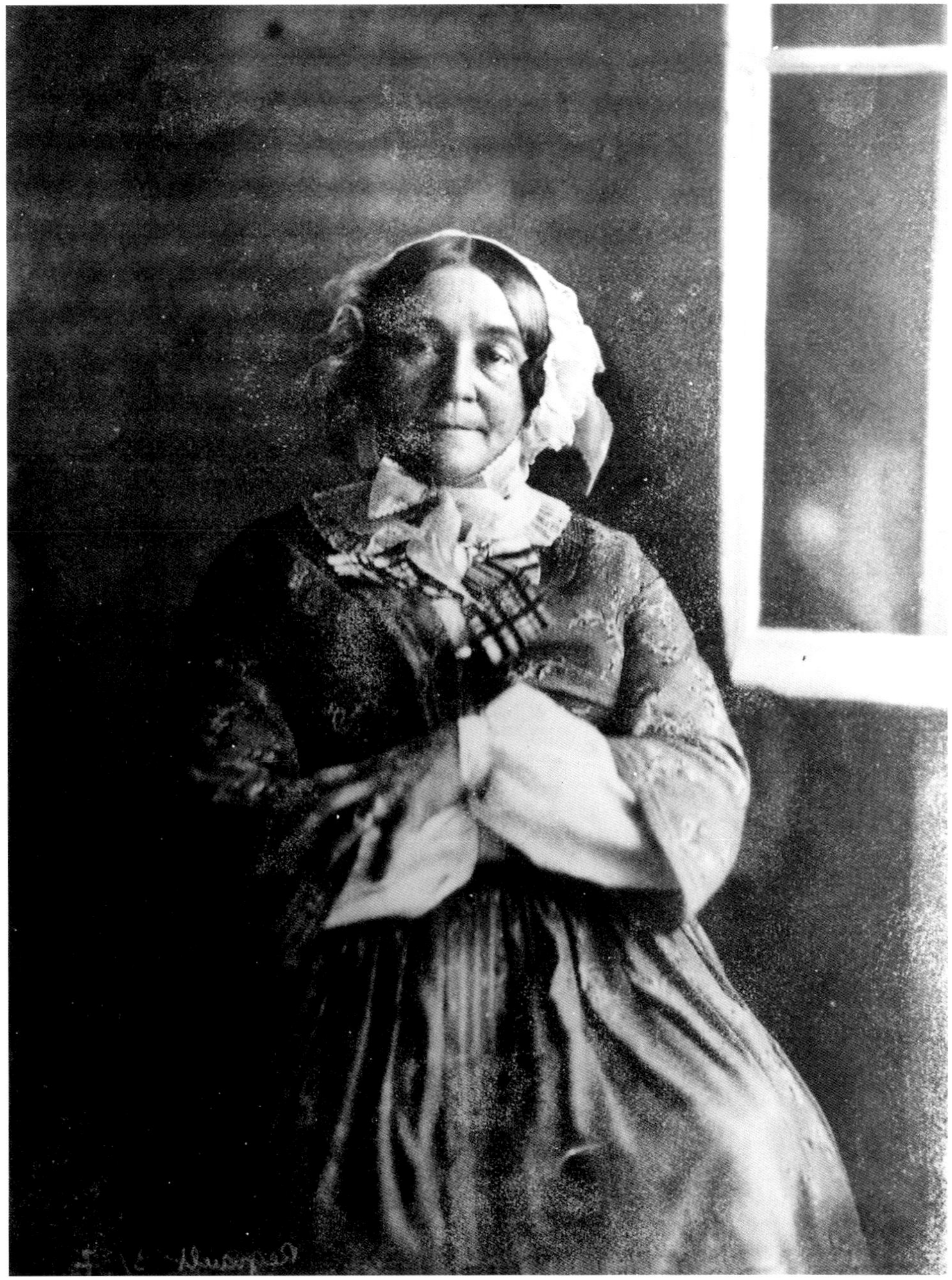

Fig. 59.

Victor Regnault, *Madame Regnault's Mother, Madame Clément*, c. 1852. Modern print from paper negative, $7^{3}/_{8}$ x $5^{1}/_{2}$ in. (18.6 x 14 cm). Société Française de Photographie, Paris. 473.37

center of her proper domain, the home. It is an iconic image that aptly portrays a recently minted social figure, the bourgeois grand-mère, an active and venerated member of the family, product of the century's economic health and the lengthening life span of bourgeois and upper-class women.[52] The widow Clément, no financial burden upon her family, enjoyed the luxury of being fully appreciated as a resource of maternal wisdom and care. With her ruffled caplet, ample bosom, soft features, and mild gaze, she presents an image of matronly goodness, although in Louise Dieterle's memory, Madame Clément's maternal passion went beyond normal limits, threatening to smother her grandchildren "in a sort of padded atmosphere by dint of abusive tenderness."[53]

The modest simplicity of this portrait is underscored by Madame Clément's simple, full-frontal pose. Many of the images of the family's adults follow the same format: a static, full-frontal treatment of the seated figure, photographed at three-quarter length. This was a formula often seen in early daguerreotypes but now discouraged by Francis Wey and other writers on photography as pedestrian and graceless, rendering the sitter more specimen than person and prone to distortion of the lower body, due to the shortness of the portrait lens.[54] Though Regnault certainly knew the admonitions against this pose—they were part of the standard instruction in most of the photographic manuals in his extensive library—he persisted in using it. He always used a direct frontal approach in posing his servants, where a more elegant pose would have seemed pretentious and inappropriate to the station of the sitter (figs. 60 and 61). But it also occurs fairly often in the academic portraits and those of the family elders. A page in the *Album Regnault,* for example, presents an interesting pair: two portraits side-by-side, both men of middle age and similar size (fig. 62). The subjects are seated in the same full frontal pose, which forces a humorous comparison upon the two. On the left is a gardener, holding a shovel, and on the right is the orientalist scholar Jules von Mohl, holding a top hat, umbrella, and a roll of papers. Whether or not this pairing of "pendant" portraits was really as teasing as it appears, it confirms that Regnault used this simple pose with all types of sitters.

Regardless of the beliefs of photographic aficionados like Wey, the full-frontal pose was not the accidental creation of uncultured photographic operators, as it was first featured in the dryly painted, idealized portraits by Jean-Auguste-Dominique Ingres (1780–1867) and his followers.[55] Regnault was himself a great fan of Ingres and the Ingristes, and the frontal pose he used so often may simply reflect this taste. In the mid-1840s Regnault commissioned portraits of himself and Clémence (now lost), painted respectively by two of the principal members of Ingres's circle: Amaury-Duval and Hippolyte Flandrin (1809–1864). Flandrin, the so-called "painter of honest women," exhibited the portrait of Madame Regnault in the Salon of 1846, where, together with portraits by Amaury-Duval and Henri

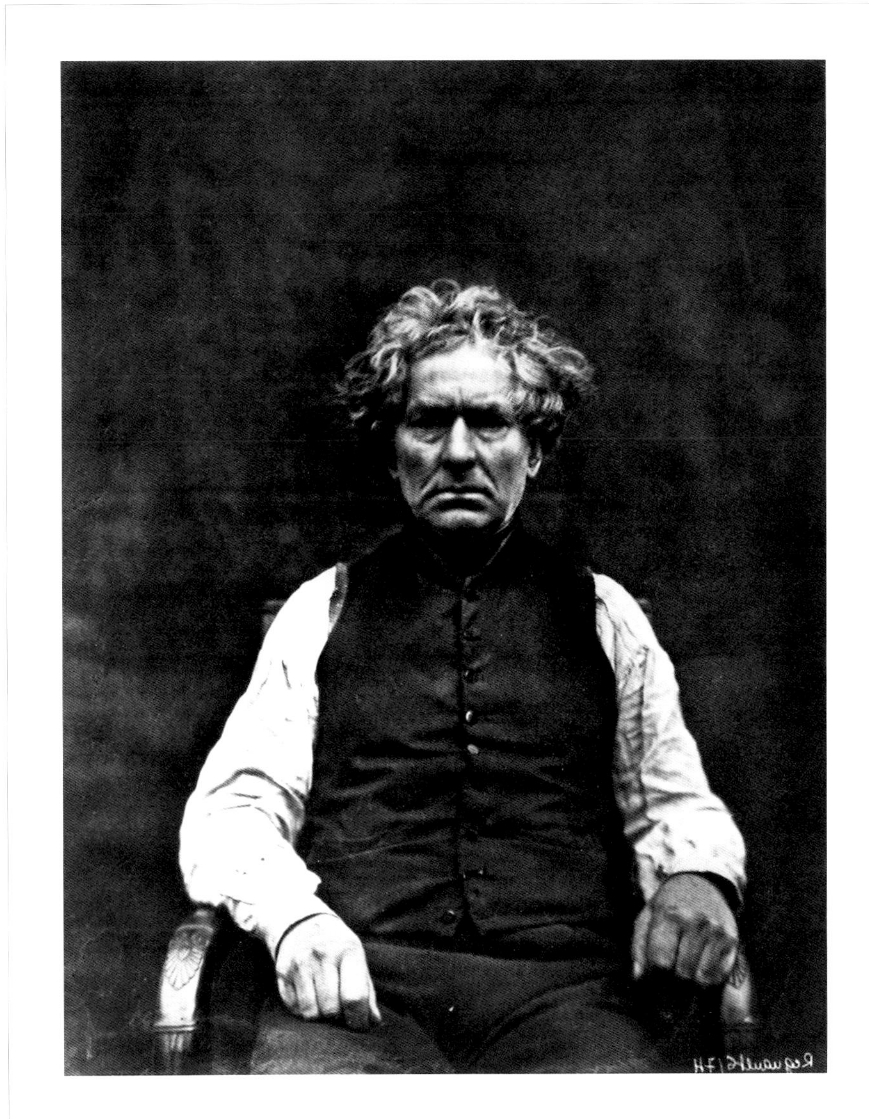

Fig. 60.

Victor Regnault, *Gardener* [?], c. 1851. Modern print from paper negative, $8^{3}/_{4}$ x $6^{3}/_{4}$ in. (22.4 x 17.2 cm). The Philadelphia Museum of Art. Purchased with funds contributed by the American Museum of Photography, 1971, 71-4-44

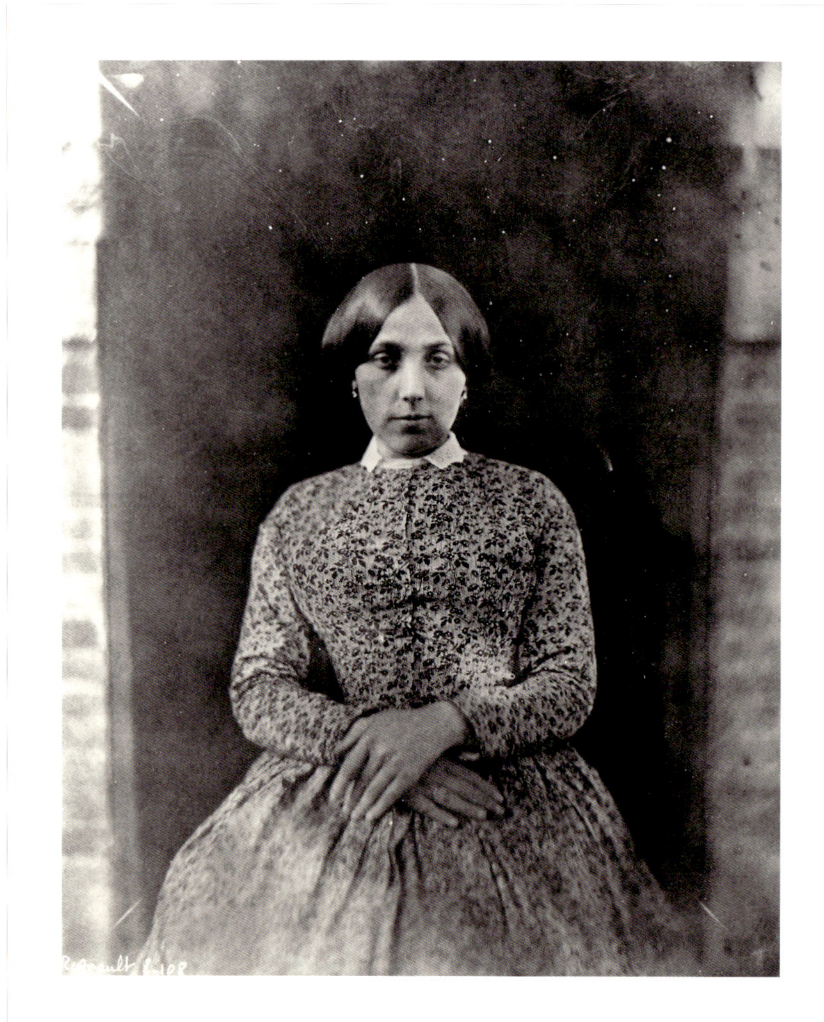

Fig. 61.

Victor Regnault, *Female Servant* [?], c. 1852. Modern print from paper negative, $8\frac{1}{8}$ x $6\frac{5}{8}$ in. (20.8 x 16.7 cm).

Société Française de Photographie, Paris. 473.108

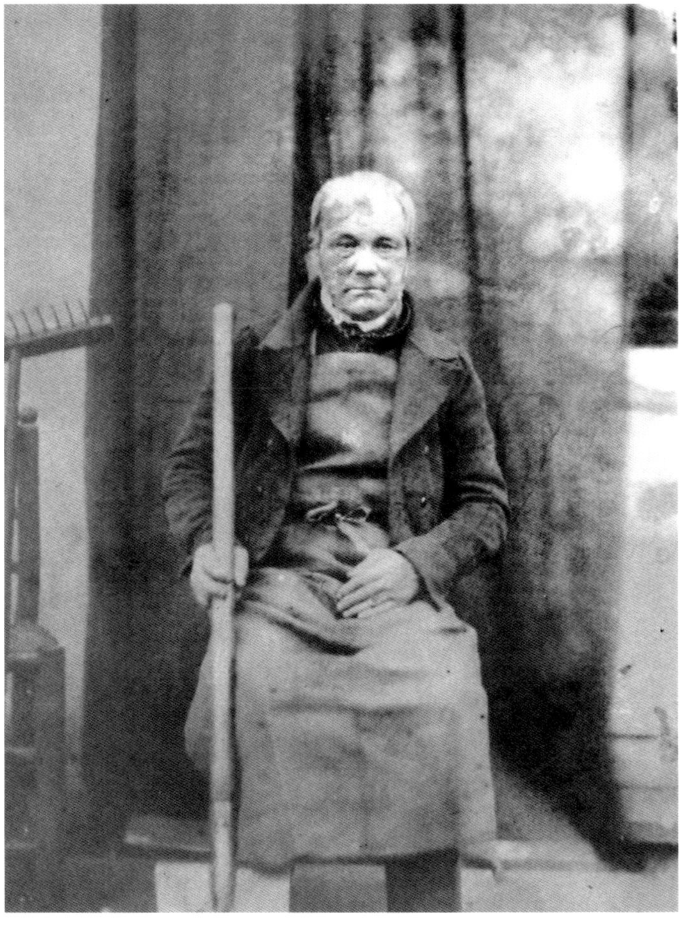

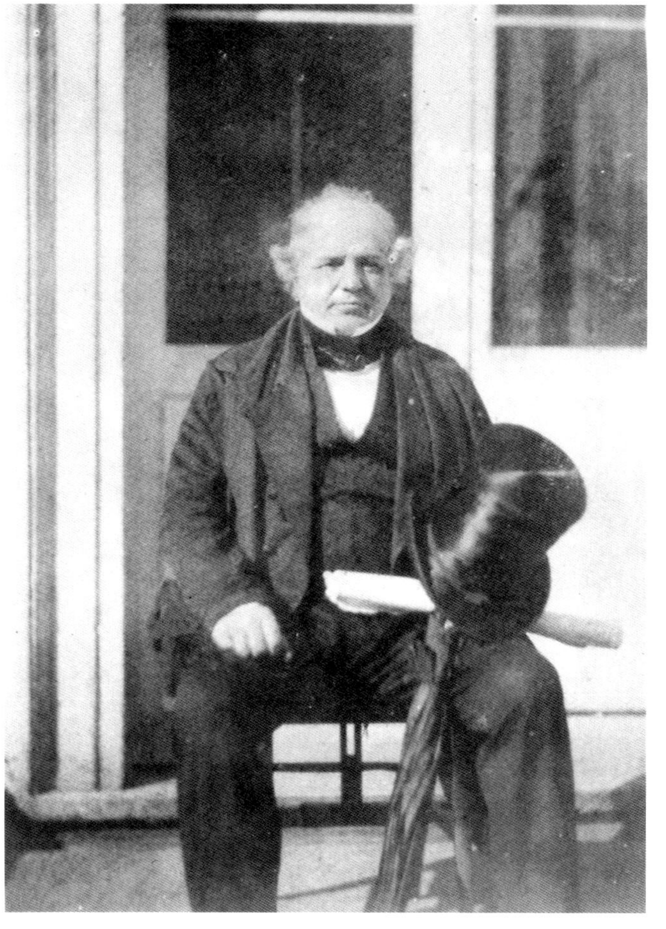

Fig. 62.

Victor Regnault, *Collège de France Gardener* and *Orientalist Jules von Mohl*, p. 26, *Album Regnault*, c. 1851. Salt prints from paper negatives; left: 6 3/4 x 5 1/8 in. (17.2 x 13.1 cm); right: 6 7/8 x 5 in. (17.6 x 12.6 cm). Société Française de Photographie, Paris. Negatives: 473.148; 473.119

Lehmann (1814–1882), it invited the ridicule of Baudelaire, who remarked, "If Dulcinea del Toboso herself were to pass through the studio of these gentlemen, she would emerge as pellucid and prim as an elegy, after a slimming diet of aesthetic tea and aesthetic butter."[56]

Clémence Regnault was by all accounts as pious and chaste as Flandrin made her out to be; after her sudden death from pneumonia in 1866, Henri described her to a friend as "so pure and so elevated, she was so completely ethereal, that it seemed to me that she must be able to escape the harsh laws that govern men."[57] Louise Dieterle also remembered her as "a ravishing young woman," cultivated, artistic, and deeply pious, and therefore "a bit mystical."[58] She specifically recalled Madame Regnault's beautiful profile, like that of "an Italian madonna."[59] Regnault made one close study of his wife's distinctive profile against a void of deep shadow in a bust-length view (fig. 63).

Regnault's pictures of his wife differ from his other portraits, whose typical formula they rarely share. In sitting after sitting, Regnault experimented with pose, gesture, background, costume, expression, lighting—those things signaled by the experts who advised a "spiritual interpretation" of the subject. He seems to have been striving to represent something about his wife that could not be achieved in four, five, or even ten attempts. Backgrounds and settings vary: a summer garden, a shallow, dimly lit interior space, a blank wall, a setting with a desk and vase of flowers. She is depicted sitting with the children, reading, and one guesses, thinking (figs. 64 and 65). It is clear, too, that she is posing; the deliberateness of the pictures, with their reductive settings and solidly centered figure, never permits the complete illusion of the photograph as a natural, omniscient view.

One of the most unusual images is the full-length portrait of Madame Regnault dressed in Spanish-style costume—a popular fashion, courtesy of the Spanish-born empress, Eugénie (fig. 66). Clémence Regnault stands in the stage like space of an interior. Light enters the frame from high above the windows to the right, streaming through the mullions and creating a dramatic pattern of diamonds and diagonals on the back wall. Raking over the figure, showing off the moiré patterns of her gown, the light casts a fine shadow pattern upon her round forehead through the lace of her mantilla. She leans upon a pedestal table and places a steadying hand to her chin in a pensive gesture, looking dreamily beyond the frame. This is not a portrait in the usual sense, much less the kind of materialist likeness disparaged by the critics, but rather Regnault's thoughtful, even literary interpretation of his wife's special quality and character.

In all, Regnault only made a few of these "high concept" portraits, all of them based on a dramatic management of available light and the creation of a moody interior setting. These stand in great contrast to the majority of his portraits. The photographer Edmond de Valicourt had advised amateurs to

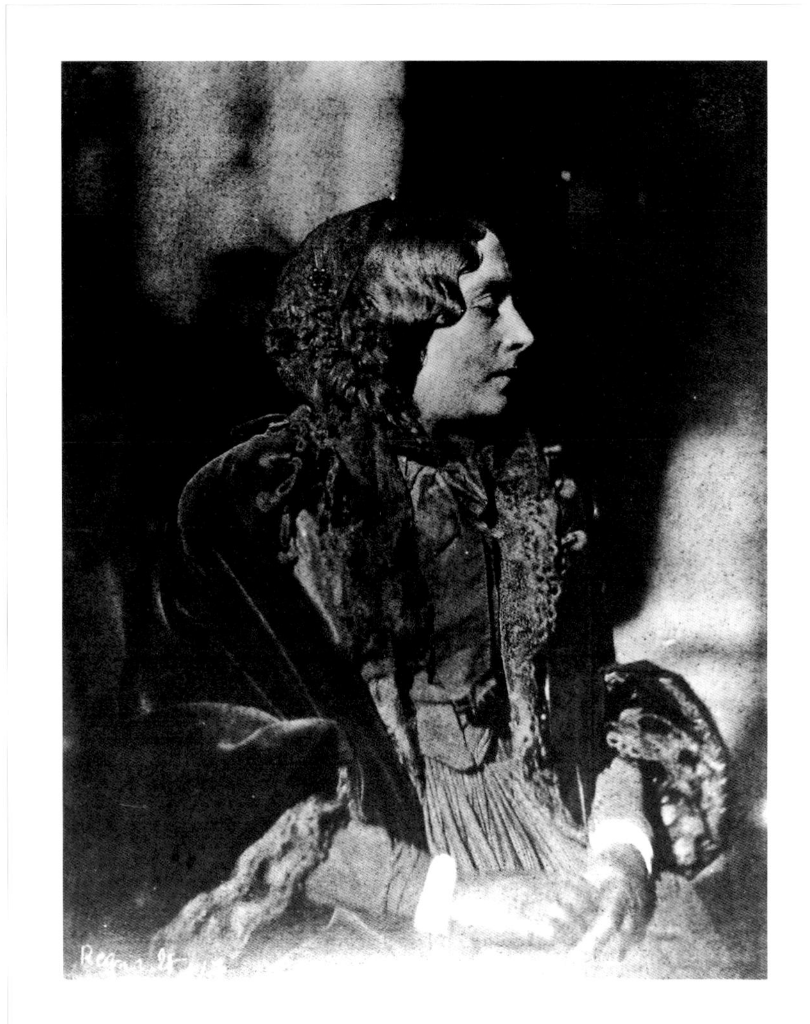

Fig. 63.

Victor Regnault, *Madame Regnault in Profile*, c. 1851. Modern print from paper negative, 6 3/8 x 5 in. (16.3 x 12.7 cm). Société Française de Photographie, Paris. 473.7

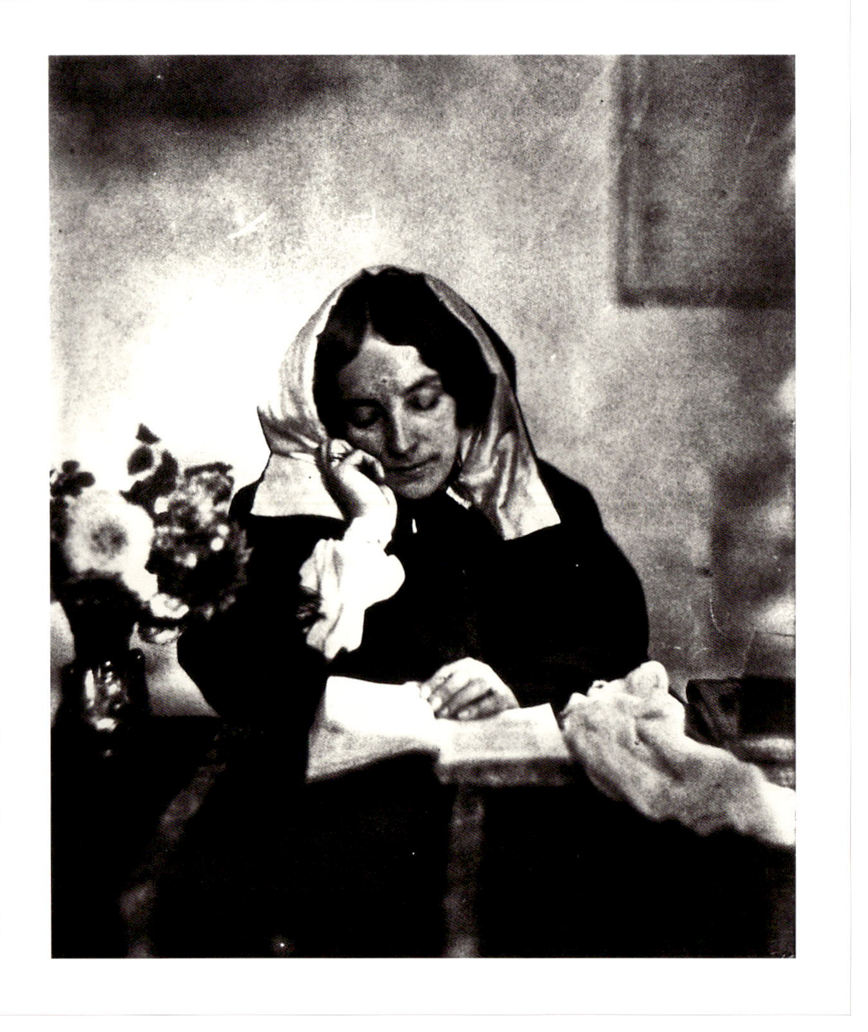

Fig. 64.

Victor Regnault, *Madame Regnault Reading*, c. 1852. Modern print from paper negative, 6 3/4 x 5 5/8 in. (17.1 x 14.2 cm).

Société Française de Photographie, Paris. 473.1

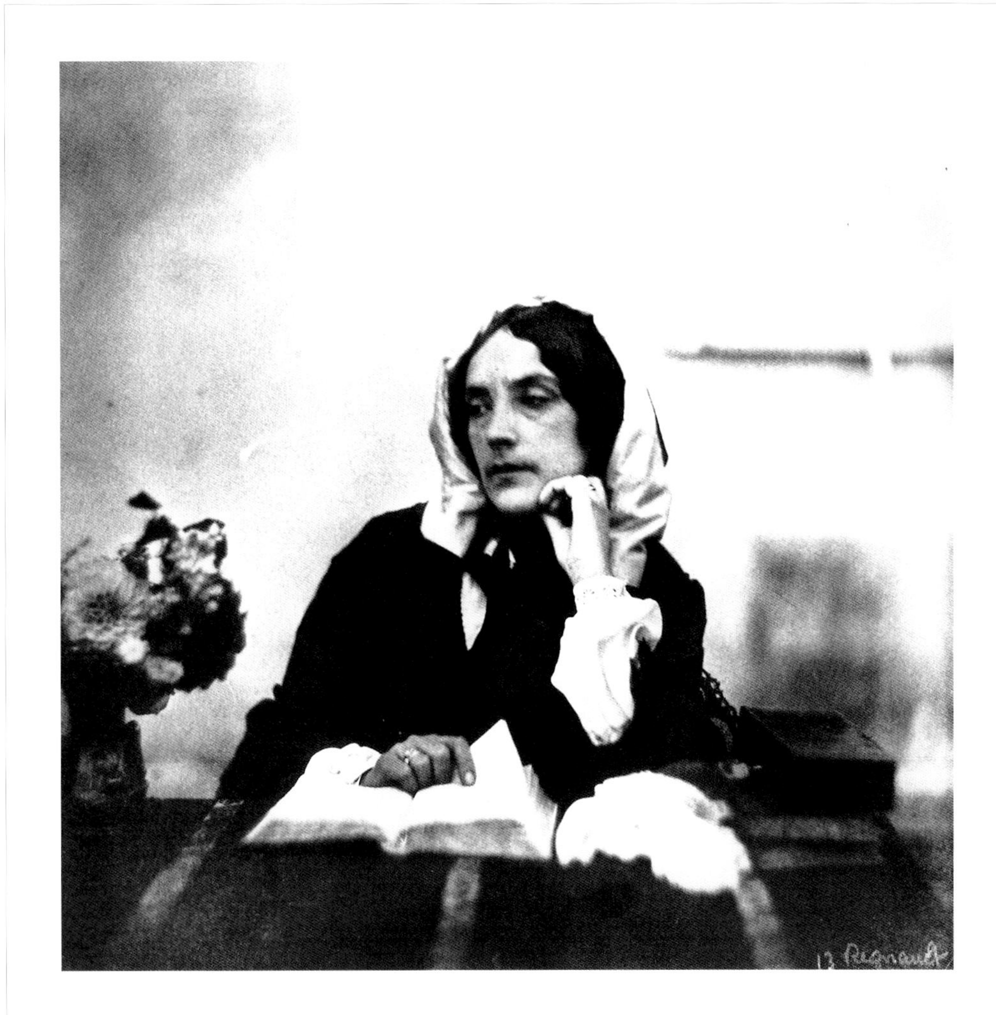

Fig. 65.

Victor Regnault, *Madame Regnault Reading*, c. 1852. Modern print from paper negative, $6^{1}/_{4}$ x $6^{1}/_{8}$ in. (16 x 15.7 cm).

Société Française de Photographie, Paris. 473.13

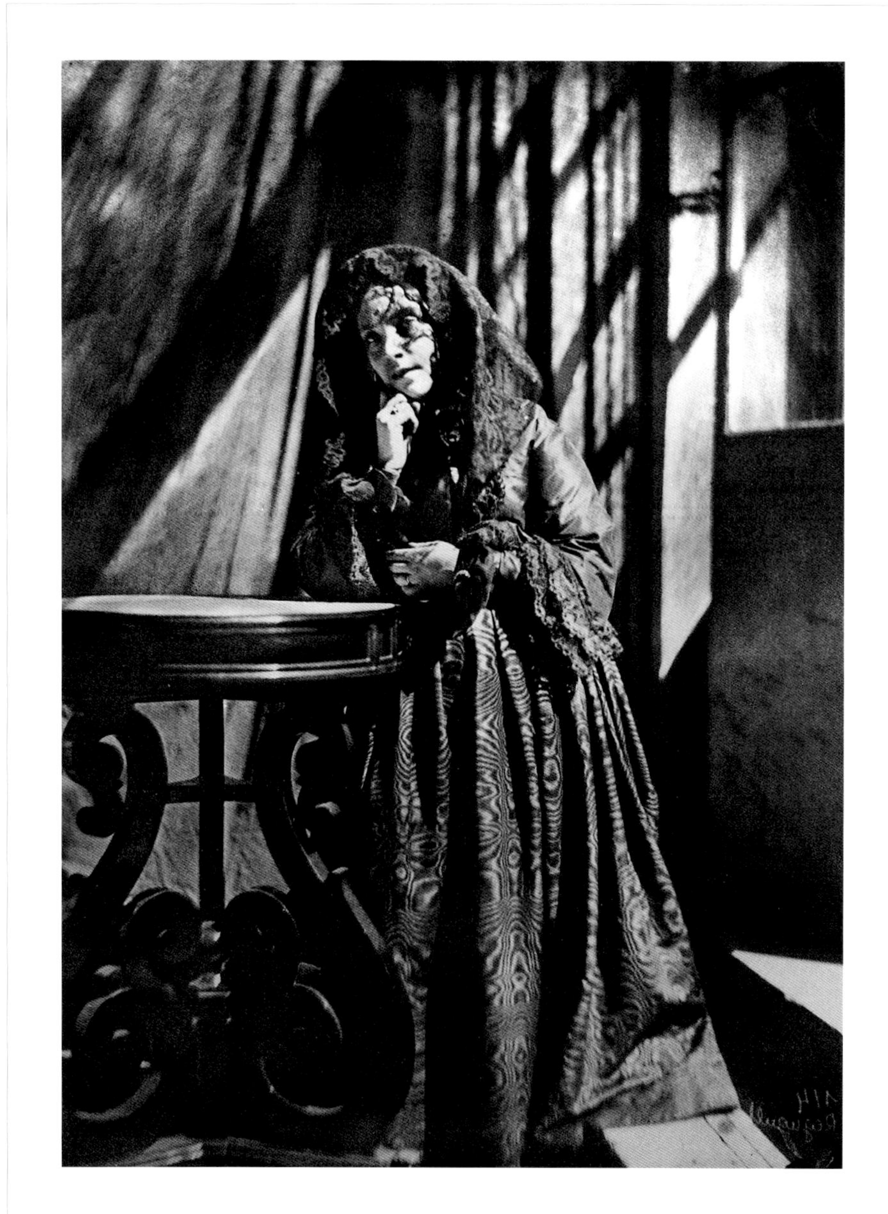

Fig. 66.

Victor Regnault, *Madame Regnault in a Mantilla*, c. 1852. Modern print from paper negative, 8 x 6¼ in. (20.5 x 16 cm).
Société Française de Photographie, Paris. 473.4

create believable settings for their portraits, because plein-air settings looked too sparsely shabby to be taken seriously, and Regnault's plein-air portraits do lack the sophisticated luster of his fewer indoor portraits.[60] The interior portraits may have taken additional time and effort to produce, but probably not a great deal more than the others. Regnault normally worked in the simpler fashion because he was satisfying documentary motives in recording family members and their relationships. Highly wrought artistry was not essential for making these private mementos.

When photography launched a new portrait industry in the 1840s, it was imagined that photographs of loved ones would be cherished as dearly as the commissioned portraits that filled the ancestral halls of the aristocracy.[61] This prediction has not been borne out, as testified by the snapshots and family albums for sale by the boxful in flea markets and antique shops. It turns out that even though photography has marginalized the business of portrait painting, family photographs are hardly comparable to painted portraits. The value of the portrait photograph normally lasts no longer than our memories of the person depicted—unless the photograph is rediscovered for historical and pictorial values that were irrelevant for its original audience. Family photographs are not kept for their aesthetic qualities, but as companions to memory, and in this sense, photography has truly been a handmaiden. Regnault's photographs were treasured by his family, but they were not substitutes for the painted, drawn, and etched portraits that the family commissioned and acquired. Writing from Italy after the death of his mother, Henri, who added some of his own drawings to the family collection, reminded his father to send photographs: "Don't forget to send me some of the family portraits. You know I don't have any of my mother."[62] He later asked for photographic copies of a sketch of his aunt and an etching of his mother.[63]

Beyond the personal significance of the pictures, there was an additional meaning and benefit to Regnault's home photography. As one of the family's "unique customs and habits" (such as he once described to Sir John Herschel), home photography fostered family identity and togetherness. The collaborative activity of posing led directly to mysterious, alchemical actions in the darkroom—and ideal opportunities to give his children hands-on lessons in chemistry and optics. The family enjoyed an intimate view of the entire process; they could watch, or perhaps participate in, the blank paper's transformation to the photographic image. We can now only speculate about the value this experience held for the Regnault family, who shared the new photographic ritual over months and maybe years.

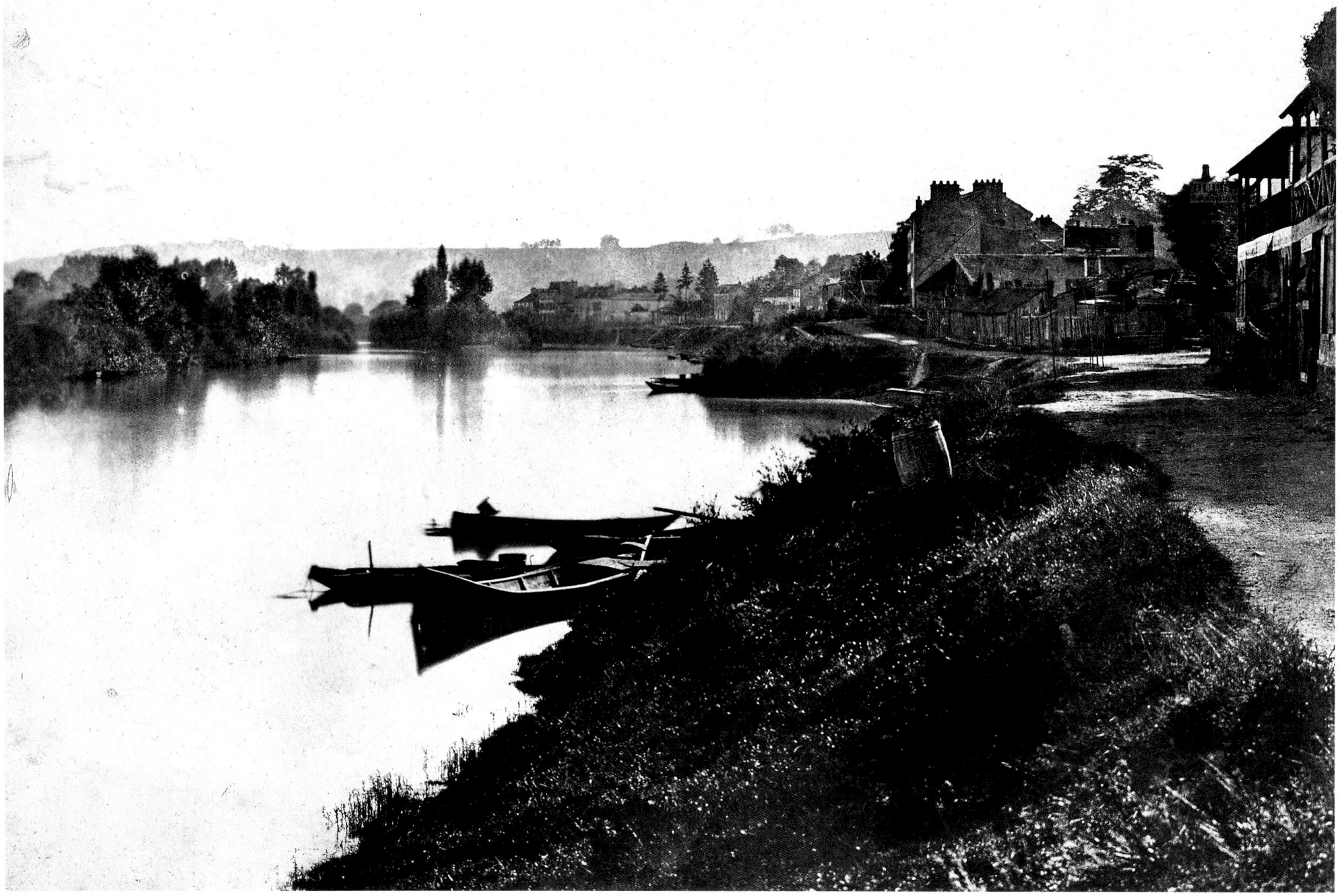

4 LANDSCAPE IN THE SHADOW OF INDUSTRY

Within the elite ranks of gentleman amateurs, landscape held special importance as a photographic subject: full of technical challenges, offering a wide variety of motifs and approaches, and rich in sentimental and cultural meaning. And although the writing of the period tends to present nature as "Nature," an absolute concept (feminine, unknowable, and utterly seductive), there was clearly some recognition that landscape (*paysage*) was not a given: it was a set of possibilities, a collection of materials interpreted poetically and/or pragmatically, a negotiated relationship between people and their surroundings, and as such, it was entirely mutable.[1] If nature was the essence, and landscape merely its vessel, it followed that not all landscapes were equal: some contained more Nature than others. Writing in the *Bulletin de la Société française de photographie* in 1855, Paul Périer reflected on the evolution of taste in landscape, which had passed from "flower beds and trellises" to something less prim in the present day: "Flora and Pomona speak less to the spirit than to the senses; but Pan and Ceres are great talkers. For us, the unwalled gardens that Providence gave lastly to her children, speak an inimitable language, the most tender and eloquent of all."[2] Périer's metaphor of Roman deities, choosing Pan, the god of woods, fields, and flocks, and Ceres, goddess of agriculture, over Flora and Pomona, the goddesses of flowers and fruit trees, reflects the Second Empire passion for the rustic, rural landscape, which urban sophisticates wistfully sought to experience as both a more authentic Nature and their patrimony as Frenchmen.[3] Like its counterpart in

Fig. 67.
Victor Regnault, *Sèvres: The Seine at Bas Meudon*, c. 1853. Carbon print by Alphonse-Louis Poitevin (1855–1860), 12 1/4 x 13 7/8 in. (31.1 x 35.4 cm). The J. Paul Getty Museum, Los Angeles. JPG 92.XM.52

painting, landscape photography became popular in the nineteenth century for many reasons, not least of which was the fact that for a large urban population, opportunities for direct experience with rural and unimproved nature were dwindling.

Following closely in the footsteps of the Barbizon painters, French photographers passionately practiced the subject of landscape-as-art in the 1850s. As Périer observed, "Nothing is more suited to the resources and limits of our art than the interiors of forests, the adorable lacework of boughs, trunks, and trifles, where nature betrays her exquisite coquetry even in her extreme dishevelment."[4] Here Périer was implying that photography's ability to render delicate detail legibly, in its reductive, monochromatic scale, was at the heart of its fitness for landscape. But as the warmth of his language indicates, there were other more affective reasons why landscape rose to the top of the S.F.P.'s hierarchy of artistic subjects. In fact, pragmatism and poetry were intermixed in the S.F.P. photographers' sense of their medium, just as these conflicting impulses were conjoined in bourgeois feelings for the land itself. This interplay between utilitarianism and emotional ardor reflects both the equivocal nature of early photography and the cultural moment of the mid-1850s, when unprecedented industrial and suburban development led to very visible changes in the French countryside. With its prodigious flexibility, photography was able not only to serve the opposing desires of developers and nature lovers but also to mediate between them. Regnault and many of his colleagues made their photographs from a position of reconcilliation.

In 1852 Regnault moved to Sèvres, a locality interwoven with commercial, industrial, residential, leisure, and agricultural uses. It was a small but busy town close to the commerce of the river, with several industries, including two breweries, commercial laundries, and of course the porcelain factory. Sèvres was also known for its bucolic setting, surrounded by farms, vineyards, and forests, and flanked on one side by the imperial Parc de Saint-Cloud, where the grounds included extensive formal gardens and fountains. Stealing time from his multitude of professional obligations, Regnault made photographs in all of these places. The record is disappointingly silent on his thoughts about the content of his subjects, although his recurring themes and compositional strategies, informed by the writings on landscape left by his contemporaries, leave room for inference. He did speak on the subject of "natural effects" and the desire to master light and atmosphere per se in his landscapes—not surprising preoccupations for a hard-bitten experimental scientist. But his rare comments also indirectly raise the problem central to all landscape art practice: how much "naturalism" is appropriate to art? Where does art leave off and science begin? Is the artist's purview strictly to record nature "as it is," or should he embellish the actual in order to achieve an effect pleasing to the eye or mind? These questions had previously interested the so-called Barbizon painters, who in the 1830s had begun their rescue of landscape from its place near the bottom of the academy's artistic hierarchy. This reversal of landscape's critical status, and the cultural factors surrounding Barbizon painting's ultimate triumph, set the stage for the importance of the landscape subject for artist-photographers of the 1850s.

THE RISE OF THE REALIST LANDSCAPE

French academic art had been slow to accept landscape as a worthy subject because it was assumed to have little historical or philosophical interest of its own, but this view began to erode in the late eighteenth century.[5] The trend was influenced by art and aesthetics from across the Channel, where the ranks of landscapists had been growing since the mid-eighteenth century, following the lead of painters like Thomas Gainsborough (1727–1788).[6] The English also produced an explicit theorization of "the picturesque," which William Gilpin (1724–1804), a clergyman and amateur artist, had described as early as 1776 as a discrete category of aesthetic experience. Gilpin's thesis was that pure, elegant beauty—found in objects of perfect regularity and ideal proportion—is not pleasing in a picture.[7] Rather, Gilpin admired what he called the picturesque landscape, the casual design of wilder nature, which was full of variation in form and texture.

Pierre-Henri de Valenciennes's treatise *Elements of Practical Perspective for the Use of Artists, Followed by Reflections and Advice to a Student on Painting and Particularly on the Genre of Landscape* (1800) signaled the nascent acceptance of landscape art in France, on grounds that essentially inverted Gilpin's thesis. Building upon ideas set forth by Roger de Piles in his *Principles of Painting* (1745), Valenciennes described two ways to envision nature—nature as it is, and nature as it could be. This real/ideal dichotomy translated into two kinds of landscape painting: the *paysage portrait* (landscape portrait) and the "pastoral" landscape (often called the "northern style" and "southern style").[8] The lowlier *paysage portrait*, which embodied Gilpin's notion of the picturesque, was a straightforward rendering of nature as it appeared to the eye, but Valenciennes argued that it did not require genius, as it dealt only in resemblance and not in invention. Still, Valenciennes recognized the distinct charm that the *paysage portrait* held at its best, namely, in the works of the seventeenth-century Dutch landscapists. Further, although he ranked the subjective, classicized pastoral form above the merely charming *paysage portrait*, Valenciennes stressed the importance of direct contact with nature, advising the artist to leave carriage travel to the "rich fools" and travel out into the country on horseback, like Jean-Jacques Rousseau's Émile, to be immersed in nature's subtle details.[9] Reflecting the rise of positivism, Valenciennes also called for the artist to have a strong grounding in the sciences, so that he might understand nature's physical laws as well as its visual effects.

Valenciennes's theories would ultimately be overtaken by the positivist view of nature that his treatise invoked only in passing. In the 1830s, the Barbizon painters expressly adopted the ethic/aesthetic of careful visual observation and naturalistic depiction, while they adamantly championed the unsung landscape of France over the pastoral landscape of antiquity (although Camille Corot would also carry on the pastoral tradition). The rise of the realist landscape was a symbolic ascendancy of the natural over the artificial, the material over the symbolic, democracy over the monarchy, and the forest of Fontainebleau over the manicured gardens of Versailles.[10] This ascendancy occurred gradually over some twenty-five years, for while topographic and exotic landscapes achieved rapid success with a travel-hungry bourgeois clientele during the July Monarchy (1830–48), certain aspects of Barbizon painting—the earthy palettes, humble subjects, and lack of dramatic viewpoints—took time to be accepted by a bourgeois public nurtured on spectacle and high-key clarity in art.[11] By the 1850s, Barbizon painting had finally become established as a popular counterpoint for academic art: a visual code of honesty and individualism predicated on direct experience with nature, modest yet sensitive rendering, and the pictorial ideals of harmony and atmosphere (figs. 68 and 69), which answered the history painter's touchstones of literary drama and design.

Writing in 1859, Baudelaire described realism as a mainstream taste run amok (thanks in part to photography), worshipped, as he put it, by the "idolatrous mob" who believed Art to be "the exact reproduction of Nature" and photography to be "the absolute of Art."[12] It was the commercial portrait, not the landscape, that Baudelaire singled out in his condemnation of photography. The ubiquitous commercial portrait epitomized the materialist excesses of popular taste: it offered transparent realism, affordability, technological wonder, democratic access, and universal currency. Photographic landscapes did not have equal public presence in the 1850s, although they became popular with artist/amateurs after 1847 once a patent-free paper process was available. This precipitated a brief movement in artistic landscape photography that lasted through the 1850s, before the landscape subject reached its ultimate popular currency in stereography and wet-plate travel photography in the 1860s.

LANDSCAPE AND THE GENTLEMAN AMATEUR PHOTOGRAPHER

With the introduction of Blanquart-Evrard's 1847 modifications to Talbot's calotype process, more French photographers began taking their box cameras and tripods out into the country and returning with studies of intimate settings and motifs in nature, images steeped in Gilpin's picturesque aesthetic and the humble naturalism of Barbizon art.[13] The painters of the original Barbizon group—Corot, Théodore Rousseau, Jules Dupré, Paul Huet, Constant Troyon, and Narcisse Diaz de la Peña—had gained

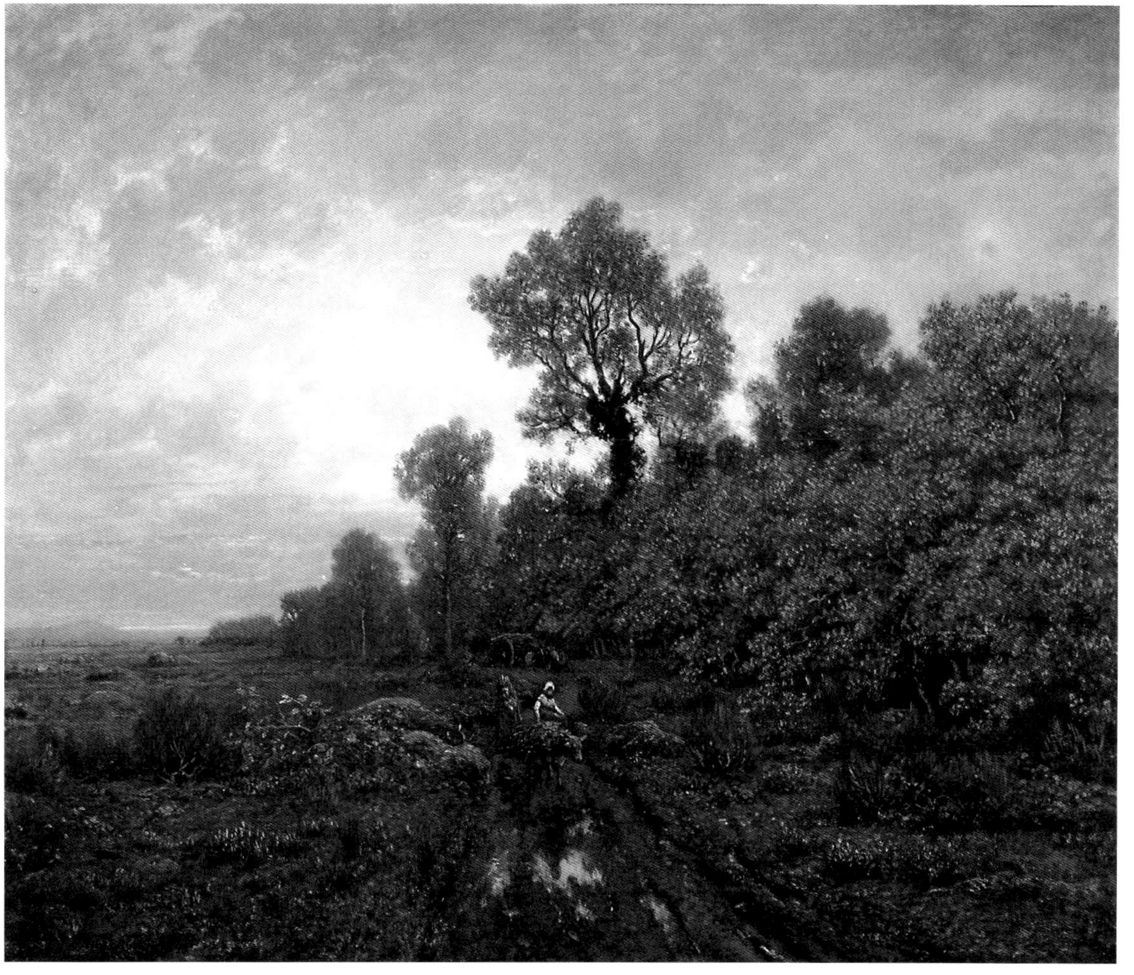

Fig. 68.

Théodore Rousseau (French, 1812–1867), *Gathering Wood in the Forest of Fontainebleau*, c. 1850–60. Oil on canvas, $21^{1}/_{2}$ x $25^{3}/_{4}$ in. (54.7 x 65.3 cm). Museum of Fine Arts, Boston. Bequest of Mrs. David P. Kimball, 23.399

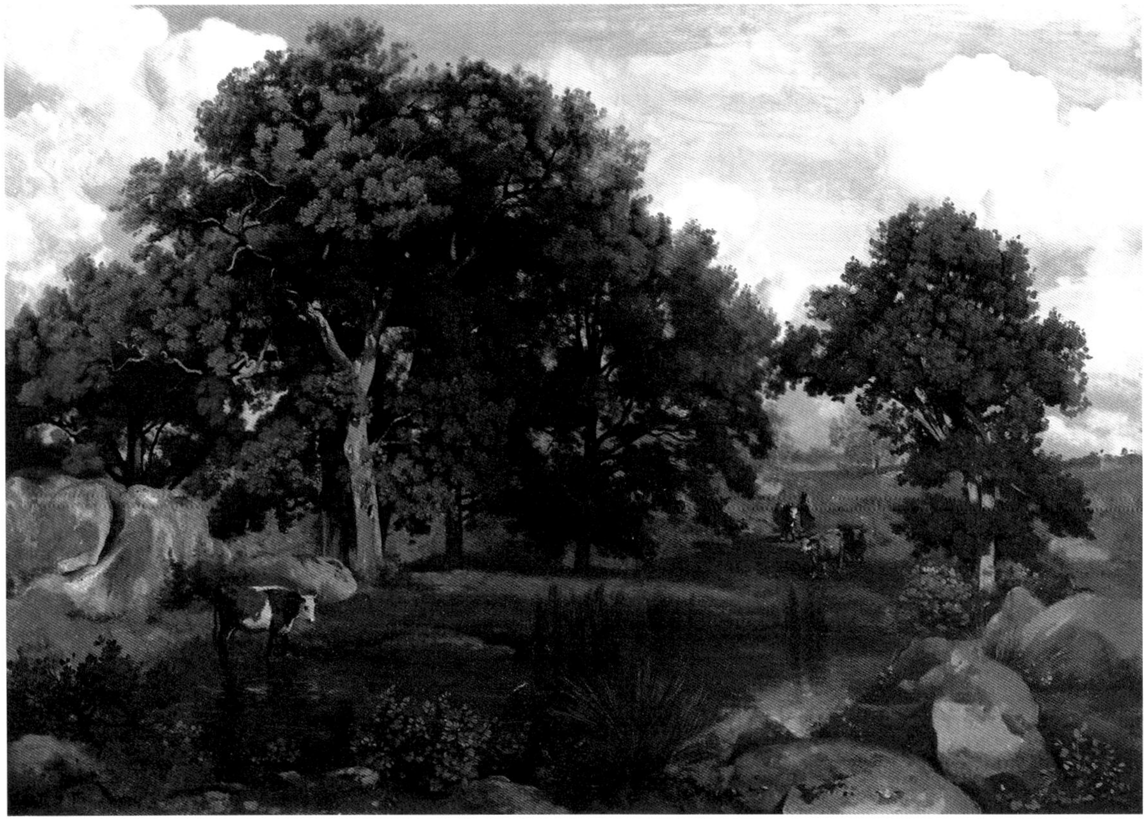

Fig. 69.

Jean-Baptiste-Camille Corot (French, 1796–1875), *Forest of Fontainebleau*, 1846. Oil on canvas, 35 1/2 x 50 3/4 in. (90.2 x 128.8 cm). Museum of Fine Arts, Boston. Gift of Mrs. Samuel Dennis Warren, 90.199

their first critical notice in the salons of 1831 and 1833 in the wake of the Revolution of 1830, when the cultural climate of romantic rebellion supported them in their struggle against academic conservatism.[14] In the 1850s, photographers joined a new generation of landscape painters (Gustave Courbet, Charles Jacque, and Charles Daubigny, among others) inspired by the "Men of 1830" at the moment when the original Barbizon painting was experiencing critical rediscovery, popular triumph, and real commercial success.

Landscape photography possessed special status in the rarefied culture of the S.F.P., where elevating photography above vulgar commerce was a key concern. Most of the society's inner circle—those who faithfully attended meetings, juried the salons, held office, and headed up committees—were avid landscapists. Gustave Le Gray (officer), Count Olympe Aguado, Paul Périer (vice-president), George Fortier (officer), Henri de La Blanchère, Louis-Alphonse de Brébisson, Marquis Raymond de Bérenger, E. Mailand (officer), Ernest Cousin (officer), Viscount Joseph deVigier, Victor Regnault (president)—these photographers and many others devoted their best efforts to producing large format landscapes (figs. 70 and 71).[15] Although most of these men were wealthy *grands bourgeois* (upper-middle class) or aristocrats, few had unlimited time for photographic travels. Regnault and many of his colleagues therefore found it practical to make picturesque views and studies of landscapes within easy reach of Paris: along the Seine, in the regional forests, or in the extensive royal parks.

Diverse as they were, Barbizon painters employed many treatments that photographers could identify with the qualities of the photographic landscape: the search for overall tonal harmony as practiced by Corot; the muted, sometimes monochromatic palette; and the unidealized, naturalistic rendering of selected fragments of nature (fig. 72).[16] Many landscape photographers consequently looked to this model, if not to the Dutch and English sources of the Barbizon style. The critical vocabulary that developed around the photographers' wild or rustic images incorporated these references immediately; indeed, the contemporary passion among some collectors for Dutch and Barbizon art frequently went hand-in-hand with an interest in fine-art photography.[17] In the judgment of connoisseurs and critics, several common elements made kindred spirits of Dutch painting, Barbizon painting, and photography.

Each had at some time been denied the respect of the French academy, and each was typically concerned with the unembellished subjects of everyday life, rendered with what was considered to be an overwhelming truth and naturalism. So linked were photography, Dutch, and Barbizon art that critics often used the terms of one reflexively to describe the others. In 1860, for example, the critic Théophile Thoré-Bürger described Dutch painting as a "a kind of photography of their great seventeenth century," while Ernest Lacan, writing in *La Lumière* in 1855, would praise a photograph by describing it

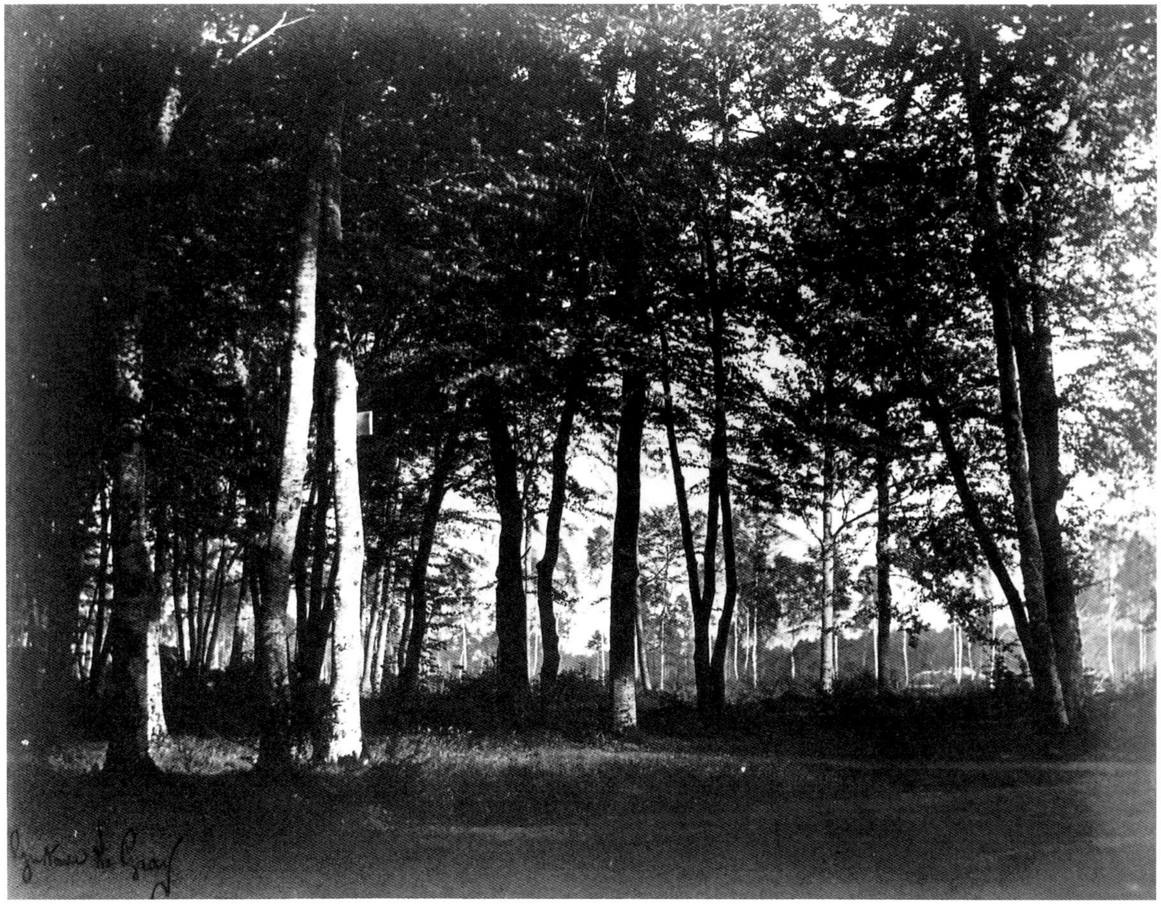

Fig. 70.

Gustave Le Gray (French, 1820–1882), *Study of Trees and Pathways*, c. 1849. Salt print from paper negative, $7^{3}/_{4}$ x $10^{1}/_{8}$ in. (19.8 x 26.4 cm). The J. Paul Getty Museum, Los Angeles. 84.xm.637.6

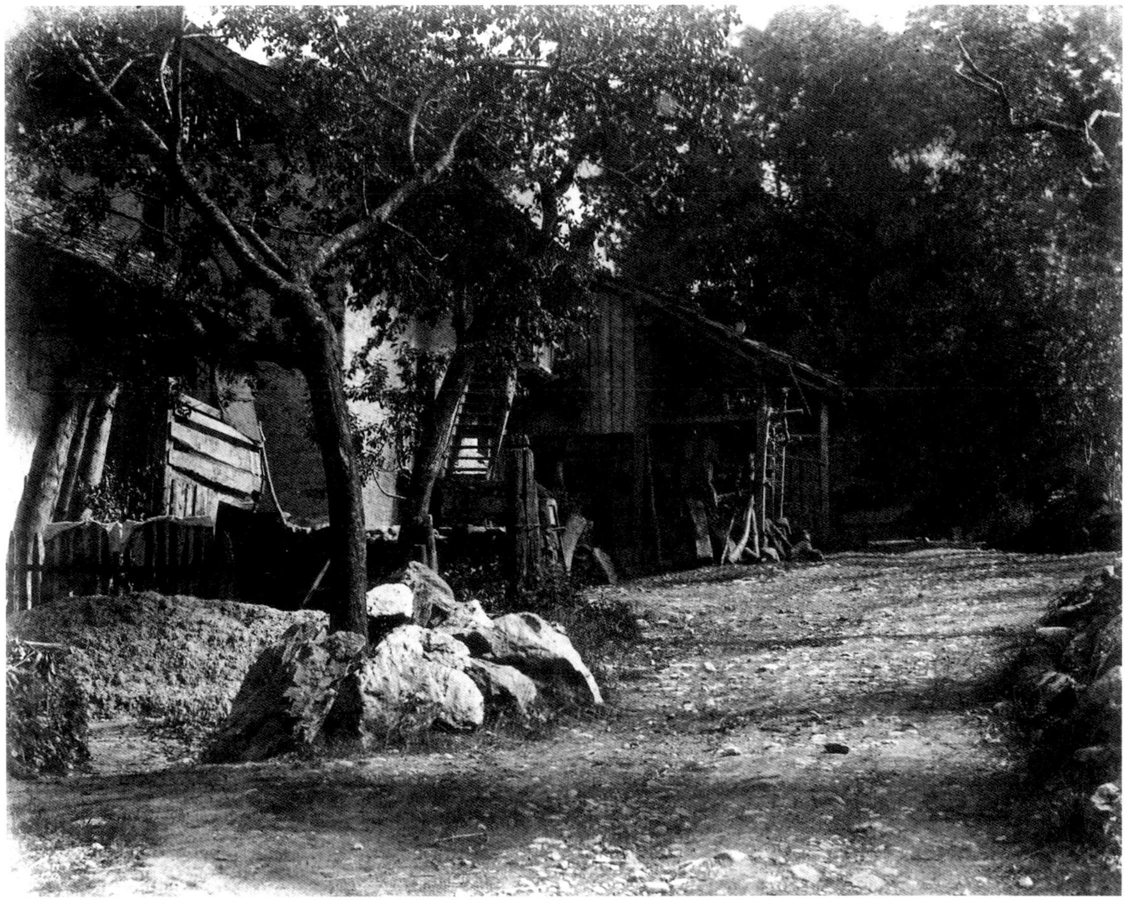

Fig. 71.

Charles-Fortunat-Paul-Casimir Périer (French, born 1812, active 1850s), *Landscape with Barns*, 1855–60. Albumen print, $7^5/8$ x $9^7/8$ in. (19.5 x 25.1 cm). The J. Paul Getty Museum, Los Angeles. 84.xm.350.20

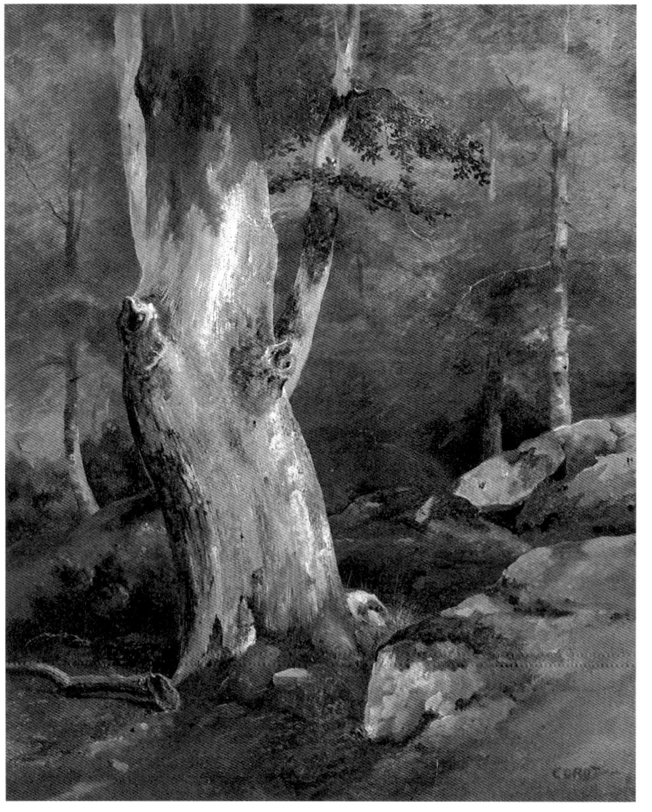

Fig. 72.
Jean-Baptiste-Camille Corot, *Old Beech Tree*, c. 1828–30. Oil on canvas, $21^{7}/_{8}$ x $18^{1}/_{8}$ in. (55.5 x 46 cm).
The Museum of Fine Arts, Boston. The Henry C. and Martha B. Angell Collection, 19.80

as "a veritable drawing by a Flemish master."[18] Speaking of the Dutch flavor of Count Olympe Aguado's photography, Lacan asked, "Where does one find more finesse of drawing, more harmony of tone, more light and air than in these masses of foliage he chooses so well? As for his *Yoked Oxen*, they recall the most celebrated canvases of Amsterdam."[19] Likewise, Lacan remarked upon the "heavy atmosphere" and "poetic sadness" of André Giroux's landscapes (fig. 73), which seemed imbued with the spirit of Barbizon and Dutch painting, while elsewhere, in the *Bulletin* of the S.F.P., Périer (an important collector of Dutch and Barbizon art) wrote that *Study of a Chestnut Tree* by Henri Le Secq (1818–1882) "could astonish Rousseau himself, Dupré, and Diaz, and recall to them the great days of Barbizon."[20]

Finally, Dutch and Barbizon art and photography shared associations with the "democratic."[21] A classical education was not needed to understand their frank realism and simple narratives, and all three modes were consequently popular with a middle-class public. However, the ostensibly democratic nature of photography was a problem for those who hoped to elevate photography's status, and the need to distinguish art photography from its popular commercial form—cheap, utterly accessible, and banal—was another reason that calotypy became the process of choice for artistic amateurs like Périer and high-minded professionals like Le Gray. Their sensitive renderings of rustic subjects signified honesty, simplicity, and the patrimony of the people, but to those in the know, their process also bespoke a finicky craftsmanship that was decidedly individualistic, time-consuming, and expensive.

In the writings of photography critics, it was never acknowledged that there might be any difference between the practice of the young romantic painters of 1830 and this upscale circle of Second-Empire landscape photographers. Rapture of the artist before nature was accepted as universal and trans-historical. But to photograph nature in 1852 signified differently than to paint nature in 1832. To audiences of the 1830s, fresh from the revolution that had overthrown the last vestiges of Bourbon rule, naturalistic landscape painting as it was practiced by Rousseau, Corot, Dupré, and others carried an implicit ideology: a radical, romantic critique of the aristocracy and theocracy. As the July Monarchy wore on, naturalism was interpreted as a rebuke to materialism and the industrialization to which it was inextricably bound.[22] Moreover, painting these rustic terrains implied a challenge to the academy's traditional bias against pure landscape.

By the opening of the Second Empire, however, Barbizon painting had been crowned by success and domesticated by its popularity with bourgeois patrons who were inclined to celebrate naturalistic landscapes as lyrical hymns of subjectivity, nostalgia, and national pride rather than as expressions of republicanism or sympathy with the peasantry.[23] If the original Barbizon painters had flung themselves against the academic tide by painting a traditionally debased subject, photographers with high art aspirations admired Barbizon painting not least for the legitimacy it had gained in the Salon in the past twenty years; by 1852 Corot, Dupré, Troyon, Diaz, and Rousseau had all received knighthoods in the Légion d'honneur.

Photographers of the 1850s were caught in the current of a different academic bias: the refusal to accept photography as a fine art. Consequently, the S.F.P. photographers with high-art aspirations were eager to choose subjects that possessed artistic cachet. Although photography's champions insisted that any subject could be treated aesthetically, all categories of photographic subjects carried special associations or biases that inflected salon criticism. Portraiture was ambivalently received, due to the market saturation by its mediocre commercial form.[24] Historical and literary work—tableau—was generally judged to be outside photography's proper domain, though it did find a niche in England.[25]

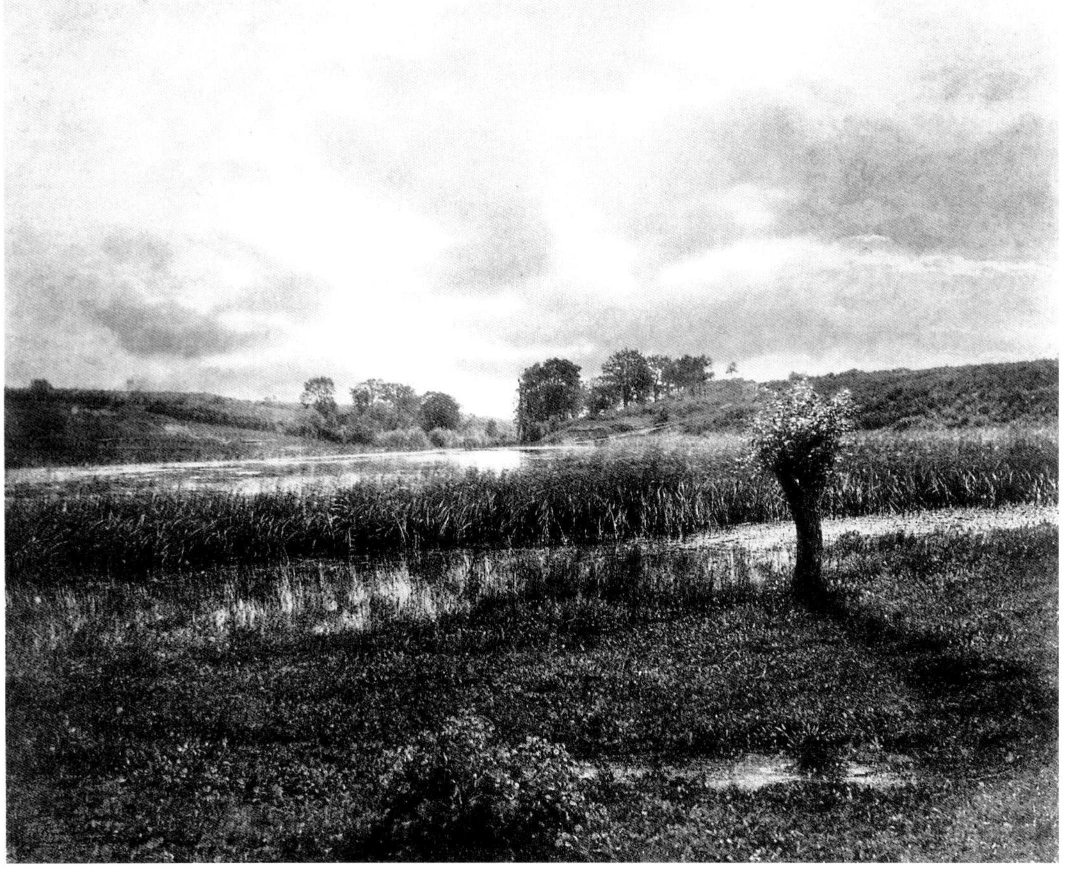

Fig. 73.

André Giroux (French, 1801–1879), *The Ponds at Obtevoz (Rhône)*, c. 1855. Salt print, 10 1/2 x 13 3/8 in. (26.7 x 33.8 cm).

The J. Paul Getty Museum, Los Angeles. 84.xp.362.3

Still lifes were often praised by the critics, but like genre subjects, their recognition was usually linked with their practical value as aides-mémoire for painting.[26] The nude would always be haunted by the spectre of pornography (S.F.P. exhibitions barred the nude).[27] Architectural photography was also well respected and represented, but it, too, had a concrete utility for historians, architects, and engineers that mingled practical use with aesthetics. In the host of photographic choices, pure landscape stood out as the subject with the greatest likelihood of gaining recognition as art. Moreover, since it encompassed more variety—seascapes, forest studies, garden corners, and so on—than the other principal genres, landscape offered photographers wider latitude for experimentation with style and form.[28]

But more important, even if it no longer signified romantic rebellion, landscape possessed something more appropriate to the respectable politics of wealthy S.F.P. photographers: spiritual feeling, based in Jean-Jacques Rousseau's philosophy of nature as the font of the soul, and a morality based in the belief that the national spirit was inseparable from the land itself. If this rarefied content was successfully conveyed in a photograph, photographers were that much closer to raising their images to the status of art. For the minority who accepted the premise that photography could embody ideas at the same time as it transcribed reality, Regnault's study of a single tree standing in a shaft of light in the forest might, for example, suggest spiritual illumination in the presence of God-in-Nature (fig. 74).

The elevated value of landscape photography did not rest solely in the end product, however. The actual experience of photographing in Nature—if approached in the spirit of communion—was itself tremendously significant, tapping into the Enlightenment concept of immersion in nature as a moral tonic for the ailing modern soul. This sentiment found a meaningful resurgence with the Second-Empire bourgeois intelligentsia who found their lives increasingly circumscribed by commerce and industry, and their leisure hours claimed by ephemeral urban entertainments. In a series of articles on the photography exhibition at the 1855 Exposition Universelle, Périer described this modern condition and expressed the importance that the nature experience held for him and his colleagues. He opened his review by defending his hierarchy of subject categories, which placed "picturesque views and landscapes" at the very top: "You will excuse us for deciding the question of which comes first according to our declared predilections for landscape," he explained.[29] He followed with a lengthy digression worth quoting:

> *The contemplation of nature, the company of the forest, fields, great clouds, and vast horizons, these thousand sweet and sad raptures that the hills and plains, the slightest green path, or the smallest brook lavish upon the melancholy* promeneur *have always seemed among the keenest of the tranquil, and therefore lasting, happi-*

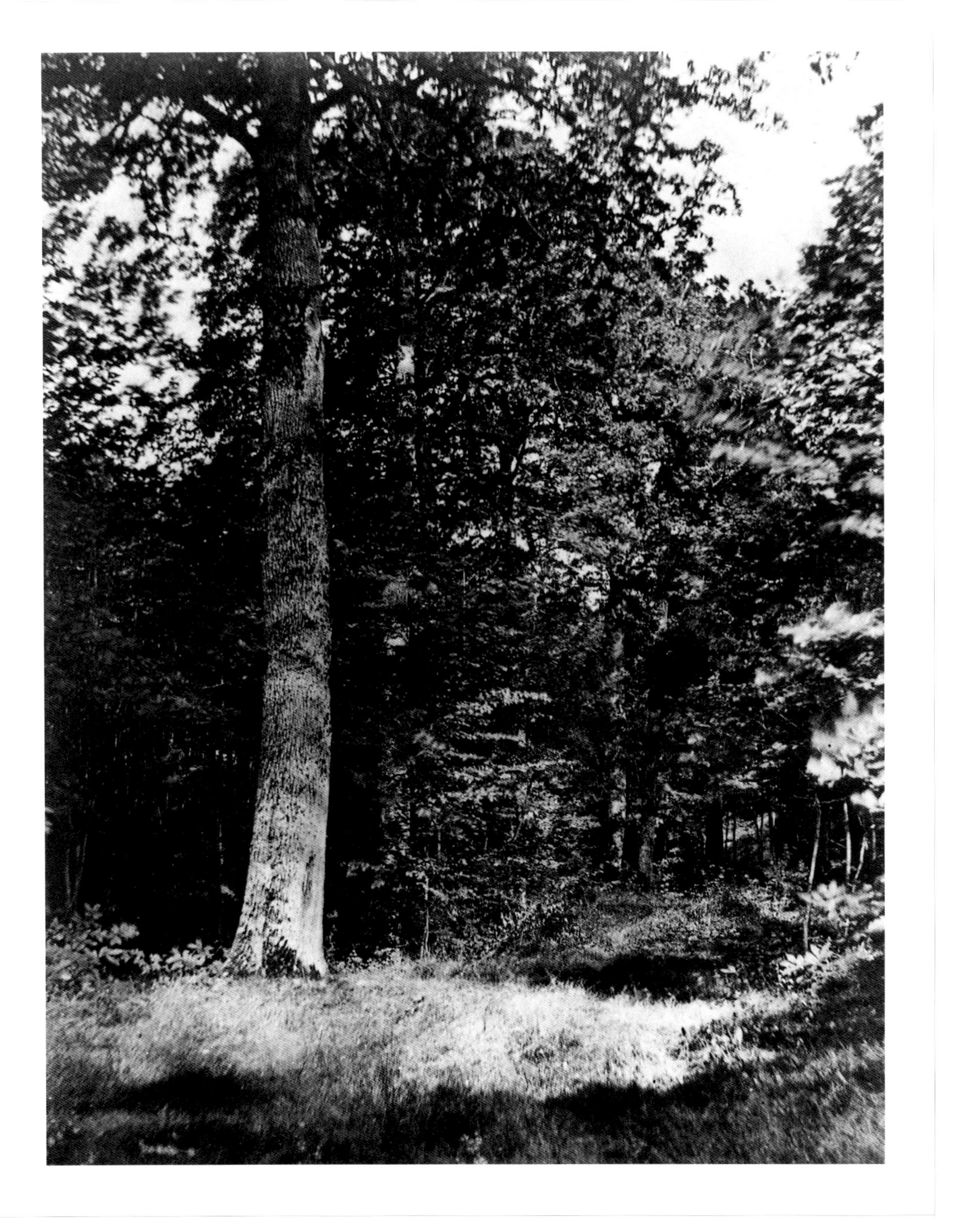

Fig. 74.
Victor Regnault, *Tree Study*, c. 1853, from *Études Photographiques* (Lille: Blanquart-Evrard, 1853). Salt print from paper negative, 11 x 8 7/8 in. (27.9 x 22.5 cm). Bibliothèque Nationale de France, Paris

nesses accorded to man on earth, some of the guaranteed joys, the best things to console us for others we have lost, and at the same time the worthiest to mingle with and multiply the greatest, purest felicities of our best days.

Undoubtedly there are some tastes that exalt and deploy the bruises of social life, and on this we speak with experience. But how many others, so bruised, are ready to reach out a hand to us! Above all, how many would thank us if we could persuade them to try an infallible remedy to ease their sorrows!

While the sight of cities and society choked with people seems designed to revive all these wounds, the harmonious and rich silence of nature and the intimacy of its many marvels elevate the soul to heights that make it immune to petty miseries, and leave nothing greater above its steadfastness.

Whether in the midst of the lively scents of springtime, in the splendid blossomings of summer, among the mute and golden predictions of autumn, or even across the brilliant harshness and poetic nakedness of winter, a single portion of the circle that the eye embraces to the horizon holds a treasure of benedictions amassed for the solitary wanderer.

And who can pride himself on never having submitted to—if that is not to love—solitude! I call it forth to you, castaways of all fortunes, to you especially, artists of vocation or avocation sadly confined to those inhabited walls! To you, more happy than we, if you fill your hours with noble works and fertile studies; but to pity a hundred times more, in the midst of the injuries that you feel so acutely and avoid so poorly, when you fill your lungs in vain for this rejuvenation of your soul! O rus! quando te aspiciam! [*Oh country life! When shall I be able to behold you!*][30]

The language of Périer's statement is familiarly romantic, summoning up the sublimely conflicting sensations of pleasure and pain, certainty and uncertainty, having and losing. For the S.F.P. landscapists, most of whom came of age in the 1830s, this sweet, sad romance with nature was exemplified in Barbizon painting, the model of sincerity and authenticity in art. But here again there was a key difference between the S.F.P. landscapists and their Barbizon predecessors. Unlike those painters, who came from more or less modest middle-class backgrounds, many of the S.F.P.'s romantic landscapists were successful capitalists who were personally involved in the economic and social transformations of their era. These photographers had a starkly different relationship to the land and themes conveyed by their chosen imagery.

Some of them, such as Le Gray and Edouard Baldus (1815–1882), were not powerful men in their own right, but they nevertheless enjoyed mutually beneficial relationships with state and corporate interests, working on photographic commissions to document and create promotional imagery of new railways, building campaigns, or army maneuvers. These commissions in turn helped them finance their other photographic work, whether it was entrepreneurial or purely personal. Le Gray, for example, was at work on a personal series of decidedly artistic landscapes in the Forest of Fontainebleau in 1852 (perhaps an influence on Regnault's Barbizon-inspired landscapes of the same year), at about the same time he was working on multiple goverment photographic commissions, such as the Mission héliographique (a mission launched in 1851 to document the country's archaeological ruins) and various documentary projects for the state bureaucracy.[31] But a number of the prominent landscapists in the S.F.P., including Regnault, Périer, Aguado, Edouard Delessert, de Bérenger, and La Blanchère, were also instrumental figures in Second-Empire government and society.[32] Aguado, for example, from a noble Spanish banking family, was close to the court and involved in railroad promotion, while Périer, the son of Louis Philippe's prime minister Casimir Périer, likewise continued to build the family's vast banking fortune in railroad speculation.[33] Well before the founding of the S.F.P., many of these men had known each other across boardroom tables and state ballrooms.[34] Given the extent of their privilege, it may be hard to imagine feeling sympathy for the "bruises of social life" described so lavishly by Périer, but this was surely part of the author's point. Périer's soliloquy was written for his constituents, this rarefied group of gentlemen who were in many ways culturally isolated by their success: their wealth, good fortune, and ceaseless responsibilities. Ingenuous though it may seem, Périer's lamentation speaks of a painful paradox: the moral void at the center of a life lived in brilliant society, invisible to those on the outside—a sentiment that echoes Regnault's disillusionment upon achieving full recognition in the A.d.S. Following in the venerable footsteps of Rousseau, Vicomte François-Auguste-René de Chateaubriand, and Jacques-Henri Bernardin de Saint-Pierre, these sophisticates looked to Nature—Périer's "guaranteed joy"—as the antidote to the artifice of the social realm.

Périer, Aguado, Delessert, and Regnault especially were strategically involved in industrial, railroad, and real-estate speculation, and their responsibilities included deciding how to use the country's material resources; they were collectively making decisions for everyone about the fate of regional forests, rivers, mineral resources, and agricultural lands. I would argue that in its ability to depict a chosen landscape in a permanent state of virginity, an ever-present "now," photography was well suited to mitigating the anxiety over the potential or actual destruction of the (picturesque) landscape. Writing in 1848, Marx had argued that the coming "bourgeois epoch" was destined to be a time of reckoning when the modern industrial world would be forced to recognize that the price of capitalist production and profit was the utter disintegration of civil society.[35] Today we recognize elements of our own social disintegration as the legacy of the profit-driven exhaustion of natural resources and environmental ruin. Looking at these romantic landscape photographs today, one is compelled to note the irony that even as Regnault and the S.F.P. elite delighted in seeking out secluded corners of nature to photograph, these were becoming measurably more rare owing to the scientific, industrial, and economic progress that they materially assisted as bankers, scientists, investors, and businessmen. Can we believe, however, that the photographers were themselves aware of this paradox?

Ecological sensitivity as we know it today hardly existed in 1850, but it has recently been noted that scientific research published in the 1840s pointed toward a new model of natural history that viewed all forms of life as interdependent.[36] Two key pieces of this research were authored by two of Regnault's closest colleagues: Justus von Liebig and J.-B. Dumas, and Regnault's own definitive research on animal respiration was meticulous proof of the biological economy of consumption, transformation, and excretion. Regnault was quite aware of the implications of this model of life as a dense skein of interdependencies, and he and his colleagues had the opportunity to observe the same principle at work in the world of business and industry. As men of power and influence, they were ideally positioned to foresee the probabilities of the near future, to recognize that these changes were really *exchanges*, that for all the economic and social good of marvels like the steam engine and rail travel, there would be losses elsewhere, as open lands receded and natural resources were depleted, especially around urban centers. As the Second-Empire government worked to galvanize the tentative beginnings of an industrial capitalist economy in France, Périer, Delessert, Aguado, and Regnault would all have been privy to high-ranking discussions of such topics as the issuing of public bonds for construction programs, governmental backing of private credit companies, and other economic incentives for all kinds of development. Their unique understanding of the repercussions of "progress," combined with their commitment to the modernization already underway, may have helped lead these S.F.P. photographers to take up the industrial medium of photography in the first place.

When prominent men took up photography and made it serve personal, expressive ends making images of undeniable beauty, they implicitly acted as standard-bearers for a progressive modernity in which technology was properly subservient to man. Far from denying the charge that photography was industrial in nature, Périer insisted that only an "intimate fusion" between the technical and the artistic in the photographer's approach to the medium could prevent the profession from being "classed among the unhealthy industries."[37] While anyone with the equipment and technical training could make photographs, true photographic success, in Périer's terms, could only be achieved by managing the techniques with the profound imagination and sensitivity acquired through the genuine worship of art. And, he asked, "Is it really necessary to point out that these faculties don't grow on trees?"[38] Artistic photography was another proof that a machine was neither good nor bad but assumed its value and character from the intelligence of its users—ideally an educated elite.

This symbolic taming of technology functioned in tandem with another means of coping with the growing split between nature and culture: imagining and depicting an immutable landscape. Under the pressures of the new economic order to which they devoted their professional lives, these men sought to depict a realm where one could deny the imperatives—even as they furthered the interests—of the world of business and industry, where anxious consciences could be eased by the illusion of a domain beyond man's control. Photography, with its assumed relationship to the "true" and the "actual," was the ideal medium to serve this symbolic representation: Nature as imagined by Périer, "guaranteed" by the magisterial gaze of photography, simultaneously accessible and unconquerable, an irresistible mistress who attracts her admirers and holds them at bay with exquisite coquetry. In this gendered refuge, the S.F.P. landscapists made photographs that were simultaneously free-floating aesthetic expressions and the grounded "proof" of nature's enduring—images that were deeply colored with nostalgia at the moment of their making.

REGNAULT AND THE MODERN LANDSCAPE

Regnault, who once joked about escaping his burdens by running away to Australia, was a model of this combination of power, privilege, and instrumentality; indeed, this condition helped motivate his election as president of the S.F.P. But if many of his colleagues chose to ignore changes occurring in the landscape in favor of creating photographic testimonials to an immutable Nature, Regnault featured industrial modernity and the rustic tradition equally in his landscapes. Photographing a range of landscapes, from sites of heavy industry to those of perfect pastoral beauty, his concerns shifted widely between documentary motives and aesthetics.

Regnault stands apart from his S.F.P. colleagues in that he was experienced in more capacities with industrial modernity and its relationship to power. He was equally an administrator and a mechanic—the man who made the machine work—and his research as a scientist and mining engineer had social, environmental, and historical impact. Regnault's state-sponsored work on two questions had a surprisingly long reach, altering the quality of French life in significant ways. First, it was his research on steam engines that made this new source of power practical, safe, and adaptable for industries of all kinds, including national defense, agriculture and food production, industry, commerce, construction, and transportation.[39] Likewise, Regnault's research on the production of coal gas made it economically feasible for Baron Georges-Eugène Haussmann to redesign Paris as it is now known—the City of Light, with its dazzling network of streetlights. Seeking to lower the price of gas charged by multiple private gas companies, Regnault was commissioned to study the problem in 1852. Establishing an experimental gas factory in

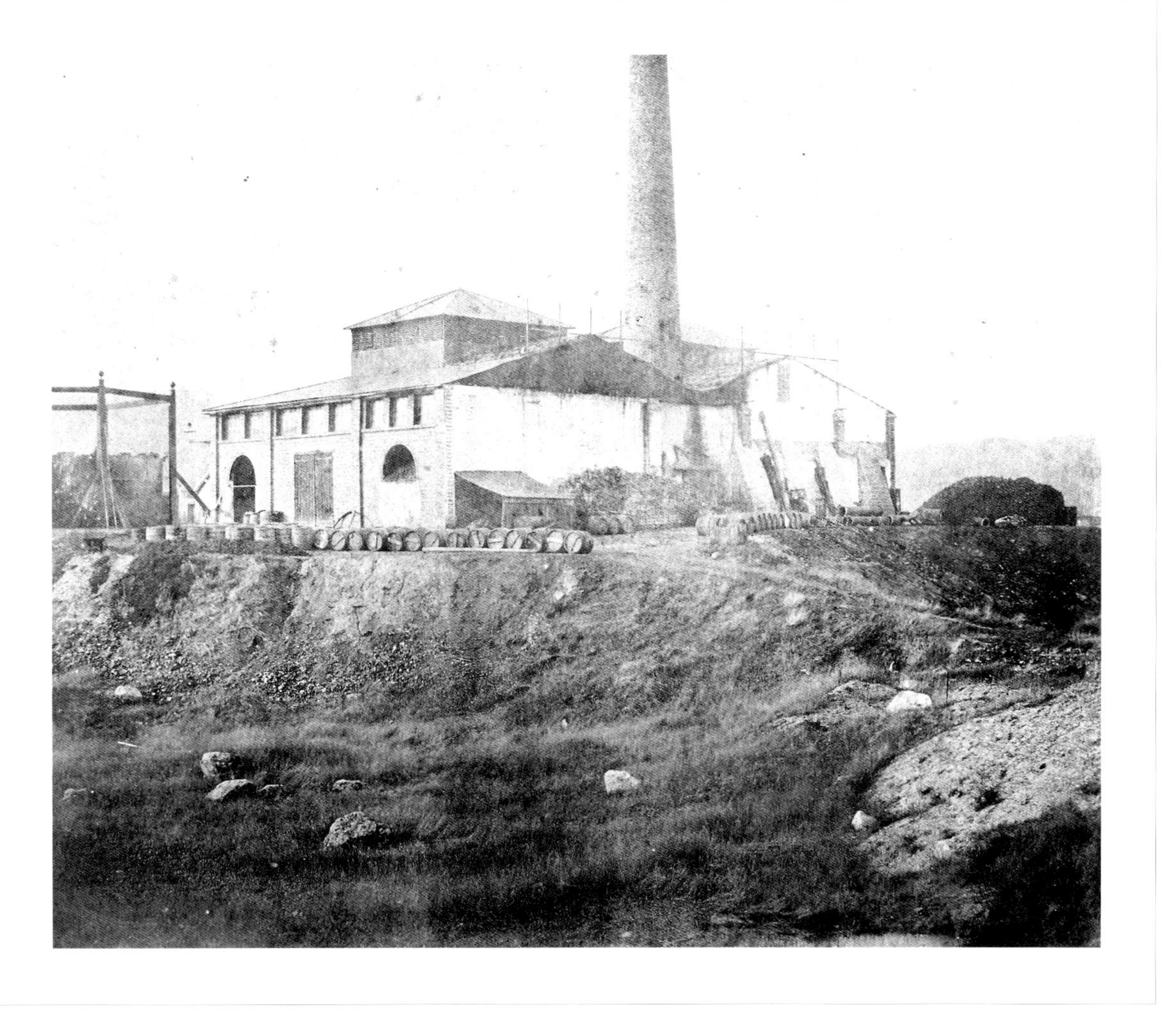

Fig. 75.

Victor Regnault, *Banks of the Seine, Gas Factory*, c. 1852. Salt print from paper negative, 13 1/8 x 16 1/4 in. (33.5 x 41.3 cm).
Musée d'Orsay, Paris. 1983.168 (Inv. 1979 D 21)

Saint-Cloud (secured by Imperial Guard to prevent sabotage), Regnault directed every detail from furnace design to fuel mixtures and proved that the current price of gas was outrageously inflated—at least five times the cost of production.[40] The government subsequently pressed the six implicated local gas companies to form one limited liability corporation, the Compagnie parisienne de l'éclairage et du chauffage par le gaz, a merger that initiated the rise of technology megacorporations in France.[41] Regnault was appointed to the board as consulting engineer, a generously paid, lifetime position.[42]

Regnault took up photography at exactly the same time as he was carrying on this work for the government. Among his large-format landscapes is an image that probably depicts the experimental gas factory at Saint-Cloud, an ugly image by almost any standard, depicting a squat brick construction with a smokestack truncated by the top of the frame (fig. 75).[43] Situated on its muddy, desolate embankment, centered claustrophobically in the frame, the building is photographed in a pedestrian manner, with no concessions to aesthetic niceties. True, little could be done to flatter this unlovely structure, except perhaps to frame the view as a vertical or at least move the camera back to include the full length of the chimney that has been unceremoniously cut off to get a closer view of the building. The photograph may have no pretensions to the pictorial, but as documentation of the factory's structural details, it may reflect some pride in the completion of this contentious and (ostensibly) publicly beneficial project. And even though it stands at the far end of the spectrum of picturesqueness in Regnault's work, its subject is not anomalous. He also photographed a few sites of construction or demolition, and motifs of modernization, particularly industrial chimneys, appear fairly regularly in Regnault's images.[44] The winter and summer views he made from an upper window at the factory, looking out over the busy town of Sèvres, took in the chimney of the Dardel brewery and sometimes other industrial objects, like the derricks used in construction.[45] In these images the tall brewery chimney harmonizes with the landscape, a strong vertical that echoes the narrow poplars in the same plane. Sometimes the chimney terminates delicately on the edge of the distant, misty tree line; sometimes it is elegantly centered in the frame (figs. 13 and 76). While they depict a burgeoning, modern townscape, these pictures still manage to convey a pleasing, natural atmosphere, in which elements of nature—masses of foliage, distant hills, misty light, or bright sunshine—have an equal presence alongside the man-made.

RURAL SÈVRES: DOCUMENTARY, TOPOGRAPHIC, PICTURESQUE

Soon after Regnault moved to Sèvres, he began exploring the local roads and fields, making pictures of structures, terrain, and activities that characterized the canton and the habits of its people. Rural views—made in a radius from the Manufacture that took in Bas Meudon to the south, Villeneuve d'Étang to the

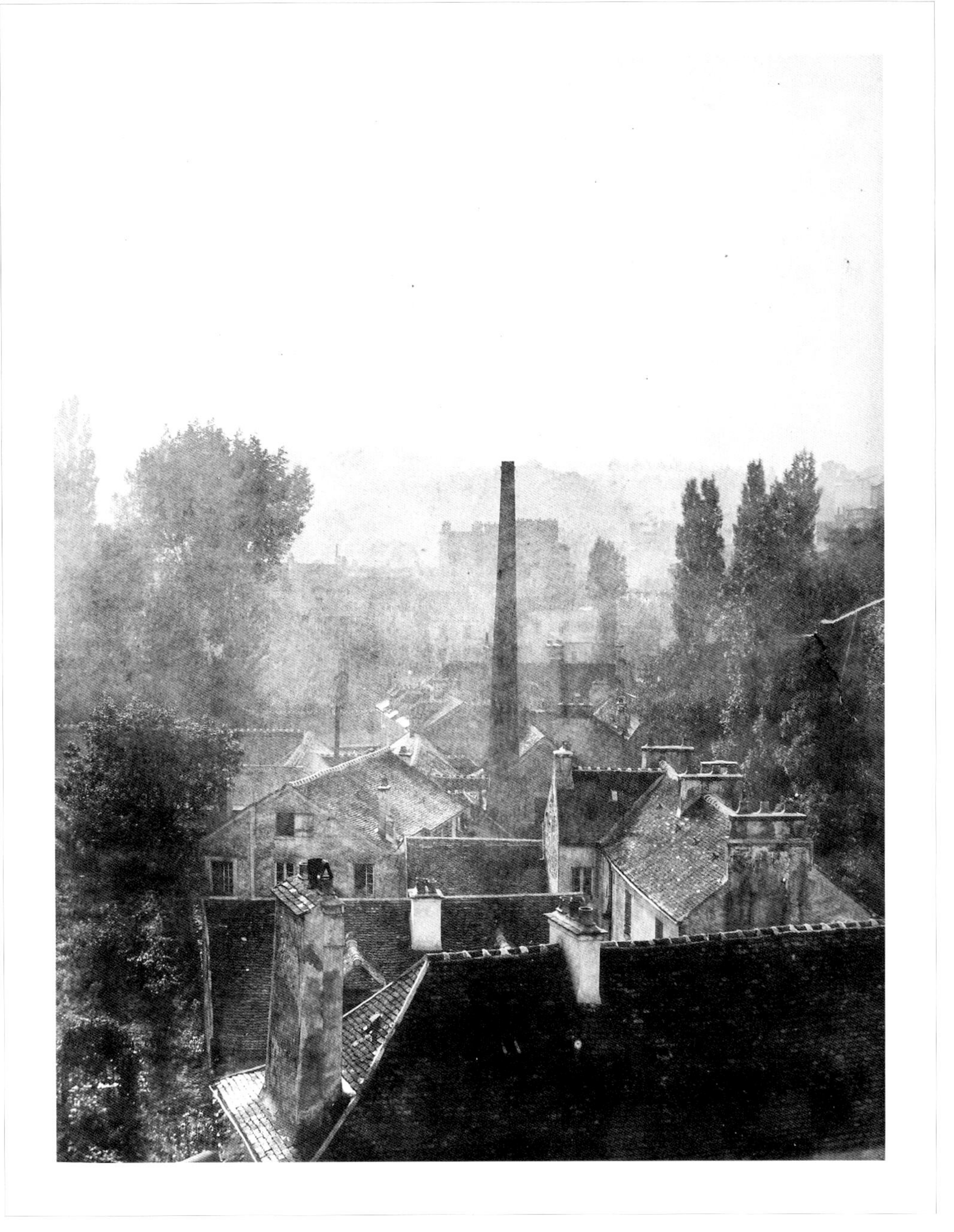

Fig. 76.

Victor Regnault, *View of Sèvres Taken from the Manufacture*, c. 1852. Salt print from paper negative, 17 x $13^{1}/_{8}$ in. (43 x 33.4 cm).
Musée d'Orsay, Paris. 1983.163 (Inv. 1979 D 26)

west, and the Parc de Saint-Cloud to the north—constitute the largest part of Regnault's work in landscape. Most are distinctly "Barbizonesque" in feeling, and it is worth noting that he was acquainted with several of these painters, particularly Corot and Troyon, who were regular visitors at the factory.[46]

Many pictures were made from a distance that emphasized topography over picturesque detail, which allowed him to show the buildings in their landscape settings, sometimes even giving a prospect of the fluvial plain stretching to the river and beyond to the suburbs of Boulogne (fig. 77). These circumspect views approach their subjects from the fields and hills, never from the road, which gives the viewer the sense of casual wandering and surreptitious discovery of the details and customs of local daily life (fig. 78). Many of them could serve equally as sociological documents and art photographs that follow the mode of unembellished realism of artists like Corot, Rousseau, and Daubigny, all of whom occasionally painted similarly modest farms from this detached middle distance. But whereas these painters frequently included some anecdotal bit of human activity, Regnault's photographs are almost always unpeopled; man's presence is implied only by his possessions and fields of labor. The photographer usually preferred to place his camera on a gentle hill overlooking some houses or a farm, where he could take in a host of quotidian minutiae: vineyards and their stakes, piles of brick, stone fences and slatted gates, hay mown and drying in the fields, logs stacked around farmyards, and laundry hung out to dry. However, the pastoral peace and quiet that reigns in these images is partly sleight-of-hand; one would never guess that the Paris/Saint-Germain railroad line (inaugurated in 1836) lies just out of view of several of these images.

One frequent theme among the rural views is the country road or path, to which Regnault returned at least eight times, usually in late fall or early spring when trees were bare (fig. 79). It was a subject much loved by landscape painters in the northern style, such as Jacob van Ruisdael and Meindert Hobbema, John Constable, or closer to home, Corot, Troyon, or almost any of the followers of Barbizon, who eagerly adapted the motif. In several photographs of these simple country lanes, Regnault used the road to create a diagonal leading to a vanishing point somewhere in the lower-third of the picture. Low horizons were common in seventeenth-century Dutch landscapes, where they provided a great stage for the drama of clouds and weather effects and invoked the notion of God's domain in heaven. However, the calotype's uneven spectral sensitivity meant it could not render earth and sky in the same exposure, so Regnault used the low horizon for other ends. In summer, it allowed him to emphasize the contour of the blank sky, shaped by masses of foliage, as in the summer view of the road to Bruyères (fig. 80), where the serpentine shape of the sky is mirrored by the road leading to the horizon. In winter views, Regnault exploited the blank sky as a flat backdrop for the graphic tracings of bare trunks, limbs,

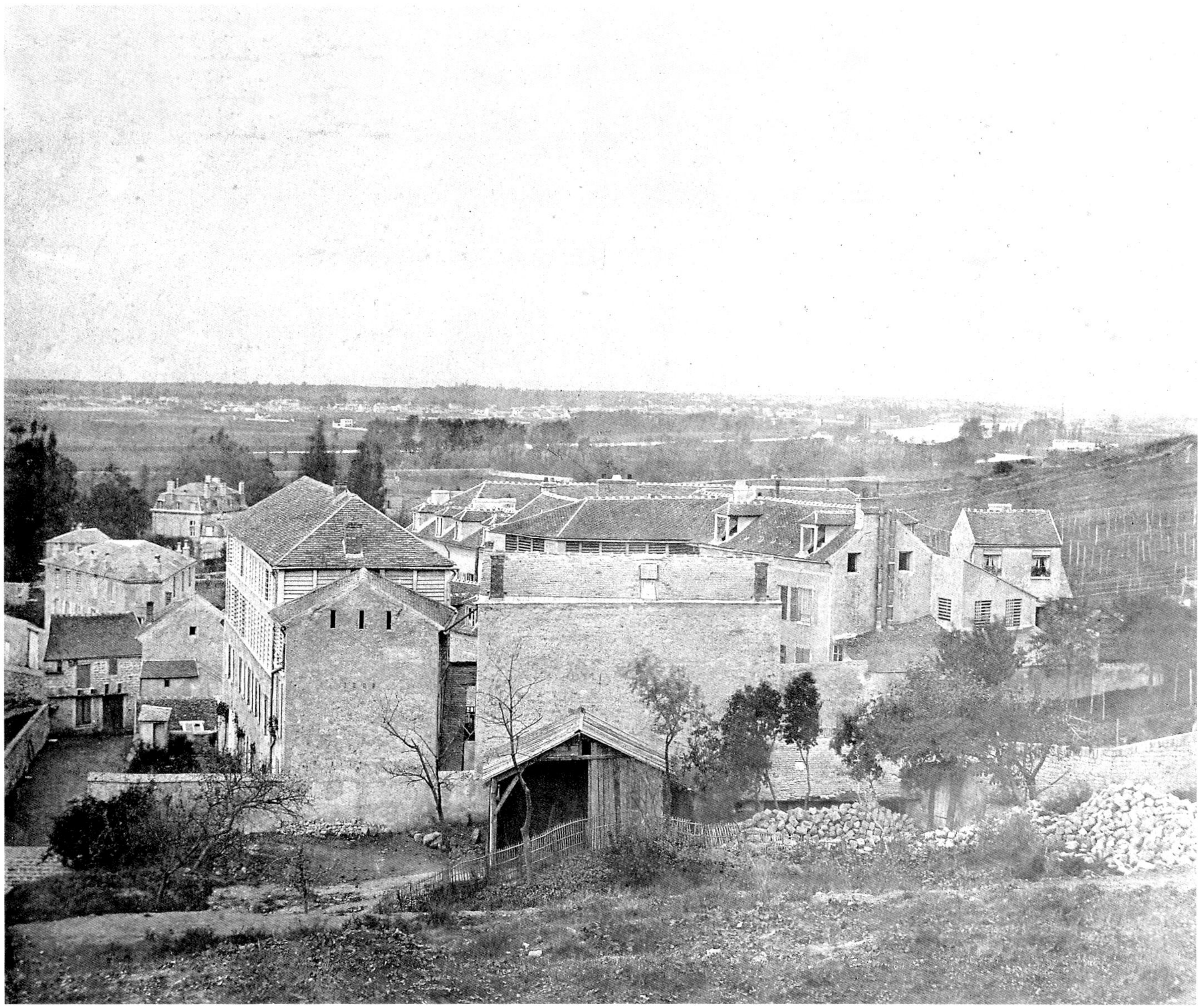

Fig. 77.

Victor Regnault, *Sèvres and Its Environs*, c. 1852. Salt print from paper negative, $14\frac{1}{8} \times 17\frac{3}{8}$ in. (36 x 44 cm).

Musée d'Orsay, Paris. 1983.172 (Inv. 1979 D 7)

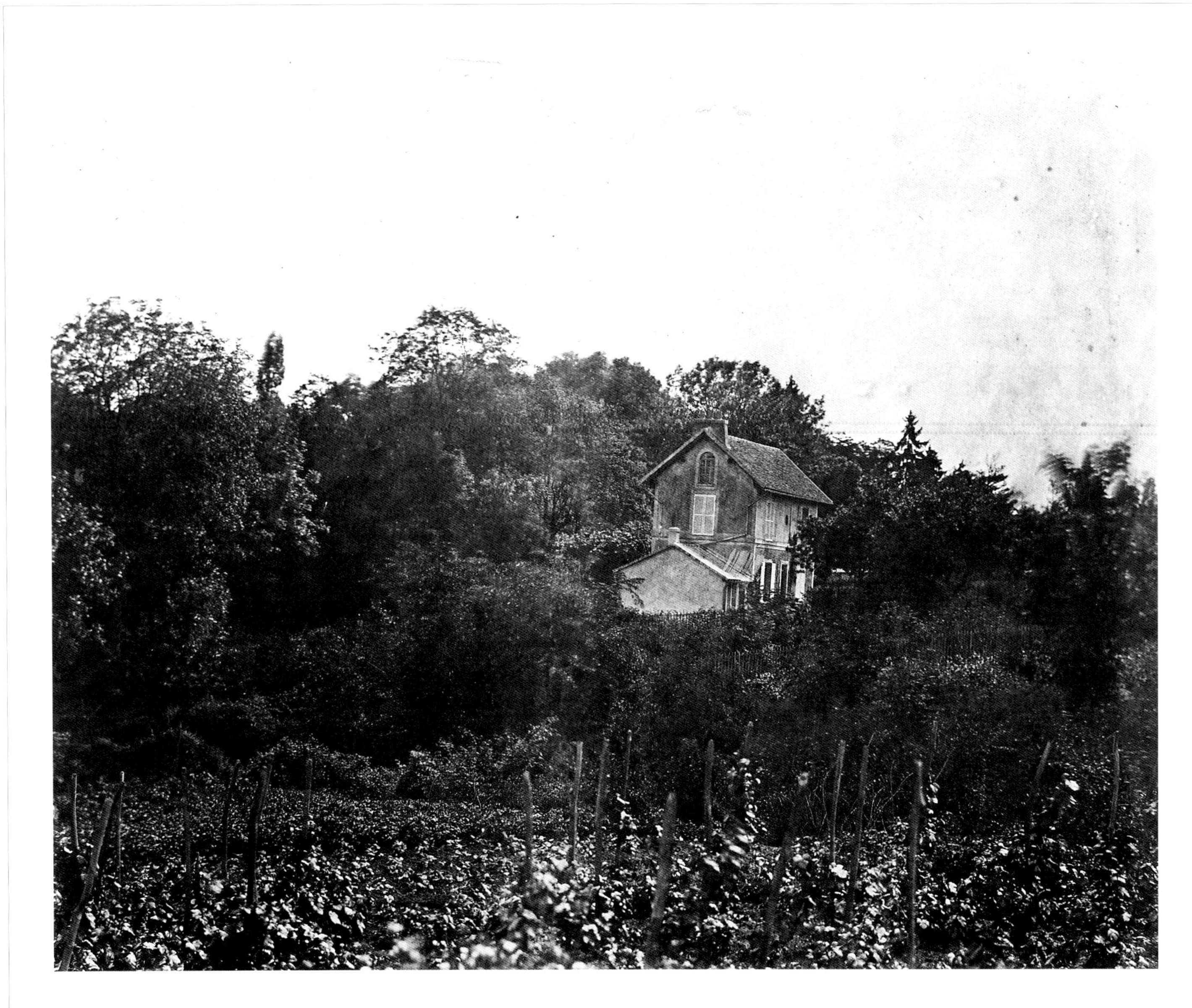

Fig. 78.

Victor Regnault, *Fields and Woods near Sèvres, the Slope Descending from Sèvres to Bellevue*, c. 1852. Salt print from paper negative, 13 5/8 x 17 in. (34.6 x 43.2 cm). Musée d'Orsay, Paris. 1983.187

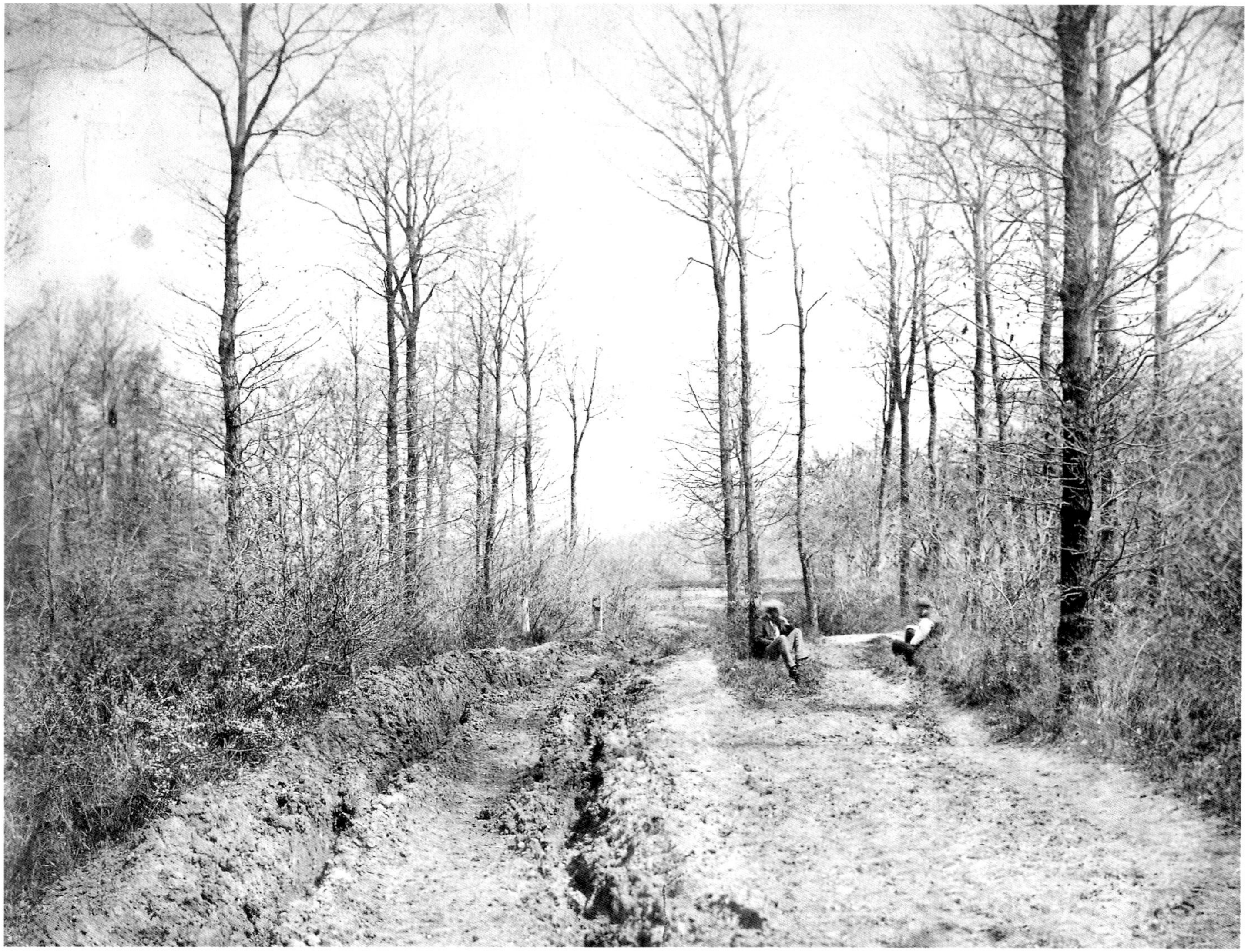

Fig. 79.

Victor Regnault, *Landscape in the Woods of Saint-Cloud*, c. 1853. Albumen print from paper negative, $12^{3}/_{4}$ x 17 in. (32.2 x 43.4 cm). National Gallery of Canada, Ottawa. P67:100 AJ

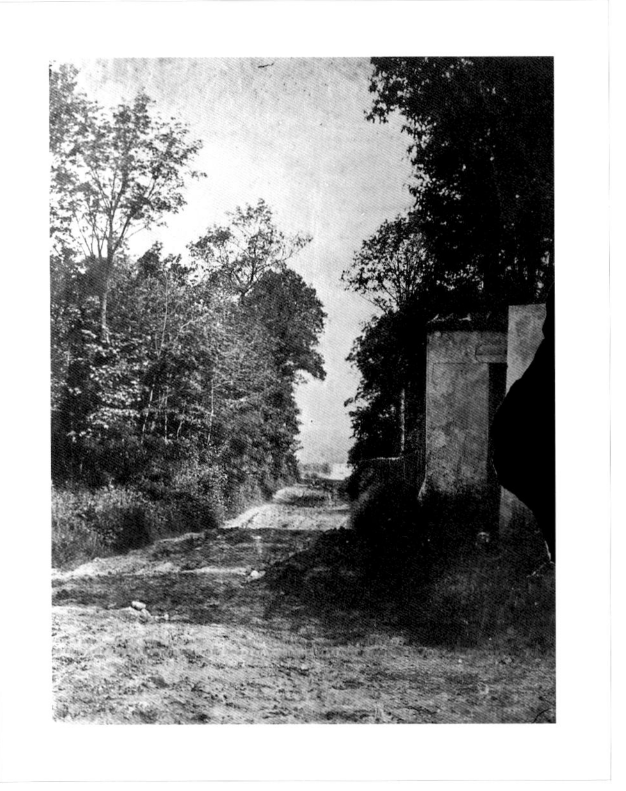

Fig. 80.
Victor Regnault, *Route de Bruyères*, c. 1852. Salt print from paper negative, 14 x 17 3/4 in. (35.5 x 45 cm).
Ville de Sèvres Archives. 5 Fi-1-2248

and branches (fig. 81). Even though natural skies were not possible, these landscapes still benefited from the calotype's typical mottled appearance in overexposed areas, which gave skies substance and weight.

He sometimes left the road for studies of trees, another subject dear to the Barbizon painters. Regnault sent several of this series to his friend Sir John Herschel in 1851, which he downplayed as "defective positive prints, already old." These are not usually like the heroic "portraits" of the country's great oaks and chestnuts by Le Gray. Rather than select a single, ancient tree, Regnault usually photographed clusters of trees in which the emphasis is on the effect of sunlight breaking through the forest, illuminating the varied textures of bark, branch, and leaf (fig. 74). Several of these appeared in Blanquart-Evrard's *Études Photographiques* (1853); like other prints in that edition, they made ideal artist's models, with their strong contrasts and sharp rendering of the overwhelming detail of the landscape setting.

Regnault made most of his landscapes around farms and open country, but he also made some pictures in the imperial Parc de Saint-Cloud, including several views of the seventeenth-century formal gardens designed by André Le Nôtre. The pictures of the gardens are long views that convey the

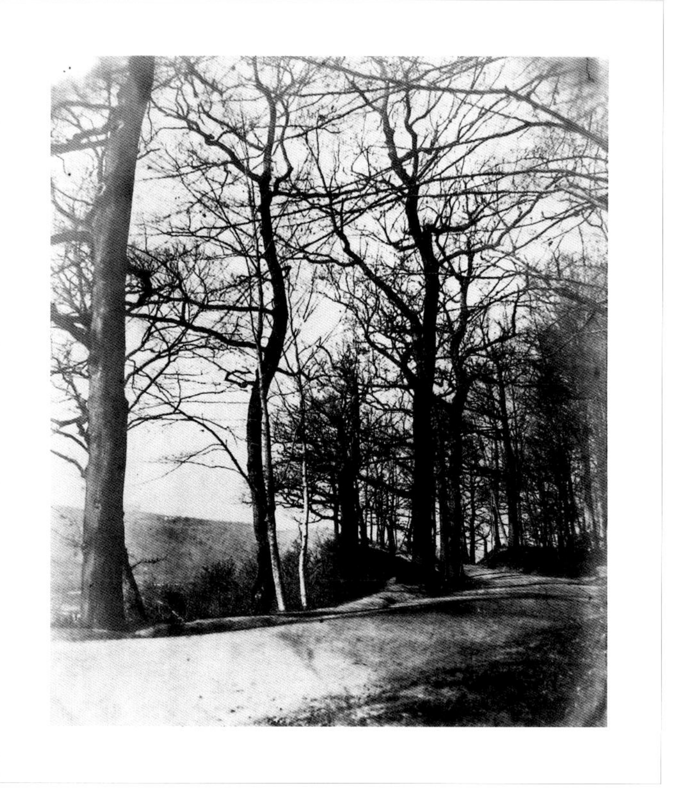

Fig. 81.
Victor Regnault, *Road in the Woods near Sèvres*, from *Études Photographiques* (Lille: Blanquart-Evrard, 1853). Salt print from paper negative, 10 x $8^1/_2$ in. (25.5 x 21.5 cm). National Gallery of Canada, Ottawa

sweeping prospects offered to the visitor walking through the park. The spatial experience of the visitor could be only roughly suggested in the two-dimensional photograph, but with its controlled perspective, the camera could adeptly render the vistas and fanciful tricks of scale and sightline that pivoted upon specific fixed points of view. Le Nôtre designed the gardens at Saint-Cloud as a complex tour de force, manipulating sightlines and vistas among plantings, parterres, fountains, and walkways in the uneven terrain through geometry and fixed-point perspective.[47] However, with its symmetries and stylization, the gardens did not offer the irregular qualities Regnault customarily sought, and his park views tend towards generalized, topographic description. On the open country roads, when he rendered the trees carving dramatically into the skies, he conveyed a sense of the strange, fortuitous design of nature; in his views of the allées of the Parc de Saint-Cloud, the effect is lessened by the uniformity of the trees.

Regnault may have photographed in the park with Louis Robert, but unlike his colleague, Regnault did not use individual pieces of statuary or architecture as a focal point.[48] One view, looking diagonally across the orangerie, was made from an elevated prospect that shows the orangerie and the

Avenue des Plate-bandes that stretches beyond it (fig. 82). From this distance, the regimented placement of the sculptures emphasizes the layout of the terraces without the sculpture acting as subject itself. Focusing on the allées of the park, Regnault could count on three things he often sought in landscapes: the open view to the horizon (which allowed him to exploit atmospheric perspective), the plunging recession of space, and great wedges of sky. The lanes of chestnut trees, however, were a problem in summer: their dense, uniformly green canopies made it difficult to render the foliage with any modulation in tonal value. In one of the views of the orangerie, lacking an adequately open exposure for highlights and shadows, Regnault adroitly added extensive highlights on individual leaves in ink on the paper negative (fig. 83). This was not the only time he adjusted the lights and darks of the negative by drawing, painting, or scraping, but it was not his usual practice.

Writing in 1792 (translated to French, 1799), William Gilpin had prescribed the components of a picturesque landscape: "Turn the lawn into a broken ground, plant rugged oaks instead of flowering shrubs: break the edges of the walk: give it the rudeness of a road: mark it with wheeltracks; and scatter a few stones, and brushwood, in a word, instead of making the whole smooth, make it rough, and you also make it picturesque."[49] This was the concept of the picturesque that informed Paul Périer's appreciation for photographs of dilapidated bridges, farmyards, rutted lanes, and "all the beauties of things that would seem to be ugly," just as it lay behind Regnault's analogous taste in subject matter: deserted lanes overgrown with brush, gnarled trees, and crumbling garden walls.[50] Subjects like these lent themselves particularly well to depiction by a light-based medium, for as Gilpin had also noted, in addition to creating a more interesting contour or profile, the rough object allowed greater play in the effects of light and shade. Gilpin's theory also called for variety and irregularity in the techniques of sketching and painting, a prescription that undoubtedly resonates in the choice of calotype by certain photographers who appreciated the process for its roughness and imperfection.[51]

The qualities of the photographic picturesque were abundantly showcased in images referred to here as "garden corners." The sub-genre of the garden corner—essentially a "found" still life arranged in an outdoor setting—was very popular with calotype photographers like Talbot, Bayard, and others (figs. 84 and 85), and it has recently attracted the interest of historians seeking to unpack the connoted meanings behind these seemingly simple arrangements of everyday objects.

Mike Weaver and Michel Frizot have each objected to the summary assessment of these compositions as merely flirtations with the picturesque.[52] Writing about Talbot, Weaver argues that to dismiss these images as simple examples of picturesque description is to miss the religious and philosophical meaning that, while subtle or even hidden, was intended to be understood by those who shared

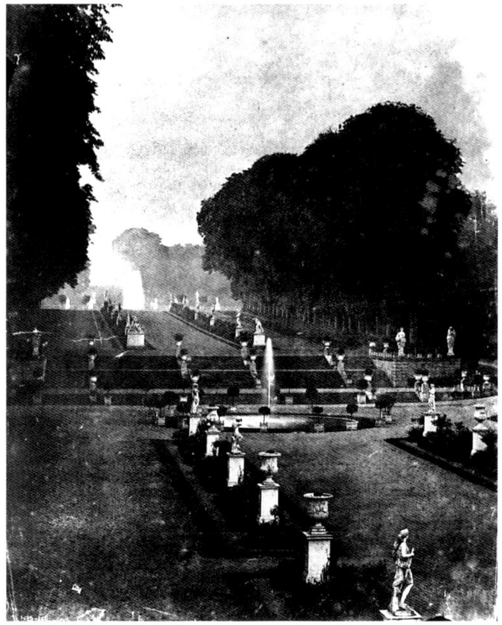

Fig. 82.

Victor Regnault, *Parc de Saint Cloud, Orangerie and the Avenue des Plate-bandes*, c. 1852. Modern print from paper negative, 16 7/8 x 13 7/8 in. (43 x 35.4 cm). Société Française de Photographie, Paris. 473.173

Talbot's cultural literacy—a convincing argument in view of Talbot's semiotic preoccupations as a passionate philologist.[53] Frizot agrees that the isolated depiction of certain everyday objects in these compositions—ladders, carts, rakes—represents "something more significant than a simple thematic picturesqueness": what he calls a "language event," a kind of naming exercise.[54] Like the pictographs in a child's alphabet primer, such pictures show the first generation of photographers using the new medium "as a method of reading and deciphering the world."[55]

However they may be been read as moral epigrams or elementary acts of photographic speech, garden corner images were in fact exercises in the picturesque idiom. While suggestively conveying human and historical presence through the arrangement of significant objects and their settings, they allowed photographers to satisfy the slow exposure requirements of the calotype and test their abilities to arrange a composition, according to received ideas of aesthetics—in this case, Gilpin's prescribed rusticity that demanded variations in form, texture, and outline. In another sense, Frizot is correct in

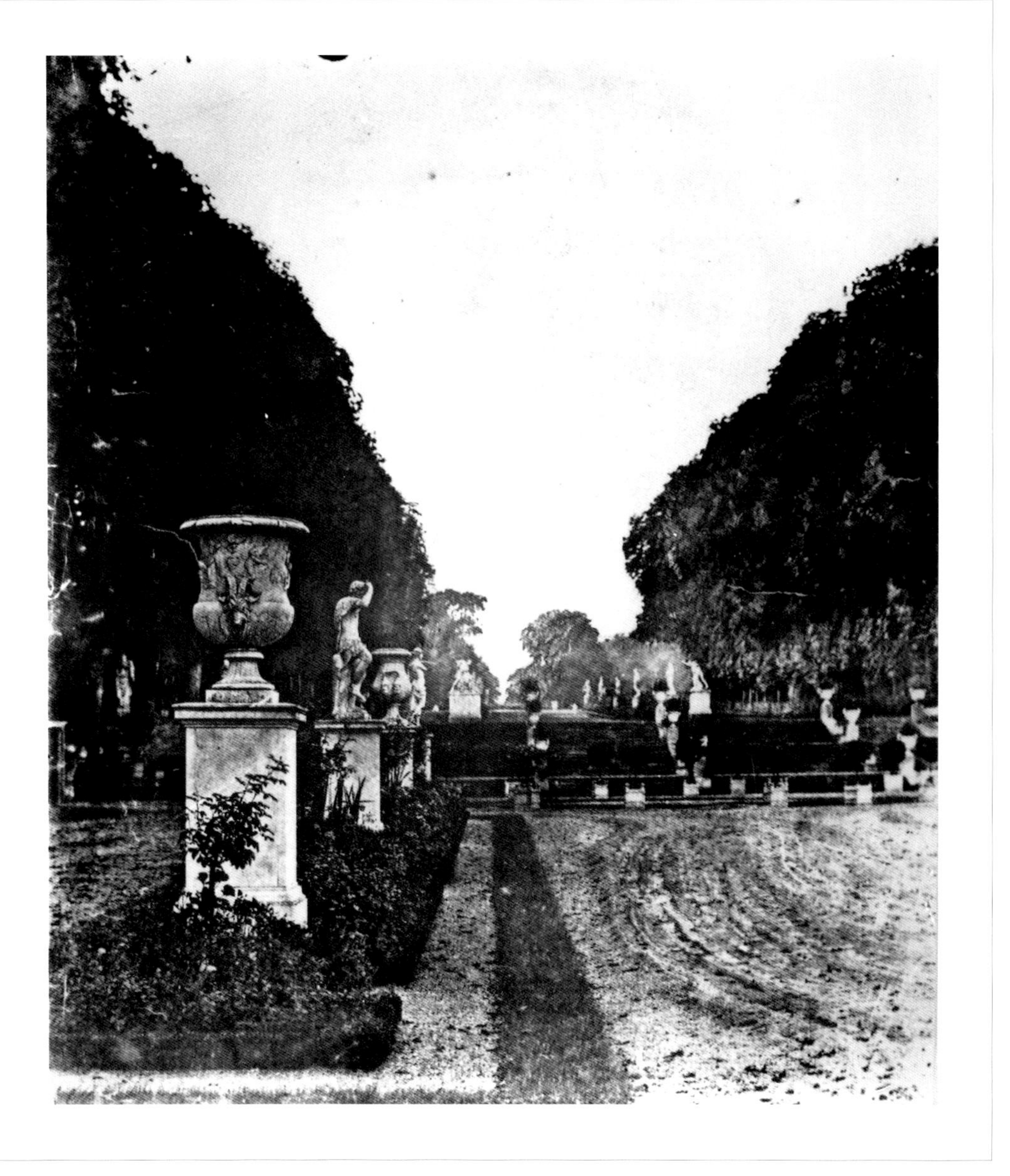

Fig. 83.

Victor Regnault, *Parc de Saint Cloud, The Orangerie*, c. 1852. Modern print from paper negative, 16 x 14 1/8 in. (40.7 x 35.8 cm).

Société Française de Photographie, Paris. 473.172

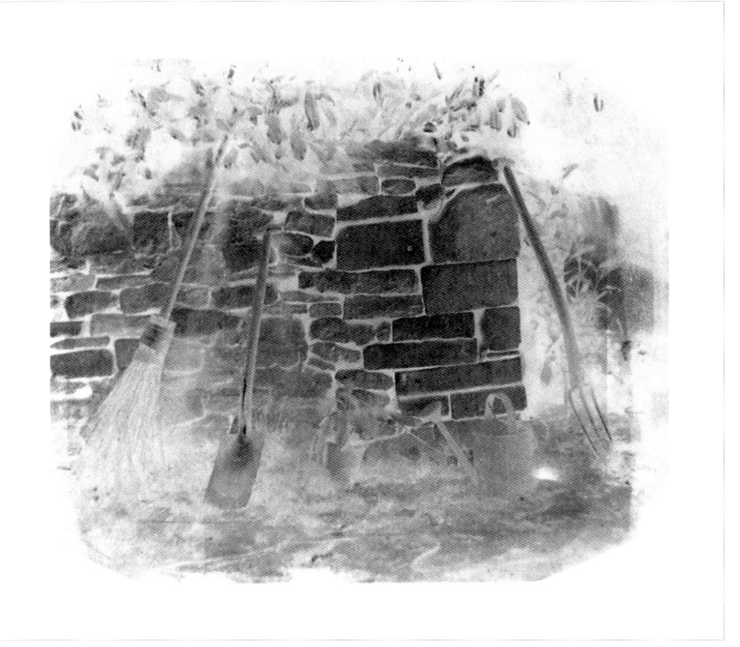

Fig. 84.
William Henry Fox Talbot (British, 1800–1877), *"Wall in Melon Ground"—at Lacock Abbey*, 1840. Paper negative, $6^{3}/_{4}$ x $8^{3}/_{8}$ in. (17.2 x 21.2 cm). The J. Paul Getty Museum, Los Angeles. 84.xm.260.6

identifying their pictographic and self-instructive nature, in that these photographs of rustic objects were sometimes made as artists' models.

Two of Regnault's garden corner pieces appear in Blanquart-Evrard's edition *Études Photographiques*, which was advertised to the public as a portfolio of models for artists' self-instruction.[56] One of these is a still life of late-summer vegetables arranged on an outdoor table (fig. 86). Like all garden corner images, this picture combines landscape with the "found" still life to create an effect of charming surprise, as if the viewer has stumbled upon a homely scene whose unexpected loveliness could be recognized only by the most sensitive eye. As such it immediately posits a knowing connection with an elite viewer. Cabbage, apples, squash, carrots, and potatoes are piled on a makeshift table; a melon has been sliced open to show the flesh of the fruit. A shovel and wicker basket on the ground implies the nearby presence of the gardener and an earthenware jug and shallow kettle stand in for the cook. The setting—the back of a kitchen garden, where a high stone wall barely holds back the beautiful, relentless growth of wild grasses and ivy—poses a contrast between cultivation and the wilder surrounding nature.

The pleasures of country life are also celebrated in *The Ladder* (fig. 87), which was photographed on the grounds of the Manufacture de Sèvres in a quiet corner between the stable and the

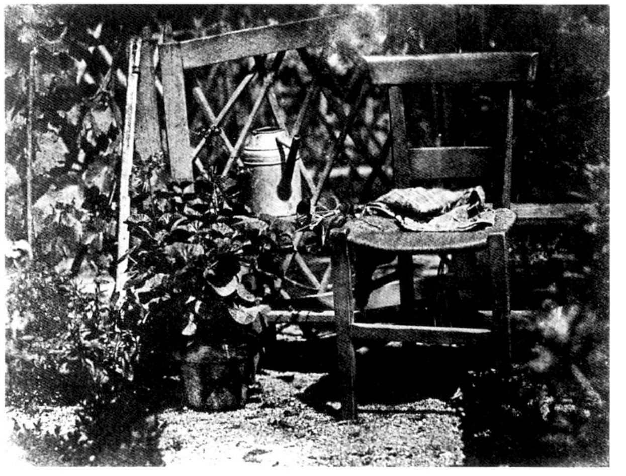

Fig. 85.
Hippolyte Bayard (French, 1801–1887), *Chair in a Garden*, 1842–52. Modern print from paper negative, 6⁵/₈ x 9 in. (17 x 22.8 cm). The International Museum of Photography and Film at the George Eastman House, Rochester, N.Y. 81:0962:4

porter's lodge. The precise vertical division of the picture into two perfect halves of shadow and light imposes order upon the piquant disarray of the scene. Humble objects of rustic labor lean or hang upon the bright, rough plaster wall of the cottage: a handmade ladder, a wicker basket, a fowl cage, some cask bands, a workman's *sabot*. A vine is trained along the corner of the building and the silhouetted leaves of an unseen tree dip down into the picture space. The paper surface of the calotype negative renders these things in all their pleasing, varied texture; their signification as objects of use adds a layer of sentimental content to the visual pleasure.

Interestingly, *The Ladder*'s motif—simple garden tools "abandoned" in a tranquil setting—is very like the painted vignettes on some of Sèvres's eighteenth-century wares, which Regnault happened to be studying at the time (fig. 88), and it also speaks of Regnault's relationship to the place.[57] He was new to country living when he made this picture, and the lush, sometimes precious views he made that first season suggest he reveled in the change of scenery from city to country. The sunny, peaceful atmosphere of *The Ladder* speaks in evangelical tones for the simple rustic life. Nature is represented as self-renewing, and through the tools of husbandry, man is implied as the contented cultivator of this nature. But Regnault could afford this romantic view, for although it appeared he was going back to a

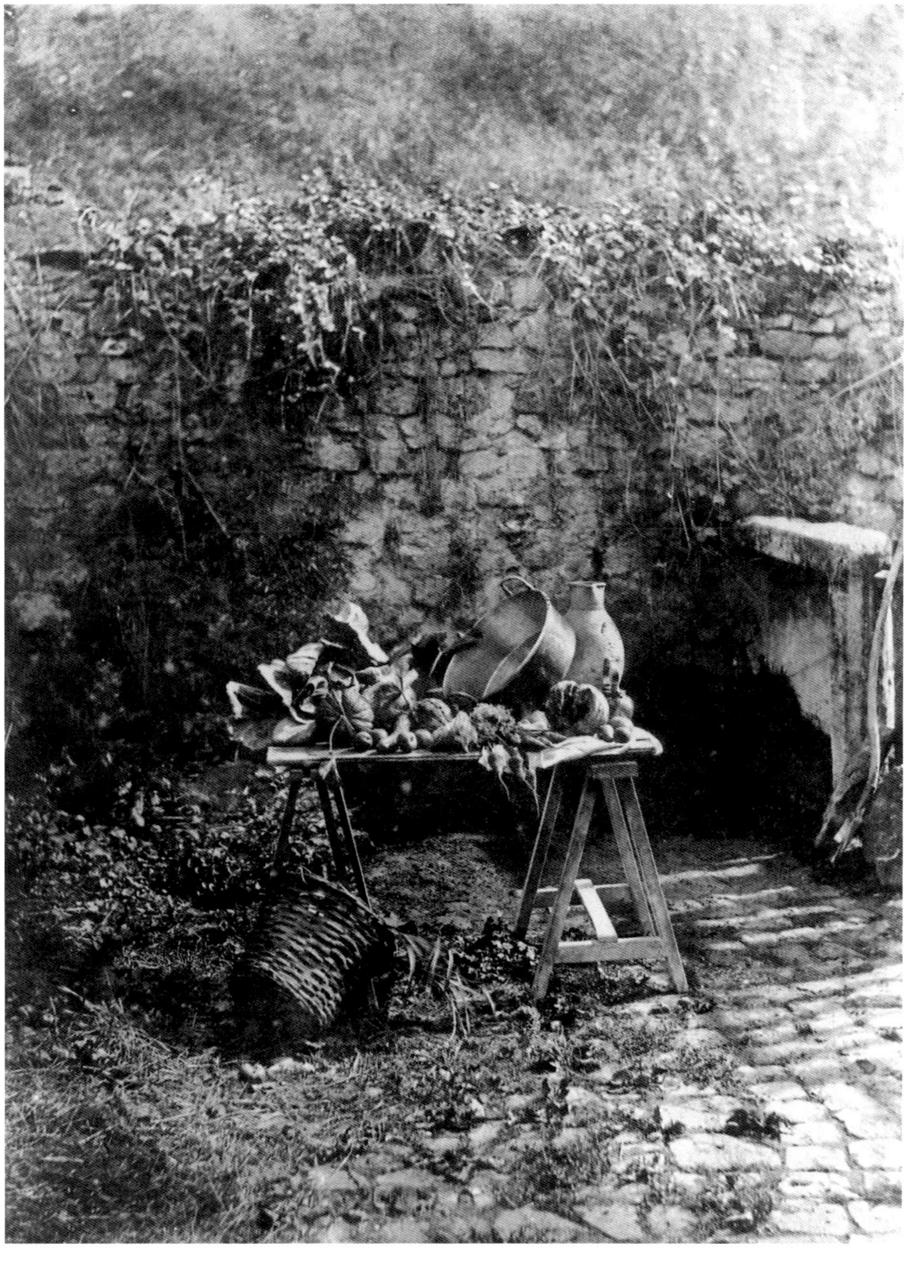

Fig. 86.

Victor Regnault, *Still Life with Vegetables*, from *Études Photographiques* (Lille: Blanquart-Evrard, 1853). Albumenized salt print from paper negative, 8 1/2 x 6 3/8 in. (21.5 x 16.2 cm). The Art Museum, Princeton University. Museum Purchase, anonymous gift, 1996-74

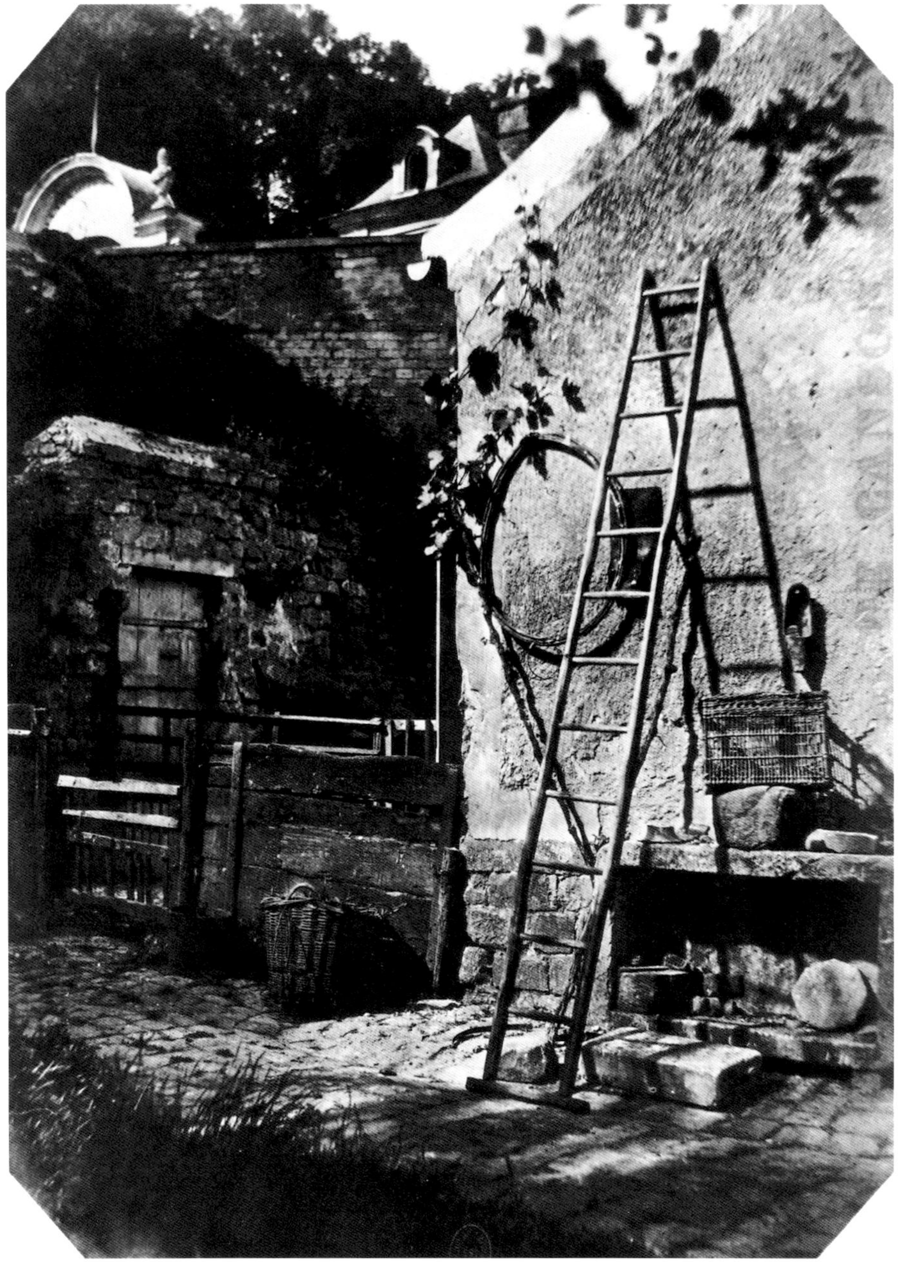

Fig. 87.

Victor Regnault, *The Ladder*, from *Études Photographiques* (Lille: Blanquart-Evrard, 1853). Salt print from paper negative, $11^{1}/_{8}$ x $8^{1}/_{8}$ in. (28.3 x 20.7 cm). Bibliothèque Nationale de France, Paris

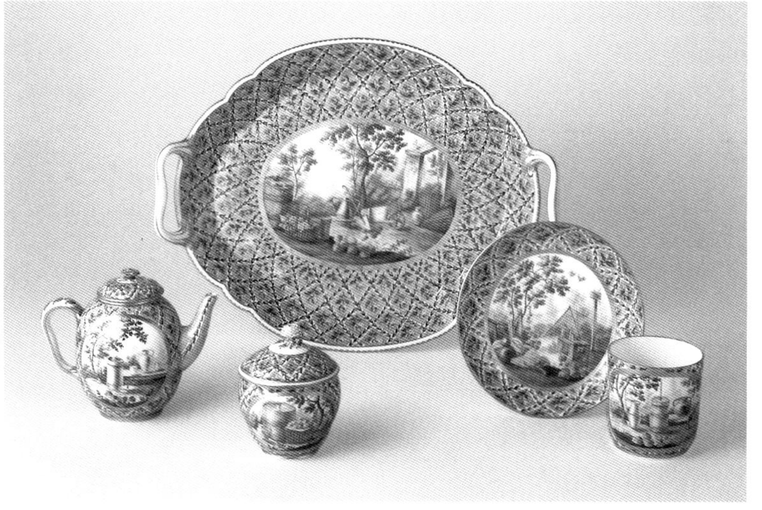

Fig. 88.

Cabaret or Solitaire with Scattered Design of Roses. Attributed to the painter Vieillard, Sèvres soft paste porcelain, 1767–72. Teapot: height 4 3/8 in. (11 cm); sugar bowl: height 3 1/2 in. (9 cm); *Calabre* cup: diameter 2 5/8 in. (6.8 cm); saucer: diameter 5 1/2 in. (14 cm); tray with handles: length 12 7/8 in. (32.8 cm). Musée Nationale de Ceramique, Sèvres. MNC 25,627 1-4

more down-to-earth existence in exchanging the artifice of academe for a life among the working people on the edge of the provinces, his move to Sèvres constituted a promotion in class. There he became the director of a factory with the population of a large village. And while his new post came with perquisites like a small orchard and large personal garden on the grounds, the factory also provided him with a gardener. It is clearly not Regnault's *sabot* that hangs emblematically on the wall.

Given Regnault's personal work ethic, it makes sense that he tended to honor the idea of work in his pictures, displaying an attitude toward labor that is frankly admiring, if somewhat naive about the struggles of rural life. The few pictures he made of thatched cottages, barns, and sheds carry on the manner of Constant Troyon and Jules Dupré in their portrayal of the quaint hardiness of peasant life and repeat the same sense of optimism and security seen in *The Ladder*. Criticizing the English taste for the picturesque in the mid-1850s, John Ruskin had argued that it was heartless to delight in the shabby appearance of huts and cottages while their inhabitants lack the most basic comforts of home.[58]

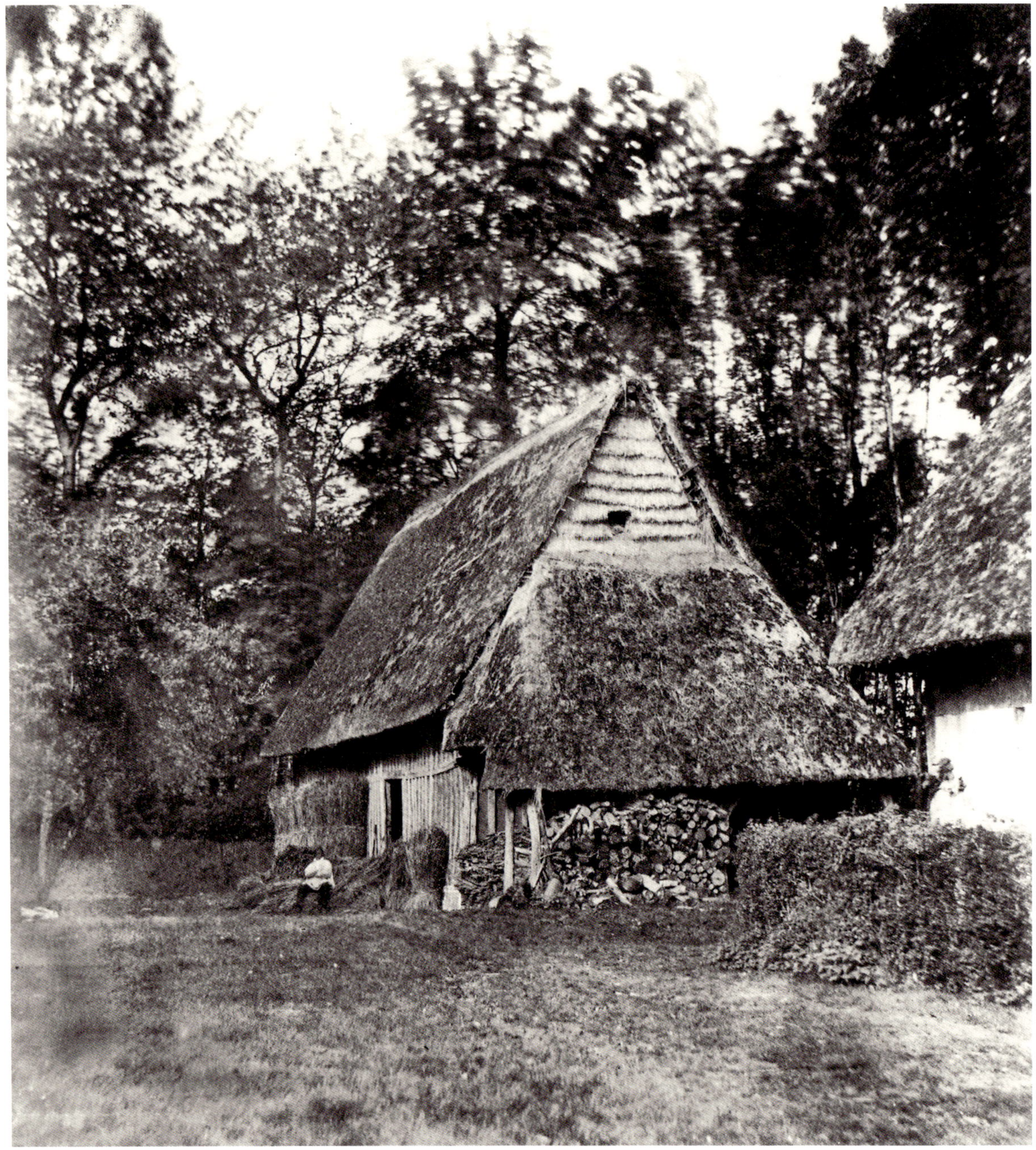

Fig. 89.

Victor Regnault, *Thatched Barn*, c. 1852. Salt print from paper negative, $8^7/_8$ x $8^1/_8$ in. (22.5 x 20.8 cm). The Royal Society, London. MS. 784.18

Yet as one would expect of someone truly enamored of these rustic traditions, there is no hint in Regnault's work of any trouble in paradise, such as the crisis of rural depopulation so acute at that time, nor is anything squalid or mean depicted, like the kinds of ancient, patched, and tumble-down peasant dwellings one finds in pictures by Henri Le Secq, Victor Prévost, or the *cahiers* (notebooks) attributed to Blanquart-Evrard.[59] On the contrary, Regnault's peasants are unmistakably prosperous, with farms that consist of numerous well-kept (if old-fashioned) buildings. In a picture of a thatched barn built at the edge of a wood (fig. 89), the structure initially looks small—it might be mistaken for a cottage—but once we notice the peasant seated at the door, the building assumes the scale of a country church. With his thatch in good repair, several cords of wood already cut and stacked for the winter, and hay stored in bundles against the outer walls of the enormous barn, this industrious farmer is the very image of rural prosperity, dwarfed by the fruits of his labor.

LIGHT AND WATER

When Regnault sent his tree studies to Herschel in 1851, he mentioned another subject of his work in photography: the study of light itself. At the same time that he referred to these pictures in the language of art, calling them "ébauches" and "études," he also described them in scientific fashion as a technical problem: "I was very busy during the last vacation that I passed in the country in researching the mode of preparation most suited to the production of landscapes, in conserving the harmony of tone and atmospheric perspective that I find lacking in the prints of our best photographers. I don't flatter myself that I have succeeded; however, I believe I have made a few steps down that path. It's on this account that I regret not being able to send you some prints of my latest tree studies."[60]

A student of optics since his days at the École Polytechnique, Regnault understood light at the highest levels explored by leading scientists like Augustin Fresnel, Sir Charles Wheatstone, J.-B. Biot, and Herschel himself.[61] In addition to his scientific understanding, he also had an artist's command (conceptually and manually) of the way light and shadow describe three-dimensional forms. An ink-wash study of the fall of light upon a Doric column—from his drawing class at the Polytechnique—shows Regnault's drafting skill and visual grasp of the workings of light as it strikes curved, flat, or angled surfaces (fig. 90). Putting his scientific understanding of light and experimental method in the service of the aesthetic aims he and his colleagues held for photography, he attempted to create a photographic method that could achieve the "harmony of tone and atmospheric perspective" still found only in the work of painters. He came closest to this goal in the slightly later series of landscapes he made along the banks of the Seine, where a luminous atmosphere was naturally enhanced by light captured in vapor from the river.

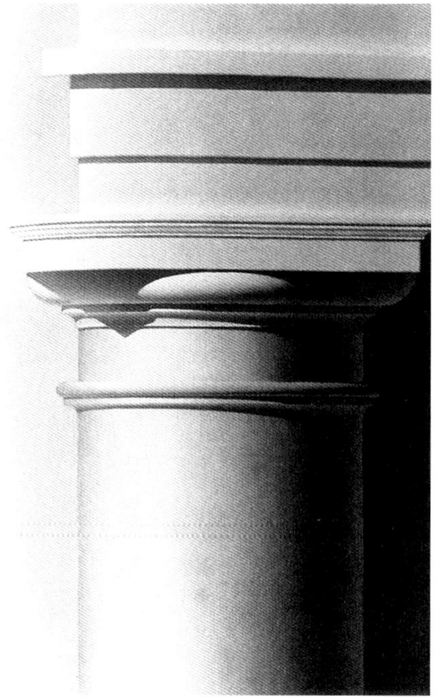

Fig. 90.
Victor Regnault, *Chiaroscuro Study*, 1832. Graphite and ink wash on paper, dimensions unknown. Institut de France, Paris. IF 2823

Regnault began photographing the river near Sèvres and neighboring Meudon soon after he moved to Sèvres. The light and scenery of the Meudon-Sèvres stretch of the river had previously attracted a number of proto-Barbizon landscapists; photographing in 1852, Regnault was revisiting the favorite haunts of these painters of some twenty, thirty, and even fifty years earlier.[62] Around 1800 Sèvres had been the home of J.-L. de Marne and J.-F. Robert, early landscapists in the area who worked at the Sèvres factory; it also hosted Paul Huet, one of the pioneers of the plein air landscape. Later, Théodore Rousseau, Corot, and Troyon (a native of Sèvres) would paint in the neighborhood, as would their friend Narcisse Diaz de la Peña, who grew up in Meudon.

Working along a stretch of the left bank between the Pont de Sèvres and Bas Meudon, Regnault made at least ten views with the large camera (approximately 14 by 20 inches). He tried both horizontal and vertical framings, and alternated facing north and south, usually choosing a point on the river's edge at Bas Meudon. In the horizontal views, the river enters the picture as a shining, oblique wedge, spreading diagonally from a lower corner toward the center of the frame, where it is separated from the sky by a narrow band of distant trees and hills (fig. 67). Spatial recession is emphasized by a progression of atmospheric veils, literally rendered as fine particulate matter by the grains of light-sensitive salts. An unusual vertical view plays upon the contrast between dark and light by sighting the river from underneath the crenellated stone arch of the Sèvres bridge (fig. 91). The technical challenge of managing large areas of deep shadow together with a clear sky and the intense light reflected on the water probably attracted Regnault to this picture, but his use of arches in other pictures suggests he also recognized them as interesting framing devices.

Reflecting his work as a whole, the pictures of the river show two motives: picturesque and documentary. In some of the photographs, nothing is permitted to impinge upon the tranquility and charm of the image. Like his views of the Sèvres countryside that carefully kept the Paris/St.-Germain railway out of sight, these views create a selective, nostalgic representation, such as a picture made just beyond the Pont de Sèvres, facing the Île Séguin where the Seine splits into two narrow streams around the island (fig. 92). Here the river is hardly recognizable as the country's major waterway; it looks more like a sleepy channel, where leisure takes precedence over labor. Regnault focused the image on a cluster of rental boats—English-style pleasure skiffs—tied loosely to a dock. The picture plays musically upon the repetition of the skiffs' graceful, attenuated shapes and their reflections on the glassy water. Forming an irregular line across the bottom of the picture, the skiffs' chance arrangement recalls the delicate disorder of Regnault's garden corners. Cast over the entire view is an ethereal, golden atmosphere, suffused with mist rising from the river.

This photograph, perhaps Regnault's most romantic effort in landscape, depicts a lush and sleepy backwater, an image of the Seine that in truth had ceased to exist more than a century ago. The docks at Sèvres were now among the busiest in the city, due in part to the fact that most of the wine shipped for Parisian consumption was stored at Sèvres.[63] Though one would never know it from this image, all kinds of craft passed through, servicing Paris or bound for other destinations: barges and transport boats of all kinds, fishing boats, and passenger steamships that offered the trip from the Louvre to Surèsnes for twenty centimes. Regnault often photographed in the early morning to catch the misty light, which also enabled him to avoid much of the activity occurring on the river. Moreover, using long exposures that precluded the photographic registration of most moving craft, Regnault was able to create a feeling of tranquility and bucolic bliss along the busiest waterway in France.[64]

Other images, while full of anecdotal interest, are not so idyllic, and in these Regnault approached the river as an active site of modern labor and commerce. Walking upriver from the Pont de Sèvres, he stopped at least twice to photograph a floating laundry, where abundant incidental details implied a narrative of life among the river's working people (fig. 93). At the lower left, the wooden structure

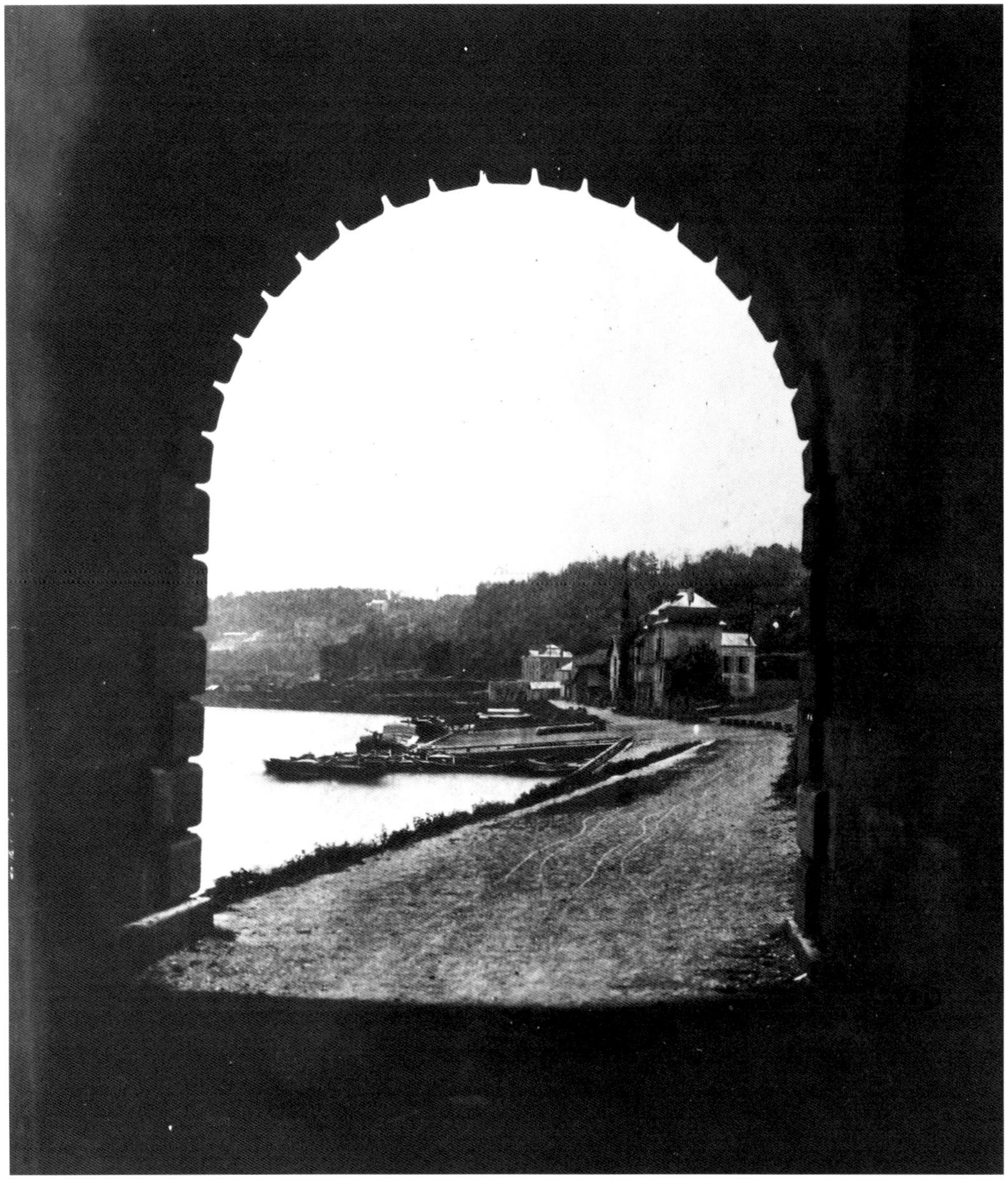

Fig. 91.

Victor Regnault, *The Left Bank from under the First Arch of the Sèvres Bridge*, 1852. Salt print from paper negative, $13^5/_8$ x $15^3/_4$ in. (34.5 x 40 cm). Ville de Sèvres Archives. 5Fi1-2205

of the laundry breaks abruptly into the corner of the frame, impeding the open view of the river. Linens hang from the clotheslines, leaving faint traces of movement. Several small boats are moored in the shallows, casting sharp reflections in the water. To the right, a large packing crate, wicker baskets, sawhorses, and other debris of the working life have been left on the bank. A dirt towpath runs parallel to the river, leading the eye past a line of houses, sheds, and warehouses, where fishing nets are stretched out to dry. Other views leave behind the picturesque entirely and show the loading and unloading of barges; their cargo, mostly barrels or lumber, sits on the muddy bank. A view of Bas Meudon, facing north, shows a blur of activity moving along a plank walkway between the bank and a small flatboat (fig. 93); a ghostly wheelbarrow, left stationary only for part of the exposure, waits at the river's edge. Regnault photographed at this sandy loading zone several times, a point of view that makes the Seine look like standing water in a wide dirt trough (fig. 95).

The views of the Seine reflect the character of Regnault's work as a whole, which resists neat interpretation and classification in its refusal to adhere consistently to either a romantic or prosaic point of view. We know that at times he actively looked for and astutely constructed images of rural splendor, while at others he did not hesitate to depict the same landscape in its transition to a semi-industrial suburb. A similar duality carries through his biography. Just when he seems to be fixed as the tough empiricist who would "banish the entire cult of the imagination" from his work, we find him putting science in the service of subjectivity. Here the *Bulletin* of the S.F.P. reported his advice on the pursuit of the ideal in photographs—in this instance, by photographically fabricating artificial moonlight:

> *Mr. President observes that in photography one can consider two different points of view: in the first case one tries to reproduce nature such as it is; in the second, one tries to obtain an effect agreeable to the eye. . . . One can also do both, and with a bit of cleverness, obtain a positive print of an agreeable effect, without dispensing with natural appearance in the least. It is thus that on a very cloudy day, by forcing the print, Mr. Regnault has been able to obtain the effects of night, of moonlight. . . . He therefore believes that with a negative that is not sufficiently developed, one can obtain an effect that will still be artistic although thoroughly different from the natural effect the camera would have furnished.*[65]

For Regnault, the landscape, too, represented the mingled virtues of functional utility and useless beauty, although in retrospect, it seems that the interpenetration of these qualities created a conflict of interest for him and others who operated as instrumental forces in French industrial development. On the one hand, he complained that the artificial life of the government functionary did not agree with his "vagabond spirit," worried about his health as a casualty of his hectic modern life of non-

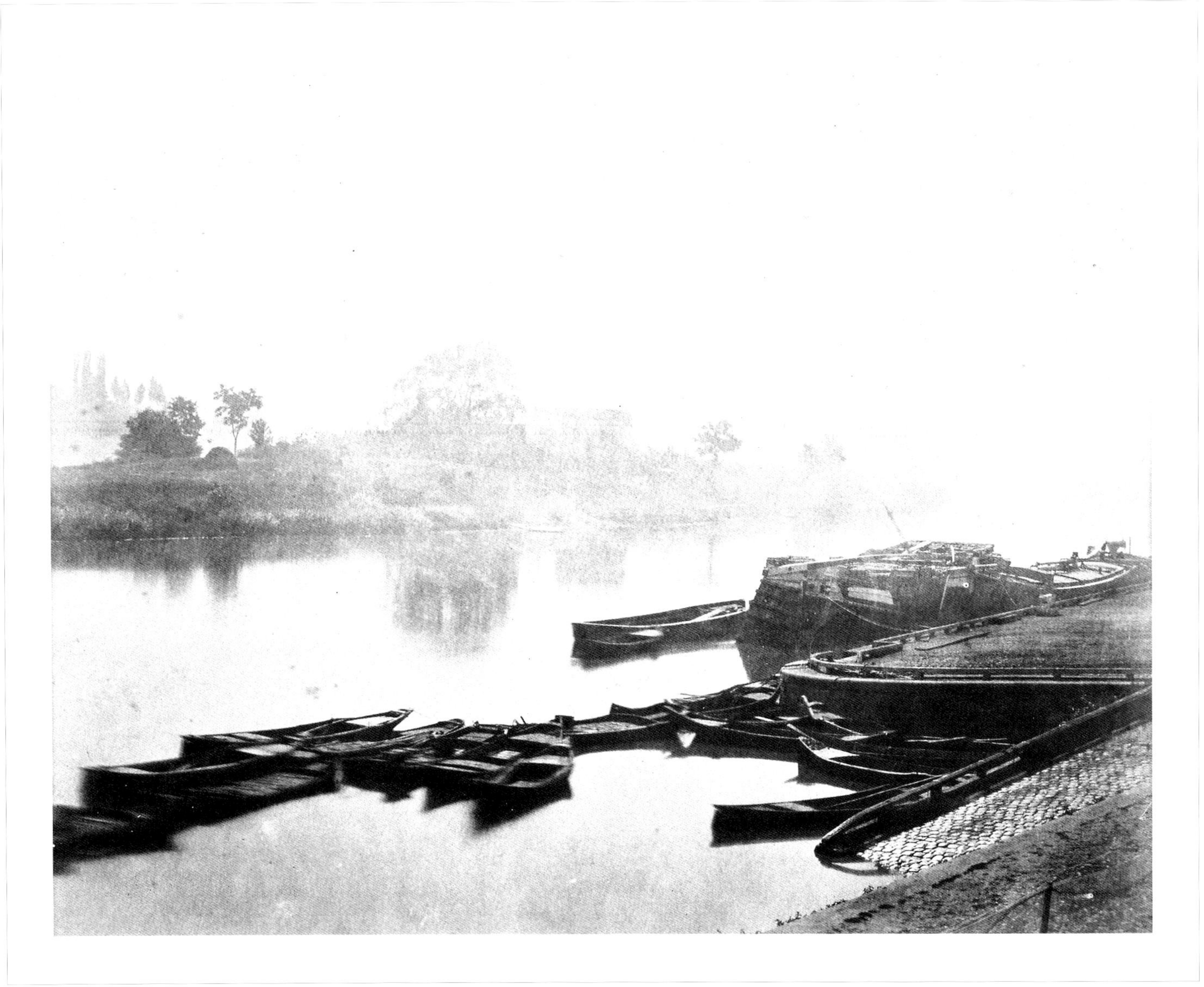

Fig. 92.

Victor Regnault, *The Seine: The Western Point of the Île Seguin*, c. 1852. Salt print from paper negative, 12 1/2 x 15 3/4 in. (31.7 x 40.4 cm). Musée d'Orsay, Paris. 1983.182

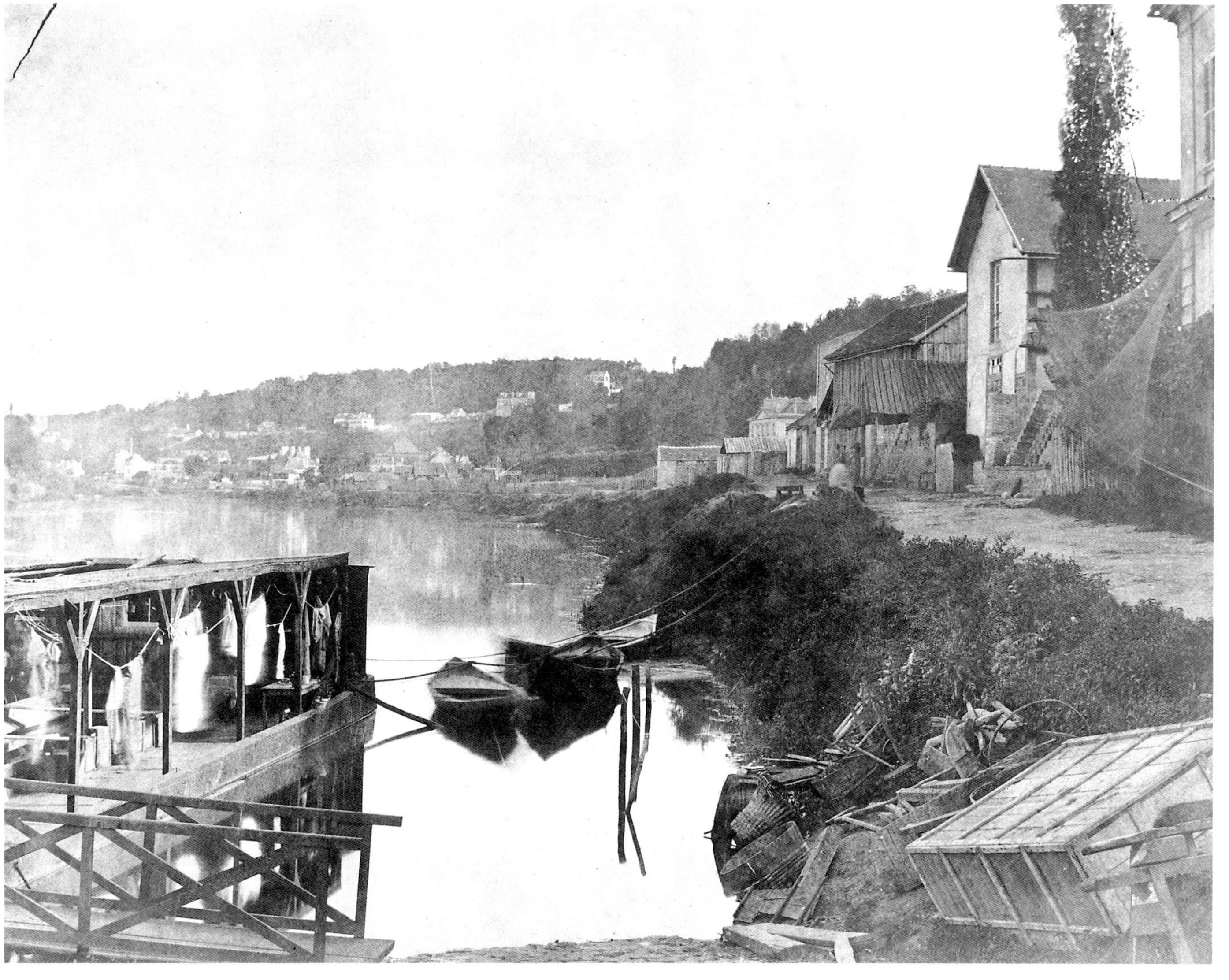

Fig. 93.

Victor Regnault, *Floating Laundry near Bas Meudon*, c. 1852. Salt print from paper negative, 13 x 16⁷/₈ in. (33 x 43 cm).

Musée d'Orsay, Paris. 1983.185

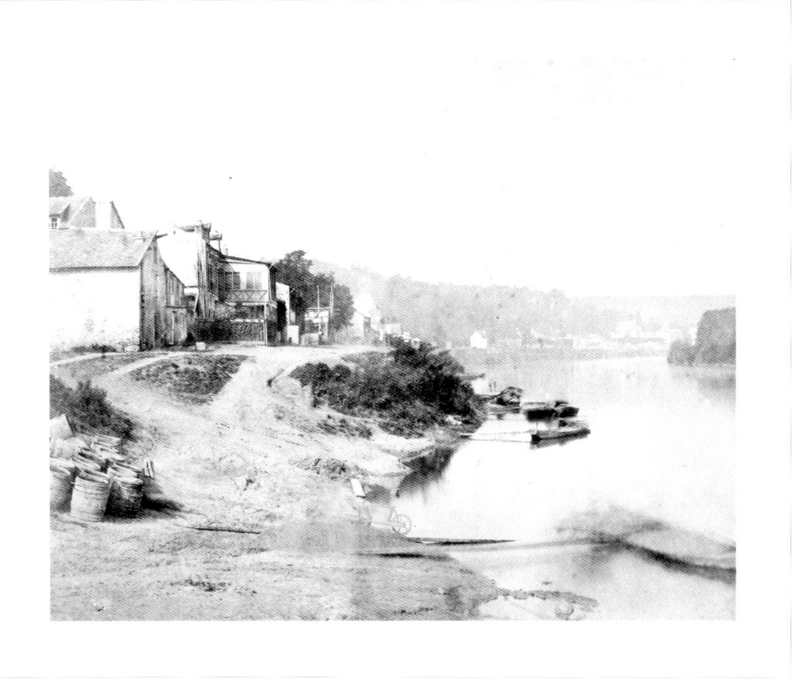

Fig. 94.
Victor Regnault, *The Left Bank between Bas Meudon and Lower Sèvres,* c. 1852. Salt print from paper negative, 13 1/2 x 17 in. (34.2 x 43.2 cm). Musée d'Orsay, Paris. 1983.170

stop responsibilities, and sought, as he said, to breathe raw sea air to "reaffirm my brain"—all of which makes him sound a lot like the alienated urban man conjured up by Périer's ruminations. Much of his photography partook of Périer's notion of a pure, restorative, rustic nature, and even ventured into that personification of Nature as fertile, flirtatious, and, naturally, feminine. Here a pair of spring and winter "portraits" comes to mind, which show an intimate, identical framing of the same tree, foliage on and foliage off, giving the subtlest hint of the eroticism or, at least, the sensuality of Nature (figs. 96 and 97).

On the other hand, Regnault seems not to have objected to modern intrusions into the landscape, and he even treated these as motifs of compositional interest, a sensibility that some have considered proto-Impressionist.[66] Yet this should not obscure the fact that much of his photography was conceived as documentary, and not expressly artistic. Nor should it be surprising that these two tendencies exist side by side, particularly with regard to landscape. Regnault's relationship to the land conjoined work and pleasure. As a mining engineer, he was trained to look at nature as a fund of material resources, full of potential for exploitation, whether in terms of timber, clay, stone, water, oil, or minerals. This training certainly did not blind him to the aesthetic qualities of the land as it met the cultured eye, and the travel notebooks he made as a student engineer in 1834 show both sensibilities comfortably side by side.[67] The pages are filled with precise pen-and-ink drawings: minute diagrams, elevations,

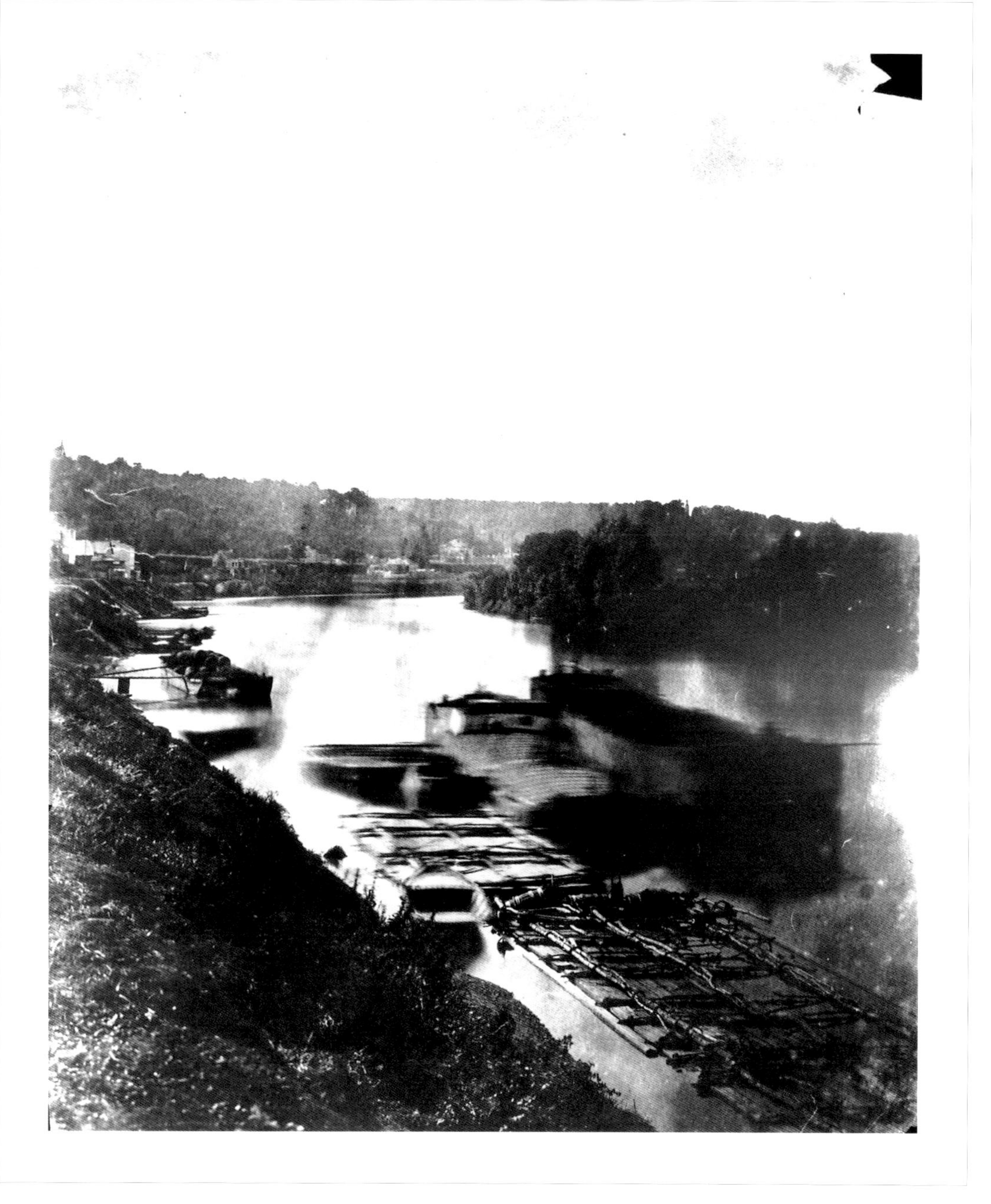

Fig. 95.
Victor Regnault, *Banks of the Seine near Bas Meudon*, c. 1852. Modern print from paper negative, 17 x 13 3/4 in. (43.1 x 35 cm).
Société Française de Photographie, Paris. 473.177

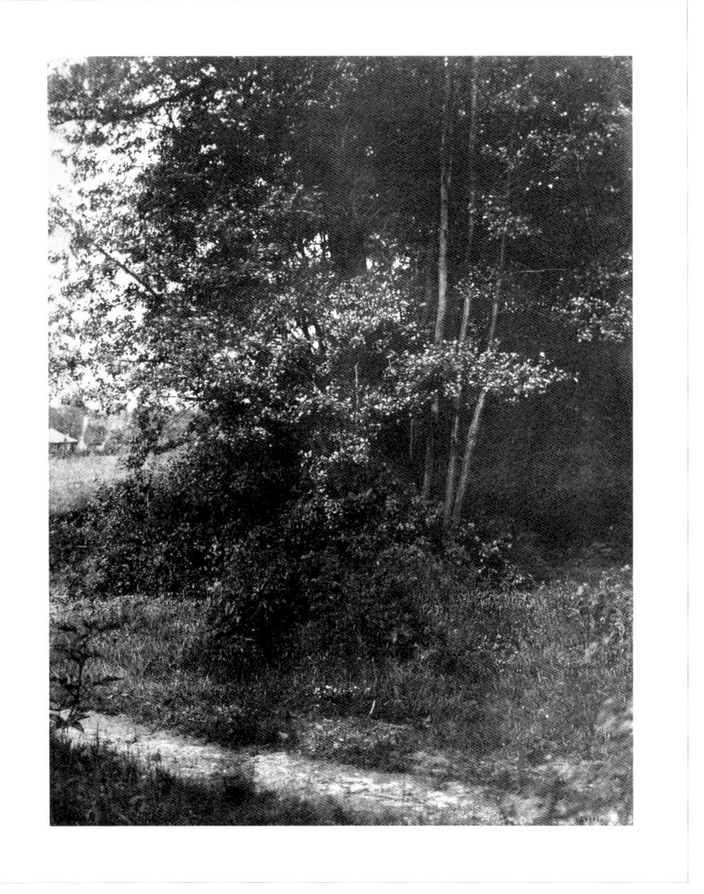

Fig. 96.
Victor Regnault, *Woods in Spring, Sèvres*, c. 1852. Salt print from paper negative, 17 1/4 x 13 5/8 in. (43.9 x 34.7 cm). Bibliothèque Nationale de France, Paris

shaded renderings in three dimensions, and cross-section drawings depicting the trappings of industry from large to small—topography, mine shafts, coal cars, pulley systems, strap hinges, down to sketches of individual bits of rock—the kind of notational work that would be vastly reduced and simplified by photography some thirty years later (fig. 98). Interspersed throughout the mechanical drawings are accomplished pencil sketches of picturesque castle ruins and landscape features (fig. 99). These were pleasure drawings, impromptu exercises, drawn on the backs of envelopes and scraps of paper, and neatly pinned or pasted into the notebooks, where he added short written descriptions. Throughout, Regnault recorded impressions of his landscape surroundings. In one entry he might remark upon the charm of "lofty mountains with the green of fir forests enclosing deep, twisting valleys, at the bottom of which runs a beautiful brook, and where one finds lovely villages or isolated houses that by their whiteness stand out pleasantly in the midst of the verdure," while in the next, he speaks of beauty of another

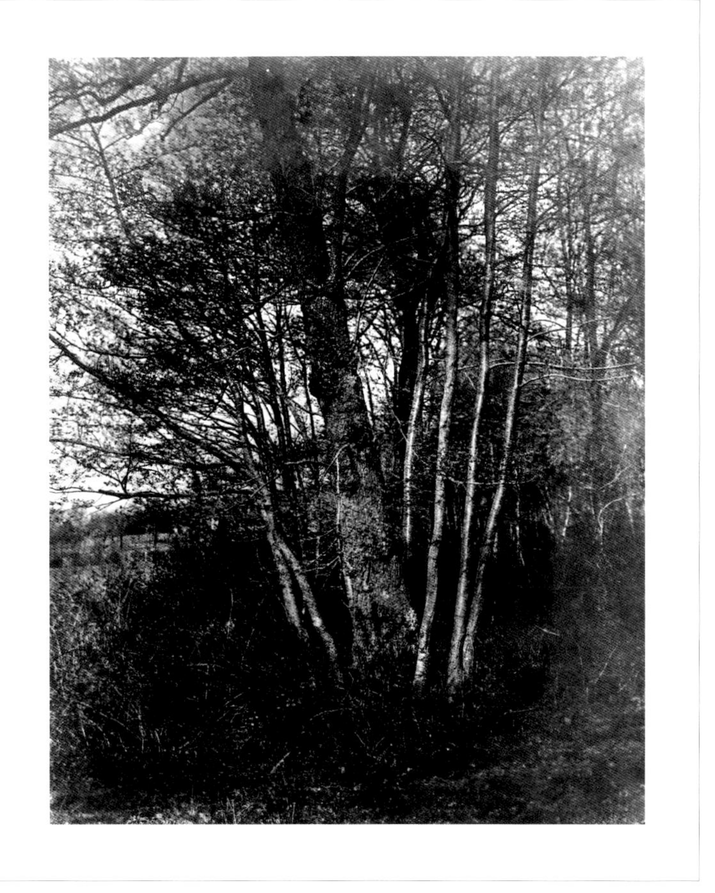

Fig. 97.
Victor Regnault, *Woods in Winter, Sèvres*, from *Études et Paysages* (Lille: Blanquart-Evrard, 1853–54). Salt print from paper negative, 15 5/8 x 12 3/4 in. (39.7 x 32.5 cm). Bibliothèque Nationale de France, Paris. Eo t. 7

kind: "Leaving Renningau ... one sees the terrain change color and one finds oneself on a fine sandstone, often much like schist, of varied nuance. One sees very beautiful quarries on the left of the road. In these quarries they exploit handsome beds of sandstone that they cut for diverse uses."[68] For Regnault, a well-engineered exploitation of the earth's rich resources had a logic and beauty of its own. The romantic gaze of the solitary wanderer and the appraising eye of the geographic engineer were not in opposition if one thought of them as complementary, as alternating faculties.

There was no reconciling the exploitation of natural resources with their preservation, just as there was no reconciling the individualistic ethos of art photography with photography's other calling as a medium for the masses; there was only learning to accept the tension that would always exist between them. Regnault's landscape practice stands apart from the work of his more romantic colleagues in its mixing of eternal nature with the modern, man-altered landscape. One can hardly believe

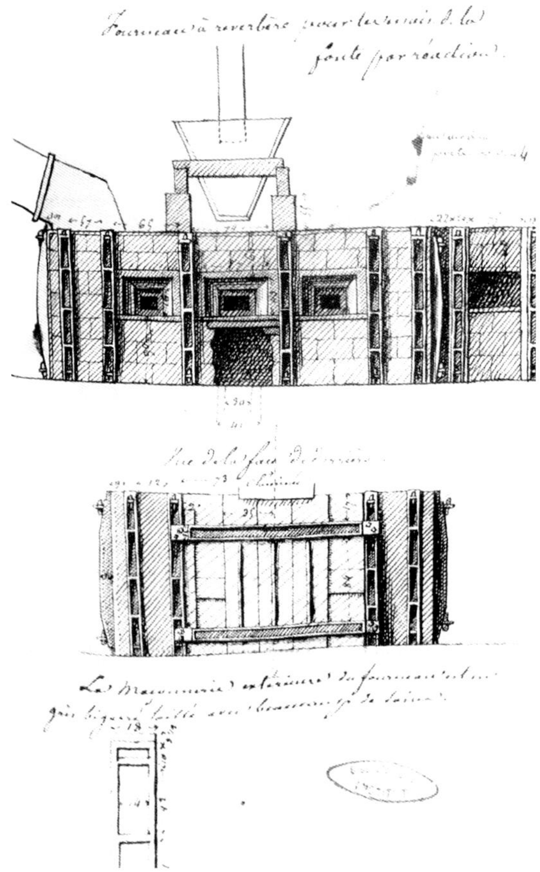

Fig. 98.
Victor Regnault, *Glass Furnace*, 1834. Pen and ink on notebook page, dimensions unknown. Institut de France, Paris. IF 2843, Regnault notebooks, *Voyage en Belgique et en Allemagne*, notebook 3

that Regnault objected to the modernization that he himself facilitated in his professional activities as physicist, chemist, and engineer. Although he was part of the means by which the technological future was arriving day by day in France, he maintained faith that there was room for a favorable coexistence of nature and technology. Photography was among the most fruitful unions of those forces, a practice that coincidentally furnished a means of extending the knowledge of both.

Writing in *La Lumière* in 1852, the critic J.-D. Du Vernay passionately articulated the teleological view of modern progress, hailing photography as one of its greatest goods: "We believe . . . with

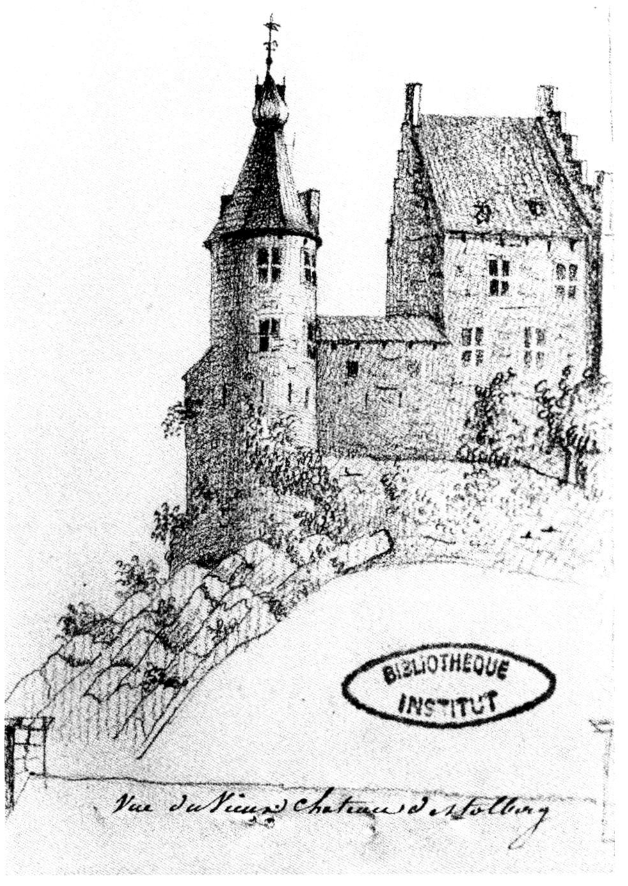

Fig. 99.

Victor Regnault, *Notebook Sketch of the Chateau de Stolberg*, 1834. Graphite on paper, dimensions unknown. Institut de France, Paris. IF2844, *Voyage en Belgique et en Allemagne*, notebook 4

all the force of our conviction, in this solemn advent of photography, as we believe in the laws of progress, as we believe in all the good things Providence has to reveal to us, at each step of the world throughout the ages, for the indefinite perfection of the generations. This holy and religious faith is a consolation—for the nameless miseries of our time—and a hope for us—for the rich treasures that will fertilize a future assuredly near."[69] Grappling with the conflict between present good and future gain would be set aside for the time being.

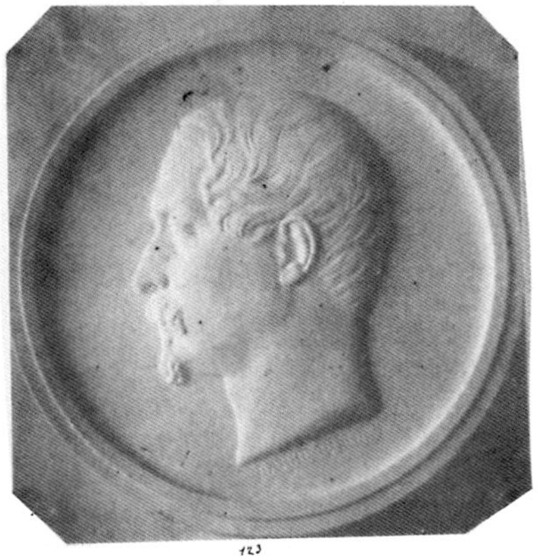

123

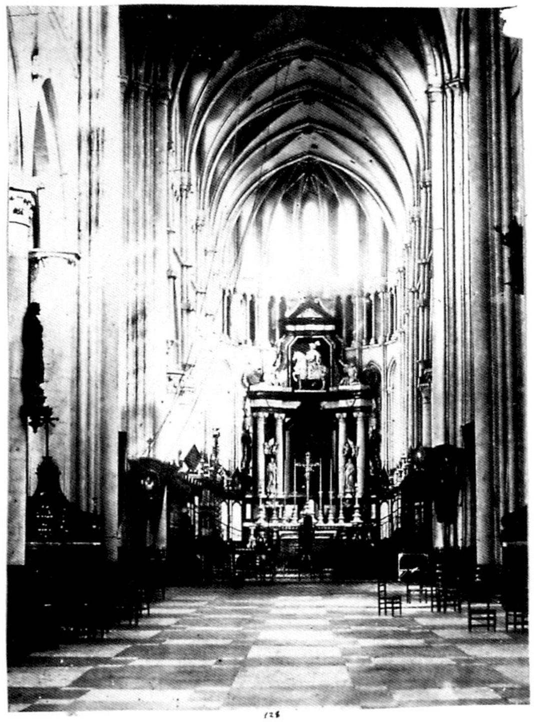

128

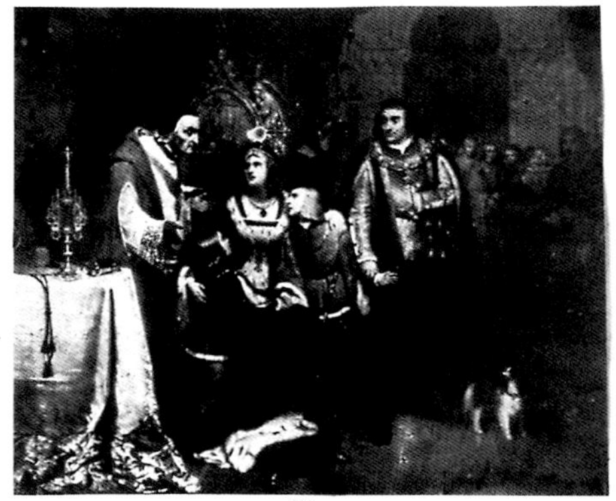

126

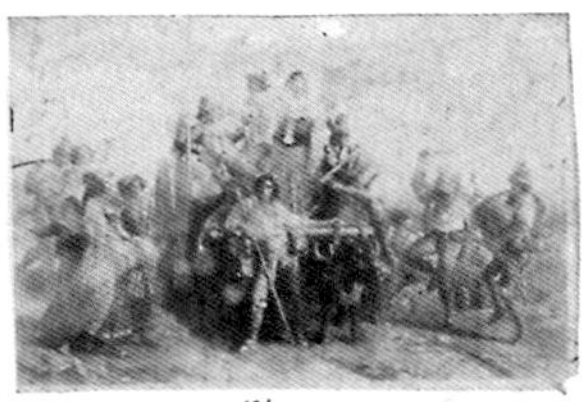

124

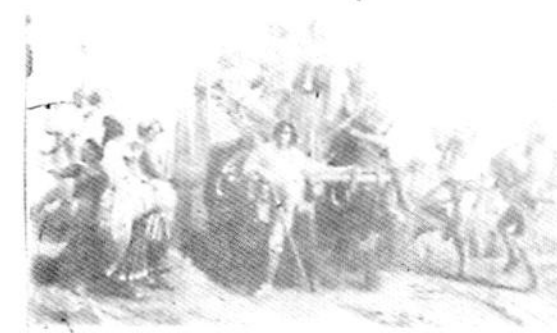

127

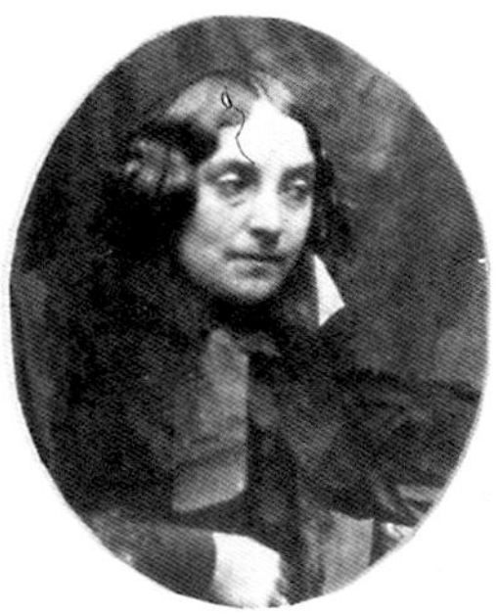

125

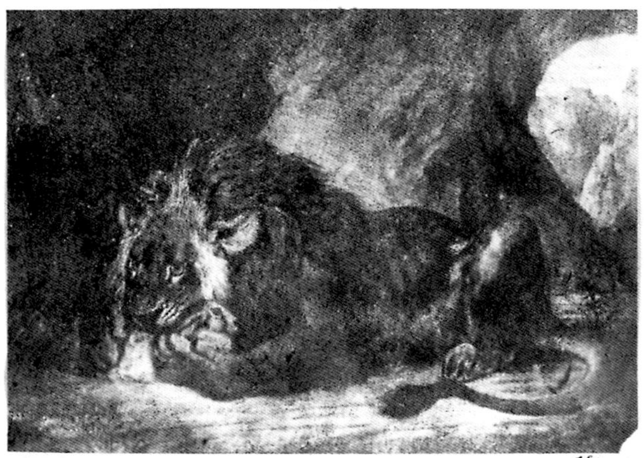

129.

Blanquart-Evrard – Procédé rapide de reproduction (avril 1851)

5 THE THREE FACES OF PHOTOGRAPHY

"Photography is at the same time a science, an art, and an industry. It thus possesses interest, charm, and beneficiality. What better condition for success and vitality?"[1] So wrote the critic J.-D. Du Vernay in *La Lumière* in 1852, proposing a "triple guarantee" of photography's success in a prognosis that proved to be fairly accurate. But no object of mass appeal escapes some measure of contempt. The criticisms lodged against photography—as the goad of shameless vanity, the lifeless product of a machine, the financial ruin of artists—were immediate and enduring, with traces that remain today. These and other complaints, however, were more than the attacks of naysayers or mediocre artists who feared for their livelihoods. As I have argued, the resistance to photography revolved around a trio of interrelated anxieties: the erosion of class boundaries, the perceived break with France's preindustrial past, and the credo of materialism, construed as the enemy of human imagination. Such concerns existed prior to the introduction of photography in 1839, but the mid-century ascendance of photography coincided with an expanding, often critical discussion of the conspicuous social, economic, and even philosophical changes of the era.[2]

The question of class in France, once clearly cut along the lines of family name, was complicated in the nineteenth century by three successive revolutions and their political aftermaths, each of which recast and to some degree expanded class opportunities and aspirations.[3] The Second Empire,

Fig. 100.
See overleaf

with its solicitous policies toward business and investment, opened the door even wider on hopes for class ascension.[4] Meanwhile, architectural and social changes in Paris were opening up more spaces where classes mixed freely, and industrial engineering had given rise to affordable goods that mimicked expensive ones.[5] While the rising middle class adopted some of the values and tastes of the nobility, aristocractic and intellectual elites (the latter, a self-made nobility) resented middle-class airs and the erosion of class distinctions.[6]

Photography was a small but ubiquitous symbol of middle-class ascension. As soon as photography became a viable portrait medium, it was vigorously marshalled in the service of building family identity. For a great middle-class population that historically lacked the wealth to commission portraits, photography now nourished notions of unity and lineage; it proudly vaunted family resemblance and asserted the family's trajectory from past to present to future.[7] The active use of photography by virtually all classes was central to the objections by some of photography's harshest critics. Victor Fournel, pained by the displays of photographs of "myriads of bourgeois of all ages and shapes" that seemed to accost him wherever he went, regarded this public display as an unredeemable vulgarity. "Look at yourself in the mirror, if you are so fond of contemplating yourself," he admonished the "Philistines." "That way you can admire yourself at your convenience, and no one has to suffer for it."[8] It was not just the bourgeoisie's putting on airs that so exasperated Fournel; it was also that they misunderstood or disrespected the upper class that they ostensibly sought to emulate, hardly realizing—or more to the point, not caring—how their vanity looked to their betters. Commercial photography was thus an important part of the growing public presence of the middle class, a demonstration of its demand for social recognition, impertinently on view in shop windows all over the city. In contrast, the lower class stood to lose as much from photography as it gained, in that photography would be increasingly deployed as a means of social control (through surveillance and promulgating ideologies of race) as time went on.[9]

As for anxieties over the anticipated demise of a preindustrial culture, resistance to new technology predated the nineteenth century. From the time of the *ancien régime*, an aggravated tension between tradition and innovation was endemic to French production in general, from manufacturing to agriculture.[10] However, by 1860, the shape of modernity in France had become much more visible. For better or worse, results of economic growth and industrial development were now becoming difficult to overlook. Population dislocation, bust and boom economic cycles, urban overcrowding, coal gas pollution, and exhaustion of natural resources could now be recognized as the price paid for new agricultural and industrial methods, improved transportation, and expanded markets. "Progress" was revealed to be

Overleaf: Fig. 100.
Album Regnault, p. 93, c. 1851. Clockwise from top left (all salt prints from paper negatives): Victor Regnault, *Biscuit Medallion of Napoléon III*, 3 1/4 x 3 1/4 in. (83 x 82 cm); Louis-Désiré Blanquart-Evrard, *St. Martin Cathedral at Ypres*, 5 7/8 x 4 1/2 in. (15 x 11.4 cm); attributed to Regnault, *Art Reproduction*, 3 3/4 x 3 1/8 in. (9.7 x 7.9 cm); attributed to Regnault, *Reproduction of Léopold Robert Painting*, 2 3/8 x 1 1/2 in. (6.1 x 3.7 cm); Blanquart-Evrard, *Reproduction of an Engraving, "procédé rapide de reproduction—Avril 1851,"* 5 1/4 x 3 5/8 in. (13.3 x 9.1 cm); Regnault, *Madame Regnault*, 2 1/2 x 2 in. (6.4 x 5.3 cm); attributed to Regnault, *Reproduction of Léopold Robert Painting*, 2 3/8 x 1 1/2 in. (6.1 x 3.7 cm). Société Française de Photographie, Paris

a complicated social and political issue, but its physical source was not difficult to locate: it was scientific knowledge that made this thing called progress possible. The resistance to science and scientific systems, growing stronger in the latter half of the century, was voiced by philosophers, popular writers, and critics such as Baudelaire.[11] Anti-scientism's complex manifestations included the reaction against photography and, similarly, the complaints against the technical feats of nineteenth-century Sèvres ware, which accompanied a nostalgia for eighteenth-century soft-paste porcelain.

Once it entered the sacrosanct domain of art, technological progress was no longer seen as an issue mainly concerning businessmen and workers, but one involving poets, artists, and men of taste and intellect. In his 1839 presentation of photography to the Chamber of Deputies, François Arago attempted to stem the fears of artists and engravers by securing the popular academic painter Paul Delaroche's blessing, a testimony that the daguerreotype would be of "immense service" to the arts, by providing aspiring artists with accurate models from which to draw.[12] Arago's argument would be taken to bolder extremes by some of photography's advocates, who welcomed the day that photography would put second-rate painters and engravers out of business, leaving only those "truly original artists" to possess the field.[13] The sniping attacks over photography's status masked a very serious anxiety: that the encroachment of technology into modern life had finally breached the battlements of art, which was to say the realm of creativity and imagination. "Poetry and progress are like two ambitious men who hate one another with an instinctive hatred," Baudelaire famously avowed, "and when they meet upon the same road, one of them has to give place."[14] By the mid-1850s, many held the case of photography to be the obvious example of the threat that technological progress posed to imagination, and photography became the symbol for the devaluation of individual, primary experience. Baudelaire asked, "Are we to suppose that a people whose eyes are growing used to considering the results of a material science as though they were the products of the beautiful will not in the course of time have singularly diminished its faculties of judging and feeling what are among the most ethereal and immaterial aspects of creation?"[15]

Baudelaire feared imagination could actually be crushed, and he located a great cause for alarm in the pernicious materialism of photography. To its critics, photography was a crude lie that was mistaken for the purest truth; the mesmerizing impression created by its record of the brute facts of the material world blinded its admirers to whatever it could not represent. But as one of the most successful new professions to arise in the 1840s and 1850s, which seemed to require no particular talent beyond the entrepreneurial spirit, photography was also associated with materialism in its second sense: money grubbing. The image of the petit bourgeois capitalist, propelling himself to the status of pseudo-artist by means of a profitable photography studio (built on his ability to flatter the gross vanities of his hideous bourgeois clients), was lampooned in cartoons and anecdotes of the 1850s. The Goncourt brothers wrote vituperatively about this social type in their journal, brought on by a chance encounter with a former mistress who now aspired to respectability as the would-be wife of a successful photographer. The woman, once a "pretty little tart" who lived the bohemian life, had been swept up in the petty capitalist orbit of the American expatriate photographer, Warren Thompson (dates unknown). Now she spent her days hand-coloring Thompson's stereo daguerreotypes, painting angel wings on deceased children in post-mortem photographs. The Goncourts' real attack was upon Thompson, whom they described as more machine than man, "regular as a Bréguet watch": an oafish dimwit with hemorrhoids, who makes love just "for health's sake," and who ought to have oil instead of blood.[16] Conflating middle-class ambition and mechanization into one despicable human form, the Goncourts found in the photographer the perfect metaphor for the tastelessness that is the progeny of industrialism. Elsewhere in their journals, the brothers observed mournfully, "Industry must kill art, for is the popularization of art anything other than its death?"[17] For these writers, under the industrial mandate of the onrushing future, imagination and fancy would be sacrificed to technological prerogatives, but the rising middle class reaping the commercial profits lacked the intelligence and sensitivity to notice what would be lost in the bargain.

As an active ambassador for technology, Victor Regnault encountered frequent resistance to the progress for which he stood. In scientific circles, insulated by the power and authority of the academic establishment, protests against the sway of positivism would have been barely audible, although we have seen how the shift in mainstream science from experimental to theoretical concerns in the 1880s demoted Regnault from the status of a true scientific thinker to that of a mere technician. But in his role at Sèvres and as the head of the most powerful photographic organization in Europe, two institutions in which critics found technology to be threatening the sovereign ground of art, he faced frequent opposition. Thus his leadership involved not only solving technical problems and finding ways to integrate new technologies with older models of artisanship, but defending the technological brand of modernity he represented. At Sèvres, he unsuccessfully proposed educating the public about the continuing artistic quality of the factory's product by publishing photographs of Sèvres wares, but persuaded the higher administration that photographic documentation was the best—and only—means to maintain an accurate record of the artists' unique output. As head of the Société Française de Photographie, his task of cultivating an educated public for photography was complicated by the volume of public attention, negative and positive, spontaneously generated by the "Daguerreotypomanie" that grew to encompass all of photography and continued to grow through the 1850s.[18]

From the moment it entered the public imagination, photography was recognized as a sleeping giant: a technology with enormous raw potential, watched warily on all sides for signs of its unknown disposition. Yet despite photography's latent power, under Regnault's leadership the S.F.P. initially sought to enter the institutional halls of art by way of supplication. Regnault was not alone in taking this deferential position. Paul Périer, for example, despite his vocal advocacy for photography-as-art, would not have dreamed of insisting that photography be granted equal rank with painting or sculpture. "We stand only for having the right of the burghers in the city," he told the *Bulletin*'s readers, "but there we shall always bow very low to the nobility; at this feast of the grand lords of art, the crumbs can satisfy us. But these crumbs are ours, and we shall claim them."[19] Périer's metaphor of class was precisely on point, but he failed to recognize that the bourgeoisie, the century's greatest sleeping giant, had already staggered to its feet and was carrying photography headlong with it as it remade standards of taste and undermined the place of the upper class as exclusive arbiter of Art. Although Périer wished to deny it, the assault upon "the grand lords of art" had already begun, and he was part of it.

Under Regnault's leadership, the more radical implications of the power of photography were softened by his patient, accommodationist stance, though all the while he was quietly working for photography's advancement from his position within the arts establishment. He and the S.F.P. continued throughout the 1850s to develop Arago's original doctrine of photography's usefulness—to so many fields, in so many ways—and assimilated fine art's teachings and values so assiduously as to make it difficult to see the medium as a real threat or a vulgar upstart challenging traditional culture. Commentaries of the 1860s by photographic writers outside the S.F.P. sometimes show patience with photography's "handmaiden" status wearing thin, but Regnault continued to focus the activities of his organization on practical matters.[20] By steering the S.F.P. away from controversy and confrontation, Regnault set a placid, pragmatic course for the S.F.P. that gave it the longevity to survive—as it does to the present day.

In his own photography, Regnault's innovations were in areas that he did not think of as art: in scientific pedagogy and in the formation of a private archive of family memory. Where he attempted to enter the discourse of art with the production of Barbizonesque landscapes, he and his colleagues showed their hopes for recognition as artists by emulating an established art style that still possessed the faint, romantic cachet of artistic rebellion and innovation. This prefigures the strategy of other photography-as-art movements, such as the Photo-Secession (1902–17), whose members attached themselves to Tonalism and Impressionism, once radical movements that were long since welcomed to the mainstream.[21] This practice combined the safety of working in a proven art style (imprinted with the trace of its avant-garde beginnings) with the photographers' own sense of breaking new ground. Working defensively under the assertion of photography's low status as an art, photographers often modeled their practices on those of their presumptive "betters"—not unlike the nouveau-riche industrialist who laid his table with Sèvres.

In 1965, sociologist Pierre Bordieu observed that the modern camera club, by now a solidly middle-class institution, was committed to culturally ennobling its members through its efforts to ennoble photography, a medium traditionally treated as an inferior substitute for the higher arts.[22] The campaign to ennoble photography began with the earliest camera clubs, but with this difference: in 1855, the leading members of the S.F.P. were certainly men who had privileged access to the higher arts, and still they chose photography. Why? Early photography began as a fairly complicated pursuit that required more education, money, and equipment than the average person could muster, hence the division of the field into professionals and well-heeled amateurs, which left out the casual, "middle-brow" users Bordieu describes. Still, photography was fundamentally different from the other arts in that it did not require a long apprenticeship to learn its techniques, and in this sense, it was well matched to the values and exigencies of the rising middle class, which had clearly infused the temper of the age. Gentlemen amateurs—even aristocrats like Count Aguado and the Marquis de Bérenger—were the products of a culture driven by bourgeois values since at least the 1830s and the reign of Louis Philippe, the so-called "citizen king." If the S.F.P. patricians no longer held themselves aloof from business, industry, and the professions, they also no longer had unlimited time to lavish on their hobbies. Photography could be learned and practiced on weekends and vacations—this was in fact how Regnault was able to accommodate it in his busy schedule.[23] The special allure of photography also bespoke a kind of bourgeois modernity, in that the purchase and mastery of technical equipment appealed to those who had prospered by technology.

Utility—or, beneficiality, as Du Vernay more positively phrased it—seemed to create the biggest problem for the medium's upper-class defenders. Romantic literary and artistic intellectuals held usefulness in contempt as part of the anti-individualistic rationalism they despised, and usefulness could not be separated from the idea of photography.[24] Photographers with artistic ambitions had to reconcile the conservative view of art-making as a sacrament of unique subjectivity with the progressive, populist implications of photography. By using the most craft-intensive process available (calotypy), some photographers hoped to distinguish their artistic intentions from more commercial or industrial motives—another strategy employed by subsequent art photography movements. Other artist/photographers denied any conflict between art and utility by insisting that photography was as flexible in the hands of the creative individual as it was adaptable to the demands of practical necessity. Many photographers, including Bayard, Robert, Blanquart-Evrard, and Le Gray, deliberately emphasized the doctrine of flexibility in the diversity of their salon entries, using the medium for practical ends (for art reproductions, scientific documentation, aide-memoire, and so on), while at the same time attempting to make photographs that produced aesthetic experience.

In many ways, Regnault was the quintessential bourgeois, although his professional success elevated him to the nobility of the academy.[25] Politically moderate, professionally ambitious, devoted to the spirit of rationalism, and optimistic about the (technological) future, Regnault consecrated his life to progress and productivity, which explains why he was so ideally suited to the needs of early photography, and vice versa. Even his moments of relaxation were tied to productive aims, and photography proved itself to be a perfect companion in this regard. When his son Henri wrote to him in 1870, well after Regnault's most active years as a photographer, he urged his father to come visit in Morocco, promising him a life of (productive) leisure: "There you will be able to do photography with Lagraine, and hunt: in the evening, you'll bring back a dozen hare and partridge, and a dozen negatives!"[26]

"THE SADDEST END IMAGINABLE"

Regnault had always been concerned about his contribution to the future. In the last decade of his life, he saw his dreams for leaving a legacy—as a father, as the director of the Sèvres manufacture, and as a scientist—collapsing in nearly simultaneous disaster. Henri Regnault's invitation to his father to visit Morocco was never accepted. In 1870, with the Second Empire government (and with it, Regnault's multiple careers) beginning to crumble and with the Prussian army advancing on Paris, Henri Regnault returned to France to enlist. Within a few months, Prussian forces had descended upon Sèvres as their base for a three-month siege of Paris, and Regnault and five of the Manufacture's *chefs* were effectively confined under house arrest. Using his fluency in German and his international reputation, Regnault secured a promise from the prince of Prussia (ensconced a few miles away at Versailles) not to molest the factory. Still, rogue soldiers surreptitiously destroyed his laboratory, smashing a lifetime's accumulation of special instruments and equipment and burning reams of unpublished research data amassed over decades; this may also explain the fate of Regnault's glass plate negatives and other photography. In December 1871, on the verge of nervous collapse, Regnault was permitted by the Prussian command to leave Sèvres to convalesce in Lassigneu, near Geneva, precipitating rumors in the press about Regnault's Prussian sympathies.[27] More bad news arrived: on 19 January 1871, literally the eve of the French surrender, Henri was killed on the battlefield of Buzenwald. Having placed his eldest son Léon in an asylum for the mentally ill, with his two other surviving children also showing signs of mental illness, Regnault, now a paralytic semi-invalid, returned to Paris, retiring to a house in the suburb of Auteuil. In a final effort to make some contribution to posterity, he had the remnants of his lab at Sèvres transported there, where he hoped to spend what remained of his life putting together a "musée historique" of his experiments.[28] He had, as Louise Dieterle recalled, "the saddest end imaginable, sick and paralyzed . . . left alone with his two poor idiot children."[29] Regnault died on the seventh anniversary of Henri's death in 1878.

The last page of the *Album Regnault* features the leitmotifs of Regnault's world (fig. 100). It presents an arrangement of seven small photographs: a portrait of his wife, trimmed as a small oval vignette; two small reproductions of a harvest scene painted by Léopold Robert (comparing photographic process variations); a photograph of a Sèvres porcelain medallion of Napoléon III; and three photographs produced by Blanquart-Evrard: the nave of the cathedral of Saint Martin at Ypres, and reproductions of two other contemporary paintings. God, country, and family: all are equally represented at the closure of this album. Photography's three faces are also present: science in the chemical process variations; art and industry in the art reproductions. Like the whole of Regnault's photographic work, this page is a patchwork of aims and intentions. Although Regnault's role directing the traffic at the center of this bustling intersection would seem to have guaranteed his memory to photography, this was not the case. As he never exhibited his work in France, there were no reviews left to recall his name to posterity, and without a great cache of vintage prints he made an unlikely candidate for museum rediscovery. Writing his substantial *Histoire de la photographie* in 1945, Raymond Lecuyer reproduced many of Regnault's images (from Regnault's negatives left at the S.F.P.), but without attribution. Only a wave of scholarly prospecting in the 1970s managed to excavate Regnault the photographer from beneath the faint memory of a scientist/functionary who once directed the S.F.P.

A century after Regnault's death, at the first solo exhibition of his work, in 1978, Henri Cartier-Bresson supposedly stood before one of the landscapes and exclaimed, "What composition! What assurance of composition, it's astounding . . . How I would love to have made that picture."[30] No one would be more surprised than Regnault to find that today, his work in photography—his guilty pleasure—seems to have received more recognition than any of his more prominent activities. This has as much to do with our continued fascination with photography as it has to do with Regnault's actual accomplishments. Regnault the scientist may have been a victim of his own success—exhausted by the demands of imperial patronage and fatally mired in the empirical philosophy that had launched his career—but no amount of success can own photography, since photography is endowed with a disinterested promiscuity that allows it to be endlessly reinvented by anyone who chooses to use it.

NOTES

INTRODUCTION

1. Françoise Heilbrun, "Nadar and the Art of Portrait Photography," in *Nadar*, exh. cat., Maria Morris Hambourg, Françoise Heilbrun, and Philippe Néagu (New York: Metropolitan Museum of Art, 1995), 38.
2. Félix Tournachon (Nadar), *Quand j'étais photographe* (Paris: Flammarion, 1900).
3. Janet E. Buerger, *French Daguerreotypes* (Chicago: University of Chicago Press, 1989), 141.
4. L. Landa and the Ville de Chalon-sur-Saône, *Commission du monument a élever a la mémoire de Nicéphore Niépce. Rapport présenté au conseil municipale dans sa Séance du 30 Mars, 1877* (Chalon-sur-Saône, France, 1877), 8.
5. Philippe Burty, *Chefs d'oeuvres of the Industrial Arts*, ed. and trans. W. Chaffers (London: Cassell, Petter, and Galpin, 1869); and Edmond de Goncourt and Jules de Goncourt, *Journal, mémoires de la vie littéraire, 1851–63*, vol. 1 (Paris: Fasquelle, 1959), 780. Charles Baudelaire, whose review of the Salon of 1859 included the era's most vituperative attack on photography, saw the new medium as the ultimate symbol of the ignorant masses' triumph over the sensitive individual. Charles Baudelaire, "The Modern Public and Photography," in *Art in Paris*, 1845–1862, ed. and trans. Jonathan Mayne (London: Phaidon Press, 1965), 149–55.
6. Allan Sekula, "The Traffic in Photographs," *Photography Against the Grain* (Halifax: The Press of the Nova Scotia College of Art and Design, 1984), 78.

CHAPTER 1: THE ART OF AVOIDING ERRORS

1. Regnault left a legacy in chemistry and physics, including the discovery of vinyl chloride, dichloroethylene, trichloroethylene, and carbon tetrachloride, compounds essential in the later development of plastics. His experiments led to a massive amount of data, which was instrumental in opening the field of thermodynamics. Robert Fox, "Victor Regnault," in *Dictionary of Scientific Biography*, ed. Charles Coulston Gillispie (New York: Charles Scribner's Sons, 1975), 11:352–53.
2. Alfred de Musset, *Confessions of a Child of the Century* (1836; reprint, New York: Current Literature Publishing Company, 1923), 17.
3. Terry Shinn, *Savoir scientifique et pouvoir social: L'École polytechnique, 1794–1914* (Paris: Presse de la Fondation Nationale des Sciences Politiques, 1980), 57.
4. Maurice Crosland, *Science under Control: The French Academy of Science* (Cambridge, U.K.: Cambridge University Press, 1992), 99.
5. Copies of the marriage certificate and of Victor's birth certificate were obtained from the Aachen (formerly Aix-la-Chapelle) municipal archives through the generous assistance of Stefanie Seib.
6. Shinn, *Savoir scientifique*, 90.
7. Henri Le Chatelier, "Discours [Centenary of Victor Regnault]," *Annales des mines* (Jan. 1911): 9.
8. Jules Janin, "Discours prononcés par des membres de l'académie, aux funérailles de M. Regnault," *Comptes rendus hebdomadaire des séances de l'Académie des sciences* 86 (1878): 131–43.
9. Robert Fox, *The Culture of Science in France, 1700–1900* (Brookfield, Vt.: Variorum, 1992), 132.
10. Jean-Baptiste Dumas, *Éloge de Victor Regnault: ingénieur en chef des mines* (Paris: Dunod, 1881), 20.
11. Ibid., 17.
12. Le Chatelier, "Discours," 11.
13. César Graña, *Bohemian versus Bourgeois* (New York: Basic Books, 1964), 94.
14. Victor Cousin, "Du Beau et de l'Art," *Revue des deux mondes* 2 (1845): 781.
15. Today the album is missing nine of the original 129 prints. Seven of those prints were missing at the time of the album's entry into the collection of the Société. The remaining two images, both portraits by Blanquart-Evrard, were among a number of images from the album that were reproduced in Raymond Lecuyer's 1945 book *Histoire de la photographie* (Paris: Baschet, 1945); it is possible they were somehow separated from the album when the photographs were rephotographed for the *Histoire*.
16. Victor Regnault/John Herschel correspondence, undated [1851], Royal Society, London, 319. Regnault was also punning on the fact that Stewart was a newlywed, having just married in May.
17. Victor Regnault/Justus von Liebig correspondence, undated [spring 1851], Staatsbibliothèque München, no. 25. While in Germany in 1834, he also found several weeks to spend in Liebig's celebrated laboratory in Giessen, not far from his hometown of Aix-la-Chapelle, which he would later recount as a formative experience.
18. Regnault/Liebig correspondence, 2 Sept. [1851], no. 24.
19. Ibid.
20. Jules Ziegler, "Société Héliographique. Séance du 18 Avril," *La Lumière* 1, no. 12 (27 Apr. 1851): 46.
21. Gilbert Beauge, ed., *Collection du journal "La Lumière"* (Paris: Jeanne Laffitte, 1995), 9.
22. The photographer Jules Ziegler, critic Francis Wey, and scientist Baron Armand Séguier have been tentatively identified among the portraits in the album (p. 13, right, p. 16, left, and p. 70, right). There are undoubtedly other figures from the photography world still to be identified.
23. Alexandre Ken, *Dissertations historiques, artistiques, et scientifiques sur la photographie* (Paris: Librairie Nouvelle, 1864), 42. Susse Frères also published Daguerre's first detailed instructions to the process, *Historique et description des procédés du daguerréotype et du diorama*, in 1839.
24. François-Victor Fournel, "Ce qu'on voit dans les rues de Paris," 1858; in *La Photographie en France*, ed. André Rouillé (Paris: Éditions MACULA, 1989), 289.
25. François Arago, "Fixation des images qui se forment au foyer d'une chambre obscure," *Comptes rendues hebdomadaire de l'Académie des sciences* 8 (7 Jan. 1839): 4–7.
26. Ibid., 7.
27. See Nancy Keeler, "Cultivating Photography: Hippolyte Bayard and the Development of a New Art," Ph. D. diss., University of Texas, 1991.
28. Jules Pelletan, "Feuilleton de la Presse, Science.-Industrie; Réclamation de M. Fox Talbot, physicien anglais, au sujet du procédé-Daguerre," *La Presse* (13 Feb. 1839): 2–3.

29. Ibid.
30. J.-B. Biot/William Henry Fox Talbot correspondence, 24 Jan. 1841, quoted in Larry J. Schaaf, *Out of the Shadows* (New Haven, Conn., and London: Yale University Press, 1992), 116–17.
31. Biot/Talbot correspondence, 13 Feb. 1839, quoted in Schaaf, *Out of the Shadows*, 59.
32. The Royal Society's prestigious Rumford Medal recognizing scientific work went to Biot in 1841, but it would be awarded to Regnault in 1848.
33. Biot/Talbot correspondence, 14 June 1841, quoted in Schaaf, *Out of the Shadows*, 182.
34. T.-J. Pelouze, C. Pouillet, E. Péligot, J.-B. Dumas, E. Becquerel, E. Chevreul, Baron Armand Séguier: these academicians were among the many who actively took an interest in photography.
35. Douglas Nickel has described the Victorian embrace and understanding of photography as being grounded in an "epistemological logic that instinctively related knowledge to sight." Photography was thus regarded as a kind of prosthetic enhancement of sight, and was, Nickel notes, quickly enlisted in the visual cataloging of a world regarded by Victorian science as "rational, knowable, and reflective of an overarching, predetermined order." Douglas Nickel, "Photography and Invisibility," in *The Artist and the Camera*, ed. Dorothy Kosinski (Dallas: Dallas Museum of Art, 1999), 35–41.
36. In 1843, the Reverend Calvert Richard Jones wrote Talbot, mentioning the calotypy he had been doing in Paris with Hippolyte Bayard and Regnault. Calvert Richard Jones/William Henry Fox Talbot correspondence, 2 Mar. 1843, quoted in Larry Schaaf, *Sun Pictures Catalogue Five: The Reverend Calvert R. Jones* (New York: Hans Kraus Jr., Inc., 1990), 11.
37. Regnault probably met Kuhlmann, who appears among Regnault's portraits (S.F.P. 473.110), through Justus von Liebig, and it is possible through these contacts Regnault was informed about Blanquart-Evrard's photographic research before 1846. Correspondence links the four men together as late as 1851. Regnault/Liebig correspondence, 15 Mar. [1851], no. 28.
38. Louis-Désiré Blanquart-Evrard, note and photographs, *pochette* (envelope) for 28 Sept. 1846, Académie des Sciences Archives.
39. In an unexplained move, the committee was jointly formed of members of the A.d.S. and the Académie des Beaux-Arts and the Académie des Inscriptions et Belles Lettres. Besides Regnault, the committee included Biot, Debret (either J.-B. or François), Baron Desnoyers, Auguste Dumont, J.-E. Gatteaux, Louis Hersent, Louis Petitot, F. E. Picot, L. H. Le Bas, and D. Raoul-Rochette.
40. Académie des Beaux-Arts, *procès verbale*, 19 June 1847, quoted in Louis-Désiré Blanquart-Evrard, *La Photographie, ses origines, ses progrès, ses transformations* (Lille, France: Imprimerie L. Danel, 1869), 21.
41. Talbot had sensitized his paper by applying the chemical solution with a brush; Blanquart-Evrard soaked the paper.
42. Louis Figuier, *Exposition et histoire des principales découvertes scientifiques modernes* (Paris: Langlois et Leclercq et Victor Masson, 1851), quoted in Blanquart-Evrard, *La Photographie*, 19.
43. Blanquart-Evrard, *La Photographie*, 20.
44. Gustave Le Gray, *Photographie: Traité nouveau théorique et pratique des procédés et manipulations sur papier-sec, humide et sur verre au collodion, à l'albumine* (Paris: Lerebours et Secretan, undated [1852]), 164. Regnault's substitution was also reported in the first issue of *La Lumière* (9 Feb. 1851): 3. Regnault may have given further technical advise to Le Gray as the latter perfected his waxed-paper process. Sylvie Aubenas, *Gustave Le Gray* (Los Angeles: The J. Paul Getty Museum, 2002), 26.
45. Victor Regnault, Notes for a "Cours d'Acoustique (1850–51)," Institut de France, Paris. File folder 2933.
46. Le Chatelier, "Discours," 15.
47. Regnault/Liebig correspondence, 15 Mar. [1851], no. 28.
48. Regnault may have actually used this method in later editions of *Cours élementaire de chimie* (Paris, 1847) or *Premiers éléments de chimie* (Paris, 1849), as the *Revue photographique* reported in 1856 that Regnault had been well-served by a process of photographic reproduction for "plates illustrating apparatus described in his *Traité de Chimie*." The writer observed that "Plates of this nature give objects a relief and perspective that singularly facilitate intelligence." The writer may have mistaken the title of the text to which he referred. *Revue photographique*, no. 6 (5 Apr. 1856): 91. Regnault's method was first reported by F. A. Rénard, *La Lumière* (9 Mar. 1851): 19.
49. See Beauge, *Collection du journal "La Lumière"*; André Gunthert, "L'institution du photographique. Le roman de la Société Héliographique," *Études photographiques* 12 (Nov. 2002): 37–63; and Janet E. Buerger, *French Daguerreotypes* (Chicago: University of Chicago Press, 1989). André Jammes and Eugenia Parry Janis also briefly discuss the Société Héliographique in *The Art of French Calotype*, exh. cat. (Princeton, N.J.: Princeton University Press, 1983).
50. Gunthert, "L'institution du photographique," 38–39.
51. Buerger, *French Daguerreotypes*, 142.
52. Ibid., 147.
53. A collection of twenty-seven works on photography, owned by Regnault, was sold in Paris in the early 1980s. Only one item, *Methode théorique et practique de photographie sur papier* (1847), by A. Guillot-Saguez, predates 1850.
54. This large exhibition was conceived and executed in barely more than a month by the Society for the Encouragement of the Arts, Manufactures, and Commerce, which included certain members of the Photographic Club (also called the Calotype Club). With time so scarce, members and friends pulled together works from their own collections for the exhibition. See Roy Flukinger, "The Calotype and the Photographic Exhibition of the Society of Arts, London, 1852–53," in *Paper and Light: The Calotype in France and Great Britain*, Richard R. Brettell et al. (Boston: David R. Godine, 1984), 64.
55. Minutes of the Council, 31 Mar. 1853, Royal Photographic Society (formerly the London Photographic Society). There are no prints by Regnault in the RPS collection, and I surmise that the offer was never followed through.
56. Around two hundred of Regnault's negatives remain from this period.
57. This mention appears at the end of Lerebours's two-part article, "Plaque, papier, ou verre?" *La Lumière* (1 May 1852): 75, which discusses the best

French photographers using the paper process.

58. His monogram appears discreetly in two of the images. See Isabelle Jammes, *Blanquart-Evrard et les origines de l'Édition photographique française* (Geneva: Librairie Droz, 1981). Thirteen works by Regnault have been identified among the editions: five from *Études et Paysages* (1853–54), see Jammes's cat. nos. 180–84; and seven from *Études Photographiques* (1853), see Jammes's nos. 201, 256–58, 260–62. A view of Peterborough Cathedral, a collaboration by Regnault and Stewart, appears in *L'Art religieux*, series 14, see Jammes's no. 84. Other images by Regnault may yet come to light in the Blanquart-Evrard editions.
59. Buerger, *French Daguerreotypes*, 143–44.
60. Eugène Durieu, who had played a very active role in that earlier society, seems to have been one of the main figures behind the new group. He was the provisional president for four months until the official election, and remained president of the administration committee thereafter.
61. "Procès-verbal de la Séance," *Bulletin de la Société française de photographie* (Mar. 1855): 62.
62. See, for example, the letter to the S.F.P. from Frederick Pollock, accepting his election as a titular member: "I hope that the generous rivalry of two great nations shall have as much brilliance and success in photography as all the other peaceful or wartime enterprises combined." "Procès-verbal de la Séance," *Bulletin de la Société française de photographie* (May 1855): 117.
63. Questions of art and commerce were taken up far more often in *La Lumière*, which continued publication after the demise of the Société Héliographique.
64. "Procès-verbal de la Séance," *Bulletin* (May 1855): 130–33.
65. Société Française de Photographie, *Prix Fondé par M. le Duc de Luynes* (Paris: Mallet-Bachelier, 1856), 6.
66. Poitevin subsequently printed one of Regnault's riverscapes by this new carbon process (Getty Museum, Los Angeles, 92.XM.52).
67. "Procès-verbal de la Séance," *Bulletin de la Société française de photographie* (June 1857): 203–4.
68. Rouillé, ed., *La Photographie en France*, 321.
69. Règlement: Beaux-arts, Exposition Universelle générale, 1855. Archives Nationale, Paris. f21 519. The man in charge of the exhibition, Frédéric Bourgeois de Mercey, was also a friend of photography, a member of the former Société Héliographique.
70. "Séance extraordinaire du 1er Mai," *Revue photographique*, no. 19 (5 May 1857): 291.
71. Ibid.
72. "Procès-verbal de la Séance," *Bulletin de la Société française de photographie* (Apr. 1855): 89.
73. Paul Périer, "Exposition universelle, 3e article," *Bulletin de la Société française de photographie* (July 1855): 199–200.
74. Victor Regnault journal, 20 July 1857, Institut de France, Paris. 2848.
75. Dumas, *Éloge de Victor Regnault*, 27.
76. Jammes and Janis, *The Art of French Calotype*, 101–4.
77. Victor Regnault, Instruction photographique faite pour Lagraine, [1869], Institut de France, Paris. 2932.
78. "Procès-verbal," *Bulletin de la Société française de photographie* (1873): 93, reprinted, *Bulletin* (Apr. 1982): 8.

CHAPTER 2: THE BULL IN THE CHINA SHOP: PHOTOGRAPHY AT THE MANUFACTURE DE SÈVRES

1. Jean-Pierre Hochet, "Tradition et novation," *Monuments historiques* 190 (Nov.–Dec. 1993): 80–83.
2. Charles Coulston Gillispie, *Science and Polity in France at the End of the Old Regime* (Princeton, N.J.: Princeton University Press, 1980), 388.
3. The Robert-Dieterle family, related by double marriages, maintains this version of events as oral history.
4. Michelle Perrot, "The Three Ages of Industrial Discipline," in *Consciousness and Class Experience in Nineteenth-Century Europe*, ed. John Merriman (New York and London: Holmes and Meier, 1979), 154.
5. A large group of Robert's calotypes—portraits, still lifes, and landscapes—exist, but it is difficult to attribute a starting date. The portraits (approximately 11 by 9 inches) date from about 1851; the landscapes, made with a larger camera (approximately 11 by 14 inches), may have followed a year or two later.
6. Speculation continues about a coterie of photographers at Sèvres. Quentin Bajac has described "a small circle of painters attached to the manufacture or working for it, gravitating around Regnault, and especially Robert," and has named Jules Ziegler, Achille Devéria (1800–1857), Jules Dieterle, Jules André, and Émile Béranger (1814–1883) as among them. Ziegler, a founder of the Société Héliographique in 1851, did make photographs, but this was certainly after 1840, when he left the factory's employ. Likewise, Devéria left the Manufacture in 1848; the earliest pictures attributed to him date from 1853. As for the others, no pictures can yet be confidently attributed to them. However, Bajac has made the recent attribution of a group of later photographs (c. 1860–65) to the painter/decorators Achille-Louis Bonnuit (dates unknown) and Jean-Charles-Gérard Derischweiler (born 1822). Formerly attributed by the Musée d'Orsay to the "atelier de Robert," Bajac is rightly cautious about ascribing any real involvement in the production of these pictures to Robert, although he believes Regnault and Robert's earlier photographic activity might have been a model or inspiration for Bonnuit and Derischweiler. Quentin Bajac, "La photographie à Sèvres sous le second Empire: du laboratoire au jardin," *La revue du Musée d'Orsay* 5 (fall 1997): 74–85.
7. Victor Regnault/Achille Fould correspondence, 25 June 1853, Archives Nationale, Paris. Cote f21-682. The minister ultimately ignored Regnault's proposals for changes to the factory regulations, which may have been behind Regnault's attempt to resign in 1853. See Marcelle Brunet and Tamara Préaud, *Sèvres: Des origines à nos jours* (Fribourg, Switzerland: Office du Livre, 1978), 270.
8. Dieterle/Victor Regnault correspondence, 7 July 1853, Archives de la Manufacture Nationale de Sèvres. T17.

9. Ibid.
10. Louise Dieterle, *Souvenirs* (Paris: privately published, 1980), 24. From 1856 to 1861, Dieterle assisted his father-in-law, the artist Charles Polycarpe Séchan (1803–1874), in decorating buildings for the Sultan Abdul-Medjid.
11. Ibid. The Dieterle descendants possessed one of the most important collections of photography from this period, including some works by Regnault, probably handed down through both Jules Dieterle and Louis Robert, who were in-laws. When Raymond Lecuyer put together his *Histoire de la photographie* in 1945, he relied heavily on Jean Dieterle's collection to illustrate the section on calotypy.
12. Victor Regnault/J.-B.-P. Vaillant correspondence, 6 Aug. 1863, Archives Nationale, Paris. f21-692.
13. Régine de Plinval de Guillebon, *Porcelain of Paris, 1770–1850*, trans. Robin R. Charleston (New York: Walker and Co., 1972), 85.
14. Shepard B. Clough, "Retardative Factors in French Economic Development in the Nineteenth and Twentieth Centuries," *Journal of Economic History* 6, supplement (1946): 102.
15. Science, revered by Napoléon as the highest order of intellectual pursuit, was the privileged discipline of the First Empire, where it inflected and informed whole programs and the philosophy of the reign. Robert Fox, *The Culture of Science in France, 1700–1900* (Brookfield, Vt: Variorum, 1992), 443–44.
16. Ibid., 5–6.
17. François Arago, "M. Arago fait l'exposition de ce procédé, dans le séance du 19 Août 1839," *Comptes rendues hebdomadaire de l'Académie des sciences* 9 (1839): 259.
18. François Arago, *Rapport à la Chambre des députés*, 3 July 1839, in *La Photographie en France*, ed. André Rouillé (Paris: Éditions MACULA, 1989), 36–43.
19. Alexandre Brongniart, *Du caractère et de l'état actuel de la Manufacture royale de porcelaine de Sèvres, et de son influence sur l'art et le commerce de la porcelaine* (Paris: Imprimerie de Amb. Firmin Didot, 1830), 14.
20. Recettes et Dépenses (1851–1860), R 55–67, Archives de la Manufacture Nationale de Sèvres. Riocreux made occasional purchases of photographs for the library in the 1850s and 1860s. The photographs included art reproductions, portraits of the imperial family, and still lifes, such as the "13 épreuves de fleur photographiée d'aprés la nature (ensemble)," by Maurel, purchased in 1856. It is most surprising that the Manufacture's library lacks a copy of the folio atlas illustrated by Émile von Marcke's lithographs after Robert's photographs, *Anciens évêchés de Bretagne* (1855).
21. Geoffrey Batchen, *Burning with Desire* (Cambridge, Mass.: MIT Press, 1997), 26–35. Around 1800, Thomas Wedgwood (1771–1805) successfully obtained photographic images on sensitized leather and other materials. Wedgwood's experiments were direct prints, obtained using flat objects like leaves as stencils. Since he did not know how to fix the images, his results were ultimately lost.
22. Antoinette Faÿ-Hallé and Barbara Mundt, *Porcelain of the Nineteenth Century* (New York: Rizzoli, 1983), 14. Printing on ceramic had been introduced in Great Britain around 1753, but even after a century of development its results were as yet comparatively crude.
23. Phillipe Burty, *Chefs-d'oeuvre of the Industrial Arts*, ed. and trans. W. Chaffers (London: Cassell, Petter, and Galpin, 1869), 171.
24. J. Turgan, *Les Grandes usines de France*, vol. 1, *Sèvres* (Paris: Michel Levy Frères, 1860), 264–66.
25. Alphonse Lafon de Camarsac, *Portraits photographiques sur émail vitrifiés et inaltérables comme les peintures de Sèvres* (Paris: self-published, n.d. [1867?]).
26. Brunet and Préaud, *Sèvres*, 19.
27. Copies of Lafon de Camarsac's 1855 treatise, *Application de l'héliographie aux arts céramiques, aux émaux, à la joaillerie, aux vitraux, ou transformation des dessins photographiques en peinture vitrifiée* (Paris: C. Chevalier, 1855), were in both Regnault's personal library and the Manufacture's.
28. Victor Regnault, "Burnt-in Pictures on Glass or Porcelain," reprinted, *American Journal of Photography and the Allied Arts and Sciences* n.s. 8, no. 3 (1 Aug. 1865): 63–64.
29. Alphonse Lafon de Camarsac, *Portraits photographiques sur émail vitrifiés et inaltérables comme les peintures de Sèvres* (Paris: self-published, [1867]), 3. Several institutions accepted Lafon's proposal to make indelible portraits for posterity of the important figures of the day, and his commissions included photographs of Thiers, Guizot, the membership of the Institut and the *titulaires* of the Légion d'honneur. Paying homage to the S.F.P. in 1867, he made the vitrified portraits of the society's officers, including Regnault.
30. Victor Regnault/Ministre d'État correspondence, 17 Dec. 1852, Archives Nationale, Paris. f21-682.
31. Adalbert de Beaumont, "Les arts décoratifs en Orient et en France," *Revue des deux mondes* 39 (1862): 807.
32. Burty, *Chefs-d'oeuvre*, 166.
33. Ibid., 159.
34. D. G. Charlton, "French Thought in the Nineteenth and Twentieth Centuries," in *France: A Companion Guide to French Studies*, ed. D. G. Charlton (London: Metheun, 1979), 293–94.
35. Burty, *Chefs-d'oeuvre*, 159.
36. Turgan, *Les Grandes usines*, 238.
37. Ibid., 211, 272.
38. Burty, *Chefs-d'oeuvre*, 166.
39. For more on the international exhibitions, see John Allwood, *The Great Exhibitions* (London: Studio Vista, 1977); Patricia Mainardi, *Art and Politics of the Second Empire* (New Haven, Conn., and London: Yale University Press, 1987); Marcia Pointon, "'From the Midst of Warfare and Its Incidents to the Peaceful Scenes of Home': The Exposition Universelle of 1855," *Journal of European Studies* 2 (Dec. 1981): 233–61; and Whitney Walton, *France at the Crystal Palace: Bourgeois Taste and Artisan Manufacture in the Nineteenth Century* (Berkeley and Los Angeles: University of California Press, 1992).
40. Walton, *France at the Crystal Palace*, 6–7.
41. Raymond Lecuyer, *Histoire de la photographie* (Paris: Baschet, 1945).
42. Jacques Werren, "Jules Ziegler, un élève oublié d'Hippolyte Bayard," *Études photographiques* 12 (Nov. 2002): 83.

43. A. J. Du Pays, "Exposition des Manufactures Impériales de Sèvres, des Gobelins, et de Beauvais," *L'Illustration* (1855): 215–18.
44. Baron Louis-Adolphe Humbert de Molard, "Exposition universelle de photographie à Bruxelles," *Bulletin* (1856): 288–89.
45. "Rapport sur l'exposition ouverte par la Société en 1857," *Bulletin* (1857): 289.
46. Elizabeth Anne McCauley, *Industrial Madness: Commercial Photography in Paris, 1848–1871* (New Haven, Conn., and London: Yale University Press, 1994), 278–80. Among the photographers given partial access to the Louvre's collections in the 1850s and early 1860s, one can name Gustave Le Gray, A.-A.-E. Disdéri, Robert Bingham, C. T. Thompson, P. A. Richebourg, and others.
47. Robert/Vaillant correspondence, 6 June 1863, A.N. f21 687.
48. Henri de Lacretelle, "Beaux-Arts: Association des artistes," *La Lumiére* (27 Mar. 1852): 53.
49. Regnault/Vaillant correspondence, 29 June 1863, A.N. f21-687.
50. Ibid.
51. Beaumont, "Les arts décoratifs," 804–40.
52. Edmond de Goncourt and Jules de Goncourt, *Journal: Mémoires de la vie littéraire, 1851–1863*, vol. 1 (Paris: Fasquelle, 1959), 780.
53. McCauley, *Industrial Madness*, 313.
54. Ibid., 292–300.
55. César Graña, *Bohemian versus Bourgeois* (New York: Basic Books, 1964), 61.
56. Burty, *Chefs-d'oeuvre*, 162.
57. For a parallel discussion of taste, social aspiration, and photography in nineteenth-century America, see Miles Orvell, *The Real Thing* (Chapel Hill: University of North Carolina Press, 1989).
58. Vaillant/Regnault correspondence, 6 July 1863, A.N. f21-687.
59. Vaillant/Regnault correspondence, 4 July 1863, A.N. f21-687. Vaillant authorized 1,200 francs to equip the studio.
60. Vaillant/Regnault correspondence, 27 Nov. 1867, A.N. f21-687.
61. Philadelphia Museum of Art, *The Second Empire (1852–1870): Art in France under Napoleon III*, exh. cat. (Philadelphia: Philadelphia Museum of Art, 1978), 177.
62. Regnault/Vaillant correspondence, 25 Feb. 1870, A.N. f21-687. The two prints that turned up at Origny were found to have been discarded test prints, surreptitiously saved from the trash.

CHAPTER 3: FRATERNITY AND FAMILY

1. "Réunion Photographique," *La Lumière* (28 May 1853): 87.
2. Janet E. Buerger, *French Daguerreotypes* (Chicago: University of Chicago Press, 1989), 52.
3. Francis Wey, "Comment le soleil est devenu peintre," pt. 2, *Musée des familles* 20 (July 1853): 298.
4. Francis Wey, "Théorie du portrait," *La Lumière* (27 Apr. 1851): 46.
5. Ibid.
6. Richard Rudisill, *Mirror Image* (Albuquerque: University of New Mexico Press, 1971), 237–38.
7. Henri de Lacretelle, "Salon de 1853," *La Lumière* (9 July 1853): 109.
8. Ernest Mayer, Fréderic Mayer, and Louis Pierson, *La Photographie* (1862; reprint, New York: Arno Press, 1979), 99–100.
9. Mayer, Mayer, and Pierson, *La Photographie*, 99–100.
10. Henri de La Blanchère, *L'Art du photographie* (Paris: Amyot, 1859), 8–9.
11. Wey, "Théorie," 51.
12. Larry J. Schaaf, *Out of the Shadows* (New Haven, Conn., and London: Yale University Press, 1992), 116–17.
13. Nancy Keeler has written on the late start calotype received in France. "The Calotype and Aesthetics in Early Photography," in *Paper and Light: The Calotype in France and Great Britain*, exh. cat., by Richard Brettell et al. (Boston: David R. Godine, 1984), 25–29.
14. N. P. Lerebours, "Plaque, papier, ou verre? Deuxième article," *La Lumière* (1 May 1852): 75.
15. N. P. Lerebours, "Plaque, papier, ou verre? " *La Lumière* (3 Apr. 1852): 58.
16. Ibid.
17. Ibid.
18. Wey, "Comment le soleil," 298.
19. Paul Périer, "Exposition Universelle, 3e article," *Bulletin de la Société française de photographie* (July 1855): 191. Périer was himself admired for his portraits, but he gave pride of place to landscape.
20. *Revue photographique* (5 July 1858): 95.
21. Alain Corbain, "Backstage," in *A History of Private Life: From the Fires of the Revolution to the Great War*, ed. Michelle Perrot (Cambridge, Mass.: Belknap Press of Harvard University, 1990), 4:491–92.
22. Ernest Lacan, *Esquisses photographiques à propos de l'Exposition universelle et de la guerre d'Orient* (1856; reprint, New York: Arno Press, 1979), 215.
23. Victor Regnault/John Herschel correspondence, [1851], Royal Society, London. 319.
24. More remains to be discovered about Regnault's connection to Talbot. The men had ample opportunity to have known each other personally; together with Biot and Herschel, they stood as the four candidates for the Royal Society's Rumford Medal in 1840 (Biot won). With Regnault's occasional visits to England to visit Herschel, it is possible that they met each other at meetings of the Royal Society, or even on social occasions. Likewise, on Talbot's long visit to Paris in 1843, the two men had many opportunities to meet. The *Album Regnault* originally contained four of Talbot's prints.
25. Victor Regnault/Justus von Liebig correspondence, 15 Mar. [1851], no. 28, Staatsbibliothèque München.
26. Regnault/Liebig correspondence, undated [1841], no. 12.
27. The S.F.P. holds more than fifty negatives that portray Regnault's academic colleagues from the Académie des Sciences or the Collège de France, and a group of twenty-six prints of the academicians is found in the S.F.P.'s *Album Regnault*. Eighteen of the portraits in the *Album Regnault* are not included among the other S.F.P. negatives, making the total number of academic portraits close to seventy. Regnault's portraits range in size from 8.7 by 7.3 cm to 21.2 by 16.1 cm.

28. Regnault/Liebig correspondence, 15 Mar. [1851], no. 28.
29. Those scientists identified include Biot, the pioneering physiologist Claude Bernard, marine scientist Auguste Bravais; Scottish chemist Thomas Graham; pisciculturist Victor Coste; German chemist Friedrich Wöhler; the Lille agriculturist Frédéric Kuhlmann; naturalist and physiologist Henri Milne-Edwards; geologist H. Hureau de Sénarmont; artillery specialist General J.-V. Poncelet; chemist Théophile-Jules Pelouze; and Regnault's closest friend and only collaborator, progressive agriculturist Jules Reiset. Fellow academics at the Collège de France include the influential Saint-Simonist economist Michel Chevalier (soon to be a named *conseiller d'État* by Napoléon III); Alexandre Chodzko, a dashing professor of slavic languages; Jules von Mohl, a scholar of Persia; and Adolphe Franck, a philosopher. Other notable sitters for Regnault's camera have been identified: the Barbizon painter Constant Troyon (1810–1865); photographic critic and writer Francis Wey; Baron Armand Séguier, who, like Regnault, was an expert in steam-engine technology and early photographic enthusiast; the painter Carl von Steuben (Regnault's drawing master at the École polytechnique); and possibly Stanislas Julien, sinologist and head administrator at the Collège de France; Jules Reiset's brother Frédéric, a curator at the Louvre; and Baron Desnoyers, an engraver and member of the institute.
30. Only two of Regnault's portraits have surfaced outside his archive (portraits of Biot and the Scottish chemist Thomas Graham, gifts to Sir John Herschel), which supports the conclusion that this collection was always a private one.
31. Graham Smith, *Sun Pictures in Scotland*, exh. cat. (Ann Arbor: University of Michigan Musuem of Art, 1989), 9.
32. Arago presented a group of Hill and Adamson's portraits of the dissenting ministers of the Free Church of Scotland (1843–47) at the Académie des Sciences in 1844, at the urging of Regnault's friend, the painter Ary Scheffer. *Comptes rendus Hebdomadaire* 19 (1844): 489. Their successful studio partnership was ended by Adamson's early death in 1848.
33. The painting (known through a photographic copy) is strongly similar in pose to Regnault's original photograph. The circumstances of this commission and the present location of the painting are not known.
34. Jacques Werren, "Jules Ziegler, un élève oublié d'Hippolyte Bayard," *Études photographiques* 12 (Nov. 2002): 64–97. Ziegler and Regnault are both associated with the Manufacture de Sèvres, but at the time of this sitting (c. 1851) Ziegler had been away from the factory for a decade (he left in 1840), and Regnault was probably not yet director.
35. Françoise Heilbrun, "Nadar and the Art of Portrait Photography," in *Nadar*, exh. cat., Maria Morris Hambourg, Françoise Heilbrun, and Philippe Néagu (New York: Metropolitan Museum of Art, 1995), 37–38.
36. Regnault/Liebig correspondence, 19 July 1840, no. 13.
37. Robert Fox, *The Culture of Science in France, 1700–1900* (Brookfield, Vt.: Variorum, 1992), 464–65.
38. Victor Regnault/Lady Herschel correspondence, undated [Nov. 1853], Royal Society, London. 315.
39. Ibid.
40. Ibid.
41. Roland Barthes, *Camera Lucida* (New York: Hill and Wang, 1981), 71–72.
42. The calotype negatives of his family and academic colleagues, dating approximately from 1850 to 1853, were found in his laboratory at the Collège de France upon his death. It is always possible that later negatives were lost in the destruction of his Sèvres laboratory in 1870.
43. Adeline Daumard, "Affaire, amour, affection: Le Mariage dans la Société bourgeoisie au XIXe siècle," *Romanticisme* 68 (1990): 33–47.
44. Jules Michelet, *La Femme, le prêtre, et la famille* (Paris: Calmann Lévy, 1846), 284.
45. Ibid.
46. By 1852, the couple would have five children: Léon, (1838–1876), Henri (1843–1871), Alice (1847–1897), Eugène (1849–1894), and Jules (1852).
47. Louise Dieterle, *Souvenirs* (Paris: privately published, 1980), 3.
48. Ibid.
49. Edward L. Wilson, "To My Patrons," 1871; reprint, *Photography: Essays and Images*, ed. Beaumont Newhall (New York: Museum of Modern Art, 1980), 129.
50. Perrot, *A History of Private Life*, 4:208–9.
51. Dieterle, *Souvenirs*, 4.
52. Jean-Pierre Bois, "L'art d'être Grand-mère, XVIIe–XIXe Siècle," *Annales de Demographie Historique* (1991): 7–19.
53. Dieterle, *Souvenirs*, 4.
54. Gustave Le Gray, *Photographie. Traité nouveau théorique et pratique des procédés et manipulations sur papier-sec, humide et sur verre au collodion, à l'albumine* (Paris: Lerebours et Secretan, [1852]), 126. Most manuals recommended the three-quarter view. Le Gray advised that at the very least, the head should always be turned slightly in relation to the shoulders.
55. Elizabeth Anne McCauley, *A. A. E. Disdéri and the Carte-de-Visite Portrait Photograph* (New Haven, Conn., and London: Yale University Press, 1985), 140. McCauley cites the possibility of mutual influence between early daguerreotype portraiture and the simple, sometimes austere, portraits by the circle of Ingres.
56. Charles Baudelaire, "The Salon of 1846: On Portraiture," ed. and trans. Jonathan Mayne, *Art in Paris, 1845–1862* (London: Phaidon Press, 1965), 89. Flandrin's portrait of Madame Regnault is lost, possibly destroyed during the siege of the Manufacture in 1870.
57. Arthur Duparc, *Correspondance de Henri Regnault* (Paris: Charpentier et Cie., 1872), 34.
58. Dieterle, *Souvenirs*, 3.
59. Ibid.
60. E. de Valicourt, *Photographie simplifiée*, quoted in McCauley, *Likenesses: Portrait Photography in Europe, 1850–1870*, exh. cat. (Albuquerque: University of New Mexico, 1980), 10.

61. Elizabeth Heyert, *The Glass-House Years* (Montclair, N.J.: Allanheld, Osmu, & Co., 1979), 42.
62. Duparc, *Correspondance de Henri Regnault*, 86.
63. Ibid., 134.

CHAPTER 4: LANDSCAPE IN THE SHADOW OF INDUSTRY

1. Greg M. Thomas, *Art and Ecology in Nineteenth-Century France: The Landscapes of Théodore Rousseau* (Princeton, N.J.: Princeton University Press, 2000), 1. Thomas puts this nicely, describing landscape as "a relationship between people and the ambient world."
2. Paul Périer, "Exposition Universelle, 3e Article—Photographes français," *Bulletin de la Société française de photographie* (1855): 191.
3. Nicholas Green, *The Spectacle of Nature* (Manchester, U.K.: University of Manchester Press, 1990), 68–70.
4. Périer, "Exposition Universelle, 3e Article," 191.
5. Françoise Cachin, "Le Paysage du peintre," in *Les Lieux de mémoire*, ed. Pierre Nora (Paris: Éditions Gallimard, 1986), 436. Cachin explains this delay as fundamentally related to the fact of France's monarchical culture and French national identity's basis in the supremacy of king and God; art was conscripted largely to their glorification. Until the emergence of a significant bourgeois land-owning class, Cachin argues, land was considered by most as a site of subsistence or production, not as an aesthetic object. See also Andrée Corvol, "Une esthetique de l'environment," in *La Nature en revolution 1750–1800*, ed. Andrée Corvol (Paris: Editions L'Harmattan, 1993), 3–14. Here Corvol explains the postrevolutionary surge in landscape painting as a pragmatic response to the volatile political environment: landscape, like portraiture, was an ostensibly neutral subject. I would add, however, that this did not stop Barbizon painting from being interpreted as ideologically driven.
6. Prosper Dorbec, *L'Art du paysage en France* (Paris: Henri Laurens, 1925), 4–5. For more on the emergence of landscape art in Britain, see Ann Bermingham, *Landscape and Ideology* (Berkeley and Los Angeles: University of California Press, 1986).
7. William Gilpin, *Three Essays: On Picturesque Beauty, and on Sketching Landscape, to Which Is Added a Poem on Landscape Painting* (London: R. Blamire, 1792), iii. Gilpin's *Three Essays* was translated into French in 1799, followed immediately by the translation of two of his books on picturesque travel.
8. Pierre-Henri de Valenciennes, *Eléments de perspective pratique à l'usage des artistes, suivi de Réflexions et conseils à un élève sur la peinture et particulièrement sur le genre du paysage* (1800; reprint, Geneva: Minkoff, 1973), 380. Borrowing from the art theorist Roger de Piles, Valenciennes also posited an even higher form, the "heroic" landscape, which was a direct quotation of the antique, but his treatise gave a privileged view of the "pastoral" form. As the paysage portrait was seen as having Dutch origins, and the "pastoral" form Italian origins, these two modes of working were also sometimes described as the northern style and southern style.

   The ascension of landscape in French aesthetic theory was technically complete by 1818, when Valenciennes's student J. B. Deperthes published his *Theory of Landscape*, which allowed no difference in value between the naturalistic landscape and the idealized landscape. Critical and academic reception of landscape in the salon, however, lagged behind artists' interest in the nascent naturalist landscape style, and would not fully embrace it until the 1850s, nearly twenty years after its most vigorous period was over.
9. Valenciennes, *Eléments*, 493.
10. Cachin, "Le Paysage du Peintre," 439.
11. Petra ten-Doesschate Chu, "At Home and Abroad Landscape Representation," in *The Art of the July Monarchy*, exh. cat., ed. Gabriel Weisberg (Columbia: University of Missouri Press, 1990), 130.
12. Charles Baudelaire, "Salon of 1859: The Modern Public and Photography," ed. and trans. Jonathan Mayne, *Art in Paris, 1845–1862* (London: Phaidon Press, 1965), 152.
13. Others who have written about Barbizon and photography include: Bernard Marbot and Daniel Challe, *Les Photographes de Barbizon* (Paris: Editions Hoëbeke/Bibliothèque Nationale, 1991); Eugenia Parry Janis, *The Photography of Gustave Le Gray*, exh. cat. (Chicago: Art Institute of Chicago and University of Chicago Press, 1987); Robert Sobieszek, "Photography and the Theory of Realism in the Second Empire: A Reexamination of a Relationship," in *One Hundred Years of Photographic History*, ed. Van Deren Coke (Albuquerque: University of New Mexico Press, 1975).
14. Steven Adams, *The Barbizon School and the Origins of Impressionism* (New York: Phaidon Press, Ltd., 1994), 93.
15. Two other important officers of the S.F.P. were landscapists, although this was not their main work: Eugène Durieu (president of the administration committee), and Hippolyte Bayard.
16. Similarly, the photograph's tonal harmony and a monochromatic, silvery palette may have been what attracted Corot, Daubigny, Huet, Millet, and others to try working with the cliché-verre technique of creating cameraless negatives on glass plates.
17. The relationship between Dutch-inspired realist painting and the rise of photography in France has further been addressed by Sobieszek in "Photography and the Theory of Realism," 146–59. André Jammes and Eugenia Janis, however, minimize early French photography's connection to Dutch models in *The Art of French Calotype*, exh. cat. (Princeton, N.J.: Princeton University Press, 1983), 18–20. Among the most prominent French collectors of Dutch art were the photographers Paul Périer, Benjamin Delessert, photography critic Philippe Burty, and the photography collectors Isaac and Émile Péreire. Périer and Burty also acquired important collections of Barbizon painting, with Périer emerging as Rousseau's most important patron. Petra ten-Doesschate Chu, *French Realism and the Dutch Masters* (Utrecht, the Netherlands: Haentjens Dekker and Gumbert, 1974), 24. See also Greg M. Thomas, *Art and Ecology*, 85–86.
18. Théophile Thoré-Bürger quoted in Chu, *French Realism*, 12. Ernest Lacan,

"Exposition Universelle, 8e article," *La Lumière* (10 Nov. 1855): 176.

19. Ernest Lacan, "Exposition Universelle, 6e article," *La Lumière* (20 Oct. 1855): 165.

20. Ernest Lacan, "Exposition Universelle, Photographie, 4e article," *La Lumière* (6 Oct. 1855): 159; Périer, "Exposition Universelle, 3e article," 196.

21. Robert Herbert, *Barbizon Revisited*, exh. cat. (New York: Clark and Way, 1964), 39. See also, Chu, *French Realism*, 14–15. In their naturalism and everyday subjects, all three were "democratic" art forms that did not require a classical education to be understood.

22. Herbert, *Barbizon Revisited*, 64–65. Herbert was among the first to study the causal relationship between the industrial, productive appropriation of open lands and the rise of naturalistic landscape painting in France.

23. Ibid., 37–40. Herbert describes the popular turn toward social consciousness during the July Monarchy, noting that Fouriéristes, Saint-Simonistes, and others attracted to programs of social progress and change called openly for "an art of actuality as a means of communicating with the masses, who were to be thus educated to inherit the power and knowledge of the moribund elite." He further argues that the Revolution of 1848 was another strong stimulus to naturalistic painting and peasant subjects, but that overtly socialist expressions in art were quickly quashed by the return of conservatism in the Second Empire. More recently, Greg Thomas has argued that the radical associations attached to Théodore Rousseau (long considered with Millet as the most openly radical of the Barbizon painters) were largely projections of contemporary critics like Théophile Thoré. Thomas, *Art and Ecology*, 11.

24. Paul Périer insisted, however, that the problem was inherited from portrait painters: the major goal was rarely to produce a good portrait, but rather, to sell many portraits. Paul Périer, "Exposition Universelle, 5e article," *Bulletin* (1855): 261–62. See chapter 3 for a full discussion of the critical ambivalence toward portrait photography.

25. "Rapport sur la section de photographie à l'exposition des arts industriels de bruxelles (suite)," *Bulletin* (1858): 109.

26. Ernest Lacan, "Exposition Universelle, Photographie, 5e article," *La Lumière* (13 Oct. 1855): 162.

27. Comité d'administration [S.F.P.], "Première exposition publique dans les salons de la société," *Bulletin* (1855): 41.

28. Françoise Heilbrun, "Appendix: The Landscape in French Nineteenth-Century Photography," in *A Day in the Country*, ed. Andrea Belloli, exh. cat. (Los Angeles: Los Angeles County Museum of Art, 1984), 349.

29. Périer, "Exposition Universelle, 3e article," 188.

30. Ibid., 190–91. Many thanks to Nina Cannizzaro for the Latin translation.

31. See Sylvie Aubenas, *Gustave Le Gray, 1820–1884*, English trans. (Los Angeles: J. Paul Getty Museum, 2002), 330–31.

32. Delessert, of another politically connected banking family, served on the boards for at least two railroads and may have been a major stockholder in the Parisian Gas Company, on whose board Regnault also served. Marquis Raymond de Bérenger was a wealthy, titled landowner; and Henri de La Blanchère was a natural scientist who received government commissions as a consultant to the emerging fisheries industry.

33. Elizabeth Anne McCauley, "Les frères Aguado, photographes amateurs, à la coeur du Second Empire," in *Olympe Aguado: Photographe*, exh. cat. (Strasbourg, France: Musées de Strasbourg, 1997), 65.

34. The era's most acquisitive industrialists, the Péreire brothers (founders of Crédit Immobilier, chief officers of the Compagnie Parisienne du Gaz, and railway magnates), were also great patrons of both Barbizon art and photography, though not photographers themselves.

35. Karl Marx and Friedrich Engels, *The Communist Manifesto*, ed. D. Ryazanoff (1848; reprint, New York: Russell & Russell, 1963).

36. Thomas, *Art and Ecology*, 5–10.

37. Périer, "Exposition Universelle, 6e article. Photographes étrangers," *Bulletin* (1855): 317.

38. Périer, "Exposition Universelle, 2e article." *Bulletin* (1855): 172.

39. Jean-Baptiste Dumas, *Éloge de Victor Regnault: Ingénieur en chef des mines* (Paris: Dunod, 1881), 21–22. Regnault's double background in mechanics and physics allowed him to analyze, measure, and control the precise action of steam, which exponentially increased the power and efficiency of these engines.

40. Henri Le Chatelier, "Discours [Centenary of Victor Regnault]," *Annales des mines* (Jan. 1911): 16. Regnault supposedly achieved this single-handedly, having designed the furnaces and distillation equipment himself to achieve the utmost precision (and economy) in the distillation of gas from coal.

41. Lenard R. Berlanstein, *Big Business and Industrial Conflict in Nineteeth-Century France* (Berkeley and Los Angeles: University of California Press, 1991), 4–5. The company ultimately became a symbol of corporate greed when continued falling production costs and the rising resale value of chemical byproducts failed to produce further savings for consumers.

42. Le Chatelier, "Discours," 17.

43. An early note on the verso of the print, not in Regnault's hand, describes this as "Sèvres et ses environs. Bords de la Seine. Usine à Gaz sur la rive droite en aval du Pont de Sèvres 18." I believe this note, like the notes on all thirty-two large-format Regnault prints in the collection of the Musée d'Orsay (formerly, collection of the Manufacture de Sèvres), was added in the early twentieth century. There are conflicting reports as to whether the first experimental gas factory was at Saint-Cloud (Le Chatelier, 1911), or as the print caption suggests, at Boulogne.

44. Quentin Bajac, "La photographie à Sèvres sous le second Empire: du laboratoire au jardin," *La revue du Musée d'Orsay* 5 (fall 1997): 79.

45. Other pictures attributed to Regnault by Franz Jayot, archivist of the Sèvres Municipal Archives, are topographic views of the Manufacture and the surrounding town, taking in structures like industrial sheds and the new train station.

46. Constant Troyon, whose parents both worked in the Sèvres factory, was a lifelong friend of Louis Robert's. Robert also made calotypes of rustic subjects that were clearly made in the Barbizon spirit.

47. F. Hamilton Hazlehurst, *Gardens of Illusion: The Genius of André Le Nostre* (Nashville, Tenn.: Vanderbilt University Press, 1980), 281. Le Nôtre regarded his work at Saint-Cloud as one of the masterpieces of his career.
48. Both men made photographs in the orangerie, steps apart from each other; they look like they could have been made on the same day.
49. Gilpin, *Three Essays*, 8.
50. Paul Périer, "Exposition Universelle, 3e article," 194.
51. Jammes and Janis, *Art of French Calotype*, 16.
52. Mike Weaver, "Henry Fox Talbot: Conversation Pieces," in *The Photographic Art: Pictorial Traditions in Britain and America*, ed. Mike Weaver (New York: Harper and Row, 1986), 11–23; Michel Frizot, "The *Parole* of the Primitives, Hippolyte Bayard, and French Calotypists," *History of Photography* 16, no. 4 (winter 1992): 358–70.
53. Mike Weaver, *The Photographic Art: Pictorial Traditions in Britain and America* (New York: Harper and Row, 1986).
54. Frizot, "The *Parole* of the Primitives," 359. Frizot doubts that the notion of the picturesque was even part of the French photographer's vocabulary before the 1850s, but this is unlikely, given the popularity of Gilpin's translated writings in France after 1799 and the currency of *Voyages pittoresques* prints in the 1830s.
55. Ibid.
56. Isabelle Jammes, *Blanquart-Evrard et les origines de l'édition photographique française, catalogue raisonné des albums photographiques édités, 1851–1855* (Geneva and Paris: Librairie Droz, 1981): 73.
57. At the time of his experimentation with these motifs in photography, Regnault was also involved in researching the old Sèvres soft-paste porcelain for a revival of rococo forms and techniques, and the time spent looking at similar delicate vignettes in porcelain might have suggested certain ideas to him for his photography. Steven Adams also finds a connection between Barbizon landscape and porcelain decoration. Adams, *The Barbizon School*, 89.
58. Wolfgang Kemp, "Images of Decay: Photography in the Picturesque Tradition," *October* 54 (fall 1990): 107.
59. For a discussion of the economic forces changing social patterns in France at mid-century, see Robert L. Herbert, "City vs. Country: The Rural Image in French Painting from Millet to Gauguin," *Artforum* (Feb. 1970): 44–55. Herbert notes the particular crisis of depopulation—and the consequent disruption of agricultural life—affecting the Île-de-France (including the department of Yvelines, where Sèvres is), which supplied most of the numbers entering the Paris workforce.
60. Victor Regnault/John Herschel correspondence, n.d., Royal Society, 319. The context of this letter suggests a date of 1851.
61. Dumas, *Éloge de Victor Regnault*, 20. For his inaugural course as the chair of physics at the Collège de France in 1841, Regnault chose the subject of optics.
62. Dorbec, *L'Art du paysage*, 12.
63. Mariette Portet, *Sèvres en Île-de-France* (Condé-sur-Noireau, France: Ch. Corlet, 1975).
64. Regnault's exposure times are not known, but they were probably comparable to those of John Stewart. In 1852, Stewart reported his success in using wet-paper negatives, following "the valuable indications of Professor Regnault," which included the use of the vacuum pump method of sensitizing paper. He reported exposure times of 10–90 minutes for landscape. J.F.W. Herschel, "Photographic Landscapes on Paper," *The Athenaeum* (11 Dec. 1852): 1363–64.
65. "Procès-verbal," *Bulletin* (18 Apr. 1856): 132.
66. Heilbrun, "Appendix," 348–62.
67. Following his studies with the chemist Gay-Lussac at the École des mines, in 1834 and 1835 Regnault was sent to Belgium, Switzerland, and Germany to study mining and other industrial sites.
68. Regnault travel notebook, 1835, Institut de France, Paris. 2847.
69. J.-D. Du Vernay, "Statistique de la Photographie," *La Lumière* (Sept. 1852), 155.

CHAPTER 5: THE THREE FACES OF PHOTOGRAPHY

1. J.-D. Du Vernay, "Statistique de la Photographie," *La Lumière* (Sept. 1852): 155.
2. D. G. Charlton, "French Thought in the Nineteenth and Twentieth Centuries," in *France: A Companion Guide to French Studies*, ed. D. G. Charlton (London: Methuen, 1979), 266.
3. Douglas Johnson, "French History and Society from the Revolution to the Fifth Republic," in *France: A Companion Guide*, 162–64.
4. Ibid., 173.
5. These two trends are by now well-documented. See, for example, T. J. Clark, *The Painting of Modern Life* (Princeton, N.J.: Princeton University Press, 1984); John M. Merriman, ed., *Consciousness and Class Experience in Nineteenth-Century Europe* (New York: Holmes and Meier, 1979); Leora Auslander, *Taste and Power: Furnishing Modern France* (Berkeley and Los Angeles: University of California Press, 1996); and Whitney Walton, *France at the Crystal Palace: Bourgeois Taste and Artisan Manufacture in the Nineteenth Century* (Berkeley and Los Angeles: University of California Press, 1992).
6. J. Blondel, "Contemporary France: Politics, Society, and Institutions," in *France: A Companion Guide*, 581–82.
7. Elizabeth Anne McCauley, *Likenesses: Portrait Photography in Europe, 1850–1870*, exh. cat. (Albuquerque: University of New Mexico Press, 1980), 20.
8. François-Victor Fournel, "Ce qu'on voit dans les rues de Paris," 1858, in *La Photographie en France*, ed. André Rouillé (Paris: Éditions MACULA, 1989), 294–95.
9. A great deal continues to be written about photography and its application to social control. See, for example, John Tagg, *The Burden of Representation* (Bassingstroke, U.K.: Macmillan, 1988); Allan Sekula, "The Body and the Archive," in Richard Bolton, ed., *The Contest of Meaning* (Cambridge, Mass.: MIT Press, 1989); Lindsey Smith, *The Politics of Focus* (Manchester, U.K.: Manchester University Press, 1998).
10. The classic study in English on France's technological transformation is

David S. Landes, *The Unbound Prometheus: Technological Change and Industrial Development in Western Europe from 1750 to the Present* (Cambridge, U.K.: Cambridge University Press, 1969). Landes's thesis that technological growth in France was retarded by a confluence of economic, material, and social factors has been recently challenged by Rondo Cameron and Charles E. Freedeman in "French Economic Growth: A Radical Revision," *Social Science History* 7 (1983): 3–30. Charles Coulston Gillispie has written extensively on science and technology in the transition from early modern to modern France, with specific attention to the eighteenth-century management of the Manufacture Royale de Sèvres. Charles Coulston Gillispie, *Science and Polity in France at the End of the Old Regime* (Princeton, N.J.: Princeton University Press, 1980).

11. D. G. Charlton, "French Thought in the Nineteenth and Twentieth Centuries," in *France: A Companion Guide*, 269–78.
12. François Arago, "Rapport à la Chambre des députés," 1839, in *La Photographie en France*, ed. André Rouillé (Paris: Éditions MACULA, 1989), 38–39.
13. Francis Wey, "De l'influence de l'héliographie sur les Beaux-Arts," *La Lumière* (9 Feb. 1851): 2 3.
14. Charles Baudelaire, "Salon of 1859: The Modern Public and Photography," trans. and ed. Jonathan Mayne, *Art in Paris, 1845–1862* (London: Phaidon Press, 1965), 154.
15. Ibid., 155.
16. Edmond de Goncourt and Jules de Goncourt, *Journal: Mémoires de la vie littéraire 1851–1863* (Paris: Fasquelle, 1959), 1:158.
17. Ibid., 126.
18. Elizabeth Anne McCauley, *Industrial Madness: Commercial Photography in Paris, 1848–1871* (New Haven, Conn., and London: Yale University Press, 1994), 1.
19. Paul Périer, "Exposition Universelle, 2e article," *Bulletin de la Société française de la photographie* (1855): 172.
20. See, for example, the demand by the Société photographique de Marseille, to have the stanchions removed that physically and symbolically separated the photography from the other fine arts in the annual Salon. E. L. [Ernest Lacan?], "Société photographique de Marseille," 1863, in *La Photographie en France*, ed. André Rouillé (Paris: Éditions MACULA, 1989), 417–18.
21. Ulrich Keller, "The Myth of Art Photography: A Sociological Analysis," *History of Photography* 8, no. 4 (1984): 249–75.
22. Pierre Bordieu, *Photography: A Middle-Brow Art*, trans. Shaun Whiteside (Stanford, Calif.: Stanford University Press, 1990), 9.
23. Bordieu, *Photography*, 5. Bordieu points to the "time-saving" aspect of photography as a key component of its success as a middle-class practice. More recently, Rosalind Krauss has questioned whether a person who practices a set of techniques without "an apprenticeship, a juvenilia, a learning of one's craft and the gaining of an individuated view of that tradition" that takes place over a period of time, can rightly be called an artist. Rosalind Krauss, "Photography's Discursive Spaces," reprint, *The Contest of Meaning*, ed. Richard Bolton (Cambridge, Mass.: MIT Press, 1989), 293.
24. César Graña, *Bohemian versus Bourgeois* (New York: Basic Books, 1964), 65.
25. Graña, *Bohemian versus Bourgeois*, 61–62. Here Graña provides a considered definition of the popular (negative) use of the term *bourgeois*.
26. Henri Regnault / Victor Regnault correspondence, 19 Jan. 1870, in Arthur Duparc, *Correspondance de Henri Regnault* (Paris: Charpentier et Cie., 1872), 340.
27. An angry exchange of letters between Louis Robert and Regnault in February and March of 1871 alludes to a letter written by Robert that was published in *Le Figaro*. Regnault adamantly argued that in the *Figaro* letter, Robert gave the impression that Regnault had abandoned his post at Sèvres, and that he, Robert, had been the one to elicit the Prussian prince's order of protection for the factory. This is supported by a statement in a letter from Henriette Robert to her father: "Everybody here was unanimous in denouncing the conduct of Mr. Regnault in having left the Manufacture, and recognized, by contrast, that your devotion has been very great." Letter from Henriette Robert Van Marcke to Louis Robert, 26 Dec. 1870. Letters of Louis Robert, Collection of Guy Watelin, Paris.
28. Édouard Laboulaye, "Discours prononcés par des membres de l'Académie aux funérailles de M. Regnault," *Comptes rendus hebdomadaires des séances de l'Académie des sciences* 86 (1878): 142.
29. Louise Dieterle, *Souvenirs* (Paris: privately published, 1980), 5.
30. J. C. Gautrand, "Victor Regnault," *Le Nouveau Photocinema* 74 (Dec. 1978): 125.

MANUSCRIPTS AND UNPUBLISHED MATERIALS

Archives de la Manufacture Nationale de Sèvres, France.

M 14–15. Administration intérieure.
Oa 4. Personnel.
Ob 11. Dossiers personnelles.
Pb 24. Travaux des ateliers.
Pb 12. Travaux des ateliers.
R 55–67. Recettes et dépenses.
T 17. Correspondence générale.
Ve. Procès verbaux des conférences.
Y 15. Conférences.

Archives Nationale, Paris. f21 series. Archives of the Administration des Beaux-Arts.

Institut de France, Paris. [8NS 20636], 2821–936 Papers of Victor Regnault.

Archives of the Académie des Sciences. Dossier Regnault.

Archives of the Académie des Sciences. Meeting files, 18 Feb. 1839; 19 Aug. 1839; 4 Jan. 1841; 28 Sept. 1846; 11 Jan. 1847; 29 Nov. 1847; 27 May 1850. Member dossiers: Arago, Balard, Bernard, Biot, Boussingault, Chevreul, Chasles, Coste, Deville (Sainte-Claire), Dumas, Edwards (Milne), Elie de Beaumont, Faye, Fremy, Gasparin, Gay, Herschel, Jaubert, Jobert, Lamé, Liebig, Liouville, Mauvais, Moquin-Tandon, Peligot, Pelouze, Pouillet, Quatrefages, Rayer, Regnault, Reiset, Séguier, de Senarmont.

International Museum of Photography at George Eastman House. Papers of Gabriel Cromer.

Musée d'Orsay, Paris. Album Dieterle.

Private collection, Paris. Papers of Louis Robert

Royal Photographic Society, London. Minutes of the Council

Royal Society, London. Sir John Herschel Collection. Victor Regnault/Herschel correspondence, 1851–61.

Staatsbibliothèque München. Victor Regnault/Justus von Liebig correspondence, 1834–56.

PERIODICALS CONSULTED

Bulletin de la Société française de photographie, 1855–68
Comptes rendus de l'Académie des sciences, 1839–60
Liverpool Photographic Journal, 1854
La Lumière, 1851–64

PUBLISHED WORKS

Académie des Sciences. "Discours prononcés par des membres de l'Académie aux funérailles de M. Regnault." *Comptes rendus hebdomadaires des séances de l'Académie des sciences* 86 (1878): 131–43.

Adams, Steven. *The Barbizon School and the Origins of Impressionism*. London: Phaidon Press, Ltd., 1994.

Aubenas, Sylvie. *Gustave Le Gray, 1820–1884*. English trans. Los Angeles: The J. Paul Getty Museum, 2002.

Auslander, Leora. *Taste and Power: Furnishing Modern France*. Berkeley and Los Angeles: University of California Press, 1996.

Bajac, Quentin. "La photographie à Sèvres sous le second Empire: du laboratoire au jardin." *La revue du Musée d'Orsay* 5 (fall 1997): 74–85.

Batchen, Geoffrey. *Burning with Desire*. Cambridge, Mass.: MIT Press, 1997.

Baudelaire, Charles. *Art in Paris, 1845–1862*. Ed. and trans. Jonathan Mayne. London: Phaidon Press, 1965.

Beauge, Gilbert, ed. *Collection du journal "La Lumière."* Paris: Jeanne Laffitte, 1995.

Beaumont, Adalbert de. "Les arts décoratifs en Orient et en France." *Revue des deux mondes* 39 (1862): 804–40.

Bermingham, Ann. *Landscape and Ideology*. Berkeley and Los Angeles: University of California Press, 1986.

Bibliothèque Nationale. *Une Invention du XIXe siècle, expression et technique: La photographie; Collections de la Société française de photographie*. Paris: Bibliothèque Nationale, 1976.

Biget, J.-L., J. Boissière, and J.-C. Hervé, eds. *Le Bois et la ville du moyen age au XXe siècle*. Saint-Cloud, France: École Normale Supérieure de Fontenay, 1991.

Blanquart-Evrard, Louis-Désiré. *La Photographie, ses origines, ses progrès, ses transformations*. Lille, France: Imprimerie L. Danel, 1869.

Bordieu, Pierre. *Photography: A Middle-Brow Art*. Trans. Shaun Whiteside. Stanford, Calif.: Stanford University Press, 1990.

Brettell, Richard R., et al. *Paper and Light: The Calotype in France and Great Britain*. Boston: David R. Godine, 1984.

Brongniart, Alexandre. *Du caractère et de l'état actuel de la Manufacture royale de porcelaine de Sèvres, et de son influence sur l'art et le commerce de la porcelaine*. Paris: Imprimerie de Amb. Firmin Didot, 1830.

Brunet, Marcelle, and Tamara Préaud. *Sèvres: Des origines à nos jours*. Fribourg, Switzerland: Office du Livre, 1978.

Buerger, Janet E. *The Era of the French Calotype*. Rochester, N.Y.: International Center of Photography at George Eastman House, 1982.

———. *French Daguerreotypes*. Chicago: University of Chicago Press, 1989.

Burty, Philippe. *Chefs-d'oeuvre of the Industrial Arts*. Ed. and trans. W. Chaffers. London: Cassell, Petter, and Galpin, 1869.

Cachin, Françoise. "Le Paysage du Peintre." In *Les Lieux de mémoire*, ed. Pierre Nora. Paris: Éditions Gallimard, 1986.

Challe, Daniel, and Bernard Marbot. *Les Photographes de Barbizon*. Exh. cat. Paris: Editions Hoëbeke/Bibliothèque Nationale, 1991.

Champa, Kermit. *The Rise of Landscape Painting in France*. Exh. cat. Manchester, N.H.: Currier Gallery of Art, 1991.

Chu, Petra ten-Doesschate. *French Realism and the Dutch Masters*. Utrecht, the Netherlands: Haentjens Dekker and Gumbert, 1974.

Cousin, Victor. "Du Beau et de l'Art." *Revue des deux mondes* 2 (1845): 773–811.

Clark, T. J. *The Absolute Bourgeois: Artists and Politics in France, 1848–1851*. London: Thames and Hudson, 1973.

———. *The Painting of Modern Life*. Princeton, N.J.: Princeton University Press, 1984.

Crosland, Maurice. *Science under Control: The French Academy of Science*. Cambridge, U.K.: Cambridge University Press, 1992.

Dahlberg, Laurie. "Victor Regnault, Louis Robert, and Photography at the Manufacture Impériale de Porcelaine de Sèvres." Ph.D. diss., Princeton University, 1999.

Daumard, Adeline. "Affaire, amour, affection: Le mariage dans la société bourgeoise au XIXe siècle." *Romanticisme* 68 (1990): 33–47.

Dieterle, Louise. *Souvenirs*. Paris: privately published, 1980.

Dorbec, Prosper. *L'Art du paysage en France*. Paris: H. Laurens, 1925.

Dörries, Matthias. "Easy Transit: Crossing Boundaries Between Physics and Chemistry in Mid-Nineteenth-Century France." In *Making Space for Science*, ed., Crosbie Smith. New York: St. Martin's Press, 1998.

Dumas, Jean-Baptiste. *Éloge de Victor Regnault: Ingénieur en chef des mines*. Paris: Dunod, 1881.

Duparc, Arthur. *Correspondance de Henri Regnault.* Paris: Charpentier et Cie., 1872.

Flandrin, Jean-Louis. *Families in Former Times*. Cambridge, U.K.: Cambridge University Press, 1976.

Fournel, François Victor. "Ce qu'on voit dans les rues de Paris," 1858. In *La Photographie en France*, ed. André Rouillé. Paris: Éditions MACULA, 1989, 289–95.

Fox, Robert. *The Culture of Science in France, 1700–1900*. Brookfield, Vt.: Variorum, 1992.

Frizot, Michel. "The *Parole* of the Primitives, Hippolyte Bayard, and French Calotypists." *History of Photography* 16, no. 4 (winter 1992): 358–70.

Gaudin, Marc-Antoine. *Traité pratique de photographie*. Paris: J. J. Dubochet et Cie., 1844.

Gillispie, Charles Coulston. *Science and Polity in France at the End of the Old Regime*. Princeton, N.J.: Princeton University Press, 1980.

Gilpin, William. *Three Essays: On Picturesque Beauty, and on Sketching Landscape, to Which Is Added a Poem on Landscape Painting*. London: R. Blamire, 1792.

Graña, César. *Bohemian versus Bourgeois*. New York: Basic Books, 1964.

Green, Nicholas. *The Spectacle of Nature*. Manchester, U.K.: University of Manchester Press, 1990.

Gunthert, André. "L'institution du photographique. Le roman de la Société Héliographique." *Études photographiques* 12 (Nov. 2002): 37–63.

Hambourg, Maria Morris, Françoise Heilbrun, and Philippe Néagu. *Nadar*. Exh. cat. New York: Metropolitan Museum of Art, 1995.

Heilbrun, Françoise. "Appendix: The Landscape in French Nineteenth-Century Photography." In *A Day in the Country*, ed. Andrea Belloli. Exh. cat. Los Angeles: Los Angeles County Museum of Art, 1984.

Herbert, Robert. *Barbizon Revisited*. Exh. cat. New York: Clark and Way, 1964.

____________. "City vs. Country: The Rural Image in French Painting from Millet to Gauguin." *Artforum* (Feb. 1970): 44–55.

Jammes, André. "Victor Regnault, Calotypist." In *One Hundred Years of Photographic History: Essays in Honor of Beaumont Newhall*, ed. Van Deren Coke. Albuquerque: University of New Mexico Press, 1975.

Jammes, André, and Eugenia Parry Janis. *The Art of French Calotype*. Exh. cat. Princeton, N.J.: Princeton University Press, 1983.

Jammes, Isabelle. *Blanquart-Evrard et les origines de l'édition photographique française, catalogue raisonné des albums photographiques édités, 1851–1855*. Geneva: Librairie Droz, 1981.

Janis, Eugenia Parry. *The Photography of Gustave Le Gray*. Exh. cat. Chicago: Art Institute of Chicago and University of Chicago Press, 1987.

Jayot, Franz. *Les débuts de la photographie à Sèvres*. Exh. cat. Sèvres, France: Archives de Sèvres, 1985.

Kemp, Wolfgang. "Images of Decay: Photography in the Picturesque Tradition." *October* 54 (fall 1990): 103–33.

Krauss, Rosalind. "Photography's Discursive Spaces." In *The Contest of Meaning*, ed. Richard Bolton. Cambridge, Mass.: MIT Press, 1989.

La Blanchère, Henri de. *L'art du photographie*. Paris: Amyot, 1859.

Lacan, Ernest. "Exposition photographique de Bruxelles." *La Lumière* (20 Sept. 1856): 145–46.

____________. *Esquisses photographiques à propos de l'Exposition universelle et de la guerre d'Orient*. 1856. Reprint, New York: Arno Press, 1979.

Landes, David S. *The Unbound Prometheus: Technological Change and Industrial Development in Western Europe from 1750 to the Present*. Cambridge, U.K.: Cambridge University Press, 1969.

Le Chatelier, Henri. "Discours [Centenary of Victor Regnault]." *Annales des mines*. (Jan. 1911): 7–19.

Lecuyer, Raymond. *Histoire de la photographie*. Paris: Baschet, 1945.

Le Gray, Gustave. *Photographie: Traité nouveau théorique et pratique des procédés et manipulations sur papier-sec, humide et sur verre au collodion, à l'albumine*. Paris: Lerebours et Secretan, undated [1852].

Lerebours, N. P. *A Treatise on Photography*. Trans. J. Egerton. 1843. Reprint, New York: Arno Press, 1973.

____________. "Plaque, papier, ou verre?" *La Lumière* (3 Apr. 1852): 58–59.

____________. "Plaque, papier, ou verre? Deuxième article." *La Lumière* (1 May 1852): 74–75.

Mainardi, Patricia. *Art and Politics of the Second Empire*. New Haven, Conn., and London: Yale University Press, 1987.

Marien, Mary Warner. *Photography and Its Critics*. Cambridge, U.K.: Cambridge University Press, 1997.

Martinez, Romeo, ed. "Victor Regnault: Premier président de la Société française de photographie." Special issue, *Bulletin de la Société française de photographie* (Apr. 1982): 1–25.

McCauley, Elizabeth Anne. *Likenesses: Portrait Photography in Europe, 1850–1870*. Exh. cat. Albuquerque: University of New Mexico, 1980.

____________. *A. A. E. Disdéri and the Carte-de-Visite Portrait Photograph*. New Haven, Conn., and London: Yale University Press, 1985.

____________. *Industrial Madness: Commercial Photography in Paris, 1848–1871*. New Haven, Conn., and London: Yale University Press, 1994.

Metropolitan Museum of Art. *After Daguerre: Masterworks of French Photography, 1848–1900, from the Bibliothèque Nationale*. Text by Jean Pierre Seguin and Weston Naef, cat. by Bernard Marbot. Exh. cat. New York: Metropolitan Museum of Art, 1980.

Michelet, Jules. *La Femme, le prêtre, et la famille*. Paris: Calmann Lévy, 1846.

Musée des Arts Décoratifs. *Victor Regnault, 1810–1878: Oeuvre photographique*. Essays by Romeo Martinez and Pierre Gassman. Exh. cat. Paris: Musée des Arts Décoratifs, 1979.

Musées de Strasbourg. *Olympe Aguado photographe (1827–1894)*. Essays by Hélène Bocard, Elizabeth Anne McCauley, and Michel Poivert. Exh. cat. Drulingen, France: Scheuer, 1997.

Museum of Art and Archaeology, University of Missouri-Columbia. *The Art of the July Monarchy*. Exh. cat. Columbia: University of Missouri Press, 1990.

Nickel, Douglas. "Photography and Invisibility." In *The Artist and the Camera*, ed. Dorothy Kosinski. Dallas: Dallas Museum of Art, 1999.

Périer, Paul. "Exposition Universelle." Parts 1–6. *Bulletin de la Société française de photographie* (May–Oct. 1855): (May) 146–48; (June) 167–76; (July) 187–201; (Aug.) 213–28; (Sept.) 256–74; (Oct.) 314–32.

Perrot, Michelle. "The Three Ages of Industrial Discipline." In *Consciousness and Class Experience in Nineteenth-Century Europe*, ed. John Merriman. New York: Holmes and Meier, 1979.

____________, ed. *A History of Private Life: From the Fires of the Revolution to the Great War*. Cambridge, Mass.: Belknap Press of Harvard University, 1990.

Philadelphia Museum of Art. *The Second Empire (1852–1870): Art in France under Napoleon III*. Exh. cat. Philadelphia: Philadelphia Museum of Art, 1978.

Pointon, Marcia. "'From the Midst of Warfare and Its Incidents to the Peaceful Scenes of Home': The Exposition Universelle of 1855." *Journal of European Studies* 2 (Dec. 1981): 233–61.

Portet, Mariette. *Sèvres en Île-de-France*. Condé-sur-Noireau, France: Ch. Corlet, 1975.

Préaud, Tamara, et al. *The Sèvres Porcelain Manufactory: Alexandre Brongniart and the Triumph of Art and Industry, 1800–1847*. New Haven, Conn., and London: Yale University Press, 1997.

Rouillé, André, ed. *La Photographie en France*. Paris: Éditions MACULA, 1989.

Schaaf, Larry J. *Out of the Shadows*. New Haven, Conn., and London: Yale University Press, 1992.

Sillevis, John, and Hans Kraan. *The Barbizon School*. Exh. cat. The Hague: Haags Gemeentmuseum, 1985.

Sobieszek, Robert. "Photography and the Theory of Realism in the Second Empire: A Reexamination of a Relationship." In *One Hundred Years of Photographic History*, ed. Van Deren Coke. Albuquerque: University of New Mexico Press, 1975.

Société Française de Photographie. "Procès-verbal de la Séance." *Bulletin de la Société française de photographie* (Mar. 1855).

____________. *Catalogue de la deuxième exposition annuelle des oeuvres des artistes et amateurs française et étrangers.* Paris: Société Française de Photographie, 1857.

____________. *Catalogue de la troisième exposition de la Société française de photographie*. Paris: Renou et Maulde, 1859.

____________. *Prix Fondé par M. le Duc de Luynes*. Paris: Mallet-Bachelier, 1856.

Stourdzé, Sam. *Louis Robert: L'Alchimie des images*. Exh. cat. Paris: NBC Editions, 1999.

Thomas, Greg M. *Art and Ecology in Nineteenth-Century France: The Landscapes of Théodore Rousseau*. Princeton, N.J.: Princeton University Press, 2000.

Tournachon, Félix (Nadar). *Quand j'étais photographe*. Paris: Flammarion, 1900.

Turgan, J. *Les Grandes usines de France*. Vol. 1, *Sèvres*. Paris: Michel Levy Frères, 1860.

Valenciennes, Pierre-Henri de. *Eléments de perspective pratique à l'usage des artistes, suivi de Réflexions et conseils à un élève sur la peinture et particulièrement sur le genre du paysage*. 1800. Reprint, Geneva: Minkoff, 1973.

Walton, Whitney. *France at the Crystal Palace: Bourgeois Taste and Artisan Manufacture in the Nineteenth Century*. Berkeley and Los Angeles: University of California Press, 1992.

Weaver, Mike. *The Photographic Art: Pictorial Traditions in Britain and America*. New York: Harper & Row, 1986.

____________. *British Photography in the Nineteenth Century*. Cambridge, U.K.: Cambridge University Press, 1989.

Weisberg, Gabriel. *The Realist Tradition*. Exh. cat. Cleveland: Cleveland Museum of Art, 1980.

Wey, Francis. "Théorie du portrait." *La Lumière* (27 Apr. 1851): 46–47.

____________. "Théorie du portrait." *La Lumière* (4 May 1851): 50–51.

____________. "Comment le soleil est devenu peintre." *Musée des familles* 20 (June 1853): 257–66.

____________. "Comment le soleil est devenu peintre." *Musée des familles* 20 (July 1853): 289–300.

Wyatt, M. Digby. *The Industrial Arts of the Nineteenth Century*. 5 vols. Exh. cat. London: Day and Son, 1851–53.

ACKNOWLEDGMENTS

Over the course of working on this project I have received generous support and active assistance from many individuals and institutions. My former dissertation advisor at Princeton, Peter C. Bunnell, gave me precious advice throughout the earlier process of writing the dissertation on which this book is based, and has continued to lend his insight and encouragement during the preparation of the manuscript. My dissertation readers, Todd Porterfield, Anne McCauley, and Esther da Costa Meyer also gave me much constructive criticism that became invaluable as I began to rethink the ungainly dissertation as a manuscript for publication. Two other former professors, Petra ten-Doesschate Chu and Alisa Luxenberg, deserve my thanks for their special encouragement and careful consideration of my work. I would further like to acknowledge the Spears Fund and the Fowler McCormick Fellowship of Princeton University, as well as the Mellon Foundation, for providing support at various stages of the dissertation.

In the research phase, many scholars, curators, collectors, and archivists made their expertise and collections available to me. It seems fitting to first thank Malcolm Daniel, Curator of Photography at the Metropolitan Museum of Art, New York, for introducing me to the photography of Victor Regnault, for generously sharing his unpublished research with me, and for following this project with interest as it has inched along. As the Lisette Model/Joseph G. Blum Fellow in Photography at the National Gallery of Canada, I was able to take advantage of the fantastic collective knowledge of the curatorial staff in the Photographs Collection, including Curator James Borcoman, Curator Ann Thomas, and Assistant Curator Lori Pauli. In France, I received crucial assistance from many patient souls, including André Jammes, MM. Guy Watelin de Lummen, Tamara Préaud at the Manufacture Nationale de Sèvres, Franz Jayot at the Archives de la ville de Sèvres, Bernard Marbot at the Bibliothèque Nationale, Françoise Heilbrun at the Musée d'Orsay, Martin Dieterle, Pierre Richard, and the late Harry Lunn. I wish to extend special thanks to Nancy Keeler for her enthusiastic encouragement and willingness to share her perceptions and special knowledge about early photography and working in French collections. Lastly, Michel Poivert and Katia Busch of the Société Française de Photographie have been so much more than generous in helping me obtain rights and reproductions.

Once I began drafting the manuscript, I was materially assisted by the Bard College Research Fund, and that process was intellectually nourished by the perceptive comments from two friends and colleagues who kindly read endless chapter drafts: Susan Bernofsky and Tabetha Ewing.

At Princeton University Press I'd like to thank my editor, Nancy Grubb, as well as her wonderful staff: Sarah Henry, Carmel Lyons, Devra K. Nelson, Ken Wong, and Kate Zanzucchi. I would also like to thank the designer, Jean Wilcox; the copyeditor, Alison Rooney; the proofreader, Laurie Burton; and the indexer, Carol Roberts.

Finally, it all comes down to the emotional support of my parents, Fred and Lorene Dahlberg, and a handful of true friends: Anne Fishbein, the fabulous L-con group, Roseann Tomko, Celia Bland, Gretchen Dietrich and Monty Paret, and Joel Smith.

INDEX

Note: Page references in *italics* refer to illustration captions. "VR" refers to Victor Regnault.